WOMEN AND RELIGIOUS WRITING IN EARLY MODERN ENGLAND

This study challenges critical assumptions about the role of religion in shaping women's experiences of authorship. Feminist critics have frequently been uncomfortable with the fact that conservative religious and political beliefs created opportunities for women to write with independent agency. The seventeenth-century Protestant women discussed in this book range across the religio-political and social spectrums and yet all display an affinity with modern feminist theologians. Rather than being victims of a patriarchal gender ideology, Lady Anne Southwell, Anna Trapnel and Lucy Hutchinson, among others, were both active negotiators of gender and active participants in wider theological debates. By placing women's religious writing in a broad theological and socio-political context, Erica Longfellow challenges traditional critical assumptions about the role of gender in shaping religion and politics, and the role of women in defining gender and thus influencing religion and politics.

ERICA LONGFELLOW is Senior Lecturer in English Literature at Kingston University. She is co-coordinator of the Performing History project in association with Hampton Court Royal Palace, which aims to reproduce early modern dramatic performances in historical settings.

WOMEN AND RELIGIOUS WRITING IN EARLY MODERN ENGLAND

BY

ERICA LONGFELLOW

CAMBRIDGE
UNIVERSITY PRESS

PUBLISHED BY THE PRESS SYNDICATE OF THE UNIVERSITY OF CAMBRIDGE
The Pitt Building, Trumpington Street, Cambridge, United Kingdom

CAMBRIDGE UNIVERSITY PRESS
The Edinburgh Building, Cambridge, CB2 2RU, UK
40 West 20th Street, New York, NY 10011–4211, USA
477 Williamstown Road, Port Melbourne, VIC 3207, Australia
Ruiz de Alarcón 13, 28014 Madrid, Spain
Dock House, The Waterfront, Cape Town 8001, South Africa

http://www.cambridge.org

First published 2004

Printed in the United Kingdom at the University Press, Cambridge

Typeface Adobe Garamond 11/12.5 pt.   *System* LATEX 2ε   [TB]

A catalogue record for this book is available from the British Library

ISBN 0 521 83758 8 hardback

Contents

Acknowledgements

Thanks are due to Malcolm Parkes, Sylvia Brown and Nigel Smith for early advice and encouragement. Elizabeth Clarke has been a continual influence, offering her advice and the resources of the Perdita Project, and being the first to introduce me to several of the writers discussed here.

I have also been encouraged by a genuinely supportive and stimulating community of scholars of early modern women, particularly the participants in the Oxford University 'Women, Text & History' seminar and the Early Modern Women's Manuscript conferences affiliated with the Perdita Project. Of these, Sarah Ross, Victoria Burke, Sister Jean Klene, Alexandra Shepard and Liam Semler sent me volumes of work-in-progress and research notes without which this study could not have been written. Along with so many scholars of my generation, I benefited from the generous advice and prodigious scholarly resources of the late Jeremy Maule. Conversations with Jane Shaw, Emma Jay, Natasha Distiller and Jonathan Gibson urged me to think further. John Carey, Peter Davidson and David Norbrook were forthcoming with advice, critique and sources. Alison Shell, Jessica Martin and Hero Chalmers all shared insightful responses to my writing samples. Andrew Gregory, Alan Le Grys and Jeremy Worthen were forthcoming with excellent theological advice. Elisabeth Dutton brought me up to speed on medieval devotional literature.

I owe a debt of gratitude to my research supervisor, Peter McCullough, for his continual enthusiasm for the project and ongoing friendship. Likewise, Tom Betteridge and Norma Clarke provided encouragement and critique at crucial moments. Emma Jay, Erica Wooff, Suzanna Fitzpatrick and Andrew Van der Vlies found the errors I could no longer see.

For graciously allowing me access to sources under unusual circumstances, I am grateful to the conservation department of the Bodleian Library, the rare books and manuscripts librarians of the Huntington Library and the Codrington Library of All Souls' College, Oxford. I also received valuable advice and assistance from the staff of the Beinecke Rare

Book and Manuscript Library, the British Library, the Greater London Record Office, the Public Record Office (now the National Archives) and the William Andrews Clark Memorial Library.

My thanks are also due to the Oxford University Graduate Studies Board and the Rector and Fellows of Lincoln College for providing me with vital financial support for research abroad, and to the Kingston University School of Humanities, particularly David Rogers and Avril Horner, for supporting this project throughout with research leave, grants and timely advice.

This book is dedicated to my parents, for always believing that I could do whatever I put my mind to.

Earlier versions of chapters 3 and 4 have previously appeared in print as: '*Eliza's Babes*: Poetry "Proceeding from Divinity" in Seventeenth-Century England'. *Gender and History* 14.2 (2002): 242–65. 'Lady Anne Southwell's Indictment of Adam'. In *Early Modern Women's Manuscript Writing: Selected Papers from the Trinity/Trent Colloquium*. Edited by Victoria Burke and Jonathan Gibson. Aldershot: Ashgate; 2004, 111–33. They are reproduced here with permission.

Abbreviations

CSPD   *Calendar of State Papers, Domestic*

CSPI   *Calendar of State Papers, Ireland*

DNB   *Dictionary of National Bibliography on CD-ROM* (Oxford: Oxford University Press, 1995)

ELH   *English Literary History*

ELR   *English Literary Renaissance*

HMC   *Historical Manuscripts Commission Reports*

LIT   *LIT: Literature, Interpretation, Theory*

MLQ   *Modern Language Quarterly*

OED   *Oxford English Dictionary Online* (Oxford: Oxford University Press, 2000)

PRO   Public Record Office (now the National Archives)

STC   A. W. Pollard *et al.*, eds., *A short-title catalogue of books printed in England, Scotland & Ireland and of English books printed abroad, 1475–1640*, 2nd edn (London: Bibliographical Society, 1991)

Wing   Donald Wing, ed., *Short-title catalogue of books printed in England, Scotland, Ireland, Wales, and British America and of English books printed in other countries, 1641–1700*, 2nd edn, New York: Modern Language Association, 1994

Note on transcription and citation

Quotations from early modern texts retain the original spelling and punctuation; only the long 's' has been regularised. In transcriptions from manuscript, brackets pointing inward > < indicate insertions above the line of text, while brackets pointing outward <> signify deletions. Square brackets [] indicate the expansion of an abbreviation or editorial interpolations. The footnotes indicate where manuscript corrections have been silently omitted or incorporated. In transcriptions from early printed books, italicisation, underlining and in some cases capitalisation have been ignored where these are used to distinguish a line or block of text (such as on title pages), but retained where they indicate emphasis.

For the ease of anyone wishing to locate a particular edition, I have included STC and Wing numbers and the names of printers, publishers and booksellers in references to all early modern books. I have followed STC convention in using short titles and capitalising only the first letter of a title.

All quotations from scripture are from the Authorised Version of the Bible.

Introduction

The poetry of Lady Anne Southwell (1574–1636) would startle anyone who believes that early modern women were constrained to be always chaste, silent and obedient. Southwell's lyrics, which she and her husband together collected into a manuscript book, were particularly critical of how men manipulated gender roles in order to keep women in their place. Consider the following poem:

> All.maried.men.desire.to.haue good wifes:
> but.few.giue good example. by thir liues
> They are owr head they wodd haue vs thir heles.
> this makes the good wife kick the good man reles.
> When god brought Eue to Adam for a bride
> the text sayes she was taene from out mans side
> A simbole of that side, whose sacred bloud.
> flowed for his spowse, the Churches sauinge good.
> This is a misterie, perhaps too deepe.
> for blockish Adam that was falen a sleepe[.][1]

Poor Adam frequently takes a beating in Southwell's poetry, as a symbol of all that is obstinate and foolish about men who crave power over women but do not understand the responsibility that comes with it. These men force women to be 'good wifes', to follow the command of St Paul's epistle to the Ephesians that wives must submit themselves to their husbands; but they refuse to follow the moral standard Paul sets for husbands, that they must love their wives to the point of self-sacrifice. Instead these husbands simply force their wives to obey, and if their wives rebel, Southwell's poem suggests, it is the husbands' own fault.

Southwell's poem is effective because it weaves a critique of the gender relations in Christian marriage into a statement about a universal Christian

---

[1] Jean Klene, ed., *The Southwell-Sibthorpe Commonplace Book: Folger MS. V.b.198* (Tempe, Arizona: Renaissance English Text Society, 1997), p. 20.

principle: men who abuse their wives are so foolish that they miss the greatest mystery of all, Christ's sacrifice on the cross. Her poem neatly demonstrates that *gendered* morals – what it means to be a good wife or a good husband – can only be understood within the context of the underlying truths of Christianity that apply to both men and women, particularly the saving capacity of sacrificial love. Any husband who misconstrues this principle will not be able to put his own privilege of headship in the right context. To his sleepy brain, the mystery is simply too deep.

But what is the 'misterie' in this poem? That the relationship between God and his people was like a marriage was an idea older than Christianity, and by the early modern period it had come to be known as 'mystical marriage'.[2] It is the strange process by which the divine Christ and the sinful human soul, made clean through his sacrifice, 'doe meet and make a mariage', as John Donne preached in one of his nuptial sermons.[3] Mystical marriage is not, in fact, a straightforward metaphor – if any metaphor ever is straightforward – but rather a cluster of Biblical descriptions of love drawn from Hosea, the Psalms, Ezekiel, 1 Corinthians 7, Revelation 22 and especially the Song of Songs. These were all read through the lens of Ephesians chapter 5, which likens the love of Christ for the Church to the love of a man for his wife and provided a loose framework under which to unite these variant texts. The Song of Songs, for example, is a collection of erotic love lyrics with only one oblique reference to God, but early modern commentators took it as read that the male speaker represented the voice of divine love and the female speaker the voice of sinful humanity.[4]

Beyond the identification of who was divine and who was human, however, it was difficult to say exactly who the players in this romance were. In post-Reformation English commentaries the speakers of the Song are variously identified as the historical King Solomon and his bride, Christ and all individual Christians, Christ and his bride the Church, Christ and the soul (always female), or even Christ and the 'Christian Man', whispering sweet nothings in each other's ears.[5] The multiplicity of allegorical players opened the way for mystical marriage in general, and the Song of Songs in particular, to be used to talk about a wide array of issues. Male theologians, particularly Puritan male theologians, most often focused on

---

[2] This was the title, for example, of a book on the subject by Francis Rous, discussed in chapter 1 below: STC 21343 *The mysticall marriage* (London: W. Jones and T. Paine for I. Emery, 1635).

[3] George R. Potter and Evelyn M. Simpson, eds., *The Sermons of John Donne*, 10 vols. (Berkeley, California: University of California Press, 1953–62), III.251.

[4] For the medieval mystical marriage tradition that established this paradigm, see Ann W. Astell, *The Song of Songs in the Middle Ages* (Ithaca, New York: Cornell University Press, 1990).

[5] The female speaker is glossed as the 'Christian man' in STC 12113 Henry Finch, *An exposition of the song of solomon*, ed. William Gouge (London: John Beale, 1615), for example pp. 79, 83, 97, 99.

the relationship between Christ and the Church, because mystical marriage provided them with a way to promote their particular ecclesiology as the true bride of Christ, all the while damning other systems, Roman, Laudian or radical Protestant, as merely whorish impostors. Following the passage in Ephesians, these writers imagined the Church as a woman, the bride of Christ, but they had no qualms about the fact that this female institution was in fact made up of both male and female believers, and controlled almost entirely by powerful men. Christ's love effectively transcended gender and blurred the distinction between the individual and the community: 'And that *Iesus Christ* is he,' George Wither asserted, 'who in this *Song* professeth an intire affection, not onely to the whole *Mysticall body* of the faithfull, but euen to euery member of it in particular.'[6]

The confusions between male and female, the believer and the Church, open up possibilities for early modern writers to negotiate gendered power relations, whether real or metaphorical. For generations of men, this meant the chance to use the feminine gender, and human marriage, as a convenient shorthand. The first chapter of this book considers the theological heritage of mystical marriage, demonstrating how Puritan male writers of the seventeenth century exploited the femaleness of the 'Bride' to invoke a traditional principle of women's utter submission to men: the Church and the soul were completely inferior to Christ, and therefore must obey him. Although this was one way, metaphorically, of imagining women's role, it was not one that had kept pace with the prevailing views on human marriage in the early modern period. These writers were in fact far more concerned with evoking the mystery than with defining marriage, and their statements about the Bride of Christ cannot be read as indicative of their standards for the brides of men.

For women writers mystical marriage offered the opportunity to do precisely what the men did not: to rewrite the human aspects of the metaphor, particularly what it meant to be a devout Christian woman. Southwell's poem demonstrates the special facility that the metaphor offered to women who had to craft a position between the conflicting gender roles of human relationships and the ultimately ungendered truths of divine love. This study is an exploration of how women writers like Southwell seized upon the fluidity of gender in mystical marriage scriptures in order to claim authority for their own religious writing. For some women, like Southwell and Aemilia Lanyer (1568–1645), mystical marriage enabled them to conceive a moral standard that was beyond gender, a Christ in whom there truly was no male or female (Galatians 3:28). For others, mystical marriage was the

[6] STC 25908 George Wither, *The hymnes and songs of the church* (London: for G. W., 1623), p. 43.

primary legitimiser of their speech: both Anna Trapnel (b. 1620) and the anonymous author of *Eliza's babes* (1652) use their metaphorical identity as the bride of Christ to justify their politically and socially subversive speech. Finally, some women use mystical marriage in much the same way as men, as a means of talking not about human marriage but about divine providence in human institutions; Lucy Hutchinson (1619/20–81), the subject of the final chapter, is the prime example, as she uses notions of divine union to talk about the new English Republic that both she and her husband had longed to inaugurate.

THEORETICAL CHOICES: FEMINIST CRITICISM AND EARLY
MODERN WOMEN

Although mystical marriage is the unifying theme of this study, *Women and Religious Writing in Early Modern England* is not a history of the mystical marriage metaphor, which would be better written as a balance of texts by both men and women. It is rather a series of case studies of five women writers that uses the common metaphor of mystical marriage as a means of bringing into focus a cross-section of early modern women's experience of authorship. This study operates within the feminist critical framework that is deliberately attentive to early modern women writers, removing them from the margins to the centre of the critical project.

At the same time, however, this study also seeks to push the boundaries of feminist critical frameworks for reading early modern women. Since the 'first wave' of such criticism in the 1980s, feminist critics have only recently begun to theorise an approach to early modern women writers.[7] We have yet to decide between the goals of historicising our own feminism and recovering the history of early modern women, or to grapple

---

[7] The 'first wave' includes Sandra M. Gilbert and Susan Gubar, eds., *The Norton Anthology of Literature by Women: The Tradition in English* (London: W. W. Norton & Company, 1985); Margaret P. Hannay, ed., *Silent But for the Word: Tudor Women as Patrons, Translators, and Writers of Religious Works* (Kent, Ohio: Ohio State University Press, 1985); Joan Kelly-Gadol, 'Did Women Have a Renaissance?', in *Becoming Visible: Women in European History*, ed. Renate Bridenthal, Claudia Koonz and Susan Stuard, 2nd edition (Boston: Houghton Mifflin, 1987), pp. 175–202; Elaine Beilin, *Redeeming Eve: Women Writers of the English Renaissance* (Princeton: Princeton University Press, 1987); Germaine Greer, *et al.*, eds., *Kissing the Rod: An Anthology of Seventeenth-Century Women's Verse* (London: Virago, 1988); Betty Travitsky, *The Paradise of Women: Writings by Englishwomen of the Renaissance* (London: Greenwood Press, 1981); Elaine Hobby, *Virtue of Necessity: English Women's Writing 1649–1688* (Ann Arbor, Michigan: University of Michigan Press, 1989); Tina Krontiris, *Oppositional Voices: Women as Writers and Translators of Literature in the English Renaissance* (London: Routledge, 1992). Of recent studies which raise theoretical questions most notable are Danielle Clarke's *The Politics of Early Modern Women's Writing* (London: Longman, 2001), and her Introduction to Danielle Clarke and Elizabeth Clarke, eds., *'This Double Voice': Gendered Writing in Early Modern England* (Basingstoke: Macmillan, 2000), pp. 1–15.

with the fact that these goals may be mutually exclusive. That there is no consistent definition of 'feminist' criticism and its aims is perhaps not surprising or even unhealthy in a movement that encompasses individuals who are a cross-section of society in all but their gender. Nevertheless, these theoretical lacunae cannot simply be ignored, for it is only in the scrutiny of such theoretical issues that the prejudices and partialities of modern criticism become apparent. What sort of early modern women are we interested in? Are we still desperately seeking Virginia Woolf's Judith Shakespeare, as so many essays on Aemilia Lanyer suggest? Or is our project one of historical recovery, with its difficult balancing act of weighing awareness of modern agendas against the desire to be as objective as possible? How do women writers fit within the confines and paradigms of modern literary studies? Should we be looking for what is unique about women writers?

These are threatening questions. They go to the heart of critical inquiry: what do we hope to gain from a study of early modern women? This book is an attempt to address this fundamental question by approaching early modern women with a deliberate awareness of such issues. It posits a method of studying women writers with a clear purpose: historicising our understanding of them, in particular how they negotiated gender and authority in religious discourse. This study works to reclaim not early modern feminists but the historical actors who until recently had disappeared from scholarly history. As a historian and a critic, I aspire to be honest about my biases, clear about my judgements, open about the strengths and weaknesses of each woman's work and careful about when a woman's work is opposed to conventional gender standards, when it is collusive and when (perhaps most often) it negotiates between these two poles.

This is painstaking business, and it requires careful, microcosmic attention to a handful of early modern women in order to historicise the categories that were once assumed. Each chapter considers elements of the author's biography, not for the sake of any simplistic equation between women's lives and their writings (characteristic of much early *anti*-feminist criticism of women writers), but for the purpose of situating these women and their writings in the precise nexus of family, factional and economic capital that went into constructing an individual's status.[8] In order to work

---

[8] The classic example of a biographical reading of a woman writer (and, in fact, Shakespeare) is A. L. Rowse's edition of Aemilia Lanyer: *The Poems of Shakespeare's Dark Lady: Salve Deus Rex Judeorum by Emilia Lanyer* (London: Jonathan Cape, 1978). For the use of biography to elucidate context, see Arthur F. Marotti, *Manuscript, Print, and the English Renaissance Lyric* (Ithaca, New York: Cornell University Press, 1995), p. 2. For the perils of assuming that early modern women writers were recoverable (auto)biographical subjects, see Clarke, *The Politics of Early Modern Women's Writing*, pp. 4–8.

against the temptation to essentialise women, the writers of this study are as diverse as possible, from widely different family, religious, geographical and educational backgrounds.[9] At the beginning of the time-scale, Aemilia Bassano Lanyer was a Londoner who aspired to move beyond her Italian-Jewish musician origins to a place in a gentry family or even a knighthood for her husband; perhaps in keeping with these aspirations, her theology is unexceptionable English Calvinism. Lucy Apsley Hutchinson, at the other end, was a staunch Independent and republican who was lavishly educated by her gentry father and married into one of the provincial elite families in Nottinghamshire. In terms of wealth, education, social connections and historical circumstances, it is difficult to imagine two more different women. The purpose of this book is, in part, to highlight these differences, to demonstrate how such identifying factors functioned along with gender to shape a woman's approach to writing.

This strategy is in keeping with the work of literary critics who are rethinking approaches to early modern gender relations and particularly the tendency to rely on outdated social history for our understanding of women's place in society.[10] Life for women in early modern England was certainly not as easy or as liberated as life for women in twenty-first-century England. There was an ethic demanding women's subordination to men

---

[9] Their one common feature, aside from their writing, is Protestantism. As a primary means of defending cloistered religious orders for both men and women, mystical marriage has such different implications for Catholic writers that the experience of Catholic women cannot be adequately addressed in this book. One example of a Catholic woman who uses mystical marriage imagery is Dame Gertrude More, one of several Englishwomen in convents in France: Wing M2631A *The holy practises* (Paris: Lewis de la Fosse, 1657); and Wing M2632 *The spiritual exercises* (Paris: Lewis de la Fosse, 1658).

[10] See especially the work of Margaret Ezell, *The Patriarch's Wife: Literary Evidence and the History of the Family* (Chapel Hill, North Carolina: The University of North Carolina Press, 1987), and *Writing Women's Literary History* (Baltimore: Johns Hopkins University Press, 1993); also Clarke, *The Politics of Early Modern Women's Writing*, and her Introduction to '*This Double Voice*'; and the Introduction to *Women, Writing, and the Reproduction of Culture in Tudor and Stuart Britain*, by Mary E. Burke *et al.*, eds., (Syracuse, New York: Syracuse University Press, 2000), pp. xvii–xxx. The early social historical texts most commonly relied on are Lawrence Stone, *The Crisis of the Aristocracy* (Oxford: Clarendon Press, 1965) and *The Family, Sex and Marriage in England 1500–1800* (London: Weidenfeld and Nicolson, 1979); also influential for critics of women's writing is Alice Clark, *The Working Life of Women in the Seventeenth Century* (London: Routledge, 1919). For a discussion of literary critical use of Stone and a bibliography of social history that revises Stone, see David Cressy, 'Foucault, Stone, Shakespeare and Social History', *ELR* 21.1 (1991): 121–33. For a revision of Clark, see Susan Dwyer Amussen, *An Ordered Society: Gender and Class in Early Modern England* (Oxford: Basil Blackwell, 1988), p. 1 and throughout. For a recent essay that cites Stone as a primary authority for early modern cultural patterns, see Mary Ellen Lamb, 'Patronage and Class in Aemilia Lanyer's *Salve Deus Rex Judaeorum*', in *Women, Writing, and the Reproduction of Culture in Tudor and Stuart Britain*, ed. Burke, pp. 38–57; earlier examples are the essays in Anne M. Haselkorn and Betty S. Travitsky, eds., *The Renaissance Englishwoman in Print: Counterbalancing the Canon* (Amherst, Massachusetts: University of Massachusetts Press, 1990).

and ridiculing their attempts to write. But this was only one of many competing strands of discourse, and it was a strand frequently contradicted or at least modified in women's actual experience, as more recent social historical work proves. Although they had considerably less access to education and official forms of power, in daily activity most women who were not servants enjoyed economic agency, and the social and intellectual accomplishments of many gentlewomen and noblewomen crucially smoothed their families' paths to elevation and preferment.[11] As these instances illustrate, 'patriarchy' was never uniform: a woman's experience of 'patriarchy' and her relation to writing in particular was always a result of economics, geography, social status and religious affiliation. In practice, women's writing seldom functioned in direct opposition to men and patriarchal culture, but rather was part of a process of negotiating gendered power roles that involved the agency of both men and women.

By locating a woman's social, economic and religious affiliations as precisely as the evidence allows, the following case studies open a way for exploring the interrelations between these identifying factors and gender and power. Through their writing, the women of this book experienced complex interactions with men and male systems of authority in which they were continually negotiating power relationships. A critical moment in Lucy Hutchinson's *Life* of her husband comes when she tells her readers that her husband was initially drawn to her *because of* her skills as a linguist and poet, while the women of their social circle urged him against the match because they believed no woman could be so studious and still be sociable and physically attractive. The example serves as a neat demonstration of the existence of competing ideals of femininity, and that men and women did not always take sides on this debate in the ways twenty-first-century readers might anticipate. This book works not to summarise or encapsulate these gender standards, but rather to expose their conflicting and fluid incarnations, and particularly how women play an active part in the constant redefinition of these ideals, in ways that are not always straightforwardly subversive.

[11] Amussen, *An Ordered Society*, and Ezell, *The Patriarch's Wife*, demonstrate the conflict between patriarchal ideals and the economic and social activity of women in early modern households. Alexandra Jane Shepard, 'Meanings of Manhood in Early Modern England, With Special Reference to Cambridge, *c.* 1560–1640' (unpublished PhD thesis, Cambridge University, 1998) explores how prescriptive writings about men's role in the family are often internally contradictory. For the experience of gentle- and noblewomen, see Diane Purkiss, Introduction, *Three Tragedies by Renaissance Women* (London: Penguin, 1998), pp. xi–xliii, and the chapter on Lady Anne Southwell below. See also Sylvia Brown, 'Godly Household Government from Perkins to Milton: The Rhetoric and Politics of *oeconomia*, 1600–1645' (unpublished PhD thesis, Princeton University, 1994).

In addition to biography, each chapter also investigates the bibliographic evidence of the writer's works to clarify how the material production of a text, whether in print or manuscript, informed a woman's experience of writing. The texts explored here cover almost all available bibliographic forms: loose papers, drafts, manuscript collections, commonplace books, presentation copies and small and large format printed books. Examining each of these objects as objects, reading the physical appearance of the texts as well as the words on the page, can yield provocative conclusions about the significance of a woman's writing within religious and social power structures. These conclusions support a model of textual exchange in which women's writing served as an important form of currency, spent in the effort to advance political religious agendas or social ambitions. Anna Trapnel's 1658 folio, for example, seems to have carried an enormous weight of authority in her circle of Fifth Monarchist sectarians, almost as if it were a new form of scripture. Lady Anne Southwell's manuscripts, on the other hand, betray evidence of husband and wife working together to exploit her poetic reputation for social and perhaps financial gain.

The case studies of Trapnel, Southwell and the other writers of this book are an effort to extend the work of social historians of texts into the realm of women's writing. Peter Beal, Harold Love and Arthur Marotti's studies of manuscript production and circulation have enhanced our view of the interplay between manuscript and print as early modern forms of publication.[12] In her 1993 book *Writing Women's Literary History*, Margaret Ezell addressed the importance of such methods to an approach to women's writing that goes beyond simple oppositional modes. Ezell demonstrated that the theoretical basis of criticism of early modern women writers was heavily dependent on Virginia Woolf's ahistorical view of women's literary past, and particularly Woolf's paradigms of women's authorship, which elevated writers of fiction who sought a 'public' audience and economic gain through commercial print. As Ezell argues in her most recent book, the feminist scholars she criticised in *Writing Women's Literary History* are not alone in conflating 'published' with 'printed' and searching for Romantic individualistic authors.[13] Despite the seminal work of these scholars, manuscript culture remains adjunct to print in the eyes of many critics. It

---

[12] Peter Beal, *In Praise of Scribes: Manuscripts and their Makers in Seventeenth-Century England* (Oxford: Oxford University Press, 1998); Harold Love, *Scribal Publication in Seventeenth-Century England* (Oxford: Clarendon Press, 1993); Marotti, *Manuscript, Print, and the English Renaissance Lyric*.

[13] Margaret Ezell, *Social Authorship and the Advent of Print* (Baltimore, Maryland: Johns Hopkins University Press, 1999).

is perhaps further confirmation of the battle of 'evidence versus agenda', as social historian David Cressy characterised the curious ahistoricism of some 'historicist' critics, including many feminist scholars.[14]

This book not only collapses the dichotomy of manuscript and print but also questions the underlying assumption of the gendering of 'public' and 'private' modes of communication. While we have for the most part moved beyond the old argument that a woman who printed her works was more daring because she had transgressed into a masculine 'public' realm, the underlying categories of 'public' and 'private' and their implicit binary gendering remain crucial to much feminist criticism, and indeed criticism of early modern literature in general.[15] The prevalence of this dichotomy is in fact evidence of the latent power of 'separate spheres' ideology in current critical discourse. Although the phrase 'separate spheres' is seldom used by early modern scholars, the paradigm still holds sway in many studies of gender relations: women's sphere of influence was confined to home and family, while men's sphere encompassed economic and political transactions. As a historical concept, 'separate spheres' is a conflation of nineteenth-century notions of domesticity (themselves now shown to be at best a partial picture) and Lockean conceptions of the family as politically 'private', in the sense that it is cordoned off from all 'public' activity and authority.[16] The effect of 'separate spheres' on historiography has been precisely the polarisation the name implies. The complex interplay between men, women and the shifting worlds of personal and political is simplified to the equations 'public' equals men and 'private' equals women.

Such a model is not only a distorted representation of the family, whether in seventeenth- or nineteenth-century England, but it is also a rather cavalier and unexamined use of the terms 'public' and 'private'. At a time when the theoretical framework of English literary history is continually under discussion, these terms have endured surprisingly little scrutiny, particularly

---

[14] Cressy, 'Foucault, Stone, Shakespeare and Social History', p. 130.
[15] For examples of recent criticism that rely on the equation of 'printed' with 'public' and 'published', see Ann Baynes Coiro, 'Writing in Service: Sexual Politics and Class Position in the Poetry of Aemilia Lanyer and Ben Jonson', *Criticism* 35.3 (1993): 357–76, especially 358–9; Pamela Benson, 'To Play the Man: Aemilia Lanyer and the Acquisition of Patronage', in *Opening the Borders: Inclusivity in Early Modern Studies: Essays in Honor of James V. Mirollo*, ed. Peter C. Herman (Newark, Delaware: University of Delaware Press, 1999), pp. 243–64; and the essays by Barbara K. Lewalski, Susanne Woods, Janel Mueller and Naomi J. Miller in *Aemilia Lanyer: Gender, Genre, and the Canon*, ed. Marshall Grossman (Lexington, Kentucky: University Press of Kentucky, 1998), pp. 49–59, 83–98, 99–127, 143–66.
[16] Susan Moller Okin, 'Gender, the Public and the Private', in *Political Theory Today*, ed. David Held (Cambridge: Polity Press, 1991), pp. 67–90.

in seventeenth-century studies.[17] The eighteenth- and nineteenth-century historian Amanda Vickery points out that scholarly use of the terms 'public' and 'private' is in fact extraordinarily vague:

The shortcomings of the public/private dichotomy as an analytical framework are many, but most obviously there is little unanimity among historians as to what public and private should be held to mean in this context. Current interpretations of 'the public' vary enormously. In a historian's hands, a public role can mean access to anything from politics, public office, formal employment, opinion, print, clubs, assembly, company, the neighbourhood, the streets, or simply the world outside the front door. However, we should take care to discover whether our interpretation of public and private marries with that of historical actors themselves.[18]

The same confusions exist in seventeenth-century studies, in which, to take the opposite term, a private role can mean interaction with family, friends, social equals, select members of a political faction, a religious mentor, a patron or God himself. David Cressy has proposed that in fact *all* life 'had public, social, or communal dimensions' in early modern England.[19] Cressy's position is perhaps extreme, and I suspect is a result of the bias of his sources, Church court records that are designed precisely to bring to the community's awareness acts that our post-Lockean culture would consider 'private', particularly sexual transgression and marital discord. But Cressy's point is well taken: it is dangerously misleading to accept as given the separation between 'public' and 'private' behaviour in early modern culture. Like the relationship between manuscript and print, the interplay between these two realms is far more complex than we have yet acknowledged.

The unwillingness to historicise these terms is particularly fraught because it is part of the attempt to maintain the fiction that these categories are value-free. In fact, twenty-first-century scholars consistently privilege the 'public' – in practice, what is masculine or political – over the

---

[17] Social historians are generally more careful with these terms than literary critics or cultural historians; see, for example, Amussen's analysis of privacy in the early modern family, *An Ordered Society*, pp. 34–66.

[18] Amanda Vickery, 'Golden Age to Separate Spheres? A Review of the Categories and Chronology of English Women's History', *The Historical Journal* 36.2 (1993): 412. Similar arguments are made by Lawrence Klein, 'Gender and the Public/Private Distinction in the Eighteenth Century: Some Questions about Evidence and Analytic Procedure', *Eighteenth-Century Studies* 29.1 (1995): 97–109.

[19] David Cressy, 'Response: Private Lives, Public Performance, and Rites of Passage', in *Attending to Women in Early Modern England*, ed. Betty S. Travitsky and Adele F. Seeff (Newark, Delaware: University of Delaware Press, 1994), p. 187. Patricia Crawford makes a similar assertion but offers little supporting evidence, 'Public Duty, Conscience, and Women in Early Modern England', in *Public Duty and Private Conscience in Seventeenth-Century England: Essays Presented to G. E. Aylmer*, ed. John Morrill, Paul Slack and Daniel Woolf (Oxford: Clarendon Press, 1993), pp. 57–76.

'private', what is feminine and often, for modern individuals, pertains to religious faith.[20] For scholarship of early modern women to subscribe to this ahistorical misconception of 'public' and 'private' does the subject a profound disservice by assuming a model of culture in which only exceptional women who transgress perceived boundaries of the male 'public' can write anything of value.[21] The vast majority of women writers who wrote works that express their 'personal' devotion, often in manuscript, are implicitly categorised in a less transgressive and therefore less interesting aesthetic. By refusing to interrogate its own notions of 'public' and 'private', such criticism effectively restricts women writers to the very categories from which it was designed to liberate them.

Through careful attention to bibliographic, documentary and literary evidence, this study uncovers some of the historical nuances of those overarching categories of 'public' and 'private' that mediate and polarise our understanding of gender, print and manuscript culture. Although no critic can claim to employ entirely value-free analytical categories, I remain cautious about the assumption that 'private' writing is less interesting because it has less impact, or that 'public' writing has more in common with political power structures. This study also begins the Herculean task, proposed by David Cressy and Amanda Vickery, of exploring how the words 'public' and 'private' have been used in history, and how our modern preoccupations affect our understanding of that usage.[22] The chapters on *Eliza's babes* and Lucy Hutchinson in particular make a case for specific historical uses of the terms that are not ones that twenty-first-century critics would expect.

MYSTICAL MARRIAGE AND WOMEN'S RELIGIOUS AUTHORITY

These disparate modes of inquiry – biographical, bibliographical and literary historical – are united throughout by the metaphor of mystical marriage. Mystical marriage serves as a way into these writers' texts that is deliberately not their gender, but rather a mode of gendered inquiry that includes both male and female. It is also deliberately a *religious* mode of inquiry. Although 'patriarchal Christianity' has been a favourite opponent of essentialist feminist critics, many now recognise that we ignore the influence of

---

[20] For a similar criticism of primarily male new historicists, see Carol Thomas Neely, 'Constructing the Subject: Feminist Practice and the New Renaissance Discourses', *ELR* 18.1 (1988): 5–18.
[21] For examples of essays in the 'exceptional woman' mode, see Haselkorn and Travitsky, eds., *The Renaissance Englishwoman in Print*.
[22] Cressy, 'Response: Private Lives, Public Performance', p. 187.

religion at our peril.[23] 'Religion' in this period was constitutive and archetypal, a fundamental agent in the construction of literary identities and the shaping of literary texts. Although it could be used to enter into other debates, religious discourse was not simply a code for concerns more secular, and to our twenty-first-century minds, more 'real'. For early modern men and women, God and belief in God were 'real', vital elements of daily life. Even for an atheist (perhaps especially for an atheist) the questions of belief were inescapable. For most men and women, such questions were both everyday and ultimate, almost invisible in the routine but technicoloured in the drama of national crisis or personal tragedy. Above all, they were historically significant questions, as this book helps to demonstrate. Whatever their personal piety or theological affiliation, all of the women of this book were sincere believers who used religious metaphors and considered religious questions because they believed both language and issues to be vital.

Christianity in this period placed such devout women in a bind. St Peter asserted that women were 'the weaker sex', and St Paul declared that it was shameful for a woman to speak in church. Nevertheless the primary duty of any Christian, male or female, was to live a godly or Christlike life; in fact St Paul himself had written that in Christ there was no male or female.[24] For many pious women, this model was difficult to reconcile with a command to be silent: was it possible to be a light to the world, as Christ had commanded, if one was not allowed to speak or write? As one early modern woman put it, 'she could not walk where she had not libertie

[23] Lynnette McGrath uses the phrase 'patriarchal Christianity' in 'Metaphoric Subversions: Feasts and Mirrors in Aemilia Lanier's *Salve Deus Rex Judaeorum*', *LIT* 3.2 (1991): 101. Some recent feminist studies that consider the role of religion include Clarke, *The Politics of Early Modern Women's Writing*, and the essays in *Early Modern Women's Manuscript Writing: Selected Papers of the Trinity–Trent Colloquium*, edited by Victoria Burke and Jonathan Gibson (London: Ashgate, 2004). There are numerous studies of the connection between religion and literature in this period, including Louis L. Martz, *The Poetry of Meditation: A Study in English Religious Literature of the Seventeenth Century* (New Haven, Connecticut: Yale University Press, 1954); Barbara Kiefer Lewalski, *Protestant Poetics and the Seventeenth-Century Religious Lyric* (Princeton, New Jersey: Princeton University Press, 1979); Nigel Smith, *Literature and Revolution in England, 1640–1660* (New Haven, Connecticut: Yale University Press, 1994); Dagmar Freist, *Governed by Opinion: Politics, Religion, and the Dynamics of Communication in Stuart London, 1637–1645* (London: I. B. Tauris Publishers, 1997); Peter McCullough, *Sermons at Court: Politics and Religion in Elizabethan and Jacobean Preaching* (Cambridge: Cambridge University Press, 1998); David Norbrook, *Writing the English Republic: Poetry, Rhetoric and Politics, 1627–1660* (Cambridge: Cambridge University Press, 1999); Alison Shell, *Catholicism, Controversy, and the English Literary Imagination, 1558–1660* (Cambridge: Cambridge University Press, 1999); and Peter E. McCullough and Lori Anne Ferrell, eds., *The English Sermon Revised: Religion, Literature and History 1600–1750* (Manchester: Manchester University Press, 2000).
[24] 1 Peter 3:7, 1 Corinthians 14:34–6; see also 1 Timothy 2:11–12, Galatians 3:28.

to speak'.[25] For such women, living a godly life and conforming to Pauline restrictions on women were fundamentally incompatible.

For the women of this book, mystical marriage was one way of negotiating this paradox. As the first chapter explains, mystical marriage mediated between human relationships where the limitations of gender were inescapable and divine relationships in which gender was ultimately irrelevant, a mere construct. For women, the mystical Christ, the ultimate lover, both exposed these inequalities and was the means to reconcile them. The sacrificial love of Christ served as a model of gendered behaviour that was not oppressive to women. His unimpeachable authority provided a means to authorise their conventionally silenced voices. The tension between his humanity and divinity, and the duality inherent in any human relationship to such a deity, offered women a means to speak of both human social issues and essential questions of faith.

'Religion', in its many, varied incarnations in the early modern period, was not solely the province of patriarchal men. Through the metaphor of mystical marriage, the women of this book worked to frame and further vital religious debates about the nature of human relationships, whether with God or to fellow human beings. Because it encompasses both human marriage and divine love, mediating between the gendered and the universal, mystical marriage provides the ideal lens through which to view women writers' religious agency. It allowed them to construct authority and negotiate competing constructs of gender; it gave them the ability to walk and the liberty to speak.

As women who were able to discover a voice for themselves within the seemingly oppressive traditions of Christianity, the writers of this study were part of a long line of women who had found a form of liberation in their relationship with the divine. From the earliest followers of Jesus to the mystic saints of medieval Europe, the history of the Christian West is replete with stories of women who combined an exploitation of the liberating texts already available in the scripture with an imaginative response to potentially oppressive traditions.[26]

The immediate forebears of the women of this study were the numerous saints and holy women of the middle ages. On the Continent, women such as Catherine of Siena and Bridget of Sweden befriended Popes, founded

[25] Matthew 5:14–16; Bodleian Library Rawlinson MS D 828, p. 28; see chapter 5 below.
[26] For feminist studies of early Christian women see the Conclusion below.

orders and advised politicians, while visionaries such as the nuns of Helfta and Beguine women imagined new models of devotion that were imitated throughout Europe.[27] In England, these women inspired Julian of Norwich and, in the next generation, Margery Kempe, who represent two distinct models of holiness. Julian, the anchoress enclosed in a cell in Norwich, expressed her devotion with her pen, writing works of speculative theology that are among the most original of the period.[28] Margery Kempe, on the other hand, expressed her devotion in subversive action, at the end of her life dictating a spiritual autobiography that set down the many experiences of the divine that marked her as a holy woman.[29]

Any connections between the early modern women of this study and their medieval forebears – or Continental contemporaries – remain tenuous. Where we can trace these women's reading, none of these Catholic works – medieval or contemporary – are included. Their main direct influences from the past are the classical and patristic works that were common in gentry libraries of the day.[30] The works of medieval mystics had largely disappeared with the Reformation, while of course Continental and English Catholic writings were generally frowned upon, although there were notable exceptions, such as the popular poetry of the Jesuit martyr Robert Southwell.[31] The difficulty of tracing influences among subsequent generations of mystical marriage writings may be evidence that several semi-autonomous interpretative traditions existed – at different points in history, or sometimes among different communities in the same period of history. Thus early modern English Catholic women approached mystical marriage as

---

[27] See the essays in Rosalynn Voaden, ed., *Prophets Abroad: The Reception of Continental Holy Women in Late-Medieval England* (Cambridge: D. S. Brewer, 1996); Barbara Newman, *From Virile Woman to WomanChrist: Studies in Medieval Religion and Literature* (Philadelphia: University of Pennsylvania Press, 1995). For editions of the texts see Roger Ellis, ed., *The Liber Celestis of St Bridget of Sweden: The Middle English Version*, Early English Text Society Original Series 291 (Oxford: Oxford University Press, 1987); Columba Hart, trans., *Hadewijch: The Complete Works* (New York: Paulist Press, 1980); Edmund Colledge, O. S. A. and James Walsh, S. J., eds., *A Book of Showings to the Anchoress Julian of Norwich*, Studies and Texts 35 (Toronto: Pontifical Institute of Mediaeval Studies, 1978); Theresa A. Halligan, ed., *The Booke of Gostlye Grace of Mechtild of Hackeborn*, Studies and Texts 46 (Toronto: Pontifical Institute of Mediaeval Studies, 1979).

[28] Nicholas Watson, 'The Middle English Mystics', in *The Cambridge History of Medieval English Literature*, edited by David Wallace (Cambridge: Cambridge University Press, 1999), pp. 558–9. It is not certain that Julian was enclosed when her text was composed: see Elisabeth Mary Dutton, 'Compiling Julian: The *Revelation of Love* and Late-Medieval Devotional Compilation' (unpublished D. Phil. thesis, Oxford University, 2002), pp. 1–5.

[29] Watson, 'The Middle English Mystics', pp. 562–4. Barry Windeatt, Introduction, *The Book of Margery Kempe* (London: Longman, 2000).

[30] A booklist is in the manuscript of Lady Anne Southwell's works, Klene, ed., *The Southwell-Sibthorpe Commonplace Book*, pp. 98–101. Lucy Hutchinson's reading is evident from her commonplace books, Nottinghamshire Archives, MSS DD/HU1 and DD/HU3. See chapters 3 and 6 below.

[31] Shell, *Catholicism, Controversy, and the English Literary Imagination*, pp. 77–88.

key to their cloistered virginity in a way that would have seemed foreign and superstitious to the Protestant women of this study.[32] The existence of such loosely connected parallel traditions makes the literary historian's work particularly difficult: in her study of medieval Song of Songs commentaries, for example, E. Ann Matter criticises Prudence Steiner for considering only Jewish traditions in her study of the Song of Songs in early modern New England, yet Matter herself seems unaware of the large body of mystical marriage literature produced in Reformation Europe.[33]

And yet, of course, these traditions are connected, not only by a common scriptural basis but also by an interpretative heritage. Despite the virtual disappearance of many medieval manuscript works from the reading of early modern individuals, a multitude of traces of the Catholic past remain in the culture: St Bernard of Clairvaux and before him Origen of Alexandria defined the basic allegorical approach to mystical marriage texts that continued to influence Protestant thinkers, and George Scheper has argued that in fact Protestant commentaries are fundamentally similar to their medieval counterparts in their conservative use of allegory.[34] Similarly, the Puritan forms of meditation that underlie much mystical marriage writing can be traced directly to Ignatian models.[35] The cultural influences of the Catholic past – and present – allowed for greater commonalities between medieval and early modern Catholic holy women and their English Protestant counterparts than many of those Englishwomen would have acknowledged.

Among those unacknowledged commonalities is the role of men in guiding and authorising women's devotional experience. The confessor of a medieval mystic was crucial as a witness that his charge was both exceptionally holy and spiritually orthodox. Holy women – even those who seem remarkably independent and outspoken – were ultimately dependent on male authorisation to escape charges of heresy. But, like their early modern descendents, medieval holy women were capable of negotiating the

[32] See for example Dame Gertrude More, *The holy practises*, and *The spiritual exercises*.

[33] 'Allegorical commentaries on the Song of Songs can be found after the Middle Ages in some specialized Christian contexts', Matter argues, *The Voice of My Beloved: The Song of Songs in Western Medieval Christianity* (Philadelphia: University of Pennsylvania Press, 1990), p. 5. Her estimate does not do justice to the more than 500 commentaries in the seventeenth century alone, as noted by George L. Scheper, 'Reformation Attitudes Toward Allegory and the Song of Songs', *PMLA* 89.3 (1973): 556. See p. 17 n. 7 in Matter, *The Voice*, for the comment on Prudence L. Steiner, 'A Garden of Spices in New England: John Cotton's and Edward Taylor's Use of the Song of Songs', in *Allegory, Myth, and Symbol*, ed. Morton W. Bloomfield (Cambridge, Massachusetts: Harvard University Press, 1981), pp. 227–43.

[34] Matter, *The Voice*, pp. 20–48 and 123–33. Scheper, 'Reformation Attitudes', p. 555.

[35] Martz, *The Poetry of Meditation*, pp. 153–75 and 331–7. See chapter 4 below.

terms of their relations with men, who were often themselves dependent upon the superior reputation of the holy woman for their own advancement. Thus, once the confessor had authorised the woman's experience as true and inspired, she was often liberated to experience God as the spirit within directed – carrying her confessor with her to fame and influence.[36] The complex symbiosis of these relationships is a warning to us not to assume that a woman writer's reliance on male authorisation is a sign of her powerlessness: Lucy Hutchinson's use of her late husband's reputation to authorise her openly republican writings, and Anna Trapnel's dependence on the male 'ear-witnesses' who transcribed more than a thousand pages of her trance-like singing, are striking examples of women who gained independence in a seeming act of submission.[37]

Women were also able to find independence in another type of submission: their devotion to God. Like many virgin saints, the twelfth-century English holy woman Christina of Markyate was empowered by her vocation to the cloister to defy her family's repeated attempts to force her to marry. The accounts of her life make clear that her defiance is a threat to her family's social honour, and thus challenges not only gendered norms of behaviour but the very social and economic system in which unmarried women served as social and economic capital, 'invested' in profitable marriages.[38] As Christina had used her commitment to God to secure her freedom from marriage in the twelfth century, so thirteenth-century beguine women exploited their status as holy women to form communities that avoided the enclosure and strict rules of conventional nunneries.[39] Their experiences demonstrate that, far from inhibiting women, devotion to God could enable women to subvert the traditional expectations of family, kinship and male authority. For their early modern descendants, defiant virginity may not have been as obvious an option – although the author of *Eliza's babes* considered it, and Anna Trapnel may not have chosen spinsterhood, but certainly exploited it – but even for married women their commitment as Christians could and did override their duties as women when the two came into conflict. The women of this study were more likely to draw on Biblical women as direct inspiration, but nevertheless, like their

[36] Janette Dillon, 'Holy Women and their Confessors or Confessors and their Holy Women? Margery Kempe and Continental Tradition', in *Prophets Abroad*, ed. Voaden, pp. 120, 129–30.

[37] See chapters 5 and 6 below.

[38] Eleanor McLaughlin, 'Women, Power and the Pursuit of Holiness in Medieval Christianity', in *Feminist Theology: A Reader*, edited by Ann Loades (London: SPCK, 1990), pp. 105–10.

[39] Newman, *From Virile Woman to WomanChrist*, p. 142; Dillon, 'Holy Women and their Confessors', pp. 119–20.

medieval ancestors, they were struggling towards a theology of Christian virtue that transcends gender.

In many ways this book resembles a collection of miniatures, detailed studies of a handful of women from a variety of perspectives. The fact that these writers are viewed more as individuals than as a group is deliberate. Many of these writers have been 'discovered' only in the last decade or two, and it is naturally much more difficult to contextualise them than the Donnes, Herberts or Miltons who have been the subjects of centuries of scholarly study. While the eagerness of early feminist scholarship for a 'big picture' of early modern women's authorship is understandable, it is a project that is not possible without historical detail, even more historical detail than we have yet uncovered. Without that detail, the picture is inevitably blurred and biased. The case studies in this book are a step towards sharpening the focus and filling in the details on that large canvas. They allow us to place these five women, at least, in perspective, and suggest ways of reading other women – and, in fact, men – whose writing or circumstances are similar. They also allow us to begin to question the historical resonance of our own analytical categories, so that we might see how women were empowered or disempowered within their own politics, not ours. The conclusion of this book demonstrates that from even a handful of such case studies it is possible to draw generalisations that radically alter current concepts of public, private, gender and religious experience in the early modern period. With many more such miniatures we can begin to assemble the 'big picture' of early modern women's writing and religious agency.

CHAPTER I

'Blockish Adams' on mystical marriage

The treatment of mystical marriage among seventeenth-century religious writers is a broad subject – the first half of the century witnessed the publication of numerous commentaries, sermon collections, translations and verse paraphrases of Biblical mystical marriage texts, particularly the Song of Songs.[1] This chapter is not long enough to consider all of these texts, or to draw generalisations about mystical marriage that cover a cross-section of early modern thinkers.[2] Instead, the men discussed here are all moderate or Puritan theologians and prose writers; their work suggests the

---

[1] In addition to works mentioned in footnotes below, the texts consulted include: STC 219 Henry Ainsworth, *Annotations vpon the five bookes of moses, the booke of the psalmes, and the song of songs, or canticles* (London: for John Bellamie, 1627); STC 2774 Robert Aylett, *The song of songs, which was salomons, metaphrased in english heroiks* (London: William Stansby, 1621); Wing B4324 John Brayne, *An exposition upon the canticles* (London: Robert Austin, 1651); Wing B4679 Thomas Brightman, *A commentary on the canticles*, in *Workes* (London: by John Field for Samuel Cartwright, 1644); STC 6042 Robert Crofts, *The lover* (London: B. Alsop and T. F. for Richard Meighen, 1638); STC 7080 John Dove, *The conversion of salomon* (London: W. Stansby for John Smethwick, 1613); Wing G436 William Gearing, *The love-sick spouse* (London: for Nevill Simmons, 1665); Wing G2206 William Guild, *Loves entercourse* (London: W. Wilson for Ralph Smith, 1657); Wing H374 Joseph Hall, *Christ mysticall* (London: M. Flesher for William Hope, Gabriel Beadle and Nathaniel Webbe, 1647) and STC 12712 *Salomons diuine arts* (London: H. L. for Eleazar Edgar, 1609); STC 13392 Samuel Hieron, *The bridegroome* (London: for Samuel Macham, 1613); Wing H2559 Nathanael Homes, *A commentary literal or historical, and mystical or spiritual*, in *Works* (London: Printed for the author, 1652); Wing H3350 Herman Hugo, *Pia desideria* (English) (London: for Henry Bonwick, 1686); Wing J542A Christopher Jellinger, *The excellency of christ* (London: I. L. for Thomas Nichols, 1641); Wing K709 Hanserd Knollys, *An exposition of the first chapter of the song of solomon* (London: W. Godbid for Livewel Chapman, 1656); Wing M1423 John Mayer, *A commentary upon the holy writings of job, david, and salomon* (London: for Robert Ibbitson and Thomas Roycroft, 1653); STC 2776 Francis Quarles, *Sions sonets* (London: W. Stansby for Thomas Dewe, 1625); STC 20542 Francis Quarles, *Emblemes* (London: J. Dawson for Francis Eglesfield, 1639); STC 21638 John Saltmarsh, *Poemata sacra* (Cambridge: Ex Academia celeberrimæ typographeo, 1636); Wing B2629A George Sandys, *A paraphrase upon the song of solomon* (London: John Legatt, 1641); Wing T2046 John Trapp, *Solomon's ΠΑΝΑΡΕΤΟΣ* (London: T. R. and E. M. for John Bellamie, 1650); Wing B2629E Richard Turner, *The song of solomon rendred in plain & familiar verse* (London: J. H. for J. Rothwell, 1659); STC 21359 Richard Verstegan, *Odes* ([Antwerp]: 1601).

[2] Barbara Lewalski's *Protestant Poetics and the Seventeenth-Century Religious Lyric* (Princeton, New Jersey: Princeton University Press, 1979) includes a summary of seventeenth-century exegesis of the Song of Songs, pp. 53–4, 59–69, but does not discuss the role of marriage as a metaphor.

intellectual context from which the women poets of this book approached mystical marriage.[3] For the most part, these 'blockish Adams' (as Lady Anne Southwell might have called them) understood mystical marriage very differently from their female contemporaries, viewing that 'misterie, perhaps too deepe' as fundamentally marked by inequality and obedience, not companionship and respect.[4]

But what is this divine mystery that attracted so much attention among religious thinkers? Following the earlier commentaries of Origen and St Bernard of Clairvaux, seventeenth-century writers used a passage in Paul's letter to the Ephesians (quoted below) as a lens through which to read other Biblical texts – Hosea 1–3, passages in Ezekiel, 1 Corinthians 7, Revelation 22, and especially the Song of Songs – that employ marriage as a metaphor for the relationship between God and his people. By beginning with the Ephesians passage, which specifically describes the Church as the spouse

---

[3] There is an ongoing scholarly debate about how to refer to the more zealous Calvinist Protestants of the late sixteenth and early seventeenth centuries. The terminology for the period of the Interregnum and Restoration was more precise as factions became more clearly defined, but in the Elizabethan and early Stuart years political and theological sympathies were both more complexly interrelated and more loosely demarcated. It was possible, for example, to be both 'moderate' politically, conforming to all ecclesiastical policy, and 'godly' theologically, preaching and writing for further (lawful) reform, as Richard Sibbes is but one example (see below). In addition, while there were loose networks of these reformers united by theology, as well as of their Arminian counterparts, the majority continued to operate under the authority of the Church of England and therefore could not be visibly organised in opposition without endangering their careers and even their lives. (See Peter Lake, *The Boxmaker's Revenge: 'Orthodoxy', 'Heterodoxy', and the Politics of the Parish in Early Stuart London* (Manchester: Manchester University Press, 2001)).

The matter is complicated by the fact that the term 'Puritan' was originally pejorative, while the term 'godly', although preferred by the enthusiasts themselves, sounds somewhat self-righteous. As Patrick Collinson has written, '"The godly" was the appellation preferred by those sixteenth-century Englishmen whose unsympathetic neighbours called them "puritans" . . . [I]t is clear that "puritan", no less than "lollard" in the past, and "huguenot" across the Channel, was a social stigma, expressing distaste for a singular way of life' (*Godly People: Essays on English Protestantism and Puritanism* (London: Hambledon, 1983), p. 1). He has, however, gone on to argue that the original insult born of exaggeration eventually developed a more stable definition that was embraced by some 'Puritans' themselves: 'The seventeenth century could recognise a puritan when it saw one', he concludes ('Ecclesiastical Vitriol: Religious Satire in the 1590s and the Invention of Puritanism', in *The Reign of Elizabeth I: Court and Culture in the Last Decade*, ed. John Guy (Cambridge: Cambridge University Press, 1995), p. 155. See also Peter Lake, *Anglicans and Puritans? Presbyterianism and English Conformist Thought from Whitgift to Hooker* (London: Unwind Hyman, 1988), especially pp. 5–7). Since this study is largely concerned with seventeenth-century writers who would have recognised a Puritan when they saw one, I refer throughout to zealous Calvinist Protestants as Puritans.

[4] Jean Klene, ed., *The Southwell-Sibthorpe Commonplace Book: Folger MS. V.b.198* (Tempe, Arizona: Renaissance English Text Society, 1997), p. 20. The poem is reproduced at the beginning of the Introduction, above. The sources and analogues in men's poetry – particularly the work of Robert Southwell, Donne, Herbert, Crashaw and Milton – are discussed in comparison to individual women writers in subsequent chapters. See also Stanley Stewart, *The Enclosed Garden: The Tradition and the Image in Seventeenth-Century Poetry* (Madison, Wisconsin: University of Wisconsin Press, 1966); Lewalski, *Protestant Poetics*, pp. 67–9, 416–25; Michael C. Schoenfeldt, *Prayer and Power: George Herbert and Renaissance Courtship* (Chicago: University of Chicago Press, 1991).

of Christ, centuries of commentators reimagined even the Old Testament passages as describing the relationship between Christ and the Church. From the early Church the metaphor had also come to encompass the relationship between Christ and the individual soul, to describe the ecstasies of mystical love that occur when the soul is 'ravished' by Christ.[5] Among Puritan writers the distinctions between the two readings – Christ married to the Church and Christ married to the soul – are often elided and confused. The blurring of the boundaries between the Church and the soul is, as we shall see, intrinsic to these writers' revisioning of the institution of the Church.

In the Ephesians passage the boundaries are clear. For Paul, the comparison is only between husband and wife, Christ and the Church:

Wiues, submit your selues vnto your own husbands, as vnto the Lord. For the husband is the head of the wife, euen as Christ is the head of the Church: and he is the sauiour of the body. Therefore as the Church is subiect vnto Christ, so let the wiues bee to their owne husbands in euery thing. Husbands, loue your wiues, euen as Christ also loued the Church, and gaue himselfe for it: That he might sanctifie & cleanse it with the washing of water, by the word, That hee might present it to himselfe a glorious Church, not hauing spot or wrinckle, or any such thing: but that it should bee holy and without blemish. So ought men to loue their wiues, as their owne bodies: hee that loueth his wife, loueth himselfe. For no man euer yet hated his owne flesh: but nourisheth and cherisheth it, euen as the Lord the Church: For we are members of his body, of his flesh, and of his bones. For this cause shall a man leaue his father and mother, and shall be ioyned vnto his wife, and they two shalbe one flesh. This is a great mysterie: but I speake concerning Christ and the Church. Neuerthelesse, let euery one of you in particular, so loue his wife euen as himselfe, and the wife see that she reuerence her husband. (5:22–33)[6]

In this curious passage, Paul draws a parallel between Christ's saving and sacrificial love for the Church and the love of a husband for his wife. Yet Paul does not make the parallel figures of Christ and the human husband perfectly analogous, or even suggest that the earthly husband strive to correspond to every aspect of the saviour, Christ. Christ, the divine husband, offers his own body as a sacrifice in order to cleanse the Church. It is true that Christ's motives, as Paul describes them, are ultimately self-seeking: 'that hee might present it to himselfe a glorious Church'. But even if Christ gains in the end, his self-seeking is marked by enormous patience and foresight, considering the horror of the sacrifice Christ endures and the time he

[5] Ann W. Astell, *The Song of Songs in the Middle Ages* (Ithaca, New York: Cornell University Press, 1990), p. 4.
[6] This extract, and any others in early modern spelling, are from the Authorised Version of the Bible in *The Bible in English* database (Ann Arbor, Michigan: Chadwyck-Healy, 1996).

must wait until his second coming, when the Church can return his love completely. By contrast, the earthly husband's love is more self-serving: he loves his wife as his own flesh, not out of self-sacrificing altruism but because it is perverse not to love oneself. As Lady Anne Southwell's poem suggests, blockish Adam on earth is neither creator nor saviour: he only needs the sense to realise that loving and respecting his wife is a form of self-preservation.[7]

The lack of complete correspondence within Paul's parallelism suggests how unwieldy the mystery itself can be, open to a host of emphases and interpretations. Just how is the earthly husband related to Christ? Is the husband meant to imitate, or is he supposed to imagine Christ's love based on his own experience of marriage? The few seventeenth-century Ephesians commentators distinguish sharply between the husband's role and that of Christ:

God will have some resemblance of Christs authority over the Church held forth in the husbands authority over the wife. I say, some resemblance only: for, the comparative particle *as*, holdeth forth not an equality, but a similitude and likenesse, and in some things only, betwixt Christs headship over the Church, and the husbands over the wife, even in those things, which I presently shew are implyed in the husbands headship, which are some shadows only of that eminency, power, and fulnesse of grace and perfections, which are in our head Christ.[8]

Despite such assured readings, the scripture itself provides no clear answers to the question of how the husband is like Christ. Ephesians 5:22–33 is inserted in the middle of a longer list of prescriptions about family relationships (chapter 6 goes on to discuss children and parents, masters and servants), and the diversion to arcane mystical imagery seems jarring amid so many domestic minutiae. As one modern commentator has argued, the themes of Christ's sacrificial love and the Church's submissive response 'are much more important to the author than that of marital relations, as can be seen from the fact that at certain points they rupture the underlying analogy'.[9] This tension is likewise apparent within the text: as so often in

---

[7] My reading of Ephesians 5:22–33 differs slightly from some modern commentaries. See Rudolf Schnackenburg, *Ephesians: A Commentary*, trans. Helen Heron (Edinburgh: T. & T. Clark, 1991), pp. 240–58. Francis Watson, on the other hand, argues that the separation between human marriage and the relationship between Christ and the Church in this passage is even more absolute: 'Is the church a Wife and Christ her Husband? Nothing compels one to read into this passage the bridal language of Revelation or the prophetic image of Israel as the adulterous wife.' Watson notes that a careful reading of the Greek demonstrates that the metaphor used to describe Christ and the church is the head-body relationship. *Agape, Eros, Gender: Towards a Pauline Sexual Ethic* (Cambridge: Cambridge University Press, 2000), p. 242.

[8] Wing F773 James Fergusson, *A brief exposition of the epistles of paul to the galatians and ephesians* (Edinburgh: Christopher Higgins, 1659), p. 376.

[9] John Muddiman, *A Commentary on the Epistle to the Ephesians* (London: Continuum, 2001), p. 256.

his letters, in the last two verses of this passage Paul seems impatient to move beyond mundane questions to heavenly mysteries. The word translated 'Neuerthelesse' in verse 33 of the Authorised Version is πλην, a 'strong adversitive' that 'signals a descent from the heights of theology to the practicalities of daily living'.[10] The higher purpose (the 'great mysterie') of the mystical marriage metaphor is not to serve as a model for human relationships (although it 'Neuerthelesse' does), but to be a reflection of the divine. Calvin emphasises this point in his argument against the Roman Catholic use of Ephesians 5:32 as a proof-text for the sacramental nature of marriage:

We see then the hammer and anvil with which they fabricated this sacrament. But they have also shown their laziness by not attending to the correction which is immediately added, *But I speak in regard of Christ and the church.* He wanted particularly to enter a caveat, in case anyone should understand him as speaking of marriage; so that he has spoken more plainly than if he had uttered the sentence without any exception.[11]

The divine image is also central to official uses of the metaphor by the Elizabethan Church, which here, as on so many other issues, followed the lead of Paul. In the marriage service, the metaphor is invoked in the opening sentences to justify the holiness of the state of matrimony, 'which is an honorable estate, instituted of God in paradise in the time of man's innocency, signifying unto us the mystical union, that is betwixt Christ and his Church'. The list of traditional Protestant justifications for marriage goes on to include the wedding at Cana and St Paul's commendation of marriage, so that the Ephesians passage becomes only one of several proof-texts in which the Bible links marriage with the divine, thus disproving the Catholic doctrine that marriage was inferior to celibacy. As the priest speaks this passage, the bride and groom standing before the minister recede and the focus falls on marriage as an institution, with no sense of the divine as a model for human behaviour.[12]

[10] *Ibid.*, p. 271. See also Max Zerwick, S. J. and Mary Grosvenor, *A Grammatical Analysis of the New Testament*, 4th edition (Rome: Editrice Pontifico Istituto Biblico, 1993), p. 589. Most male theologians (although few women) would have had access to the Greek New Testament.
[11] *Calvin's Commentaries: The Epistles of Paul the Apostle to the Galatians, Ephesians, Philippians and Colossians*, trans. T. H. L. Parker (Edinburgh: Oliver and Boyd, 1965), p. 210.
[12] John Booty, ed., *The Book of Common Prayer 1559: The Elizabethan Prayer Book* (Charlottesville, Virginia: University of Virginia Press, 1976), p. 290, see also pp. 296–8. Many preachers argued that the metaphor of mystical marriage proved the holiness of human marriage; see for example Thomas Becon's *The boke of matrimony*, printed in STC 1710 *The worckes of thomas becon* (London: John Day, 1564), vol. I, ff. CCCCClxx^iv–CCCCClxxii^r, also Donne's sermon for Sir Francis Nethersole's marriage, in George R. Potter and Evelyn M. Simpson, eds., *The Sermons of John Donne*, 10 vols. (Berkeley, California: University of California Press, 1953–62), II.335–347.

Later in the service, the model is made more explicit in one of the prayers for the new couple:

O God, which by thy mighty power hast made all things of nought, which also after other things set in order, didst appoint that out of man (created after thine own image and similitude) woman should take her beginning, and knitting them together didst teach that it should never be lawful to put asunder those whom thou by matrimony hadst made one: O God, which hast consecrated the state of matrimony to such an excellent mystery, that in it is signified and represented the spiritual marriage and unity betwixt Christ and his Church, look mercifully upon these thy servants, that both this man may love his wife, according to thy Word (as Christ did love thy spouse the Church, who gave himself for it, loving and cherishing it even as his own flesh), and also that this woman may be loving and amiable to her husband . . .[13]

In intricate parallelism typical of his collects and prayers, Cranmer imbeds the mystical marriage of Ephesians 5 in God's divine ordering of creation; like the creation of Adam and Eve that serves as a model for all marital relations, God's blessing on the state of matrimony ultimately reflects the unity and sovereignty of a God who has 'made all things of nought'. Although Cranmer glances here at the example that Christ is meant to be for husbands, like Paul (whom he closely paraphrases), Cranmer's focus is on the 'great mysterie' of God's sovereign love and purpose. Surprisingly, there is no attempt in the marriage service to dissect the human elements of the metaphor, to consider what mystical marriage might mean for men and women pledging themselves to one another. Even the appointed homily on marital duties merely cobbles together paraphrases of Ephesians 5 and other New Testament passages on marriage into a blandly prescriptive list of duties that offers little consideration of the nature of marital love or why it might be an appropriate metaphor for divine love.[14]

Cranmer was not alone in resorting to the 'great mysterie' of the metaphor of marriage. Among seventeenth-century Puritan male writers, it is most often this Pauline use of the mystical marriage metaphor that is invoked. In order to understand Christ's love, the theologian imagines an ideal married love, freely assigning characteristics to the divine husband, Christ, that would not be ascribed (or even prescribed) to human husbands. With the exception of William Gouge, who attempts to literalise the mystical marriage metaphor, in most Puritan writers the mystery of mystical marriage has very little connection to human marriage. This discontinuity between the

[13] Booty, ed., *The Book of Common Prayer 1559*, p. 296.
[14] Mary Ellen Rickey and Thomas B. Stroup, eds., *Certain Sermons or Homilies* (Gainesville, Florida: Scholars' Facsimiles and Reprints, 1968).

ideal and the earthly is vital to an understanding of the gender differences in readings of mystical marriage. It is in delineating this discontinuity that male divines, unlike the women poets, come to emphasise the inequality in the relationship between Christ and the Church.

The separation of the metaphor from its anthropomorphic origin is paralleled in the radical separation of symbolic and literal meaning in the reading of mystical marriage texts. The detailed readings of individual writers at the centre of this chapter demonstrate that Biblical mystical marriage texts were especially fruitful for reforming writers because they offered an opportunity to imagine the relationship between Christ and the Church, often with only a very tenuous connection to the original text and the human aspects of the metaphor. Because of the hyper-allegorical tradition of reading these texts, the individual elements of the allegory – the kisses, watchmen, gardens, winds, doors – were made to represent almost anything the commentator could imagine.

At the heart of these allegorical readings is the Old Testament book of the Song of Songs. Most of the mystical marriage scriptures served as minor glosses or augmentations of the mystery, but the Song of Songs, a collection of intensely erotic love lyrics that contains only one oblique reference to God, was read as a detailed chronological narrative of the relationship Paul alludes to in Ephesians. Unlike other scriptures about mystical marriage, the Song is not self-consciously allegorical, but it is in fact this secularism that demands an allegorical reading in order to fit the poem into the Biblical canon. From Jewish scholars of the second and third centuries onwards commentators stressed that the erotic love lyrics must be approached with a mature faith for their true meaning to be understood.

The traditional Christian solution to the problem of the Song's eroticism began with Origen of Alexandria, who drew on Jewish exegesis to establish the book as an allegory of spiritual love between God and the Church or the Christian soul. Origen's reading was 'crucial for all subsequent Christian interpretation' because it established a pattern for exploiting the eroticism of the text for spiritual means.[15] In the twelfth century Bernard of Clairvaux developed Origen's interpretation into a comprehensive model of devotion for his Cistercian brethren. The love lyrics of the Song of Songs became

---

[15] E. Ann Matter, *The Voice of My Beloved: The Song of Songs in Western Medieval Christianity* (Philadelphia: University of Pennsylvania Press, 1990), pp. 28, 25. See also Astell, *The Song of Songs*, pp. 1–4. Another classical writer who influenced the allegorisation of erotic texts for moral purposes was Ovid. See Danielle Clarke, *The Politics of Early Modern Women's Writing* (London: Longman, 2001), pp. 193–8.

'a dynamic guide to the quest of each human being for union with God'.[16] Bernard can thus be credited with popularising the connection between mystical marriage theology and daily devotional practice that is crucial to the religious poetry of early modern women, for whom mystical marriage was one of many vehicles for imagining their life with God, and the Christian dimensions of their relationships with others.

Bernard and his Cistercian followers, as well as the parallel school of St Victor in Paris, were influential in inspiring 'bridal mysticism' among medieval holy men and women. As Nicholas Watson has argued, these works 'helped to create a remarkable climate of spiritual ambition throughout western Europe, with their teaching that a state of union with God was attainable, however briefly, in this life'.[17] Forms of 'bridal mysticism' based on Bernard's homilies influenced Catherine of Siena, Bridget of Sweden and the English mystics Richard Rolle and Walter Hilton.[18] These men and women advocated a complex devotional process in which the soul of the believer seeks ever closer union with God, although individual writers differ on the question of whether union with God can be achieved in mortal life.[19]

As Ann W. Astell has argued, such traditions encourage a symbolic feminisation of the reader, aligned with the beloved bride in her 'receptive surrender' to her lover, Christ. Seekers on this path are characterised by childlike service and loving obedience, enacting 'a romance of rescue and ravishment' in their longing for Christ, the great prince and knight.[20] For feminist scholars it is tempting to conclude that this feminisation of devotion opened up possibilities for women to speak, but such arguments must be approached with extreme caution. Caroline Walker Bynum, for example, has argued in a number of influential studies that connections between the increasing medieval emphasis on devotion to Christ's dying yet nurturing body imparted power to women who were traditionally identified with the flesh and feeding.[21] But David Aers has demonstrated that the parallels

---

[16] Matter, *The Voice of My Beloved*, pp. 39, 123.

[17] Nicholas Watson, 'The Middle English Mystics', in *The Cambridge History of Medieval English Literature*, ed. David Wallace (Cambridge: Cambridge University Press, 1999), pp. 545.

[18] For further reading on these figures see the essays in Rosalynn Voaden, ed., *Prophets Abroad: The Reception of Continental Holy Women in Late-Medieval England* (Cambridge: D. S. Brewer, 1996); Astell, *The Song of Songs*, pp. 105–18; and Watson, 'The Middle English Mystics', throughout.

[19] Watson, 'The Middle English Mystics', pp. 548–9, 555.

[20] Astell, *The Song of Songs*, pp. 138, 76–7.

[21] Caroline Walker Bynum, *Holy Feast and Holy Fast* (Berkeley: University of California Press, 1987) and *Fragmentation and Redemption: Essays on Gender and the Human Body in Medieval Religion* (New York: Zone Books, 1991).

between the body of Christ and female bodies are frequently tenuous, and moreover wonders whether '"feminizing" the tortured body of Christ as material, for instance, may not actually reinforce some basic premises and fantasies in traditional patriarchal constructions of "women"'.[22] The mere availability of ways of identifying with the feminine may not in itself be empowering to women, and may at times act as part of the process of controlling women, who are encouraged to imagine their devotional life in stereotypically subordinate ways. Both Aers's and Bynum's arguments are also complicated by the fact that men as well as women exploited these 'feminised' models of devotion.

For some medieval women the relatively passive female role in bridal mysticism was not sufficiently robust to express their ecstasies of divine love. As Barbara Newman has demonstrated, thirteenth-century Beguine holy women such as Hadjewich of Brabant, Mechtild of Magdeburg and Marguerite Porete combined the role of Bernard's 'receptive' bride with the more active wooing role of the *male* lover in contemporary courtly love lyrics. Hadjewich, for example, follows the conventions of German *Minnesang* so closely 'that only initiates will recognize her Beloved as God' and that the speaker is a pious (female) soul, not a male lover.[23] The metaphorical and symbolic gender identifications of the mystical marriage tradition are thus continually in flux: by the seventeenth century in England, it is primarily male poets who fuse the gender conventions of mystical marriage and the contemporary 'courtly' form, Petrarchism, although Aemilia Lanyer is a notable female exception.[24]

Although they also draw their basic interpretative model from Origen, Bernard and the tradition of bridal mysticism, early modern commentators on the Song of Songs tend to be considerably less experimental in their approach to the literal, gendered meaning of the text. These writers often discount the gender identifications drawn from the Song of Songs as insignificant: 'The speech indeed is of man and woman', as Thomas Myriell admitted in a sermon, 'and the bare letter sounds humane loue and affection; but this is but the *shell*, the sweet *kernell* is within in the sense, where you shall find more sung of then the loue of man to woman, euen the loue of God himselfe to man.'[25] For some readers uncomfortable with

---

[22] David Aers, in David Aers and Lynn Staley, *The Powers of the Holy: Religion, Politics, and Gender in Late Medieval English Culture* (University Park, Pennsylvania: The Pennsylvania State University Press, 1996), pp. 30–4, 35.

[23] Barbara Newman, *From Virile Woman to WomanChrist: Studies in Medieval Religion and Literature* (Philadelphia: University of Pennsylvania Press, 1995), p. 148, 137–67.

[24] See chapter 2 below.

[25] STC 18322 Thomas Myriell, *Christs suite to his church* (London: for Nathaniel Butter, 1613), p. 5.

the hyperbolic imagery of the Song, the entire literal signification of the
text could be discarded as nonsense: 'how absurd and monstrous were some
of [the author's] comparisons' wrote the Lincolnshire divine John Cotton,
offering a list of hyperbolic imagery that probably did seem absurd to a
Puritan literalist.[26]

For many, the habit of reading the Song of Songs as an allegory of Christ
and the Church had become so commonplace that the literal erotic meaning
of the text disappeared. The Canterbury preacher Thomas Wilson's oft-
reprinted *A christian dictionarie* (1612) included 'A Dictionary, specially
made, to giue some light to the darkesome Booke of Salomons Song, called
the Canticles'. While his title acknowledges the difficulty of understanding
the Song of Songs, Wilson's dictionary entries consistently erase literal
meaning, glossing phrases such as 'no Breasts' entirely metaphorically: 'No
true doctrine or sincere milke of the word'. Curiously, Wilson provides no
gloss on the male speaker of the poem, presumably because it is obvious that
the speaker is Christ.[27] The eminent Glasgow Presbyterian James Durham
went even further in his *Clavis cantici* (1668), attempting to theorise this
well-established practice: 'I grant [the Song] hath a literal meaning, but
I say, that literal meaning is not immediat, and that which first looketh
out, as in Historical Scriptures, or others which are not figurative, but that
which is spiritually and especially meant by these Allegorick and Figurative
speeches, *is* the Literal meaning of this Song.'[28] For such Puritan readers,
the breasts of the bride and other sensuous elements of the song were almost
invisible, obscured by the more 'immediat' theological meaning.

Puritan commentators went to such convoluted exegetical lengths
because the eroticism of the Song was spiritually dangerous if not
approached in the proper frame of mind.[29] In his 1623 hymnal *The hymnes
and songs of the chvrch*, George Wither insists repeatedly of his various
translations of the Song of Songs that they should not be sung without
spiritual preparation: 'This *Canticle* we may sing to the stirring vp of our
spirituall *Loue*; having first seriously meditated' on a dauntingly long list
of Christ's divine attributes.[30] Thomas Myriell likened reading the Song to

[26] Wing C6410 John Cotton, *A brief exposition of the whole book of canticles* (London: for Philip
Nevil, 1642), pp. 4–5. See also John Collinges, Wing C5323, *The intercourses of divine love* (London:
A. Maxwel for Thomas Parkhurst, 1676), sig. a2ᵛ–a3ʳ.
[27] STC 25786 Thomas Wilson, *A christian dictionarie* (London: W. Iaggard, 1612), pp. 173, 177.
[28] Wing D2802 James Durham, *Clavis cantici* (Edinburgh: George Swintoun and James Glen, 1668),
p. 6, emphasis added.
[29] See, for example, STC 12113 William Gouge ed., *An exposition of the song of solomon* (London: by
John Beale, 1615), sig. A3ʳ; STC 22476 Richard Sibbes, *Bowels opened* (London: G. M. for George
Edwards, 1639), pp. 3–4.
[30] STC 25908 George Wither, *The hymnes and songs of the church* (London: for G. W., 1623), p. 33.

entering the Holy of Holies, and demanded similar spiritual preparation: 'Hence therefore all prophane eyes and eares; and come not neare'.[31] These writers use images of darkness, earth and the heavy elements to explain the difference between the 'carnall sense' of earthly love and the mystery of divine love:[32]

In our meditation of this mysterie, let vs conceiue no carnall, no earthly thing of it, because it is a mysterie: it is altogether spirituall and heauenly . . . but if because of these comparisons we draw this which is only and wholly spirituall, to any carnall matter, we shall make that to be a thicke mist, and darke cloud, which is giuen for a light.[33]

The dichotomy between the heavy sinfulness of the flesh and the heights of contemplation was conventionally Pauline; yet, as E. Ann Matter has pointed out, Christian commentators since Origen have used allegorical interpretation as a way of celebrating 'the erotic desiring, seduction, and wounding' of the individual searching for God.[34]

Similarly, among medieval Catholic Song of Song commentators there was a long tradition of 'identif[ying] sexual union itself as the *foremost* aspect of the spiritual marriage metaphor'.[35] During the sixteenth and seventeenth centuries such eroticised models of mysticism flourished as the post-Tridentine Church sought to reinvigorate the devotion of Catholic laity. In Spain in particular mystics such as John of the Cross and Teresa de Jesús helped to popularise passionate forms of bridal mysticism, and Spain experienced an unprecedented flowering of holiness, particularly among women.[36] While most of these writings included the standard warnings about the carnal dangers of literalising the text, Catholic mystics were nevertheless unafraid to exploit the metaphoric potential of erotic detail in a way that would have seemed extreme and superstitious to the women of this study, although their own writings drew on the same interpretative traditions.

---

[31] Myriell, *Christs suite*, pp. 4, 5.
[32] Wither, *The hymnes and songs of the chvrch*, p. 33; and STC 21343 Francis Rous, *The mysticall marriage* (London: W. Jones and T. Paine for I. Emery, 1635), pp. 3–6.
[33] STC 12119 William Gouge, *Of domesticall dvties* (London: John Haviland for William Bladen, 1622), p. 125.
[34] Matter, *The Voice of My Beloved*, p. 32.
[35] George L. Scheper, 'Reformation Attitudes Toward Allegory and the Song of Songs', *PMLA* 89.3 (1973): 559.
[36] Stephen Haliczer, *Between Exaltation and Infamy: Female Mystics in the Golden Age of Spain* (Oxford: Oxford University Press, 2002), pp. 4, 9–13, 28–35. See also Matter, *The Voice of My Beloved*, pp. 181, 185–6; and Catherine Medwick, *Teresa of Avila: The Progress of a Soul* (London: Duckworth, 2000).

English Protestant commentators, on the other hand, usually avoided the erotic play of their Catholic counterparts. George Scheper suggests that these writers instead substitute the 'domestic hierarchical relation of husband and wife' for the erotic desire of the bride for her bridegroom.[37] In fact, even this seemingly benign aspect of human marriage is rarely mentioned in Puritan mystical marriage texts. Puritan writings focus on two aspects of the mystical marriage relationship: the complete faithfulness and utter submission of the Church to her husband Christ, and the overwhelming and undeserved love Christ showers upon the Church. The dynamics of this relationship are dependent upon the vast difference in spiritual purity between Christ and the Church. The Church is obedient to the point of self-abnegation because she cannot possibly be worthy of the love extended to her. Christ, on the other hand, offers himself from such a lofty height that he cannot expect an equal return from her. In the knight–lover allegories of the medieval period, this relationship was often likened to the devotion between lovers of great social inequality, a trope that is echoed in the host–guest relationship of George Herbert's 'Love bade me welcome' and in Petrarchan courtly love lyrics.[38]

Among Puritan commentators, this social separation had its allegorical value: the Church's faithfulness in mystical marriage is a means of defending the Church of England as the true Church, who (unlike the Roman Church) has not strayed from her true husband; and the sacrificial devotion of Christ is a means of moving both the body of the Church and the individual believer to obedience. But, despite its allegorical facility for describing the relationship between humans and the divine, a match of such insurmountable inequality was anathema to the Puritan concept of human marriage, with its focus on reciprocal duties and the social and spiritual unity of husband and wife. The traits that moderate and Puritan commentators appropriate for Christ the lover and husband and his submissive spouse are radically different from those desirable for Puritan husbands and wives.[39] 'For what man being to marry', wrote Thomas Myriell, 'would chuse a deformed, blacke, and adulterous wife? Or hauing chosen such a

---

[37] Scheper, 'Reformation Attitudes', p. 559.
[38] Frances Beer, *Women and Mystical Experience in the Middle Ages* (Woodbridge, Suffolk: The Boydell Press, 1992), pp. 56–77; Astell, *The Song of Songs*, p. 14.
[39] See Sylvia Brown, 'Godly Household Government from Perkins to Milton: The Rhetoric and Politics of *oeconomia*, 1600–1645', (unpublished PhD thesis, Princeton University, 1994); she has also allowed me to consult an unpublished seminar paper, 'Puritan Family Values', presented at Keble College, Oxford, in February 1996. See also the discussion of Daniel Rogers and other Puritan writers on marriage in the next section of this chapter.

one in marriage, would loue her so much as to dye for her?'[40] Even the strictly prescriptive William Gouge, whose literal reading of Ephesians leads him to insist on the complete submission of wives, nevertheless backs away from giving husbands a Christ-like authority to punish their wives.[41]

For all of their well-documented interest in controlling domestic relations, Puritan theologians of mystical marriage are much less interested in husbands and wives than they are in the future of the Church. Over the course of the century the mystical marriage metaphor became crucial to Puritan ecclesiology, as is evidenced by the sheer number of commentaries, sermons and paraphrases of these texts.[42] The value of the metaphor lay in its flexibility; for it came to encompass all of the central tenets of the Puritan community: the Westminster *Annotations* valued the Song of Songs 'for the very splendour and evidence shining so clear and bright, even through all its clouds, that the dimmest eye may read Christ in it . . . And not him onely, but likewise his glory and benefits and treasures dispenced to the Church; and her duty and office, and affections to be returned towards him.'[43] Glossing this complicated allegory in their sermons and commentaries opened up possibilities for theologians to shape a comprehensive vision of the Church that was not outright polemic.

The next three sections of this chapter explore this tradition in detailed readings of three Puritan mystical marriage commentators from the first half of the century: *Of domesticall dvties* (1622) by William Gouge, the sermons of Richard Sibbes and Francis Rous's *The mysticall marriage* (1635). These case studies serve as an introduction to a body of material that deserves further study. The opening section considers William Gouge's treatment of mystical marriage in his domestic handbook alongside the work of other prescriptive writers on marriage. Uniquely, Gouge does not discard the human institution in his reading of the divine ideal, but labours throughout his text to connect human and divine.

Sibbes and Rous, on the other hand, draw on the two strands of mystical marriage commentary that concentrated on the divine elements of the metaphor: the ecclesiastical and the personally mystical. The ecclesiastical readings, focused on the relationship of the institutional Church to

---

[40] Myriell, *Christs suite*, p. 40.   [41] Gouge, *Of domesticall dvties*, pp. 389–93.

[42] George Scheper has documented more than five hundred commentaries on the Song of Songs in seventeenth-century Europe, and has argued that Protestant Reformers were as preoccupied with the Song of Songs as High Medieval theologians, 'Reformation Attitudes', p. 556.

[43] Wing D2064 *Annotations upon all the books of the old and new testament* (London: Evan Tyler, 1657), sig. 7G^r.

Christ, were by far the most common among Puritan commentators from the first half of the seventeenth century, who used the genre to articulate an ideal of the reformed Church. The sermons of the archetypal Puritan minister Richard Sibbes offer a paradigm of this type of reading, dense with exquisitely detailed, verse-by-verse explication of the Church in the text. Francis Rous's slim book is, by contrast, one of the few personal mystical readings of the text among early Puritan commentators; Rous dispenses with textual detail to write his own allegory of the intense desire between Christ and the individual soul. In only a few cases (and not with any of these particular texts) is it possible to detect direct textual influences between the texts of 'blockish Adams' and the Eves of this study, but the ideas of these works, so common in such a wide variety of texts, would have been available generally to educated men and women.[44]

As an epilogue, the final section of the chapter examines the fate of the mystical marriage metaphor in the second half of the century. In the 1650s the leading Presbyterian and Independent thinkers emphasised the importance of mystical union with Christ for individual salvation. Drawing on the personally mystical interpretations of the Song of Songs, men such as John Owen and Samuel Annesley developed an elaborate affective language to describe the relationship between Christ and believers. In the 1670s a heated debate sprang up around these texts, demonstrating the continuing vitality of mystical marriage and the centrality of the metaphor in the struggle between Calvinists and anti-Calvinists to define the true Church of England. The issue at stake – the use of imaginative language in devotional writing – would have profound significance for the relationship of women's writing to orthodox theological texts.

WILLIAM GOUGE

Unlike the other texts discussed in this chapter, William Gouge's (1578–1653) book *Of domesticall dvties* (1622) is focused primarily on human marriage relations, and it is worth pausing to compare this work with other texts concerned with marriage as a subject, not a construct. Like Gouge, other writers on marriage invoke the concept of mystical marriage; but, perhaps surprisingly, none of these focus on the connections between human and divine marriages. Like the marriage service and St Paul, the three sermons on marriage in Donne's *Fifty sermons* (1649) use the metaphor to draw

---

[44] Lady Anne Southwell's library, for example, contained numerous volumes of Puritan sermons and commentaries; see Sister Jean Carmel Cavanaugh, S. L., 'The Library of Lady Southwell and Captain Sibthorpe', *Studies in Bibliography* 20 (1967): 243–54.

Donne's audience from the notion of human union to the higher concept of union with the divine.[45] The distinction between these two unions is more apparent in *A treatise of salomons mariage* (1612), a text written to commemorate the wedding of Princess Elizabeth and Frederick, the Elector Palatine, by Andrew Willet. Willet sets prescriptive advice about marriage alongside mystical marriage readings of Psalm 45, but draws distinctly different pictures of the two relationships, advocating a respect and reciprocity between husband and wife, who are both expected to offer advice to one another, but absolute submission for the Church, who is to obey Christ unquestioningly.[46]

Similarly, in his marriage handbook *Matrimoniall honovr* (1642), Daniel Rogers also uses mystical marriage to shift the focus from human to divine, insisting that both husband and wife must possess a soul that 'delight[s] in denying her selfe' for her divine husband.[47] Like the mystical marriage commentaries of Sibbes, Rous and others, *Matrimoniall honovr* demonstrates the radical differences between the characteristics ascribed to the bridal soul and the attributes desired for an ideal human bride. Rogers's bridal soul possesses a 'whorish hard heart' that is absolutely foul and sinful and entirely estranged from her perfect husband. Once her hard heart is broken by his love and she recognises her sinfulness, she abases herself before him: 'I say, at length, she is convinced, and casting her selfe downe at his feet, as one that is loath to dishonour that love which she so much abused; with a trembling and selfe-despairing heart, begins to touch the hem of his garment.' This bride that crawls and pleads at the foot of her beloved stands in sharp contrast to the ideals Rogers holds for human wives and husbands, who are both enabled through their humbled relationship with Christ to become like Christ to one another, earning from their abasement 'the fellowship with Christs holy nature, by which the soule partakes the properties of Christ, qualifying it with wisedome, influence, strength, meeknesse, patience, holinesse, cheerfulnesse, long-suffering and compassion; which graces, as they make him a meet head and husband for the Church, so they make married couples meet heads and helpers for each other.'[48] Significantly, Rogers envisions both partners in the human marriage taking the roles of the partners in the divine marriage: husband and wife are both first bridal soul in their relationship to Christ, then

---

[45] In Potter and Simpson, eds., *The Sermons of John Donne*, II.335–47, III.241–55, V.113–29.

[46] STC 25705 Andrew Willet, *A treatise of salomon's mariage* (London: F[elix] K[ingston] for Thomas Man the elder and William Welby, 1612), pp. 1–27, especially compare readings on pp. 6–8, 21–4.

[47] Wing R1797 Daniel Rogers, *Matrimoniall honovr* (London: Th. Harper for Philip Nevil, 1642), p. 23.

[48] *Ibid.*, pp. 22, 23, 25.

divine Christ in their relationship to one another. In practice wives may be exhorted to submit and husbands to love and direct, but neither the radical subjection of the soul nor the supreme headship of Christ is a gendered model for the married couple.

The ideal of corresponding – if unequal – duties for husbands and wives was particularly appealing for more reforming Protestants: far more handbooks and sermons on marriage were written by Puritans and Calvinists like Rogers and Willet than by religious conservatives like Donne. For early modern English Calvinists, the family was '*the Seminary of the Commonwealth*' where the religious instruction that would aid salvation began.[49] Maintaining order in the family was the first step towards creating a Puritan society in which each person could live out his or her calling and perform his or her duty to God.

While there is not room here to list all of the attributes of the ideal Puritan household, the prescriptive writings emphasise three elements relevant to the concept of mystical marriage: that spouses should come from similar backgrounds, that love was a duty of both spouses equally and that wives, although exhorted to submit, exercised some economic authority within the household.[50] Economic and social parity in spouses was vital to prevent marital strife – 'Those matches doe seldome proue but vncomfortable, where this rule is not obserued', wrote William Whately in *A care-cloth: or a treatise of the cvmbers and trovbles of marriage* – and also to preserve the social order. But, Whately asserted, 'the maine matter to be desired, is vertue and godlinesse'.[51] Similar religious inclinations meant that spouses could support one another in faith and religious duties and instruct children and servants in the fundamentals of faith. Without such agreement in faith the more pious partner might be brought to sin by the one weaker in faith.

Such a position was especially difficult for wives, who were exhorted to submit and obey in all but the most extreme situations and might find themselves forced to choose between obedience to their husbands and obedience to God.[52] Even the strict William Gouge, who as the following

---

[49] *Ibid.*, p. 7. On the importance of sermons as a means to salvation for English Calvinists, see Lake, *The Boxmaker's Revenge*, pp. 53–66.

[50] The most recent study of Puritan marriage writings is Christine Peters, *Patterns of Piety: Women, Gender, and Religion in Late Medieval and Reformation England* (Cambridge: Cambridge University Press, 2003), pp. 314–2. See also Brown, 'Godly Household Government'; John Morgan, *Godly Learning: Puritan Attitudes towards Reason, Learning and Education 1560–1640* (Cambridge: Cambridge University Press, 1986), pp. 142–71.

[51] STC 25299 William Whately, *A care-cloth: or a treatise of the cvmbers and trovbles of marriage* (London: Felix Kyngston for Thomas Man, 1624), p. 73, 71.

[52] Peters, *Patterns of Piety*, p. 319.

analysis demonstrates was considerably more thorough than his contemporaries in his emphasis on women's submission, allowed that 'If an husband shall command his wife to goe to Masse, to a stage play, to play at dice, to prostitute her body to vncleannes, to goe garishly and whorishly attired, to sell by scant weights, short measures, or the like, she ought not to doe so.'[53] But such necessary disobedience would create great strife in the home, and would be best prevented by the pious woman marrying a man equally devout, '[a]s if of heaven, he were elect', as the author of *Eliza's babes* (1652) writes of her unexpectedly supportive husband.[54]

For most writers, the next two elements of the marriage ideal similarly served to soften the emphasis on women's submission and men's authority. The priority given to mutual duties the couple were both required to perform was frequently seen as lessening the impact of gender inequality. William Whately, for example, asserts that the husband's authority is 'Gods authoritie inuested in his person', therefore 'he must not permit (vnlesse hee will wrong God) that it bee troden downe and despised'. Similarly, he advises the wife to 'set downe this conclusion within her soule: Mine husband is my superiour, my better: he hath authoritie and rule ouer me, nature hath giuen it him'. But these harsh assertions of duties specific to husband and wife follow nearly a hundred pages extolling the duties spouses hold in common, including chastity (sexual fidelity), 'Due Beneuolence' (satisfying one's spouse sexually so that he or she will not be tempted) and 'the life and soule of marriage', mutual love.[55] Although the second half of *A bride-bush* elaborates on the gendered division of authority in marriage, at the end of the book Whately returns to mutuality, advising both husbands and wives to look first to their own faults before criticising their partners.[56]

Daniel Rogers, similarly, emphasises the mutual duties of religious faith and married love over the gendered requirements of authority and submission. Rogers argues explicitly that gendered duties flow from those which are common such as love: 'so, let the married parties once be united in the former duties which stande in equality: it wilbe no difficulty to mainteine

[53] Gouge, *Of domesticall dvties*, p. 329. For similar limitations to submission see Rogers, *Matrimoniall honovr*, pp. 262–3; STC 25297 William Whately, *A bride-bvsh: or, a direction for married persons* (London: Felix Kyngston for Thomas Man, 1619), p. 206.

[54] Wing E535C, *Eliza's babes* (London: M. S. for Laurence Blaiklock, 1652), 'The Change', p. 44, l. 9. Edited by L. E. Semler as *Eliza's Babes: or The Virgin's Offering (1652): A Critical Edition* (Madison, Wisconsin: Fairleigh Dickinson University Press, 2001). See chapter 4 below.

[55] Whately, *A bride-bush*, pp. 98, 189, 2–13, 14–28, 31. Pages 1–97 cover mutual duties.

[56] *Ibid.*, pp. 217–18. Pages 97–216 cover specific duties of husbands and wives.

these which are peculiar'.[57] If spouses love one another, there will be fewer conflicts to make a husband's rule or a wife's submission more difficult. Such framing of the command to wives to submit serves to mitigate some of the harshest possible consequences, although ultimately each of these writers expects a wife to acknowledge her inferiority even to an immoral or ungodly husband.

Many commentators also mitigate the harshness of women's subjection by allowing women economic power and authority within the household. John Dod and Robert Cleaver's oft-reprinted *A godlie forme of householde government* (first published 1598), Rogers's *Matrimoniall honovr* (1642) and before them Thomas Becon's influential works on matrimony in the mid-sixteenth century, all assigned corresponding realms of decision to husbands and wives: for example, husbands are to bring home goods to support the family, while wives are to manage those goods.[58] Rogers, for example, asserts that a wife has control over 'the Bestowing & safe storing up, preserving & improving those commodities which her husba[n]d hath brought to her hand'.[59] Although none of these texts are notably liberating for women by modern standards, or free of misogyny, they do at least allow the wife a degree of autonomy. Within her own (smaller) realm the wife acts independently on behalf of her family; she must obey her husband, but she need not consult him on every decision.

For all of these writers marriage is a balance between equality in love and sexual fidelity and inequality in authority. William Gouge, on the other hand, emerges as unusual in his thorough exploration of the inequality between husbands and wives. For Gouge, it is the gendered duties of authority and submission that come first and define the shape of the marriage, not the equalising force of love. Gouge's distinction arises out of his attempt to apply the mystical marriage metaphor in Ephesians 5: 22–33 to the realities of human marriage. In order to connect the roles of a human wife and husband to the roles of the feminine Church/soul and masculine Christ, Gouge has to imagine a wife more extremely submissive, obedient and self-abnegating than other Puritan writers would conceive.

The extremes of Gouge's marriage handbook, *Of domesticall dvties*, are perhaps not surprising given the context of its writing. Like his close contemporary Richard Sibbes, Gouge was an influential moderate voice in

---

[57] Rogers, *Matrimoniall honovr*, p. 203.
[58] STC 5384 John Dod and Robert Cleaver, *A godlie forme of hovseholde government* (London: Felix Kingston for Thomas Man, 1600), especially pp. 61–97; STC 1710 Becon, *The boke of matrimony*, in *The worckes*, vol. 1, ff. DClxvi^v–DClxxviii^r, DClxxv^v–DClxxvi^r; see also his *A new catechisme*, also printed in *The worckes*, vol. 1, f. CCCCCxv^r.
[59] Rogers, *Matrimoniall honovr*, p. 292.

the London Puritan community. Both were members of the Feoffees for Impropriations, a group of men who organised financial backing for embattled Puritan clergymen, endowing lectureships and schoolmasters to support their cause.[60] At the end of his life Gouge served on the Westminster Assembly and helped pen the new annotations to the Bible meant to replace the marginal glosses of the old Geneva translation.[61] *Of domesticall dvties* began as a series of sermons delivered to the fashionable Puritan congregation at St Anne's, Blackfriars, where Gouge held a coveted lectureship for most of his career. The lectures were most likely written in response to a meeting of London clergy called by bishop John King to issue an 'expresse commaundment from the King to will them to inveigh vehemently and bitterly in theyre sermons against the insolencie of our women'. The command had an immediate effect; a few weeks later John Chamberlain reported that 'Our pulpits ring continually of the insolence and impudence of women".[62]

Gouge was one of those who took James's misogyny to heart; his book seemed so adamant about the 'vttermost' subjection of wives to their husbands that it caused a minor uprising among the women of his congregation. Gouge was forced to modify his most extreme statements in the dedicatory epistle to his parishioners. Even the exemplary Puritan men and women of St Anne's, who included such notables as the future Civil War hero Sir Robert Harley and his third wife, Brilliana, considered the strictures Gouge placed on women too severe; their harsh criticisms are implied in Gouge's protest: 'This iust Apologie I haue beene forced to make, that I might not euer be iudged (as some haue censured mc) *an hater of women.*'[63]

Despite this initial apology, Gouge is more thorough than his contemporaries in his emphasis on the subjection of wives to husbands. In response to James's command, Gouge's sermons address the pressing question of the

[60] Nicholas Tyacke, *Aspects of English Protestantism, c. 1530–1700* (Manchester: Manchester University Press, 2001), pp. 116, 121–2; Paul S. Seaver, *The Puritan Lectureships: The Politics of Religious Dissent 1560–1662* (Stanford, California: Stanford University Press, 1970), p. 237.

[61] Wing D2062 *Annotations upon all the books of the old and new testament* (London: John Legatt and John Raworth, 1645). The work was enlarged and reprinted in 1651 (Wing D2063) and 1657 (Wing D2064).

[62] Letters from John Chamberlain to Dudley Carleton, dated 25 January 1619/20 and 12 February 1619/20, *The Letters of John Chamberlain*, ed. Norman Egbert McClure (Philadelphia: The American Philosophical Society, 1939), II:286, 289; quoted in Lindsay A. Mann, 'Misogyny and Libertinism: Donne's Marriage Sermons', *John Donne Journal* 11.1–2 (1992): 113. Because James issued the command through the bishop there is no record of it among royal proclamations, and John King's own papers do not survive.

[63] Gouge, *Of domesticall dvties*, sig. ¶4ʳ. On the 'small but fashionable' congregation of St Anne's, Blackfriars, see Patrick Collinson, *The Birthpangs of Protestant England: Religious and Cultural Change in the Sixteenth and Seventeenth Centuries* (London: Macmillan, 1988), p. 71; Seaver, *The Puritan Lectureships*, pp. 50, 182, 274.

place of women within the world of men. Using Ephesians 5 and 6 as the text for his treatises, Gouge imagines the role of husband and wife arising out of the command to all Christians in Ephesians 5:21 to submit themselves to one another. Although modern commentators frequently see this verse as an assertion of equality in Christ that 'relativizes differences, but [ ] does not erase them', for Gouge as for many other early modern writers the exhortation to submit to one another reflects the fact that each early modern individual was positioned within a hierarchical social order.[64] Gouge's ideal husband and wife are a loving authority figure and an obedient subordinate whose relationship parallels not only the love of Christ and the Church but the interaction between a king and his magistrates, magistrates and the people, masters and their servants. In doing so, Gouge establishes a hierarchical family structure that is of unimpeachable authority, derived from the example of Christ himself, which both establishes women's position in the male hierarchies of the world and imagines women's subjection as a model of subjection to higher authority.

Gouge imagines the family as a series of power relationships that are a kind of microcosm of the state: 'a little Church, and a little commonwealth', or 'at least a liuely representation thereof'.[65] His model of society is an ordered chain of authority, with clear steps from one individual to the next:

Yea, God hath so disposed euery ones seuerall place, as there is not any one, but in some respect is vnder another. The wife, though a mother of children, is vnder her husband. The husband, though head of a family, is vnder publike Magistrates. Publike Magistrates one vnder another, and all vnder the King. The King himselfe vnder God and his word deliuered by his Ambassadours, whereunto the highest are to submit themselues. And Ministers of the word, as subiects, are vnder their Kings and Gouernours.[66]

More important in this passage than the fact that women's place is near the bottom of the chain, just above children, is the fact that she is part of the chain at all. Gouge establishes the relationship between husband and wife as a relationship of political authority and submission that mirrors all other such relationships (all of which are between men), in effect making adherence to gendered family power structures a matter of obedience to public authority.

Gouge does not hesitate to connect domestic duties with public duties: for men, because family duties test and form men's ability to govern with love, and for women because in the family they learn submission and

---

[64] Watson, *Agape, Eros, Gender*, p. 226.   [65] Gouge, *of domesticall duties*, p. 18.   [66] *Ibid.*, p. 5.

obedience to the commonwealth, to the Church and ultimately to God. The chief duty of the wife is to submit to her husband, whereas the chief duty of the husband is to love his wife, in other words, to govern justly and mercifully the creature that submits to him. Thus the particular calling, both publicly and privately, of the entire female sex is to submission within the home, and it is from these duties that women are to derive satisfaction and a sense of usefulness:

This is to be noted for satisfaction of certaine weake consciences, who thinke that if they haue no publike calling, they haue no calling at all; and thereupon gather that all their time is spent without a calling. Which consequence if it were good and sound, what comfort in spending their time should most women haue, who are not admitted to any publike function in Church or commonwealth?[67]

By making a women's domestic duties equivalent to her 'publike calling', Gouge establishes the public role of the woman's submission, and raises the stakes for any women who would disobey by implying that she risks her very salvation if she cannot learn Christian submission within the home. Although the connection between order in the home and the good of the commonwealth may be commonplace, for Gouge the force of the mystical marriage metaphor adds to the impact of this connection on women. Unlike men, who enjoy a variety of callings and forms of Christ-like authority, a woman's religious duty in public and at home is defined by her Church-like submission. The connection Gouge draws between 'private' submission in the home and 'publike' submission to Church and state also provides evidence of the fluidity of public and private behaviour in this period. Private disobedience has public consequences in Gouge's commonwealth.[68]

Although he recognises that women have a function within the family and even within the state, Gouge controls women's active role by making them in all matters subject to the male head of the family. He distinguishes three orders of a family, or three power relationships: husbands/wives, parents/children, masters/servants. In two of these relationships, Gouge assumes that the superior actor in the relationship is male – a husband, a master. In Chapter Eight on the duties of masters, for example, Gouge makes no mention of the relationship between a wife and her servants, as if he can assume that in a smoothly run household the wife will follow the direction of her husband. When writing of the third relationship, between

---

[67] *Ibid.*, p. 18.
[68] See Introduction, above, and David Cressy, 'Response: Private Lives, Public Performance, and Rites of Passage', in *Attending to Women in Early Modern England*, ed. Betty S. Travitsky and Adele F. Seeff (Newark, Delaware: University of Delaware Press, 1994), p. 187.

parents and children, Gouge does encourage children to be obedient and respectful to both parents equally.[69] But this allowance does not constitute a distinct authority for the wife, for in this section Gouge speaks almost entirely of parents as a unit, with the implicit assumption that the mother, as a good wife, will submit herself to the authority of the father. The two act together as one mind – his. Tellingly, only nine of seventy-nine sections in Chapter six, on the duties of parents, refer specifically to the duties of mothers. Eight of these nine discuss the duties of the pregnant or nursing mother, duties restricted to a mother by her biology. Even in these sections Gouge instructs husbands how to influence their wives towards good practices in pregnancy or nursing.[70] Section 38, 'Of mothers particular care in nurturing young children', the only section devoted to mothering that does not draw on a mother's biologically determined duties, exhorts her to teach her children the fundamentals of the Christian faith. Yet even this section ends by referring all matters to the father's guiding authority: 'Fathers therefore must doe their best endeuour, and see that mothers doe theirs also, because he is a gouernour ouer child, mother, and all.'[71]

In Gouge's ideal family, unlike that of other early modern marriage writers, women are left with tiny amounts of independent agency. They are always submissive to and even dependent upon the will of their husbands. Chapter Three of *Of domesticall dvties*, on the duties of wives, does allow as other commentators do that wives have the power to dispose of their own goods, those given expressly to her in trust for her family, and common goods designated to provide for the household and give to the poor. Yet unlike other commentators who recount the areas in which the wife has autonomy, Gouge details meticulously all of the cases of specific household decisions in which she must consult and conform to her husband's will, even to 'ordering seruants and beasts'. Gouge may be merely more thorough in his assertion of a wife's inferiority, but if so his thoroughness has the practical effect of limiting any autonomy the wife has to almost nothing. In her acts of charity, for example, she may 'giue a bit of bread, or scrap of meat to a poore body, or make a messe of broth or caudle for a sicke body' without asking her husband – but Gouge makes this concession for wives of 'tender consciences' concerned about their own level of submission, a wording that implies that it is more laudable for a wife to err on the side of caution than to make autonomous decisions.[72]

---

[69] Gouge, *Of domesticall dvties*, pp. 484–7.
[70] *Ibid.*, pp. 497–588. Sections 9–16 pertain to birth and nursing.
[71] *Ibid.*, p. 547.   [72] *Ibid.*, pp. 291–2, 292–311, 310, 292.

Gouge's emphasis on a wife's submission and limitation of her authority arises out of his attempt to connect human and divine marriage. Gouge likens the submission of a wife to her husband to the Church's submission to Christ, and he gives the simile the force of a command: 'A wife must submit her selfe to an husband, because he is her *head*: and she must doe it *as to the Lord*, because her husband is to her, as Christ is to the Church.'[73] Gouge emphasises the likeness between the husband and Christ, both in positions of power, and both ordered to love their (sometimes undeserving) spouses. In doing so, he neatly avoids the confusion of gender roles – male Christians imagining themselves 'married' to a male Christ – that is inherent in the mystical marriage metaphor, without needing to resort to the gender blurring of writers like Francis Rous, who imagines a female soul acting the role of a male lover.

Gouge places the husband one step closer to Christ and removes the wife from direct relationship to Christ by insisting that her relationship to Christ is through her husband:

Wiues in subiecting themselues aright to their husbands are subiect to the Lord. And on the contrary side,

Wiues in refusing to be subiect to their husbands, refuse to be subiect to the Lord.[74]

Christ is at the top of a ladder of male power relationships, ruling over the whole Church through her (male) authorities, kings, magistrates, ministers, masters, servants, with the wives of each of these neatly placed one rung below their husbands: 'Let Kings and Queenes, Lords and Ladies, Ministers and their wiues, Rich men and their wiues, Poore men and their wiues, Old men and their wiues, Young men and their wiues, all of all sorts take them [the treatises] as spoken to them in particular.'[75] The universality of domestic relationships allows Gouge to construct a kind of Christian egalitarianism that embraces men of all stations, while never transgressing the line of difference between those stations. All husbands, no matter where their place in the chain of power, are, by virtue of being male, reflections of Christ.

And all women, by implication, are farther from an understanding of God. Despite the fact that their submission within the home is supposed to teach them submission to God, it is the husband, not the wife, who enjoys a close bond with Christ: 'in being an head, he is like Christ. So as there is a kinde of fellowship and copartnership betwixt Christ, and an husband: they are brethren in office, as two kings of seuerall places.' The likeness persists despite the infinitely greater glory of Christ:

[73] *Ibid.*, p. 29, italics original.   [74] *Ibid.*, p. 29.   [75] *Ibid.*, p. 130.

Two kings may be more different in estate then a subiect and a king; yet those two kings brethren and fellowes in office. There may be a resemblance where there is no parity, and a likenesse where there is no equality . . . So then an husband resembleth not only the head of a naturall body, but also the glorious image of Christ, and is that to his wife which Christ is to his Church.

Gouge makes a remarkable departure here from the standard readings of mystical marriage outlined above: instead of emphasising the difference between men and the lover Christ, who is 'Lord, Master, head, guide' to them, Gouge focuses on the similarities, prefiguring Milton in his equation of the husband to the divine. Gouge contends that the husband is closer to Christ because he understands Christ's actions. Indeed, 'by vertue of his place he is *the Image and glory of God*'.[76]

In his reading of the relationship between Christ and the Church, William Gouge is not unlike his male contemporaries, emphasising the fundamental inequality between the two actors. But Gouge is unusual among Puritan writers in following this reading to its logical conclusion: submission as a wife's primary duty and her exclusion from secular and spiritual realms of power. The fact that Gouge's conclusions are unique is suggestive both about how we read early modern prescriptive writings on marriage, and how we read the ideals of marriage and other family relationships expressed in metaphors. It is easy to read Gouge as a normative representative of Puritan beliefs about marriage, regarding his strict and misogynistic position as typical of a masculine need to control women that prevailed in the early modern period.[77] But when Gouge's rules of marriage are regarded in light of his theological position on mystical marriage, it becomes clear that both these elements of his work are extreme and unusual. Neither the 'uttermost subiection' of women in the home, nor their utter displacement in the kingdoms of earth and heaven, were mainstream ideals of the early modern period. Although misogyny certainly did prevail among early modern writers on marriage, we must be sensitive to the context of prescriptive writings in order to understand the ideals they disseminated.

RICHARD SIBBES

Richard Sibbes (1577–1635) was an 'establishment revolutionary', one of the many moderate Puritans who favoured further reform of the Church

---

[76] *Ibid.*, pp. 344, 353, 349.
[77] See for example, Anthony Fletcher, *Gender, Sex & Subordination in England 1500–1800* (New Haven, Connecticut: Yale University Press, 1995), pp. 112–17, 205–10.

rather than separation. From his pulpits in Cambridge and London, Sibbes's preaching was staunchly Calvinist and indirectly challenged the ecclesiastical policies of James I and particularly Charles I; yet he never advocated nonconformity, and always believed Church government to be subordinate to the vital issue of salvation. By the time of Sibbes's death in 1635, Archbishop Laud's vigorous anti-Calvinist programme had brought these issues closer together, as Arminian ceremonialism threatened to interfere with Calvinist means to salvation.[78] Thus in 1639 it was possible for men far more radical than this lifelong conformist to appropriate Sibbes's words to their own cause. His 'hardline' nonconformist contemporary John Dod and the younger radicals Philip Nye and Thomas Goodwin ushered in their colleague's works as a kind of Puritan answer to Bishop Andrewes's *XCVI sermons* (1629), appropriating the words of a respected man after his death to speak to a perceived current crisis.[79] As Dod writes in the preface, 'the whole frame of all these Sermons, is carried with such Wisdome, Gravity, Piety, Iudgment and Experience, that it commends it self unto all that are godly wise'.[80] Like *XCVI* sermons, Sibbes's posthumous works are fronted with engraved portraits of the author, beaming the wisdom of moderate ecclesiastical policy from beyond the grave.[81]

These posthumous sermons demonstrate the facility of the mystical marriage metaphor for promulgating – and concealing from the censors – a polemical vision of the Church. At least four of Sibbes's published works, *A fountain sealed* (1637), *The spouse, her earnest desire after Christ her husband* (in *Two sermons*, 1638), *The brides longing* (1638) and *Bowels opened* (1639), are sermons on mystical marriage texts. The first three of these are single works that were edited from one or more sermons; the last is a fat collection of twenty sermons. In the well-established Puritan tradition, Sibbes's sermons extract volumes of theology from tiny amounts of text: each individual sermon is a detailed, phrase-by-phrase allegorical reading of

---

[78] Mark E. Dever, *Richard Sibbes: Puritanism and Calvinism in Late Elizabethan and Early Stuart England* (Macon, Georgia: Mercer University Press, 2000), p. 93. Sibbes was Master of Katherine Hall, Cambridge, and held lectureships at Holy Trinity, Cambridge, and Gray's Inn in London; on the disputed evidence that he was deprived of the Holy Trinity lectureship for nonconformity, see Dever, *Richard Sibbes*, pp. 38–48. On Arminianism and Calvinism, see Nicholas Tyacke, *Aspects of English Protestantism*, pp. 132–55.

[79] Tyacke, *Aspects of English Protestantism*, pp. 67, 122–3.   [80] Sibbes, *Bowels opened*, sig. Aᵛ.

[81] For the political implications of the publication of *XCVI sermons*, see Peter McCullough, 'Making Dead Men Speak: Laudianism, Print, and the Works of Lancelot Andrewes, 1626–1642', *The Historical Journal* 41.2 (1998): 401–24. On Sibbes's ecclesiology, see Dever, *Richard Sibbes*, especially pp. 85–95. On Arminianism and the Stuart Church, see Nicholas Tyacke, *Anti-Calvinists: the Rise of English Arminianism c. 1590–1640* (Oxford: Oxford University Press, 1990), and McCullough, 'Making Dead Men Speak', pp. 414–15, for the restriction of interpretation to a select few.

a single verse, or sometimes only a part of a verse. The 495 pages of *Bowels opened* cover less than two chapters of the Song of Songs, verses 5:1–6:2. Like the texts of many other Sibbes sermons, these verses are about longing for Christ and restoration to him; in this passage the woman does not open the door for her lover in time, and must search for him throughout the city, where she is abused by the watchmen. Since antiquity, commentators had read this passage as a description of the falling away of the Church/soul into sinfulness, and then her renewed desire to be united to her lover, Christ. By the medieval period this reading was so institutionalised that it was almost impossible to read the text any other way. As James Durham would argue a generation after Sibbes, the allegory had become the literal meaning.[82]

For Sibbes and other Puritan writers, this passage had a special usefulness because it described the Church fallen away from the true path and then reformed, thus opening the way for criticism of various 'fallen' Churches and a vision of a new Church. In the more extreme independent commentaries several fallen Churches are criticised in detail; most often the attacks are directed at Rome.[83] In *Bowels opened*, the fallen Church is clearly an enemy much closer to home: the Jacobean and Caroline institution that was never reformed enough for Puritan ministers like Sibbes. Although they are carefully worded – and perhaps edited – to avoid overt polemicism, the sermons of *Bowels opened* describe a Church that is noticeably unhierarchical. The Church Sibbes imagines is a community of believers, governed by ministers who rule and guide her but do not tyrannise over her: 'So *Ministers* are *Christs Ambassadors* and should carry themselves even as Christ would do, they should strengthen the feeble knees and bind up the broken hearted, nor discourage and not sow pillowes vnder the arme-holes of wicked and carnall men.'[84] Such sentences attack the growing tendency of the Church to restrict power – particularly interpretive power – to a clerical elite. Sibbes's ministers are first and foremost servants, who assist the laity rather than wield power over them.

In Sibbes's cogent prose, England's embellished, hierarchical Church is quickly reduced to her contingent members. The two are so closely related that they can be interchanged in allegorical readings; everything that is said of the Church could be said of the individual believer, and vice versa:

---

[82] Astell, *The Song of Songs*, pp. 17–18. On Durham and the reliteralisation of the text, see note 28 above.

[83] For attacks on various reformed churches see, for example, Cotton, *A brief exposition*, pp. 215ff.

[84] Sibbes, *Bowels opened*, p. 297.

This Observation must carrie strength through this whole *Song*, That, *there is the same regard of the whole Church, & of every particular member in regard of the chiefest Priviledges and Graces that accompany salvation.* There is the same reason of every drop of water, as of the whole *Ocean* all is water; and of every sparke of fire, as of the whole Element of fire, all is fire: of those Homogeneall bodies, as we cal them, there is the same respect of the part and of the whole.[85]

A drop of water is the same as the ocean, and every believer is the whole Church: the effect is to demystify the highly ceremonialised Church power structure, which becomes no more than the sum of its homogenous human parts, and partaking of all of the qualities of all of those parts. Sibbes's church possesses power and authority not institutionally, transferred from the divine through the hierarchy, but communally, through the action of 'Homogeneall' members.[86]

In contrast to the institutional power of an elite clergy, the ornaments of Sibbes's Church are preaching ministers, gifted by God to 'moove all stones' through 'their severall gifts' and to unite the members of the community to one another through Christ.[87] Their sermons and lectures were the primary means of preparing the elect for salvation, rather than the sacraments and ceremonies that were the means of grace in the Laudian Church: 'they are Christs mouth, as wee said of the pen-men of holy Scripture; they were but the hand to write, Christ was the head to indite. So in preaching and unfolding the Word, they are but Christs mouth and his voyce, (as it is said of *Iohn*,) Now he is in heaven, he speakes by them'. Given the restrictions on preaching in the 1630s, these were strong words indeed.[88]

These virulent critiques of the Stuart Church are neatly bound together in the metaphor of mystical marriage, which also serves as an ostensible subject to distract the censors from the work's polemic. All of the sermons begin with the metaphor of marriage, in which the spirit 'sets out the union that wee have with Christ, by the union of the Husband with the wife; and that wee might the better understand what this union is'.[89] Sibbes does acknowledge that the sensuous imagery of the Song could be misinterpreted, but he argues that these earthly comparisons, rightly interpreted,

[85] *Ibid.*, p. 5. See also Sibbes's *Two sermons*, STC 22519 (London: T. Cotes for Andrew Kembe, 1638), p. 13.
[86] See Peter Lake, 'Feminine Piety and Personal Potency: The "Emancipation" of Mrs Jane Ratcliffe', *The Seventeenth Century* 2.2 (1987): 144.
[87] Sibbes, *Bowels opened*, p. 144. On the importance of sermons in Calvinist soteriology, see Lake, *The Boxmaker's Revenge*, pp. 53–66.
[88] Sibbes, *Bowels opened*, p. 143. See also *Two sermons*, p. 28. Dever, *Richard Sibbes*, pp. 128–31. Tyacke, *Aspects of English Protestantism*, pp. 120–6, 143–4, 149–51.
[89] Sibbes, *Two sermons*, p. 2. Compare also STC 22495 Richard Sibbes, *A fountain sealed* (London: Thomas Harper for Lawrence Chapman, 1637), pp. 130–1.

draw the spirit to contemplation of higher things. Significantly, however, he warns that the reader should not be misled by too close examination of the human aspects of the metaphor, which are meant only to serve the divine image:

The *Mystery* of *Mysteries*, the *Communion* betwixt *Christ* and his *Church*, is set out in the familiar comparison of a *Marriage*: that so we might the better see it in the glasse of a comparison, which we cannot so directly conceive of, as we may see the *Sun* in water, whose beames we cannot so directly looke upon: Onely our care must be, not to looke so much on the *colours*, as the *Picture*: and not so much on the Picture, as on the *Person* it selfe represented: that we looke not so much to the *resemblance*, as to the *Person resembled*.[90]

Sibbes's prose in this passage draws the reader's attention progressively away from the human element of the metaphor: not only must we not be too concerned with the details ('*colours*') of human marriage, nor the institution in general ('the Picture'), but we must even be careful not to focus on the aspects of the human relationship that *resemble* the divine relationship, lest these likenesses draw us away from the true object of contemplation. Thus, even as Sibbes establishes the marriage metaphor as the basis for his text, he warns us not to be diverted by any likeness between divine marriage and human marriage. 'Marriage' here is little more than a convenient construct.

It is not surprising, then, that in each of these texts the metaphor of marriage fades rapidly away, to be replaced by other more pliable allegorical elements. In all 495 pages of *Bowels opened*, Sibbes devotes two pages to the similarities between human marriage and divine marriage. (As a matter of comparison, he devotes five pages to the relationship between bodily sleep and spiritual sleep, and six pages to the conceit of knocking.)[91] The first two connections between earthly marriage and mystical marriage Sibbes notes are: first, that wives take their husbands' name, as Christians are named after Christ; and second, that husbands must take over their wives' debts and share riches with them, as Christ takes all of the sins of Christians and shares his kingdom with them. Both of these connections rest on basic legal aspects of early modern marriage that Sibbes neither questions nor comments upon; he accepts them as natural fact much like the other elements of allegory he draws upon, as 'whatsoever is excellent in the whole world, is borrowed to set out the excellencies of these two great Lovers' Christ and the Church. The third connection, a common one in mystical marriage texts, is even more obviously a stretching of the allegorical bounds:

[90] Sibbes, *Bowels opened*, p. 4. [91] *Ibid.*, pp. 88–92, 140–5.

Those that bring together these two different parties, are the friends of the Bride; that is, the Ministers, as it is *Iohn* 3:23. They are the *paranymphi* the friends of the Bride, that learne of *Christ* what to report to his *Spouse*, and so they wooe for *Christ*; and open the Riches, Beauty, honour, and all that is lovely in him, which is indeed the especiall duty of Ministers, to lay open his unsearchable Riches, that the *Church* may know what a Husband she is like to have, if she cleave to him, and what an one she leaves, if she forsake him.[92]

Here the relationship between human and divine, between signifier and signified, is clearly coincidental, a convenient excuse for Sibbes to return to one of his favourite subjects, the role of preaching ministers in the Church. In all of these connections the focus, significantly, is on institutional aspects of marriage, not on a loving relationship that mirrors the loving relationship between Christ and his Church.

Sibbes's casual use of mystical marriage raises questions about the function of the metaphor: why invoke it at all? In Sibbes's case, as for many other early modern commentators, the answer seems to be simply that mystical marriage had become so integral to his text, the Song of Solomon, that no reading could escape it. But if it is inescapable, why not mine it for allegorical readings, using the human relationship to imagine the divine? Why does Sibbes spend so much time explicating other allegorical elements while all but ignoring the allegorical vehicle of mystical marriage?

The answer to this question lies in the relationship Sibbes imagines between Christ and the Church, which is not at all like the Puritan ideal of marriage. The radically human and unceremonial Church witnessed in Sibbes's writings is utterly unlike her divine husband; she is both unclean and unworthy, and in need of cleansing from her perfect husband. Using the same conceit as Lady Anne Southwell but reversing the emphasis, Sibbes argues that the Church 'rose out of [Christ's] Bloud, and Death', taken directly from his wounded side because we Christians, her members, were 'in such a Condition, that *Christ* must Redeeme us, before he could wed us'. Like most commentators, Sibbes employs this conceit especially to describe the condition of the Church before she is redeemed by Christ, but his language also suggests that a continual reform and cleansing are necessary: 'so before the *Church* (which is not *Heathenish*, but indeed *Hellish* by nature, and led by the spirit of the world) be fit to be the Spouse of *Christ*, there must be an alteration and a change of nature'. This 'Hellish' Church that imperatively 'must be' remade points directly at the Stuart Church that is 'led by the spirit of the world'.[93] In order to castigate the

[92] *Ibid.*, pp. 2, 48–9.   [93] *Ibid.*, pp. 47, 49.

sinfulness of the institution, Sibbes makes the fallen English Church utterly unlike her holy and perfect saviour, and in the process creates a mystical bride and bridegroom of such dramatic difference in station that no Puritan minister would sanction their marriage. Sibbes cannot concern himself with the human aspects of the metaphor because the relationship he imagines in fact bears little resemblance to human marriage as Puritan ministers imagined it.

FRANCIS ROUS

Francis Rous's (1579–1659) slim allegory, *The mysticall marriage*, represents the opposite strain of readings, the personally mystical. Unlike Sibbes's ecclesiastical reading, in Rous's book the bride of the metaphor is not the institutional Church but the individual soul. In these 'Experimentall Discoveries of the heavenly Mariage betweene a Soule and her Saviour', as the subtitle calls them, Rous offers a narrative description of the progress of the soul's love for Christ, borrowing imagery from the Song of Songs, Ephesians and many other Biblical texts. The focus is intensely personal, an exhortation to each individual to imagine (his) soul as a lover of Christ.

Given his political background – Rous was a vocal politician and reformer, Member of Parliament throughout his adult life and Speaker in 1653, as well as author of numerous polemical works against Catholicism and Arminianism – it is perhaps surprising that this outspoken man should forego a reforming ecclesiastical reading in order to write such a volume of personal piety.[94] Or perhaps it is not surprising: as for many of the zealous of his times, for Rous the source and foundation of a reforming spirit was a personal relationship with Christ. In 'A Reason of this Worke', his prefatory remarks to *The mysticall marriage*, Rous explains the connection between personal piety and societal action. Rous opens 'A Reason' by arguing that his descriptions of divine love bring joy to the reader, which is necessary for the strength and peace of the individual soul. This 'excessively conquering, and unconquerable safety' is not only a haven for the afflicted, but also the means of spurring to action, warming the cold hearts of the world's decadent:

And surely with these last times of the world it hath too great a fitnesse; For it hath beene foretold that in these times the love of many should waxe cold: And what fitter remedie is there for love when it hath taken cold, than to kindle a fire to it; even that spiritual fire, which issueth from the spirit that baptiseth with fire?

94 DNB.

In 1635 Rous may have foreseen the 'last times' of the civil wars and desired a spiritual renewal among the saints that would lead them to action on behalf of the kingdom of God. He ends 'A Reason of this Worke' with a call for more stirring up of the elect: 'it may provoke others of this Nation to bring forth more boxes of this precious oyntment, even of that mysticall love which droppeth downe from the Head Christ Iesus, into the soules of the Saints, living heere below'.[95]

The fire that heats the spirits of the saints is lit by the unimaginable love of Christ; it is the greatness of God that inspires humans to reform their base and sinful world. Thus it is that Rous, even more than Sibbes, concentrates on the vast gulf between the human soul and her divine lover, which can only be surmounted by his divine sacrificial love. The soul Rous imagines is 'a low, and measured, and weake spirit' overflowing with 'a high, and large, and mightie joy' poured out by Christ: 'she is too narrow and feeble to contain and beare a joy that is too large and strong for her; and therefore having filled her to the utmost capacity, it goes beyond, and runnes over'. The divine love of Christ so overwhelms the soul that her very identity is lost in the outpouring of affection, her very baseness merely a means of throwing into relief the greatness of God: 'Fulnesse is glorified most by filling the greatest emptinesse, and majesty by succouring greatest infirmity'.[96]

Like his medieval predecessors, as well as some poetic contemporaries, Rous expresses the vast difference between the soul and Christ in the language of courtship. While the soul is on earth, she is wooed by Christ but cannot enjoy full consummation with him; all of the commentators agree that the consummation of mystical marriage occurs in heaven, but Rous emphasises this point, stressing that the 'inchoate marriage' of life on earth may 'seeme but like to a betrothing'. Like a giddy courting couple, the soul and Christ exchange seals and tokens, suffer the torments of separation and quarrels, and even whisper 'mysteries and secrets' 'in the bed of love'. At times Rous plays gender games with the language of courtship; curiously enough, he does not use the medieval conceit of the lover-knight who rescues the unworthy woman, but reverses the gender role of the bride. The female soul who 'hath him by whom the worlds were made' behaves like a courtly lover who abases himself in the service of his royal beloved and is overwhelmed by her condescension. At one point Rous makes the comparison to a male lover explicit: 'Looke but to a carnall lover, and see how he affects the title of a servant, and is more than glad, (even proud) to

[95] Rous, *The mysticall marriage*, sigs. A3ʳ, A3ᵛ, A4ᵛ.   [96] *Ibid.*, pp. 47, 8.

receive and fulfill the commands of his beloved. Give then spiritual love to a soule, and she will rejoyce also to perform the spiritual commands of her beloved.'[97]

The conceit of the courtly lover allows Rous to voice passionate desires that would be inexpressible in the moderate language of Puritan marriage. Puritan writers on marriage counselled that desire between husbands and wives should not be too excessive, slavish or disorderly; but in *The mysticall marriage* the love of the soul for Christ 'brings her to an extasie' of ravishing heat.[98] The soul is allowed transports of love that no Puritan commentator would deem appropriate for a sober wife: 'Shee that loveth Christ much, may embrace him much, and kisse him much, and holde him much; and if any man doe trouble her, hee himselfe will say, *Why trouble yee the woman?*' Moreover, the inequality of their relationship presents a model that no Puritan couple would want to follow: she 'hath him by whom the worlds were made, and therefore she hath also the worlds made by him', an act no sober human husband could replicate. She also has her own will completely subsumed by his: 'Behold how the soule married unto Christ delights in the law of her husband; and no wonder if she love his law, when she loves him; neither if her heart be to his law, when his law is written in her heart.'[99] Not only is the 'wife' of Christ utterly obedient to him, but any sense of individual agency is almost literally overwritten, inescapably inscribed by the will of her husband. This 'wife' Rous conjures up to inflame the saints combines both a passionate 'lust' for her husband and creator and an entire self-abnegation to his cause, useful traits for inspiring action but entirely undesirable in the Puritan human wife, who was valued for her temperance and self-control, her ability to act wisely and moderately within her sphere of duties.[100] For all of his emphasis on individual human relationships to God, Rous sidelines the most human aspects of the marriage metaphor.

Reading Rous, Sibbes and other Puritan commentators suggests that we must exercise care in analysing idealised representations of family relationships in theological texts. Despite surface appearances, for Puritan male writers mystical marriage has little in common with human marriage. The standards imagined for the divine husband Christ and his wife the

[97] *Ibid.*, pp. 43, 175, 56, 72.
[98] Gouge, *Of domesticall dvties*, pp. 221–6; Rogers, *Matrimoniall honovr*, pp. 152–3; Rous, *The mysticall marriage*, p. 174.
[99] Rous, *The mysticall marriage*, pp. 114–15, 56, 70–1.
[100] See Brown, 'Godly Household Government'.

Church/soul are radically unlike Puritan standards for a human husband and wife. The metaphor has, ultimately, scant connection to its human source. Such a profound dislocation between the metaphorical and the literal, the divine and the human, suggests that we ought to be cautious when reading metaphorical representations for their implications of standards of human behaviour, and that we should be ready to compare metaphors in theological contexts with prescriptive texts about family relationships. God the father may be invoked as an ideal for a human father, but are these two fathers expected to perform the same role in the family, human or divine?[101]

EPILOGUE: THE RESTORATION

In 1674 a young clergyman fired a shot into the nonconformist camp with the publication of *A discourse concerning the knowledge of jesus christ, and our union and communion with him*.[102] William Sherlock was a product of Peterhouse, Cambridge, an Arminian seminary before the civil wars that selected an anti-Calvinist Master, old-member Joseph Beaumont, shortly after the Restoration.[103] Sherlock remained faithful to the anti-Calvinism of his alma mater, preaching numerous controversialist sermons carefully aimed to please the Church hierarchy, but his advancement had been slower than he might have hoped. His first preferment came in 1669, six years after graduating MA, and in 1674 he was still the relatively unknown Rector of St George's, Botolph Lane, London.[104] His first venture into print was deliberately provocative, designed to make a name for its author in the fiercely competitive world of London divinity.[105] For *A discourse* attacked the very core of English nonconformity: the doctrine of the believer's union with Christ, and through it the foundations of the Calvinist theology of salvation.[106]

---

101 For a reading that conflates these two figures, see Debora Shuger, *Habits of Thought in the English Renaissance: Religion, Politics, and the Dominant Culture* (Berkeley, California: University of California Press, 1990), pp. 218–49.

102 Wing S3288 William Sherlock, *A discourse concerning the knowledge of jesus christ, and our union and communion with him* (London: J. M. for Walter Kettilby, 1674).

103 Beaumont was appointed master the year Sherlock graduated MA, 1663. DNB and Tyacke, *Aspects of English Protestantism*, pp. 333–4.

104 Biographical information is from the DNB.

105 Polemical disputation had long been a means to advancement for young ministers; for earlier examples see Lake, *The Boxmaker's Revenge*, especially pp. 221–46.

106 Elizabeth Clarke kindly suggested I consider these texts, discussed in the Introduction to *The 'Centuries' of Julia Palmer*, edited with V. Burke (Nottingham: Trent Editions, 2001), pp. xii–xiii, and in her forthcoming book, '*Re-writing the Bride': Politics, Authorship and the Song of Songs in Seventeenth Century England* (London: Macmillan).

His targets in 1674 were the classics of nonconformist practical theology, many first printed in the 1640s and 50s.[107] In that period the metaphor of union with God became one of the key motifs of Calvinist, anti-episcopal theologians. Sherlock's principle opponent, the eminent Dr John Owen, defined communion generally as 'the mutuall Communication of such good things, as wherein the Persons holding that Communion are delighted, bottomed upon some union between them'.[108] Using this broad definition, Owen and others applied the numerous mystical union metaphors in the scriptures to the Calvinist doctrine of grace: 'Communion with God is nothing else but the communication of grace between God and the Soul', explained noted Presbyterian Samuel Annesley.[109] It was through communion with God that human beings could share in Christ's righteousness, and this imputation of righteousness was central to Calvinist soteriology.

Sherlock does not attack such a significant target directly, but rather approaches it through an argument about nonconformist use of language. '[I]nstead of those substantial duties of the love of God, and men, and an universal holiness of life,' Sherlock contended, the nonconformists

have introduced a fanciful *application* of Christ to our selves, and *Union* to him, set off with all those choice Phrases of *closing with Christ, and embracing Christ, and getting into Christ, and getting an interest in Christ, and trusting, and relying, and rowling our Souls on Christ:* And instead of obedience to the Gospel, and the Laws of Christ, have advanced a kind of Amorous and Enthusiastick devotion, which consists in a passionate love to the Person of Christ, in admiring his *Personal excellencies, and perfections, fulness, beauty, loveliness, riches, &c.*[110]

Sherlock maintains that nonconformists have become 'fanciful' in their understanding of Christ, urging believers to have a personal knowledge of

---

[107] Wing B4919 Thomas Brooks, *The unsearchable riches of christ* (London: Mary Simmons for John Hancock, 1657); Wing J119 Thomas Jacomb, *Several sermons preach'd on the whole eighth chapter of the epistle to the romans* (London: W. Godbid for M. Pitt, R. Chiswel and J. Robinson, 1672); Wing O777 John Owen, *Of communion with god the father, sonne, and holy ghost* (Oxford: by A. Lichfield for Philemon Stevens, 1657); Wing S3118 Thomas Shepard, *The sincere convert* (London: T. P. and M. S. for Humphrey Blunden, 1641), also his *The saints jewel*, printed with *The sincere convert* from 1652, Wing S3123A (London: E. Cotes for John Sweeting), and his *The sound beleever*, Wing S3133 (London: for R. Dawlman, 1645); Wing V428 Thomas Vincent, *Christ the best husband* (London: for George Calvert and Samuel Sprint, 1672); Thomas Watson, *Christs lovelinesse*, in Wing W1145 *Three treatises* (London: for Ralph Smith, 1660). Also relevant are Wing A3227 Samuel Annesley, *Communion with god. In two sermons* (London: Evan Tyler for Nathanael Web and William Grantham, 1655); and Wing M337 Thomas Mallery, *The inseperable communion of a believer with god* (London: for R. D., 1674).

[108] Owen, *Of communion with god the father, sonne, and holy ghost*, p. 4.

[109] Annesley, *Communion with god*, p. 34.

[110] Sherlock, *A discourse concerning the knowledge of jesus christ*, pp. 12–13. 'Rowl' is from the Hebrew 'galal', meaning to rest or trust; see OED.

Christ that was not in fact possible. All we could know of Christ, Sherlock argued, was 'what he hath been pleased to reveal to us' in the Gospel.[III] The nonconformist insistence that believers must 'finde out experimentally, what it is to enjoy God' was nothing more than an 'Amorous' fancy that distracted Christians from their true duties of obedience, which could be known clearly from scripture.[112] As Sherlock wrote in *A defence and contin-uation of the discourse concerning the knowledge of jesus christ* (1675), 'I reject such a notion of our Union to the Person of Christ, as is unintelligible, such as the Great Patrons of it cannot explain, nor anyone else understand[.]'[113]

Sherlock's argument strikes at the heart of nonconformist faith, implying that all nonconformists' professions of love for God are only imagined, and that they have no true knowledge of the gospel. He was not alone in his criticisms: in 1670 Samuel Parker had made similar claims about noncon-formist use of language, and Parker himself was drawing on earlier Latitu-dinarian texts that defended a rational and simple approach to Christianity as opposed to what were seen as the 'Amorous' excesses of Calvinist non-conformity.[114] Their concern was that nonconformist religion depended upon an emotional response from the believer, and thus contradicted the principles of reason. If, as John Owen cautioned, seeking Christians must ask themselves 'hath Christ his *due place* in your hearts? is he *your all*? does he dwell *in your* thoughts? do you know him in his *excellency* and desireablenesse?' then confidence in salvation was contingent upon emo-tion rather than reason.[115] '[A]ll this may be no more', Sherlock argued, 'than the working of a warm and Enthusiastick fancy, and no man ought to think himself ever the more experimentally acquainted with Christ, unless he find the power of it in governing his life[.]'[116]

Mystical marriage was only one metaphor among many that expressed the notion of mystical union, but it enjoyed a central place because the Song of Songs was seen as the most developed description in the Bible of the believer's union with God. The interpretative tradition had shifted slightly since the beginning of the century, and the spouse of the text was now more frequently read as individual believers than as an institutionalised Church, a change that sat more comfortably with the increasing difference

---

[III] *Ibid.*, p. 34.   [112] Annesley, *Communion with god*, p. 25.

[113] Wing S3281 William Sherlock, *A defence and continuation of the discourse concerning the knowledge of jesus christ* (London: A. C. for Walter Kettilby, 1675), pp. 35–6.

[114] Wing P459 Samuel Parker, *A discourse of ecclesiastical politie* (London: for John Martyn, 1670), pp. 74–5. Isabel Rivers, *Reason, Grace, and Sentiment: A Study of the Language of Religion and Ethics in England, 1660–1780*, vol. 1 (Cambridge: Cambridge University Press, 1991), pp. 53–9, 123–4.

[115] Owen, *Of communion with god the father, sonne, and holy ghost*, p. 57.

[116] Sherlock, *A discourse concerning the knowledge of jesus christ*, pp. 140–1.

of opinion about the nature of the true Church. Thus personally mystical readings like Francis Rous's *The mysticall marriage* grew more common, and the mystical union treatises of Owen, Annesley, Watson and others are essentially a development of this trend. Within this tradition the Song of Songs became a history of the personal relationship between a believer and Christ, and thus could be read as a paradigm of how a Christian should relate to his or her God. John Owen reads Song of Songs 2:1–7, for example, as evidence of the characteristics of this relationship (sweetness, delight, safety and comfort), and glosses verse 6, 'His left hand is under my head, and his right hand doth embrace me', as 'to lye in the Armes of Christs Love, under a perpetuall influence of *supportment* and *Refreshment*, is certainly to *hold communion with him*'. He concludes the reading by asserting, 'In briefe this whole Book is taken up in the description of the *Communion* that is between the Lord *Christ* and his saints, & therefore it is very needlesse to take from thence any more particular *instances* thereof.'[117]

The centrality of the Song of Songs and the reliteralisation of the metaphor were so accepted by nonconformists as to be almost undeniable, but for men like Sherlock these interpretations verged on the ridiculous. In one passage that aroused comment, Sherlock quoted Thomas Watson, '*Christ saith to a believer with my body, yea with my blood I endowe thee, and a Believer saith to Christ, with my Soul I thee worship*', then added in scathing parenthesis, 'as if Christ and a Believer were marryed by the Liturgy'.[118] Sherlock views such imaginative literalism as dangerous because it allows nonconformists to defend almost any interpretation using a Biblical passage as proof: 'if they can find any words in Scripture, which chime to the tune of their private conceits, without ever considering the use of the words in those places where they are found, they clap their own sense on them, and then they serve for very solid and substantial proofs'.[119]

Ultimately, Sherlock's position is an attack on the fundamental hermeneutic of interpreting scripture according to the analogy of faith, which had been the governing principle for Reformed theologians for more than a century and a half.[120] The essence of the analogy of faith was that all

---

[117] Owen, *Of communion with god the father, sonne, and holy ghost*, pp. 47, 48.

[118] Sherlock, *A discourse concerning the knowledge of jesus christ*, p. 67. The quotation is from Thomas Watson, *Christs lovelinesse*, in *Three treatises*, p. 462 misnumbered 460.

[119] Sherlock, *A discourse concerning the knowledge of jesus christ*, p. 102.

[120] Scheper, 'Reformation Attitudes', p. 555. For references to the analogy of faith, see Sherlock, p. 101; Wing O821 John Owen, *A vindication of some passages in a discourse concerning communion with god* (London: for N. Ponder, 1674), p. 204; Wing F740 Robert Ferguson, *The interest of reason in religion* (London: for Dorman Newman, 1675), p. 350.

interpretations of scripture must accord to the principles of gospel faith; in other words, that one scripture could not contradict either another scripture or the accepted doctrines of the faith. While almost all theologians of the period – including Catholic and Arminian – would have assented to this interpretative model generally, what Sherlock and others disliked in the nonconformist tradition was what they saw as the imaginative rethinking of both Old and New Testament passages in order to adapt them to a particular image of Christ and the doctrine of the atonement. For example, Sherlock comments sarcastically on nonconformist readings of 1 John 5:12: '*He that hath the Son hath life, and he that hath not the Son, hath not life.* For what can *having the Son* siguifie [*sic*], but having an Interest in him, being made one with him; though some will be so perverse as to understand it, of believing and obeying his Gospel[.]'[121]

For many of his respondents (not all of them nonconformist), Sherlock's attack on the interpretation of scripture is almost not worth answering, because the allegorical reading of the Song of Songs (and mystical union in general) had become so pivotal to the faith: 'Indeed to deny it, is to renounce the Gospel, and the Catholick Faith', John Owen asserted.[122] As Vincent Alsop wrote in a response that established his reputation as a satirist:

Now in this our Author speaks more Truth than he is aware of: *What can* [having the Son] *signifie* (says he) *but having an Interest in Him? Being made* one with Him, *especially when we remember, that it is called* [being in Christ] *and* [abiding in him] *which must signifie a very near Union between Christs Person and ours?* It must so! If [the Son] signifie the *very Son of God*, we must *have Him*, as he is *capable* of *being had;* and that's only *by Interest* and *Propriety*, through Compact agreement, and the Constitution of God in a Gospel Covenant. Ay, but (says our Author) *Some will be so Perverse as to understand it of believing, and Obeying his Gospel.* Well, and if they will be *so Perverse* without a Reason, we shall take the freedom to be *as Perverse* as they can be, and believe no more than we have proof for.[123]

Alsop similarly regarded as perverse Sherlock's sarcastic remark about Christ and believers being 'marryed by the Liturgy'. 'That Christ does really *endow Believers* with his Body and Blood, and all *the Benefits* procured by his Sacrifice, is out of doubt to all that are not Infidels', Alsop insisted.[124]

---

[121] Sherlock, *A discourse concerning the knowledge of jesus christ*, p. 103.

[122] Owen, *A vindication of some passages in a discourse concerning communion with god*, p. 203.

[123] Wing A2905 Vincent Alsop, *Anti-sozzo, sive sherlocismus enervatus* (London: for Nathanael Ponder, 1676), p. 310. Square brackets are original.

[124] *Ibid.*, p. 239.

John Owen, likewise, felt that Sherlock's arguments against Song of Songs interpretations in particular did not deserve an answer:

> if he either deny, that that whole Book doth mystically express the conjugal Relation that is between Christ and his Church, with their mutual affections and delight in each other; or that the places particularly insisted on by me, are not duly applyed unto their proper intention; I can at least confirm them both, by the Authority of such persons as whose Antiquity and Learning will exercise the utmost of his confidence in calling them *Fools* for their pains.[125]

Just as Sherlock's respondents are almost unanimously united in viewing mystical marriage and mystical union central to the faith, they are equally united in setting aside Sherlock's contentions about language in order to take up his attacks against key Calvinist principles, such as the imputation of Christ's righteousness. Alsop's extensive response, for example, frequently ignores Sherlock's critique of metaphor altogether. In responding to Sherlock's section 'Concerning the nature of our Union to Christ', Alsop omits the opening pages about the 'conjugal relation' between Christ and believers, opening instead with Sherlock's argument pages later that human beings are not entitled to share in Christ's personal righteousness.[126] Owen's *Vindication*, and Edward Polhill's *Answer*, the two other lengthy responses, likewise devote considerably more pages to soteriology than to language.[127] The single exception to this rule is Robert Ferguson, whose *Interest of reason in religion* (1675) is in effect a treatise on religious metaphor that responds not only to Sherlock but to Samuel Parker and others. Ferguson's book attempts to defend nonconformist use of metaphorical scriptures by demonstrating that their methods are in fact governed by reason, and that those, like Sherlock, who criticise nonconformist affective language are themselves guilty of misinterpreting scripture.[128]

Even Ferguson does not really answer Sherlock's oppositions to mystical union writings, and particularly to interpretations of the Song of Songs. For all of these men it seems it was impossible to imagine that the Song of Songs was *not* a love-song between Christ and the believer, nor was it

---

[125] Owen, *A vindication of some passages in a discourse concerning communion with god*, pp. 204–5.

[126] Alsop's response begins on p. 579 of *Anti-sozzo, sive*, Sherlock's chapter 4, section 3 is on pp. 279–337 of *A discourse concerning the knowledge of jesus christ*; pp. 279–87 discuss the conjugal relation metaphor, pp. 320–37 the imputation of Christ's personal righteousness.

[127] Wing P2749 Edward Polhill, *An answer to the discourse of mr william sherlock* (London: for Ben. Foster, 1675).

[128] See Ferguson, *The interest of reason in religion*, pp. 278, 288–90. Owen, *A vindication of some passages in a discourse concerning communion with god*, pp. 199–200, and Alsop, *Anti-sozzo, sive*, pp. 302–4, similarly argue that Sherlock's own use of metaphors is irrational.

easy to acknowledge the plethora of interpretations possible within this allegorical system. That the dove's eyes of Song of Songs 1:15 might not in fact be proof of '*Christs giving himself to the Soul with all his Excellencies, Righteousness, Preciousness, Graces, Eminencies*' (as Sherlock claimed Owen had argued), was a premise few theologians were prepared to admit.[129]

That said, their reading of the mystical marriage metaphor is not fundamentally different from the earlier writings of Richard Sibbes. For if these later writers tended to focus on the personal elements of the allegory, they are nonetheless not inclined to be too literal in connecting human marriage with the divine. Vincent Alsop, although he defends Thomas Watson's statement that 'Christ saith to a Believer, *with my body, yea with my blood I thee endow*, and a believer saith to Christ, *with my soule I thee worship*', nevertheless points out that this little ceremony does not precisely parallel the marriage ceremony: 'for Mr *Watson* brings in *the Spouse* saying to Christ, *With my soul I thee worship*; but *the Liturgy* teaches *the Man* to use those words to *his Spouse, With my Body I thee worship*: So that I see *no great Danger* that ever *Christ and a Believer* should be *marryed by the Liturgy*'.[130] Indeed, all of these writers emphasise that the mystical marriage metaphor can only ever be a partial representation of the relationship between Christ and believers, and thus it was important not to read the divine relationship as entirely and only like the human: '[T]he *Headship of the Husband over the Wife*, will not *exactly measure* the *Headship of Christ over Believers*; we must call in assistance from *another Similitude*, that of *the Head in the Natural Body over the Members*[.]'[131] All metaphors, in fact, 'come short of the Mystical Union which they refer to: they may *illustrate* it but they cannot *reach* or *equalize* it'.[132]

One seeming exception to this rule is Thomas Vincent's *Christ the best husband: or an invitation of young women unto Christ. Delivered in a sermon to young women* (1672). Vincent preached to his female audience on Psalm 45, which was generally read as companion to the Song of Songs. Using verses 10–11, which begin 'Hearken, (O daughter)', Vincent argued that the Psalm's invitation to be married to Christ was 'particularly applicably [*sic*] unto the Daughters o[f] men', but admitted immediately after that it was 'not so as excluding the sons of men any more than when God speaketh unto the sons of men, he doth exclude the daughters'.[133] Sherlock argued that Vincent's sermon 'would have sounded much better in a *Popish Nunnery*,

---

[129] Sherlock, *A discourse concerning the knowledge of jesus christ*, p. 284.
[130] Watson, *Christs lovelinesse*, in *Three treatises*, p. 462 misnumbered 460; Alsop, *Anti-sozzo, sive*, p. 240.
[131] Alsop, *Anti-sozzo, sive*, pp. 351–2.   [132] Jacomb, *Several sermons*, p. 52.
[133] Vincent, *Christ the best husband*, p. 2.

than among such *pretenders to reformation*.[134] His chief critique of *Christ the best husband* was that it violated the convention that the allegory should not be read too literally:

[Vincent preaches] to his *She-Hearers* in particular, which is a very *spiritual* conceit; because he knew that Women, not Men, wanted Husbands: He has in the same Pamphlet a distinct Exhortation to *young Men*, but does he invite *them* to chuse Christ for their *Husband*? by no means; the conceit would not do there; for young Men are more for Wives than Husbands, and therefore his Exhortation to them is only to give God their Hearts; which is a plain confession of guilt, that he had so debased and carnalized the notion of that *spiritual* Marriage between Christ and his Church, that it was not so properly applicable to men, as to Women, as if there were any regard to the difference of Sex in this Spiritual Marriage[.][135]

Sherlock's criticism demonstrates how vital it was for all Christians that the mystical marriage metaphor not be too strongly gendered; the access to God implied in the metaphor must be available to both men and women. In fact Vincent includes very little in his text that could not be applied to both genders. Only once does he address his audience of young women in gender-specific language, exhorting 'Come, Virgins, will you give me leave to be a Suiter unto you, not in my own name, but in the name of my Lord?' But only a few sentences later he reminds his female hearers that what is appropriate for them in human courtship is not appropriate in their relationship to Christ: 'Be not coy, as some of you possibly are in other Loves: Modesty and the Virgin blush may very well become you, when motions of another kind are made unto you; but here coyness is folly, and backwardness to accept of this motion is a shame[.]'[136] Similarly, Vincent reiterates the argument made by Rous and other mystical marriage writers that the believing soul is utterly inferior to her husband, Christ: 'He doth not expect a portion and dowry with you, as many, yea, most great persons do in their applications to any upon this account, they expect something answerable to their degree and estate; but none have any thing answerable unto Christs degree[.]'[137] Christ is the *best* husband, Vincent argues, precisely because he is not governed by the same conventions as human husbands and wives.

But if even Sherlock and his enemies do not connect mystical marriage to its human counterpart, then what is the significance of their work to the writing of early modern women? The answer lies in the argument about

---

[134] Sherlock, *A discourse concerning the knowledge of jesus christ*, pp. 144–5.
[135] Sherlock, *A defence and continuation*, p. 62.   [136] Vincent, *Christ the best husband*, p. 18.
[137] *Ibid.*, pp. 25–6.

metaphorical language that was so quickly pushed to the side as the debate progressed. The unwillingness of so many of Sherlock's opponents even to consider the constructed nature of their own theology demonstrates the near-complete reliteralisation of the mystical marriage metaphor and its ubiquitous and integral function in nonconformist and Puritan theology. The existence of this established imaginative framework was vital for women writers, who inherited an orthodox language through which they could construct devotional subject positions. For many women writers, particularly Anna Trapnel and the author of *Eliza's babes*, the imaginative use of metaphor opened up new interpretative possibilities which enabled them to contribute to debates about gender and devotion. For these women, the facility of the mystical marriage metaphor lay in being able to do what the men do not: to connect human and divine, to demonstrate how marriage to Christ authorises their speech as human women. These women utilise the gaps in the metaphor that are frequently denied or elided by male writers in order to imagine, more literally, what it meant for a woman to be the bride of Christ. The possibilities of interpretative play opened up by mystical marriage enabled these women radically to redefine gender roles using entirely orthodox language.

Yet lest we believe that all women were primarily concerned with gender issues, the example of Lucy Hutchinson, in the last chapter of this book, provides an important corrective. Hutchinson is closest in spirit and theology to the nonconformist writers discussed above, and her use of the mystical union metaphor to canonise her husband and his political cause draws closely on the paradigm established by Owen and Annesley. Hutchinson's writing demonstrates that women as well as men could use gendered metaphors to discuss ungendered subjects, whether the true form of the English Church or the future of the English Republic, and should remind us not to reconfine women to the ghetto of gender through our critical attention to the subject.

CHAPTER 2

Ecce homo: the spectacle of Christ's passion in Salve deus rex judæorum

Aemilia Lanyer's passion poem *Salve deus rex judæorum* (1611) presents a familiar dilemma for historians of women's literature. Although Lanyer was not the first woman writer to print a poem, there were not many to precede her, and although other women had added dedications to their poems, none had so clearly inscribed the search for patronage into their work.[1] Perhaps most significantly, few women writing before her were as concerned with vindicating women's virtue and questioning contemporary constructions of gender.

Given these facts, it is easy to see why many critics have hailed Aemilia Lanyer as a pioneer: 'the first woman writing in English who clearly sought professional standing as a poet'; a radical thinker with 'a vision that yearns toward a feminist space'.[2] Yet while it is important to acknowledge that

---

[1] Ann Lock had printed a sonnet sequence in 1560, Isabella Whitney had printed poems in 1567 and 1573 and Mary Sidney Herbert's translation of the Psalms had circulated in manuscript in the 1590s, and is mentioned in Lanyer's dedication. STC 4450 Ann Lock, *Sermons of john calvin* (London: John Day, 1560); the sonnet sequence is appended to the translation, both edited in Susan M. Felch, ed., *The Collected Works of Anne Vaughan Lock* (Tempe, Arizona: Renaissance English Text Society, 1999). All subsequent references are to this edition. STC 25439 Isabella Whitney, *The copy of a letter* (London: Richard Jones, 1567) and STC 25440 *A sweet nosgay* (London: Richard Jones, 1573). Margaret P. Hannay, Noel J. Kinnamon and Michael G. Brennan, eds., *The Collected Works of Mary Sidney Herbert Countess of Pembroke*, 2 vols. (Oxford: Clarendon Press, 1998).

[2] Susanne Woods, *Lanyer: A Renaissance Woman Poet* (Oxford: Oxford University Press, 1999), p. vii; Lynnette McGrath, '"Let Us Have Our Libertie Againe": Aemilia Lanier's 17th-Century Feminist Voice', *Women's Studies* 20.3–4 (1992): 345. Woods mentions Lock, Whitney and Sidney Herbert, but rejects each as a "professional" poet. See also similar statements in Pamela Benson, 'To Play the Man: Aemilia Lanyer and the Acquisition of Patronage', in *Opening the Borders: Inclusivity in Early Modern Studies: Essays in Honor of James V. Mirollo*, ed. Peter C. Herman (Newark, Delaware: University of Delaware Press, 1999), p. 243; Barbara Lewalski, 'Seizing Discourses and Reinventing Genres', in *Aemilia Lanyer: Gender, Genre, and the Canon*, ed. Marshall Grossman (Lexington, Kentucky: University Press of Kentucky, 1998), p. 49; and in the same volume Naomi J. Miller, '(M)other Tongues: Maternity and Subjectivity', p. 144, and Achsah Guibbory, 'The Gospel According to Aemilia: Women and the Sacred', p. 192. Other references to Lanyer's 'feminism' include McGrath, 'Metaphoric Subversions: Feasts and Mirrors in Aemilia Lanier's *Salve Deus Rex Judaeorum*', *LIT* 3.2 (1991): 101–13; and Janel Mueller, 'The Feminist Poetics of "Salve Deus Rex Judaeorum"', in *Aemilia Lanyer: Gender, Genre, and the Canon*, ed. Grossman, pp. 99–127. Those who focus on Lanyer's

Lanyer had few female poetic contemporaries, and that her attention to gender was not common, celebrating her achievement within those circumstances is much more problematic. The difficulty with such readings is that they tend to isolate Lanyer from history and her contemporaries by emphasising her exceptionalism. Susanne Woods, for example, justifies her own valorisation of Lanyer not through Lanyer's uniqueness among *all* poets, but the fact that she 'has no obvious challengers among Englishwomen'.[3] Such readings could be said to be fundamentally *anti*-feminist because they privilege one woman at the expense of all of her contemporaries who were not as bold or as 'feminist' as she. Significantly, Aemilia Lanyer herself speaks out against this way of advancing one woman to the detriment of the rest: 'Often have I heard,' she begins her epistle 'To the Vertuous Reader', 'that it is the property of some women, not only to emulate the virtues and perfections of the rest, but also by all their powers of ill speaking, to ecclipse the brightnes of their deserved fame[.]'[4]

Yet the fact remains that Lanyer, like other women writers of her time, has few female contemporaries with whom to share her fame. There were only a handful of works by women in print in the early seventeenth century, and while many more women wrote in manuscript, much of their work has not survived, or only in fragments. The case of Aemilia Lanyer thus epitomises the conundrum posed to scholars by the work of every woman writer in this book. In a very real sense, each is unique; and it is difficult to write into literary history someone who has few direct parallels among other writers.

The fact of their relative isolation is of course a vital part of these women's literary history, and it is the project of this chapter to situate Lanyer in the

---

opposition to patriarchy without using the term 'feminist' include Barbara K. Lewalski, 'Of God and Good Women: The Poems of Aemilia Lanyer', in *Silent But for the Word: Tudor Women as Patrons, Translators, and Writers of Religious Works*, ed. Margaret Hannay (Kent, Ohio: Kent State University Press, 1985), pp. 203–24, and her 'Imagining Female Community: Aemilia Lanyer's Poems', in *Writing Women in Jacobean England* (Cambridge, Massachusetts: Harvard University Press, 1993), pp. 213–41; Susanne Woods, 'Vocation and Authority: Born to Write', in *Aemilia Lanyer: Gender, Genre, and the Canon*, ed. Grossman, pp. 83–98; Elaine Beilin, 'The Feminization of Praise: Aemilia Lanyer', in *Redeeming Eve: Women Writers of the English Renaissance* (Princeton: Princeton University Press, 1987), pp. 177–207; Theresa M. DiPasquale, 'Woman's Desire for Man in Lanyer's *Salve Deus Rex Judaeorum*', *Journal of English and Germanic Philology* 99.3 (2000): 356–78.

[3] Woods, *Lanyer*, p. vii.

[4] *The Poems of Aemilia Lanyer: Salve Deus Rex Judaeorum*, ed. Susanne Woods (Oxford: Oxford University Press, 1993), p. 48. All quotations below are from this edition. Page and line numbers for the dedicatory material are given in the notes; line numbers of the title poem are given parenthetically in the text.

context available to us without denying the ways in which she is anomalous.[5] For Lanyer, as for other women writers, that context must include the work of male writers, for the traditions into which many women were writing were informed and even dominated by men. Placing Lanyer in both male and female traditions opens a way of interpreting her poetry that is beyond the binary oppositions of earlier criticism. Many of these readings invoke 'standing dichotomies' – 'public/private, mind/body, culture/nature, [and] reason/passion' – to demonstrate that *Salve deus rex judæorum* argues for the impact of women in a domain that is assumed to be exclusively masculine – and implicitly superior.[6] Such oppositional readings of Lanyer and other women poets assume that there is always a clear line between male and female in the early modern period, part of an omnipresent ideological system in which women are on the losing side.[7]

Recent social and literary history has demonstrated that it was rarely easy to construct simple lines of demarcation between the genders, whether in prescriptive literature or in practice.[8] The most recent criticism of Lanyer has taken these developments into account, scrutinising the ways in which her poetry incorporates existing traditions rather than directly opposing them.[9] This chapter furthers the project of contextualising Lanyer by reading her account of Christ's passion as a patronage poem, and alongside other passion narratives of the period, establishing that many of the most

[5] A number of recent studies have begun the project of contextualising Lanyer's complex poem: Su Fang Ng, 'Aemilia Lanyer and the Politics of Praise', *ELH* 67.2 (2000): 433–51; Patricia Phillippy, 'Sisters of Magdalen: Women's Mourning in Aemilia Lanyer's *Salve Deus Rex Judaeorum*', *ELR* 31.1 (2000): 78–106; Kari Boyd McBride and John C. Ulreich, 'Answerable Styles: Biblical Poetics and Biblical Politics in the Poetry of Lanyer and Milton', *Journal of English and Germanic Philology* 100.3 (2001): 333–54.

[6] Mueller, 'Feminist Poetics', p. 117; see also Lewalski, 'Seizing Discourses', p. 49; Guibbory, 'The Gospel According to Aemilia', p. 193; Mary Ellen Lamb, 'Patronage and Class in Aemilia Lanyer's *Salve Deus Rex Judaeorum*', in *Women, Writing, and the Reproduction of Culture in Tudor and Stuart Britain*, ed. Mary E. Burke *et al.* (Syracuse, New York: Syracuse University Press, 2000), p. 41.

[7] The existence of these 'dominant ideologies' is seldom historicised beyond references to long-superseded social histories. As Lamb's essay suggests, the appeal of 'dominant ideologies' is part of larger trends in criticism that extend beyond feminism. For a critique of these frameworks see David Cressy, 'Foucault, Stone, Shakespeare and Social History', *ELR* 21.1 (1991): 121–33.

[8] See the Introduction above.

[9] Danielle Clarke, *The Politics of Early Modern Women's Writing* (London: Longman, 2001), p. 159; Ann Baynes Coiro, 'Writing in Service: Sexual Politics and Class Position in the Poetry of Aemilia Lanyer and Ben Jonson', *Criticism* 35.3 (1993): 357–76; Judith Scherer Herz, 'Aemilia Lanyer and the Pathos of Literary History', in *Representing Women in Renaissance England*, ed. Claude J. Summers and Ted-Larry Pebworth (Columbia, Missouri: University of Missouri Press, 1997), pp. 121–35; Lisa Schnell, '"So Great a Difference Is There in Degree": Aemilia Lanyer and the Aims of Feminist Criticism', *MLQ* 57.1 (1996): 23–35 and 'Breaking "the rule of *Cortezia*": Aemilia Lanyer's Dedications to *Salve Deus Rex Judaeorum*', *Journal of Medieval and Early Modern Studies* 27.1 (1997): 77–101.

challenging elements of Lanyer's poetry have their roots in collaboration between men and women, particularly in the male-authored passion tradition. The mystical marriage motifs of the passion narratives provide Lanyer with the materials for a model of ungendered virtue for all followers of Christ, male and female, rich and poor. Reading Lanyer alongside her male contemporaries suggests far more exciting conclusions than reading her poem in opposition to men: that the most radical elements of her text are not unique, but are in fact constructed out of a conventional and orthodox tradition.

PATRONS AND PRINT

As with so many texts by early modern women, the contextualisation of *Salve deus rex judæorum* begins with the circumstances surrounding its publication.[10] The mechanisms of patronage are fundamental to understanding the poem: the dedicatory material is nearly as long as the title poem itself, and within the passion poem the verse and marginal notes continually address Aemilia Lanyer's chief patron, Margaret Clifford, Countess of Cumberland.[11] *Salve deus rex judæorum* is thus inscribed as an act of supplication to a group of patrons, and the theology of the passion that influences the poems is imbedded in this context. In her pursuit of advancement, as well as in her reading of the passion, Aemilia Lanyer was not as oppositionally 'feminist' as she might seem: the alliances between men and women and across lines of status that are vital to the poem's model of ungendered virtue are also crucial to the author's bid for patronage.

Salve deus rex judæorum is addressed to nine specific royal and noblewomen – Queen Anne, Princess Elizabeth, Lady Arabella Stuart and the Countesses of Kent, Pembroke, Bedford, Cumberland, Suffolk and Dorset – as well as the catch-all 'To all vertuous Ladies in generall'.[12] None of these patrons is a surprising or unusual choice for a woman writer or in fact for any of Lanyer's contemporaries. Mary Sidney, Countess of Pembroke, and Lucy, Countess of Bedford, both maintained circles of client-poets,

---

[10] Because Lanyer's life has been studied in detail elsewhere, this chapter forgoes an extended biographical narrative. For detailed biographies of Lanyer, see Woods, *Lanyer*, pp. 3–41; and the Introduction to her edition of *The Poems of Aemilia Lanyer*, pp. xv–xxx.

[11] On the mechanisms of patronage that influence Lanyer's poem, see the essays in *Patronage in the Renaissance*, ed. Guy Fitch Lytel and Stephen Orgel (Princeton, New Jersey: Princeton University Press, 1981), especially Marotti, 'John Donne and the Rewards of Patronage', pp. 207–34; also his '"Love is not love": Elizabethan Sonnet Sequences and The Social Order', *ELH* 49.2 (1982): 396–428.

[12] The dedications are pp. 3–50 in Woods's edition.

including Spenser, Daniel, Donne and Jonson.[13] Aemilia Lanyer's chief patron, Margaret Clifford, Countess of Cumberland, was one of the dedicatees of Spenser's *Fowre hymnes* (1596), a principal source for Lanyer's evocation of Christ's beauty.[14] Women patrons also received dedications from other women: the Countess of Pembroke dedicated her own works to Queen Elizabeth, and Ann Lock addressed her translation and sonnet sequence to Catherine Willoughby, Duchess of Suffolk (to whom Lanyer alludes in her dedication to Willoughby's daughter, Susan Bertie, Countess of Kent).[15]

That Aemilia Lanyer chose to address her book exclusively to female patrons has been cited frequently as her attempt to establish a 'community of good women', but it may in fact have been as much a matter of exigency as a sign of consciousness of gender.[16] The men who receive dedications from women writers tend to be close relatives or family associates: the Cavendish sisters' address of their poems and play to their father is a fit example.[17] Aemilia Lanyer had no such powerful men on whom she could call; her former lover and protector, the Lord Hunsdon, had been dead since 1596, and her own family were immigrant court musicians, not landed gentry or titled nobility. It would have been immodest for her or any other woman of her station to seek patronage from an unknown man. Male writers might expect remuneration from both male and female patrons who could offer financial sums, household positions or indirect incomes, like the patent for weighing hay and grain won by Alfonso Lanyer.[18] A married woman, on the other hand, was less likely to have gained anything directly for herself from a male patron. Any financial rewards would have gone to her husband, as head of the household, while the sort of positions a woman client might take in a household would probably have been at the disposal of women patrons only.

---

[13] Margaret P. Hannay, *Philip's Phoenix: Mary Sidney, Countess of Pembroke* (Oxford: Oxford University Press, 1990), pp. 106–42; Leeds Barroll, 'The Court of the First Stuart Queen', in *The Mental World of the Jacobean Court*, ed. Linda Levy Peck (Cambridge: Cambridge University Press, 1991), pp. 191–208.

[14] Einor Bjorvand *et al.*, eds., *The Yale Edition of the Shorter Poems of Edmund Spenser* (New Haven, Connecticut: Yale University Press, 1989), pp. 683–752. The other dedicatee is Margaret Clifford's sister, Anne Dudley, Countess of Warwick. See also Woods, *Lanyer*, pp. 54–61.

[15] 'Even now that Care', in Hannay, *et al.*, eds., *The Collected Works of Mary Sidney Herbert*, I. 102–4; Felch, ed., *The Collected Works of Anne Vaughan Lock*, pp. 4–8.

[16] Lewalski, 'Of God and Good Women', p. 207. For a critique of this reading, see Ng, 'Aemilia Lanyer and the Politics of Praise'.

[17] Margaret Ezell, '"To Be Your Daughter in Your Pen": The Social Functions of Literature in the Writings of Lady Elizabeth Brackley and Lady Jane Cavendish', *Huntington Library Quarterly* 51.4 (1988): 281–96.

[18] Woods, Introduction, *The Poems of Aemilia Lanyer*, p. xxv.

Lanyer's appeal to important women patrons is thus less daring and unconventional than the fact that her book made its way into the libraries of two influential men, Prince Henry and Thomas Jones, Archbishop of Dublin. As Leeds Barroll's work has suggested, the survival of these copies points to the intriguing possibility that *Salve deus rex judæorum* may have been a joint attempt on the part of Aemilia and Alfonso Lanyer to gain advancement. We know from Aemilia Lanyer's visits to the astrologer Simon Foreman that one of the hopes she shared with her husband was that he might receive a knighthood.[19] Barroll's work has demonstrated that Alfonso had a number of influential connections, including Henry Wriothesley, Earl of Southampton, and Sir Robert Wroth, later Earl of Montgomery, through whom he pursued preferment for himself, and by association, his wife. On at least one occasion Alfonso used his wife's literary talent as part of that search for advancement: Archbishop Jones's copy of *Salve deus rex judæorum* is inscribed 'guift of Mr Alfonso Lanyer', and the presentation copy of *Salve deus rex judæorum* is much more likely to have reached Prince Henry through one of Alfonso's many documented patrons than through Aemilia Lanyer's possible tangential court acquaintances.[20]

A knighthood for Alfonso would have made Aemilia Lady Lanyer, so that with her husband's excellent connections it would have been expedient and mutually beneficial for the two to work together to promote her book. The title-page designation of the author as 'Wife to Captaine *Alfonso Lanyer* Servant to the Kings Majestie', is thus less a sign of a patriarchal printer than the pooling of joint social capital.[21] As a collaborative effort, *Salve deus rex judæorum* might be compared to Alice Sutcliffe's volume, *Meditations of man's mortalitie* (1634).[22] Like Lanyer's work, Sutcliffe's book includes intimately phrased dedications to women, the Duchess of Buckingham and Countess of Denbeigh. The dedications are followed by a collection of encomia by male poets flattering the author, including poems by Ben Jonson and George Wither that demonstrate connections to a circle of esteemed writers that Lanyer, in her lower social position, could not have claimed. Sutcliffe's book also displays her husband's name and office on its title page, much like *Salve deus rex judæorum*. Both books seem gauged to

[19] Woods, *Lanyer*, p. 25.
[20] Leeds Barroll, 'Looking for Patrons', in *Aemilia Lanyer: Gender, Genre, and the Canon*, ed. Grossman, pp. 36–41. Woods, Textual Introduction to *The Poems of Aemilia Lanyer*, p. xlix.
[21] Schnell argues that the subtitle is 'an attempt by the printer, it would seem, to present the poet as a thoroughly respectable woman, thus erasing any traces of the reputation she might have earned as Hunsdon's mistress', in 'Breaking "the rule of *Cortezia*"', p. 80.
[22] STC 23447 Alice Sutcliffe, *Meditations of man's mortalitie* (London: by B. Alsop and T. Fawcet for Henry Seyle, 1634).

garner advancement for both the writer and her husband by trading on her accomplishments and virtues as a gentlewoman writer, a project in which both husband and wife are active.

The chief difference between the two women and their books is that Alice Sutcliffe and her husband already enjoyed the favour of the king (John Sutcliffe was a Groom of the Privy Chamber), while Aemilia Lanyer had only a slim claim to patronage. Leeds Barroll has demonstrated that the simple facts of Lanyer's birth and station, as well as details of her physical location at specific times, make the relationships to Susan Bertie and Margaret and Ann Clifford posited in the dedications highly unlikely.[23] It is possible to make much, as Susanne Woods has done, of Aemilia Lanyer as a 'gentlewoman' by both parentage and marriage.[24] In practice, however, she would have seemed little more than an educated servant to her aristocratic dedicatees, rather like Maria, Olivia's 'gentlewoman' in *Twelfth Night*, whose marriage to Sir Toby Belch is such a coup. Whatever her claims by birth, Lanyer visited Foreman in the late 1590s because she was in serious financial difficulty.[25] Given these economic troubles, Lisa Schnell speculates that Lanyer fictionalised the relationships with her patrons, since there is absolutely no corroborative evidence.[26]

I agree with Schnell and Barroll that it is unwise to take Lanyer at her word. Evidence does disappear, but given the voluminous material available on Anne Clifford alone, it seems significant to have not a single mention of Aemilia Lanyer in connection with any of the women she claims to have known. But fictionalising such connections would have been pointless if the goal of the volume was to gain advancement; surely pretended intimacy would only have angered the implicated person and disgusted any other potential patrons. It seems more likely that Lanyer greatly exaggerated small favours received from these women and imagined a more sustained relationship. Such exaggeration was not, perhaps, an unusual practice among poets seeking patrons: Spenser's dedications of several of his *Complaints* to his distant relations the Spencer sisters of Althorp are a case in point.[27] If Aemilia Lanyer had been the mistress of Lord Hunsdon, it is not unlikely that she had some similarly tangential contact with ladies at court, and she seems to have hoped to lever herself upwards on the basis of these former associations.

---

[23] Barroll, 'Looking for Patrons', throughout.   [24] Woods, *Lanyer*, p. 8.   [25] *Ibid.*, pp. 21–5.
[26] Schnell, 'Breaking "the rule of *Cortezia*"', pp. 81–2; '"So great a difference"', p. 30 n. 9.
[27] 'The Teares of the Muses', p. 268; 'Prosopopoia: *or* Mother Hubberds Tale', p. 334; 'Muiopotmos: *or* The Fate of the Butterflie', p. 412; all in Bjorvand, *et al.*, eds., *The Yale Edition of the Shorter Poems of Edmund Spenser*.

Whatever her hopes to connect herself to the great and wealthy, the material format of *Salve deus rex judæorum* may suggest Aemilia Lanyer's distance from exclusive court circles. As Susanne Woods has demonstrated, the existence of copies of *Salve deus rex judæorum* with specially tailored prefatory material suggests that different versions of the book were printed for different patrons, much like a series of presentation manuscripts. The physical appearance of Prince Henry's copy supports this theory; its fine binding stamped with Henry's emblem clearly marks it as a book intended for the prince alone.[28] The question remains of why Lanyer, if she imitated a practice of manuscript culture, did not use a scribe to create copies of her book. The answer, I would suggest, lies not in Lanyer's daring desire to 'publicise' her writing – she would not have earned anything from sales of the book, nor would she have been likely to garner patronage through a copy purchased in a bookshop – but rather in her strained financial circumstances.

The financial motives behind the choice of print or manuscript are seldom explored, but a brief glance at the available evidence suggests the economic gulf between scribal and print publication. A printed book in this period cost approximately one halfpenny per sheet, unbound.[29] Lanyer's book, at 14.5 sheets quarto, would have cost between 7 and 7.5 pence per copy in a bookshop.[30] Lanyer may not have paid anything to her printer and bookseller, or they may have paid her a small sum for the manuscript; the detailed imprint indicates that Richard Bonian had some hope of selling copies in his St Paul's bookstall, and in any case the book was not printed 'for the author'.

Whether she paid or was paid, printing would have been a considerably cheaper option than hiring a scribe. Although as yet no study has calculated the average cost of preparing a manuscript, collating scraps of evidence demonstrates that it would have been much more than the cost of setting up the press. Sir Edward Dering paid one penny per sheet to a 'mr carington' for copying Shakespeare's *Henry IV*; this wage amounted to twice or possibly eight times the price of a printed book, since a 'sheet' in this context may have the more conventional meaning of 'page', or one side of a folio, rather than four sides of a bifolium. Copies of a letter sent to

---

[28] Woods, Textual Introduction, *The Poems of Aemilia Lanyer*, pp. xlvii–xlix.

[29] Francis R. Johnson, 'Notes on English Retail Book-prices, 1550–1640', *The Library* 5.5 (1950): 83–112, especially p. 90. I have ignored the cost of binding in this analysis since it would have been similar for both manuscript and printed volumes.

[30] The price of a book for sale may of course have been more than the cost of having it prepared; although see note 32 below.

Buckingham about the Spanish match or a defence of the Earl of Salisbury were priced by Humphrey Dyson at 18 pence and 2 shillings respectively. Several extant manuscripts of these texts average around three folios in length, approximately one-tenth the size of *Salve deus rex judæorum*.[31] Even taking into account that the cost of preparing these manuscripts would have been somewhat less than the selling price, and that the notoriety of the subject matter might have inflated that price, preparing these manuscripts must have cost several times more than print, far more than Aemilia Lanyer could afford or expect from her patrons in return. Unless she chose to undertake the arduous task of producing eleven autograph manuscripts (one for each of the nine women, Prince Henry and Archbishop Jones), print was the only option for Aemilia Lanyer if she wanted to reach her patrons.[32]

In addition to emulating the manuscript circulation of her patrons by the only affordable means, Lanyer had to use every poetic faculty at her disposal to create the illusion of intimacy. It is a delicate project, balancing the demands of praise, humility and self-presentation integral to successful patronage poetry. The fact that Lanyer explicitly addresses her book to women, and that she carefully establishes her book as a defence of women's virtues in the prose epistle 'To the Vertuous Reader', may be part of one strategy to overcome the disadvantages of social status. Common values and concerns based on gender become one way of uniting Lanyer to her otherwise distant patrons.

The gulf between Lanyer and her patrons points to another way in which her poem is not as oppositional as it may seem. As Coiro, Schnell and Lamb have argued, *Salve deus rex judæorum* is at least as concerned about constructions of status as it is about constructions of gender.[33] Lanyer's anxieties about status can be glimpsed in her epistle 'To the Vertuous Reader'; although degree is not explicitly mentioned, Lanyer clearly has her eye on unbalanced power relations within her own gender. Some women have disproportionate power to control others' actions, and Lanyer fervently hopes 'they will rather, cherish, nourish, and increase the least sparke of

---

[31] H. R. Woudhuysen, *Sir Philip Sidney and the Circulation of Manuscripts, 1558–1640* (Oxford: Clarendon Press, 1996), pp. 86, 178–80. Humphrey Dyson's Booklist is in All Souls' MS 117; I am grateful to the librarian of the Codrington Library at All Souls' College, Oxford, for lending me a microfilm of the manuscript while the library was closed for construction. A list of manuscripts of the letter to Buckingham is in Woudhuysen, *Sir Philip Sidney*, p. 180; Sir Walter Cope's dialogue or character of the Earl of Salisbury is in Bodleian Library Tanner MSS 74, 265, 278, and 283 (autograph).

[32] Even if she had chosen to copy the text herself, Lanyer would only have saved about 25 per cent on the cost of print, since the cost of paper (a necessary expense for either medium) amounted to up to 75 per cent of the price of a book. See Tessa Watt, *Cheap Print and Popular Piety 1550–1640* (Cambridge: Cambridge University Press, 1991), p. 1.

[33] See note 9; Lamb, 'Patronage and Class', p. 40.

virtue where they find it, by their favourable and best interpretations, than quench it by wrong constructions'.[34] That this is an *interpretative* power is clearly significant in the introduction to a volume of poems. Lanyer indirectly raises the possibility that her own virtue will be quenched by the wrong constructions of women more powerful than she. Her poem and its elaborate epideictic apparatus exist to guide both men and women to 'best interpretations' of the possibilities for virtue in women.[35]

Such fears of misinterpretation and slander were not, perhaps, unwarranted, given Lanyer's origins. As the daughter and wife of court musicians, Lanyer could claim the title of gentlewoman, but in status, income and influence she dwelt far below her nine women dedicatees, all monarchs or wives of peers of the realm. This difference in status led directly to differences in expectations of feminine behaviour. A woman like Anne Clifford, '[w]hose birth and education both combines', and a woman untitled and financially struggling, would have experienced different status-specific definitions of how a woman should form and express her opinions.[36] For daughters of the upper gentry and nobility, writing was often seen as an appropriate feminine accomplishment. In the Tudor period, Lady Jane Fitzalan Lumley and the women of the Cecil family were honoured for their ability to turn Latin and Greek verse, while in the Caroline era, Lady Anne Southwell's poetry was framed by her husband as a sign of both her piety and her gentility.[37] As Jane Stevenson has pointed out, the evidence is growing that an early modern gentlewoman was expected to be 'chaste, obedient, and mistress of an appropriate poetic discourse'.[38] In the case of Lanyer, it may in fact be her social status and not her gender that makes her writing so daring. Lanyer's use of printed poetry to approach her patrons is, I would suggest, less an act of feminist subversion than it is an act of social audacity. *Salve deus rex judæorum*, and the accompanying dedications,

[34] 'To the Vertuous Reader', p. 50.
[35] Lorna Hutson considers 'interpretive virtue' in *Salve deus rex judæorum* in 'Why the Lady's Eyes are Nothing Like the Sun', in *Women, Texts, and Histories 1575–1760*, ed. Claire Brant and Diane Purkiss (London: Routledge, 1992), pp. 13–38.
[36] 'To the Ladie *Anne*, Countesse of Dorcet', p. 45, l. 91.
[37] Jan van Dorsten, 'Literary Patronage in Elizabethan England: The Early Phase', in *Patronage in the Renaissance*, ed. Guy Fitch Lytel and Stephen Orgel (Princeton, New Jersey: Princeton University Press, 1981), pp. 195–9; Louise Schleiner, *Tudor and Stuart Women Writers* (Bloomington, Indiana: Indiana University Press, 1994), pp. 30–51; Diane Purkiss, Introduction, in *Three Tragedies by Renaissance Women* (London: Penguin, 1998), pp. xiii–xv, xx–xxi; 'Mildred Cecil, Lady Burghley: Poet, Patron, Politician', paper given by Jane Stevenson at the Women, Text and History seminar at Mansfield College, Oxford, November 1998. For a discussion of Lady Anne Southwell see the next chapter.
[38] Jane Stevenson, 'Women, Writing and Scribal Publication in the Sixteenth Century', paper given at the Trinity–Trent Colloquium, Trinity College, Cambridge, 29 November 1997.

are an attempt by Lanyer to prove that she can speak the language of her patrons, and to raise herself to the degree of the noblewomen she addresses.

It is important, however, not to read too much oppositional radicalism into this strategy. While Lanyer may make complex use of the interconnections of gender and virtue, her bid for patronage is a fundamentally conservative one. There is no hint that she wishes to destroy a hierarchical system – the dedications, in fact, are a clumsy attempt to inscribe the hierarchy into her book – but rather that she wishes to move up the ladder through her husband's knighthood.[39] It is telling that the opening dedication of her poem is addressed 'To all vertuous *Ladies* in generall' (italics mine), a term used specifically to isolate only those readers with titles. In it the author is careful to excuse herself for elevating one member of the peerage above another, lest she offend a potential patron:

> Yet some of you me thinkes I heare to call
> Me by my name, and bid me better looke,
> Lest unawares I in an error fall:
>   In generall tearmes, to place you with the rest,
>   Whom Fame commends to be the very best.[40]

Lanyer excuses herself by arguing that the titled women themselves have distinguished certain ladies above all others, and this itself is testimony to their virtue. Nowhere in the volume does she extend her community of flattery to women of her own status.[41]

Rather than urging an egalitarianism that would have been alien to early modern society, Lanyer instead subtly insists that the ideals underpinning the hierarchy ought to be enacted. Drawing on the prescriptive literature considered in the previous chapter, Lanyer takes advantage of the fact that social and gender hierarchies were justified by the benevolent example of Christ's authority. By emphasising that the resurrected king is also the Christ of the passion, a model of passive resistance, patient suffering, generosity and all-encompassing forgiveness, Lanyer creates a Christ who radically bridges gender and status yet never departs from her Biblical text or Christian ideals of authority. Her Christ demonstrates how the privilege of her patrons – and, implicitly, the power men have over women – can only be justified when the powerful rule in Christ-like benevolence.

---

[39] Barroll comments on how Aemilia Lanyer seems to have mistaken the order of her dedications, 'Looking for Patrons', p. 40.

[40] P. 15, lines 73–7.

[41] For more on the disruptions of social status in Lanyer, see Lisa Schnell, '"So Great a Difference"', and 'Breaking "the rule of *Cortezia*"'.

THE PASSION AND MYSTICAL LOVE

Lanyer's account of Christ as an ideal authority draws on a long history of retellings of the story of his arrest, trials, torture and crucifixion, beginning, of course, with the four Gospel narratives that were the source for all later accounts. By Lanyer's own time new passion narratives were considerably less common than they had been for medieval Christians. The veneration of Christ's wounded body seemed idolatrous to English Calvinists, who included crucifixes among the church images removed in the late 1540s.[42] Dwelling too much on the crucified Christ might lead one to forget the grace of the risen Christ that was central to reformed theology. 'The Church of Rome, so fixes her selfe (in her adoration) vpon the Crosse of Christ, as if shee forgat his glory', Joseph Hall argued in the preface to his 1609 passion sermon. Yet, he continued, 'Many of vs so conceiue of him glorious, that we neglect the meditation of his Crosse, the way to his glory and ours'.[43] Despite Hall's urging, Debora Shuger counts only a handful of passion sermons between the Edwardian reformation and the civil wars, a tiny number compared with the dozens of contemporary sermons, commentaries and paraphrases of the Song of Songs and other mystical marriage texts examined in the previous chapter.[44]

But if '[t]he figure of the crucified Jesus slips to the margins of English Protestantism' in terms of the volume of texts it inhabits, the passion sequence naturally maintains a significant influence on English religious thought.[45] The poems of the Jesuit martyr Robert Southwell operated on the margins of the passion story and inspired a number of imitations and responses from Protestants and Catholics alike.[46] For English Protestants, the act of Christ's sacrifice and resurrection, if not the narrative detail, was central to pivotal contemporary debates about the nature of salvation.[47] There is even a sense in a number of the reformed passion narratives that

[42] Eamon Duffy, *The Stripping of the Altars: Traditional Religion in England c. 1400–c.1580* (New Haven, Connecticut: Yale University Press, 1992), pp. 480–1.

[43] STC 12694 Joseph Hall, *The passion sermon, preached at pavles crosse on good-friday* (London: W.S. for Samuell Macham, 1609), sig. A4ʳ.

[44] Debora Kuller Shuger, *The Renaissance Bible: Scholarship, Sacrifice, and Subjectivity* (Berkeley, California: University of California Press, 1994), p. 89.

[45] *Ibid.*

[46] Alison Shell, *Catholicism, Controversy, and the English Literary Imagination, 1558–1660* (Cambridge: Cambridge University Press, 1999), pp. 77–88.

[47] Nicholas Tyacke, 'Puritanism, Arminianism, and Counter-revolution', in *Aspects of English Protestantism c. 1530–1700* (Manchester: Manchester University Press, 2001), pp. 132–55.

the tradition has become so omnipresent as to be exhausted; some writers excuse themselves from recounting details 'because this theme hath beene admirably discoursed and discussed' by earlier writers.[48] While it is impossible to know if Lanyer read any particular passion sermon or poem, it is likely that she inherited these frequently 'discoursed and discussed' embellishments and elaborations to the Gospel narratives which imputed theological significance to each event in the passion story.

A number of these motifs in the passion story were borrowed from the mystical marriage tradition, which shared with the passion the key theme of the sacrificial love of Christ, enacted in his death and allegorised in his marriage to the Church. These shared motifs included many of the elements commonly considered radical in Lanyer's own passion poem: her exhortation to desire Christ, her erotic blazons of Christ's body, her emphasis on the fluidity of Christ's gender. In the passion narratives, these motifs all point to the paradoxical nature of Christ's role in the passion, simultaneously both powerful and meek, in control of the situation and yet suffering in silence. Underlining these episodes enables Lanyer to recall the radicalism of that paradox: the Christ of the gospels in whom 'Poverty and Riches met together, / The wealth of Heaven, in our fraile clothing' (1114–15). Thus, although he is entirely in keeping with conventional passion narratives, Lanyer's Christ provides a model for love that transforms not only individual sin, but the excesses and abuses of power hierarchies.

Lanyer's exhortation to her patrons to gaze upon and desire the body of Christ as a symbol of grace is one of the most frequently discussed aspects of her poem, but the roots of this motif in English devotional literature have not yet been explored fully.[49] Passion sermons and poems, like many mystical marriage texts, are primarily devotional, offering a pattern for contemplation and prayer. They rely on the visually arresting spectacle of Christ's death to move readers to pity, sorrow, guilt and, ultimately, redemptive worship. Within this tradition Debora Shuger has identified a number of distinct devotional strands, arguing that while late medieval iconography

---

[48] STC 24996a Samuel Walsall, *The life and death of iesus christ* ([Cambridge]: for I. Porter and L. Greene, 1607), sig. C4ʳ; STC 4946.9 Bartholomew Chamberlaine, *The passion of christ, and the benefits thereby* (London: for Thomas Pauier, 1612), sig. A8ʳ; first printed 1595 (STC 4946.8).

[49] Phillippy, 'Sisters of Magdalen', pp. 97–101; Ng, 'Aemilia Lanyer and the Politics of Praise', pp. 442–3; Clarke, *The Politics of Early Modern Women's Writing*, pp. 160–1; Wendy Wall, *The Imprint of Gender: Authorship and Publication in the English Renaissance* (Ithaca, New York: Cornell University Press, 1993), p. 322; Kari Boyd McBride, 'Sacred Celebration: The Patronage Poems', in *Aemilia Lanyer: Gender, Genre, and the Canon*, ed. Grossman, p. 64; and McGrath, 'Metaphoric Subversions', throughout.

focused on the intense suffering of Christ's last days, the early reformers, and Calvin himself, never depict Christ's pain, concentrating instead on the love offered in the passion. The later English Calvinist passions return to the Catholic tradition, 'dwell[ing] with an almost Ignatian vividness on the horrific agony of Christ's tortured body'. For these writers, Shuger suggests, 'Christ's inner struggle' becomes the means of describing the development of the elect soul, an 'exemplary subtext for Calvinist representations of Christian selfhood'.[50]

Lanyer, in keeping with her mixed devotional heritage as the daughter of an Italian Catholic family who had become Protestants in England, embraces elements of each of these strands, offering her readers both the tortured Calvinist Christ and the beautiful Saviour of medieval Catholics and the early reformers.[51] All of these writers exhort their readers to gaze at Christ's body, not merely to feel sorrow for his suffering but to contemplate their own sin. Lancelot Andrewes, for example, closes one of his passion sermons with a meditation on looking at Christ's 'piercing', but does not offer any vivid descriptions of Christ's damaged body.[52] In Andrewes's Ignatian meditation gazing at Christ leads through conviction of sin to belief, hope and receipt of grace. For the Calvinist Joseph Hall, on the other hand, genuine conviction of sin is the key sign of election, and a true embracing of Christ's body should lead not to comfort but the stoic conviction of the early martyrs:

I call you not to a weake & idle pitty of our glorious Sauiour: to what purpose? His iniurie was our glory. No, no; *Yee daughters of Ierusalem, weepe not for me; but weepe for your selues*: for our sins, that haue done this, not for his sorrow that suffered it: not for his pangs, that were, but for our own, that should haue been, and (if we repent not) shall be[.][53]

Perhaps not surprisingly, Lanyer's poetic bid for patronage prefers Andrewes's reading to Hall's; repeatedly emphasising the sinfulness of her patrons might not have been the best means to earn their favour. Instead, Lanyer urges her readers to be transformed by the spectacle of Christ presented in her poem. Rather than offer her own abilities as a poet, over and over in the dedications Lanyer urges her patrons to accept Christ as their

[50] Shuger, *The Renaissance Bible*, pp. 95, 89–90.
[51] Susanne Woods discusses the religious heritage of Lanyer's family, the Bassanos, including the possibility that they were Jewish or radical Protestants, in *Lanyer*, pp. 5–7.
[52] Lancelot Andrewes, 'A sermon preached at the court, on the xxv. of March, A. D. MDXCVII. being Good-Friday', in STC 606 XCVI *sermons* (London: George Miller for Richard Badger, 1629), pp. 333–48.
[53] Hall, *The passion sermon*, p. 50.

gift: 'I present unto you even our Lord Jesus himselfe[.]'[54] She figures
Christ's mystical love – and by extension her own poetic account of that
love – as desirable for her patrons, urging them to accept and embrace
him, and in 'entertaine[ing] this dying lover' they also accept his example
of sacrificial love.[55]

Lanyer's metaphorical packaging of the spectacle of Christ's crucifixion
works within the gift–exchange system that created and sustained religious
and social alliances in early modern England.[56] Although gifts were often
material, the language of the system was also inscribed into patronage
poetry. Spenser begs Ralegh, for example, to accept *Colin clouts come home
againe* 'in part of paiment of the infinite debt in which I acknowledge my
selfe bounden unto you'.[57] In such exchanges, the gift of poetry is accorded
a value, even if an inferior one, allowing the poet-client to assume a degree
of control of the relationship that would not be possible if he or she were
always on the receiving end. For a poet like Lanyer, well below her patrons
in station, assuming such rhetorical control was vital. As a religious poet, she
could also manipulate the tactic of conflating the identities of poet, subject
and text into one united gift in order to 'borrow' the virtue of her divine
subject matter. This was also a common practice; Ann Lock's dedication
of her translation of Calvin reminds Catherine, Duchess of Suffolk of the
agency of both author and translator, even while claiming that the work
originates from God: 'This receipte God the heavenly Physitian hath taught,
his most excellent Apothecarie master John Calvine hath compounded, and
I your graces most bounden and humble have put into an Englishe box,
and do present unto you.'[58]

Lock's preface focuses on the visible merits of her translation, reminding
her patron 'howe we sawe Ezechias healed, whome we imagine in this Boke
to see, both dying, revived, and walking after health recovered'.[59] Like a
painting of a Biblical scene, the text both delights and instructs primarily

[54] 'To the Ladie *Margaret* Countesse Dowager of Cumberland', p. 34. For examples of similar formulas in other dedications, see also 'The Authors Dreame to the Ladie *Marie*, the Countesse Dowager of *Pembrooke*', p. 31, lines 218–19; 'To the Ladie Susan, Countesse Dowager of Kent, and Daughter to the Duchesse of Suffolke', p. 19, lines 37–42; 'To the Ladie *Catherine* Countesse of Suffolke', p. 38, lines 42–45.
[55] 'To the Ladie *Lucie*, Countesse of Bedford', p. 33, line 16.
[56] Jane Donawerth, 'Women's Poetry and the Tudor–Stuart System of Gift Exchange', in *Women, Writing, and the Reproduction of Culture*, ed. Burke *et al.*, pp. 3–18.
[57] Bjorvand, *et al.*, eds, *The Yale Edition of the Shorter Poems of Edmund Spenser*, pp. 525–6; see also the dedication of *Foure hymnes* to the Countesses of Cumberland and Warwick, p. 690.
[58] Felch, ed., *The Collected Works of Anne Vaughan Lock*, p. 5. Susanne Woods demonstrates that Lanyer may have been acquainted with Ann Lock, whose brother Stephen Vaughan was the executor of Lanyer's mother's will. *Lanyer*, p. 7.
[59] Felch, ed., *The Collected Works of Anne Vaughan Lock*, p. 8.

through the eyes. Lanyer's construction of her poem is also overwhelmingly visual: 'Here may your sacred Majestie behold / That mightie Monarch both of heav'n and earth'; 'Heere they may see a Lover much more true', 'your Saviour in a Shepheards weed, / Unworthily presented in your viewe'.[60] Lanyer uses such formulations to control the gaze of her readers, directing their eyes toward her picture of Christ and by implication to her poetry itself. Her patrons' own virtue is implicit in their approval of this portrait. Lanyer's text becomes a mirror of both the beauties of Christ and of the nobility of her patrons, who can 'peruse[]' either at any time in the convenient form of the book.[61]

Lanyer may draw this element of mirroring directly from the passion sermons, where Christ is frequently depicted as directing 'his deiected countenance and languishing eyes vnto vs miserable and most vnthankfull caitifes, that neyther sympathize with him in his calamity, nor so much as remember, that hee himselfe stood in the vantguard of the battell, and with his helmet of *Patience* sheltered vs from the gunneshot of his Fathers indignation'.[62] In these texts Christ returns virtue for vice, meeting the eyes of those who have harmed him, forcing them to acknowledge their sin and simultaneously offering forgiveness. The healing power of Christ's eyes was especially significant in the episode of Peter's denial, for it was commonly thought that a single glance from Christ had saved Peter from falling away: 'so nowe when he walked in the paths of death, and was nigh swallowed in the gulfe of perdition, Christ saued him with a respecting and recalling and reclayming eye'.[63] This motif of Christ's 'reclayming eye' became the excuse for a long digression on the beauty of Christ's 'unspotted eyes' in Robert Southwell's influential poem 'Saint Peter's Complaint'.[64] In *Salve deus rex judæorum*, Lanyer narrates Christ's prediction of Peter's denial rather than the event itself, but when Peter responds angrily to the prediction in her version of the story, 'Wisdoms eyes did looke and checke his crime' (358), alluding to the way Peter will be recalled to the flock after the crime is committed.

[60] 'To the Queenes most Excellent Majestie', p. 5, lines 43–4; 'To the Lady *Catherine*', p. 38, line 52; 'The Authors Dreame', p. 31, lines 218–19.
[61] 'To the Ladie *Margaret* Countesse Dowager of Cumberland', p. 35. On mirror images in Lanyer see McBride, 'Sacred Celebration', throughout; McGrath, 'Metaphoric Subversions', throughout; Ng, 'Aemilia Lanyer and the Politics of Praise', p. 448.
[62] STC 13039 Daniel Heinsius, *The mirrovr of hvmilitie*, translated by John Harmar (London: Bernard Alsop, 1618), p. 65. First printed in Latin as *Dan. heinsii in cruentem christi sacrificium, siue domini passionem, homilia* (Leyden: Ludovicum Elzervirium, 1613).
[63] Walsall, *The life and death of iesvs christ*, sig. D4^v-E^r.
[64] James H. MacDonald and Nancy Pollard Brown, eds., *The Poems of Robert Southwell, S. J.* (Oxford: Clarendon Press, 1967).

The emphasis on the ability of Christ's gaze to recall and to heal is part of a larger motif of vision and blindness that permeates all passion narratives, including Lanyer's poem. Those who see the crucifixion truly, like Peter after he has been reclaimed, are 'appaled and affrighted at the view of so doleful a spectacle'.[65] Similarly, in Spenser's 'An Hymne of Heavenly Love', the truly sighted believer should be moved to 'pittifull remorse' '[a]t sight of [Christ's] most sacred heavenly corse', whereas the earthly and sinful will be blinded by the 'durt and drosse' of 'earthes glorie'.[66] By exchanging looks of true vision with Christ himself, believers are liberated both to see and be seen, as Peter says in Southwell's poem: 'By seeing things, you make things worth the sight, / You seeing, salve, and being seene, delight.'[67]

By contrast, those who do not see truly delight in the wrong objects and are in danger of damnation. Lanyer's passion narrative refers repeatedly to the failure of Christ's crucifiers and even his disciples to see him clearly. In the garden of Gethsemane, for example, Peter, James and John 'shut those Eies that should their Maker see' (420). When the soldiers come to arrest him, Christ 'Presents himselfe, that they might take a view' (515), but they are unable to look at him with discernment because 'Sinnes ugly mists, so blinded had their eyes' (681). Lanyer's concept of true vision also draws on the Calvinist duty of 'watchfulness', the idea that the believer must be continually conscious of his own tendency to sin. Peter, James and John remember in the garden that they should 'Watch and Pray' lest they be tempted (423), a Biblical motif prominent in Calvin's commentary on this episode.[68] Lanyer thus borrows from the passion tradition a model of devotional vision that includes the possibility of self-understanding as well as of understanding the divine, a difference that is significant within the reflexive nature of her poem. To know Christ, her patrons must also look to their own virtues, and emulate his generous love.

Lanyer uses this dual model of vision in order to reconsider the implications for women of seeing and being seen by men. In her 'Invective against outward beuty unaccompanied with virtue' (185–248), she mingles the stories of temptresses – Helen of Troy, Cleopatra and Rosamund – with the tales of the virgin martyrs Lucretia and Matilda.[69] Like the figure

---

[65] Heinsius, *The mirrovr of hvmilitie*, pp. 56–7.
[66] Bjorvand, *et al.*, eds., *The Yale Edition of the Shorter Poems of Edmund Spenser*, pp. 733–4, lines 247, 249, 276, 275. See also Woods, *Lanyer*, pp. 54–61.
[67] MacDonald and Pollard Brown, eds., *The Poems of Robert Southwell*, p. 87 lines 377–8.
[68] STC 2962 Jean Calvin, *A harmonie vpon the three euangelists*, translated by Eusebius Paget (London: George Bishop, 1584), p. 708.
[69] On Lanyer's use of Cleopatra, see Ng, 'Aemilia Lanyer and the Politics of Praise', pp. 437–8, 440–1.

of Bathsheba, many of the temptresses had traditionally been blamed for their own tragedies because they exposed their beauty to men's sight. But for Aemilia Lanyer, the crime of these women is that they could 'no better see' (219) that beauty is only worthy when coupled with virtue. When added to the stories of the virgin martyrs who prove with their lives that they understand the value of chastity, this reversal has the effect of imparting power to women, who are no longer merely objects of a man's gaze but possess vision of their own which can vindicate them if used truly. Lanyer tells the Countess of Cumberland, for example, 'Your perfit sight could never be so blind, / To entertaine the old or yong desires / Of idle Lovers' (1549–51), and compares her with the Queen of Sheba, whose

> . . . Desire did worke a strange effect,
> To drawe a Queene forth of her native Land,
> Not yeelding to the nicenesse and respect
> Of woman-kind[.]   (1601–4)

For these women, the reciprocity of true vision – the fact that they can see as well as be seen – imparts power to transcend the limits placed on women by men who cannot see their true worth.

Both Margaret Clifford and the Queen of Sheba earn Lanyer's praise because they have discerned the highest object of devotional vision: wisdom, or Christ himself.[70] Like the passion narratives and mystical marriage texts, *Salve deus rex judæorum* signals the desirability of Christ through blazons on his body drawn from the Song of Songs. Hall reminds his readers that Christ is the one 'of whome is said; *Thou art fairer than the children of men*', while Heinsius quotes a long list of Christ's attributes,

fayrest among men, being both white and ruddie, the chiefest among ten thousand. His head is as the most fine golde, his lockes bufoie [sic] & blacke as a Rauen: His eyes are the eyes of doues by the riuers of waters, washed with milke, and fitly set: His cheekes as a bed of spices, as sweet flowers; his lips like Lillies, dropping sweet smelling myrrhe[.][71]

The purpose of inserting these descriptions of Christ's beauty in the midst of his passion is to point out the depths of his suffering, and the disfigurement that results from his assumption of the burden of human sin.

---

[70] Solomon, as the author of the Song of Songs and the possessor of wisdom, was frequently cited as a type of Christ. See Michael Schoenfeldt, 'The Gender of Religious Devotion: Amelia Lanyer and John Donne', in *Religion and Culture in Renaissance England*, ed. Claire McEachern and Debora Shuger (Cambridge: Cambridge University Press, 1997), p. 220.

[71] Hall, *The passion sermon*, p. 34; Heinsius, *The mirrovr of hvmilitie*, p. 62. The references are to Song of Songs 5:10–13.

As Heinsius continues, 'Hee that was thus set out, and embellished with so many gracefull ornaments, lyeth now disfigured with wounds, weltering and panting in a crimson riuer of his owne bloud.'[72] The descriptions of Christ's beautiful body are frequently juxtaposed with reverse blazons of his bloody and dying body. For Hall Christ's fair face 'is all besmeared with the filthy spettle of the Iewes, and furrowed with his teares; those eyes, clearer than the Sunne, are darkened with the shadow of death; those eares that heare the heauenly comforts of Angels, now are filled with the cursed speakings & scoffes of wretched men'.[73]

In *Salve deus rex judæorum*, Christ is similarly both 'God in glory' (1329) and 'man in miserable case' (1330), beautiful precisely because he is bloody and dying. As Lanyer explains in her dedication to the Countess of Suffolk:

> No Dove, no Swan, nor Iv'rie could compare
> With this faire corps, when 'twas by death imbrac'd;
> No rose, nor no vermillion halfe so faire
> As was that pretious blood that interlac'd
>   His body, which bright Angels did attend[.][74]

For Lanyer, the fairness of Christ's dying form lies in the virtue of his sacrifice, not in any idealised image of suffering. Although she does not dwell on Christ's pain with the relish of the Calvinist sermonisers, her account of Christ's death hints at the ugliness of the crucifixion:

> His joynts dis-joynted, and his legges hang downe,
> His alabaster breast, his bloody side,
> His members torne, and on his head a Crowne
> Of sharpest Thorns, to satisfie for pride:
> Anguish and Paine doe all his Sences drowne,
> While they his holy garments do divide:
>   His bowells drie, his heart full fraught with griefe,
>   Crying to him that yeelds him no reliefe.   (1161–8)

This glimpse of suffering is balanced by a celebration of Christ's triumph in the culmination of her poem. This passage, designated in the margin 'A briefe description of his beautie upon the Canticles', draws the head-to-toe blazon of the lover in Song of Songs 5 that also appears in the passion sermons:

---

[72] Heinsius, *The mirrovr of hvmilitie*, p. 62.   [73] Hall, *The passion sermon*, p. 34.
[74] 'To the Ladie Catherine Countesse of Suffolke', p. 39, lines 79–83.

This is that Bridegroome that appeares so faire,
So sweet, so lovely in his Spouses sight,
That unto Snowe we may his face compare,
His cheekes like skarlet, and his eyes so bright
As purest Doves that in the rivers are,
Washed with milke, to give the more delight;
   His head is likened to the finest gold,
   His curled lockes so beauteous to behold;

Blacke as a Raven in her blackest hew;
His lips like skarlet threeds, yet much more sweet
Than is the sweetest hony dropping dew,
Or hony combes, where all the Bees doe meet;
Yea, he is constant, and his words are true,
His cheekes are beds of spices, flowers sweet;
   His lips, like Lillies, dropping downe pure mirrhe,
   Whose love, before all worlds we doe preferre.

                            (1305–20)

For Lanyer, both the beautiful and the dying Christs are intimately tied up with the quest for patronage, as both become gifts that she offers to Margaret Clifford, to behold 'with the eie of Faith' (1169), and keep 'Deepely engraved' in her heart (1327). The passages from the Song of Songs that describe the beauty of Christ are particularly useful for Lanyer because they encode virtue in visual metaphors. Christ's white purity reflects his innocence, his scarlet lips his blood and sacrifice, his perfumed cheeks his precious divinity. All these virtues combine to visual effect, allowing Lanyer to guide Margaret Clifford rhetorically to gaze on Christ's beauty and moral worth simultaneously. But she must also gaze on his death: implicit in Lanyer's praise of Margaret Clifford is the idea that the Countess sees clearly because she understands that the true beauty of Christ's love is intimately linked with his suffering and sacrifice. '[H]ere both Griefe and Joy thou maist unfold' (1171), Lanyer advises her patron of the spectacle of Christ 'Bowing his head, his bloodlesse body cold' (1173). The mystical marriage is worthy of devotion only because the bridegroom died. As Samuel Walsall explained, 'we see CHRIST IESVS that bride-groome of bloud celebrates a marriage with his Church vpon the geniall bed of the crosse, his head resting vpon a pillow of thornes, and himselfe attired with the rich wedding garment of loue . . . Let the Church therefore (as the spouse in the Canticles) be sick and faint for loue[.]'[75]

---

[75] Walsall, *The life and death of iesvs christ*, sig. E2ᵛ.

Lanyer similarly urges Margaret Clifford to be consumed with love for her saviour. In his death and triumph Christ becomes emblematic of a particular kind of sacrificial virtue. In the stanza following the blazon quoted above (labelled in the margin 'To my Ladie of Cumberland'), Lanyer excuses any flaws in her description of Christ by metaphorically depositing the burden of gazing upon Christ in the heart of Margaret Clifford:

> Ah! give me leave (good Lady) now to leave
> This taske of Beauty which I tooke in hand,
> I cannot wade so deepe, I may deceave
> My selfe, before I can attaine the land;
> Therefore (good Madame) in your heart I leave
> His perfect picture, where it still shall stand,
> > Deepely engraved in that holy shrine,
> > Environed with Love and Thoughts divine.
>
> There you may see him as a God in glory,
> And as a man in miserable case;
> There you may reade his true and perfect storie,
> His bleeding body there you may embrace,
> And kisse his dying cheekes with teares of sorrow,
> With joyfull griefe, you may intreat for grace;
> > And all your prayers, and your almes-deeds
> > May bring to stop his cruell wounds that bleeds.
>
> > > > (1321–36)

In a clever use of the humilitas topos, Lanyer asks her patron to take up the task that the author cannot complete, inviting her to 'embrace' and 'kisse' the body the poet has just described, in order that his image shall continue to be venerated. The beauty of Christ ultimately becomes a reflection of the countess's own inward beauty, since the 'holy shrine' of her heart is 'Environed with Love and Thoughts divine' that enable her to witness the 'true and perfect storie' of Christ. It is the very purity of Margaret Clifford's piety that enables Lanyer's unfinished image of Christ to be completed and sustained, for it is in the countess's heart that 'His perfect picture' 'still shall stand'.[76]

As also in Spenser, in this passage vision implies interpretative power; Margaret Clifford is able to 'reade' Christ's story merely through the image of his physical beauties. Underlying this assertion is the hope that she will also 'read' the virtues of Lanyer's poem and her bid for patronage, and reward them with prayers and 'almes-deeds'. Near the end of her passion

---

[76] The line echoes Spenser's 'And in thy brest his blessed image beare', 'An Hymne of Heavenly Love', in Bjorvand *et al.*, eds., *The Yale Edition of the Shorter Poems of Edmund Spenser*, p. 733, line 259.

poem, Lanyer praises the countess's ability to recognise and emulate the
true virtues of Christ, even when he comes to her disguised:

> Sometime h'appeares to thee in Shepheards weed,
> And so presents himselfe before thine eyes,
> A good old man; that goes his flocke to feed;
> Thy colour changes, and thy heart doth rise;
> Thou call'st, he comes, thou find'st tis he indeed,
> Thy Soule conceaves that he is truely wise:
> > Nay more, desires that he may be the Booke,
> > Whereon thine eyes continually may looke.
>
> Sometime imprison'd, naked, poore, and bare,
> Full of diseases, impotent, and lame,
> Blind, deafe, and dumbe, he comes unto his faire,
> To see if yet shee will remaine the same;
> Nay sicke and wounded, now thou do'st prepare
> To cherish him in thy dear Lovers name:
> > Yea thou bestow'st all paines, all cost, all care,
> > That may relieve him, and his health repaire.
> >   (1345–60)

True interpretation is a sign of election in this passage. Unlike Christ's
persecutors who fail throughout the poem to see what is before their eyes,
and like the good 'sheep' of Matthew 25, Margaret Clifford's virtuous sight
will pierce through any dirt or disguise to distinguish genuine need.

Implicit in this exchange is a powerful and potentially radical role reversal. Christ himself takes on the meekest, most helpless of human forms,
and asks for the healing and care that he himself displayed in his ministry.
Margaret Clifford is pictured offering succour to the sick and wounded
'in thy dear Lovers name'; out of desire for Christ, the ideal Lover, she
emulates his self-sacrificing charity and becomes herself the bestower of
ultimate love. A few lines after this passage, Lanyer explicitly hands the
authority of the Church, derived from Christ, to Margaret Clifford: 'These
are those Keyes Saint *Peter* did possesse, / Which with a Spirituall powre are
giv'n to thee' (1369–70). Unlike their Biblical counterparts, whose power
was to forgive sins, the keys in Lanyer's poem offer the power 'To heale
the soules of those that doe transgresse, / By thy faire virtues' (1371–2). The
hurt and sinful who look upon Margaret Clifford are not only forgiven but
healed by the sight of her virtue and generosity. This is an extraordinary
rewriting of the nature of Church authority, both in the gender of the
bearer and in the nature of authority itself. Rather than simply being able
to forgive and punish, Margaret Clifford receives the power of Christ to

heal and regenerate. Not only can Christ's authority be conferred upon a woman, but it becomes nurturing rather than dictatorial.

Imbedded in Lanyer's praise of Margaret Clifford's Christ-like generosity is a reminder of Lanyer's own needs as a client. Lanyer commends Clifford for ignoring the differences of degree when bestowing her gifts:

> Thou beeing thus rich, no riches do'st respect,
> Nor do'st thou care for any outward showe;
> The proud that doe faire Virtues rules neglect,
> Desiring place, thou sittest them belowe:
> All wealth and honour thou do'st quite reject,
> If thou perceiv'st that once it prooves a foe
>   To virtue, learning, and the powres divine[.]
>   (1385–91)

Although this passage appears to advocate a egalitarian society in which wealth is not a marker of virtue, a close reading reveals that it in fact recalls the ideals that underpin the social hierarchy based on wealth and birth. Lanyer's lines reject the sinful possession of wealth that betrays these ideals. Margaret Clifford is praised as one who does not respect the 'outward showe' of the proud, who neglect virtue by being concerned only about their place at the table. She also rejects 'All wealth and honour', but only if 'once it prooves a foe'; in other words, she renounces the trappings of material wealth only if they conflict with virtue. She does, however, implicitly reward the virtuous, learned and pious – categories which glance at Lanyer's self-presentation in *Salve deus rex judæorum* – by seating them above the vain and proud. Alternatively, 'thou sittest them belowe' may imply that Margaret Clifford herself, not 'Desiring place', chooses to sit below the wealthy and status-conscious, as Christ advised his disciples to take the lowest place so that they he might exalt them (Luke 14:7–11). Both readings imply a distinction between virtuous and sinful wealth that is significant because Margaret Clifford herself, as well as 'beeing thus rich' in her likeness to Christ, is also comparatively rich in material wealth, and capable of bestowing it upon clients like Lanyer. In this passage, Lanyer's praise carefully and cleverly reminds her patron that she should not be moved only by 'outward showe' (of which Lanyer could produce little) without implying that Clifford's own wealth is sinful or suspect.

Sacrificial love, constancy, justice, mercy, bounty, charity – the virtues that Lanyer extols in Christ, and by extension in Margaret Clifford – are all virtues that any client would desire in a patron. This is not to suggest that Lanyer's piety is not sincere, or that she uses the figure of Christ solely out of greed and ambition; but rather that in repeatedly urging her patrons to identify with a particular image of Christ, she simultaneously urges them to embody particular values that might alter their attitude toward herself as a client. She also returns their attention to her own goodness and piety. In recognising Christ's virtues (as she must in order to write of them), Lanyer herself performs the pious acts of worship for which she praises Margaret Clifford and her other dedicatees. Displaying Christ's love so prominently is also a means of displaying her own religious virtue.

Several critics have argued that Lanyer's display of Christ's love to her woman patrons is particularly effective because of its erotic appeal. Michael Schoenfeldt, for example, sees Lanyer as a 'divine procuress, arranging relationships between these noble ladies and her heavenly lord'.[77] Lanyer's Christ is explicitly a lover in the mystical marriage tradition. She uses the titles 'Love', 'true-love', 'Bridegroome' and 'Lover' nineteen times in the poem, and her visual imagery relies heavily on the Song of Songs and Petrarchan love poetry. It is easy to conclude from a twenty-first-century perspective that Lanyer's strategy is a 'distinctly female approach to Christ', in which 'she holds him up to the desiring gaze of women'.[78] Curiously, Aemilia Lanyer is the only woman I have found who focuses so intensely on looking at Christ as a lover. The other women writers in this book are far more concerned with the authority imparted to them by Christ as a husband than with his physical beauty or attraction as a lover. What Lanyer's poetry does draw upon, however, is a long tradition of mystical marriage writing by men which extols the desirability of Christ for other male readers. The difference between Lanyer's writing and that of the other women in this study lies in her self-conscious emulation of the patronage poetry, passion poems and sermons of her male contemporaries, who described their desire for Christ using the imagery of love poetry.

Read within this context, the eroticism of the gaze in Lanyer's poetry becomes problematic, neither straightforwardly heterosexual, nor even clearly about sex at all. As the previous chapter documents, portrayals of Christ as a lover using the language of love lyrics were in fact extremely common in both poetry and prose. Such erotic portraits were often written by male writers for the contemplation of male readers, and betray little if any anxiety that such language was sexually transgressive in its expression

---

[77] Schoenfeldt, 'The Gender of Religious Devotion', p. 216. See also Catherine Keohane, '"That blindest Weakenesse be not over-bold": Aemilia Lanyer's Radical Unfolding of the Passion', *ELH* 64.2 (1997): 372; DiPasquale, 'Woman's Desire for Man', pp. 362–3; Wall, *The Imprint of Gender*, pp. 327–9; and Guibbory, 'The Gospel According to Aemilia', pp. 202–3.

[78] Woods, 'Vocation and Authority', pp. 87, 92.

of the desire of one man for another. The poet Giles Fletcher, for example, describes himself in an aside in his poem *Christs victorie, and triumph* as 'One of ten thousand soules',

> and more,
> That of his eyes, and their sweete wounds complaine,
> Sweete are the wounds of loue, neuer so sore,
> Ah might he often slaie me so againe.
> He neuer liues, that thus is neuer slaine.
> > What boots it watch? those eyes, for all my art,
> > Mine owne eyes looking on, haue stole my heart,
> In them Loue bends his bowe, and dips his burning dart.[79]

Fletcher's language of slaying and sweet wounds draws on the Petrarchan conventions of masochistic male love, although in this case the beloved is an ultimately kind male Christ rather than a cruel mistress. Fletcher's poem owes much to 'Saint Peters Complaint' by Robert Southwell, who inverted the tropes of Petrarchism in order to argue that divinity was the proper subject of poetry.[80] The language of Petrarchism is especially apparent in the lengthy paean to Christ's eyes in 'Saint Peter's Complaint'. In entirely conventional love images, Southwell's Peter compares the saviour's eyes to 'springs of living light', 'liquid pearle', a pair of turtle doves and the 'spotlesse Sunne'. In their effect on Peter, Christ's eyes act much like the eyes of a Petrarchan mistress:

> You nectared Aumbryes of soule feeding meats,
> You graceful quivers of loves dearest darts:
> You did vouchsafe to warme, to wound, to feast:
> My cold, my stony, my now famishde breast[.][81]

Like the lady of Spenser's *Amoretti* sequence, Christ's eyes are to Peter both cruel and instructive. By convincing him of his own sinful inadequacy, they cause him pain but yet draw him towards repentance and reform. That Christ can be both a male lover and a female beloved underlines the fluidity of gender identifications in mystical marriage writing. The question of who is loved and who is loving, who is male and who is female, is unstable in this tradition precisely because the primary subject is not human erotic desire. The fact that Aemilia Lanyer offers a beautiful lover

---

[79] STC 11058 Giles Fletcher, *Christs victorie, and triumph* (Cambridge: C. Legge, 1610), p. 28.

[80] Shell, *Catholicism, Controversy, and the English Literary Imagination*, pp. 70–1.

[81] MacDonald and Pollard Brown, eds., *The Poems of Robert Southwell*, p. 86, lines 331, 357, 433–8, 336, 351–4.

Christ to her female readers does not mean that she is appealing to them solely on heteroerotic terms.

I do not suggest that the poetry of Aemilia Lanyer or Robert Southwell is devoid of eroticism. Erotic language provided a powerful, provocative metaphor for religious longing that is forever unconsummated in this life, and the connection to forbidden sexual longing was not coincidental. But there was a level on which erotic language was clearly a shorthand for a love that had little to do with sexuality. The use of the conventions of love poetry to describe Christ had in fact become so common that, in one dimension at least, it was arguably no longer erotic at all by the time Lanyer was writing. If Puritan ministers could speak unflinchingly of the desirable body of Christ, the spiritual connotations of this particular code may have seemed so self-evident that other more suggestive meanings were easily ignored. The shocking strength of Donne's sonnet 'Batter my heart, three-personed God' lies in the fact that it eroticises divine love without using the language of Petrarchism. The loving Trinity of Donne's poem is no figure of courtly grace or conventional beauty, but a ravaging erotic force that breaks, captivates, enthrals and ravishes the tormented soul. Donne's poem captures the devastating link between erotic and spiritual desire only by breaking away from conventional expressions of such desire.

By contrast, Lanyer's evocation of Christ never veers from the conventional; the 'desire' she calls upon is a longing for spiritual union and for virtue, spurred and mediated by the provocative language of erotic love poetry. Lanyer employs the figure of Christ as a lover both because he is desirable – and therefore so is her poem – and also because, in the tradition of lovers representing patrons, he is the ideal Lord. Christ represents a fluidly gendered, utterly desirable virtue which Lanyer both presents as a gift to her patrons and urges them to emulate in their own lives.

The fluidity of Christ's gender in Lanyer's poem has led to the critical commonplace that the Christ she describes is 'feminised' 'according to the period norms set out in conduct books and doctrinal tracts'. Lanyer never in fact uses explicitly feminine images of Christ, not even the metaphor of God as a mother available to her in the Old Testament, but her Christ is 'silent except when induced to speak, and modest and taciturn when he does', behaviour critics contend embodies the instruction that women be silent and obedient.[82] The argument relies on the assumptions that prescriptive literature is a straightforward representation of contemporary gender relations, rather than a contested ideal, and that the virtues some

---

[82] Mueller, 'The Feminist Poetics', p. 112. See Deuteronomy 32:11, Psalm 131:2, Isaiah 42:14, 49:15, 66:13.

writers extolled for women were always recognisable as exclusively feminine. Such readings expect Lanyer and her early modern readers to acknowledge Christ's 'gentle, mild, peaceable, and submissive' behaviour as textbook femininity.[83]

In fact, descriptions of Christ as 'gentle, mild, peaceable, and submissive' were extremely common in this period, and did not necessarily represent a feminising of his image. Prose passion narratives focused on the tender, frightened and ultimately passive nature of Christ, who came to represent Protestant victimhood glorified in the act of sacrifice.[84] 'In his teaching it is sayd hee opened his mouth in parables', wrote Samuel Walsall, 'but at his cōdemning it is said hee opened not his mouth[.]'[85] Christ's silence is paradoxically a sign that he is in control of his situation; if he did not willingly submit to suffering, his persecutors could not harm him. 'Behold, he himself must giue *Pilate* power against himselfe', Joseph Hall asserted, 'else hee could not be condemned: he will be condemned, lifted vp, nailed; yet no death without himselfe.'[86]

Poems on the passion similarly underline the humility of Christ and his pacifist response to suffering. In Abraham Fraunce's *The countesse of pembrokes emanuel* (1591), Christ's gentleness throws the depravity of his tormentors into relief. Fraunce's verses describe an incident in the gospel of John (18:19–23), in which Christ is struck when his answers to the high priest are unacceptable:

> Soe from a woord to a blow, with a sinfull fyste hee defyled
> That synles sweete mouth, which these woords peaceably vttred;
> Fryend, if I haue sayd yll, beare witnes, let mee be punisht,
> Y[f] but well, why then doest thou vnworthyly stryke mee?[87]

All such descriptions of Christ's humility and passivity in the passion are ultimately derived from Biblical tradition. Throughout the story of Christ's passion, in episodes such as the trial before Caiaphas and the arrest in the garden of Gethsemane (Matthew 26:47–56; Mark 14:43–52; Luke 22:47–53; John 18:1–11), Gospel accounts all emphasise that Christ is passive in his

---

[83] Mueller, 'The Feminist Poetics', p. 112; see also Michael Morgan Holmes, 'The Love of Other Women: Rich Chains and Sweet Kisses', in *Aemilia Lanyer: Gender, Genre, and the Canon*, ed. Grossman, p. 178; Lynette McGrath, '"Let Us Have Our Libertie Againe"', pp. 342–3; Schoenfeldt, 'The Gender of Religious Devotion', p. 211; Clarke, *The Politics of Early Modern Women's Writing*, p. 160.

[84] Shuger, *The Renaissance Bible*, pp. 91–95.   [85] Walsall, *The life and death of iesus christ*, sig. D3^r.

[86] Hall, *The passion sermon*, p. 77. See also Calvin, *A harmonie*, p. 747; Chamberlaine, *The passion of christ*, sig. B2^v.

[87] STC 11339 Abraham Fraunce, *The countesse of pembrokes emanuel* (London: Thomas Orwyn for William Ponsonby, 1591), sig. C1^v–C2^r.

suffering; he allows it to happen. Thus the 'gentle, mild, peaceable, and submissive' behaviour of Christ in his passion is more akin to traditional Christian depictions of the paradoxical humility of the Messiah than of any feminising of Christ.

Instead of drawing on a prescriptive definition of womanhood, such representations of Christ by Aemilia Lanyer and other religious writers seem to be struggling towards a definition of ungendered virtue. Debora Shuger, in her study of passion narratives in Calvinist sermons, has argued that the images of 'male abjection' in such narratives indicate a 'crisis of manhood' in the early modern period. The reader is exhorted to identify himself with both the cruel tormentors and the passive Christ, and these two extremities, as 'psychological projections of [the reader's] own malice and impotence', depict a wider struggle in the nature of Christian manhood, meant to be paradoxically strong and warlike yet meek and suffering.[88]

'Crisis' is perhaps too strong a word, and suggests a dichotomy of opposing values where in fact there were a series of competing definitions of manhood. Alexandra Shepard has demonstrated in her study of prescriptive and medical literature that several models of manhood existed in the early modern period, each invoked in particular contexts, so that one man might, in practice, simultaneously embody several different concepts of his own nature as a man.[89] The meekness and humility represented in the suffering Christ is thus only one of many possibilities for what a man might be, and should be balanced with the figures of Christ the King or the Christ of judgement day as paradigms of Christian manhood. In addition, the 'gentle, mild, peaceable, and submissive' Christ of the passion could also be invoked as a model for women, or for both genders, depending on the context. Lady Anne Southwell makes this point when she demonstrates that Christ embodies virtues that in some men would be scorned as effeminate, but which, in Lady Southwell's rewriting, become the pinnacle of manhood.[90]

For Aemilia Lanyer, both men and women are capable of following Christ, although some members of both sexes fail to live up to his standard. In her oft-quoted preface 'To the Vertuous Reader' Lanyer describes her purpose as to celebrate and encourage 'all virtuous Ladies and Gentlewomen of this kingdome' in the face of aspersions upon female virtue. The slanderers of women are not only 'evill disposed men' but other women. '[A]ll women deserve not to be blamed', Lanyer declares, 'though some forgetting they

[88] Shuger, *The Renaissance Bible*, pp. 116–17.
[89] Alexandra Shepard, 'Meanings of Manhood in Early Modern England, With Special Reference to Cambridge, c. 1560–1640' (unpublished PhD thesis, Cambridge University, 1998).
[90] See the next chapter.

are women themselves, and in danger to be condemned by the words of their owne mouthes, fall into so great an errour, as to speake unadvisedly against the rest of their sexe[.]'[91] In addition to separating virtuous women from those who slander their own sex, Lanyer also carefully distinguishes between 'evil disposed men' – those who speak ill of women – and 'honourable minded men' who promote women's virtue.[92]

The possibility that there are 'honourable minded' members of both sexes holds throughout the poem. Many critics have noted that Lanyer 'stresses male guilt and complicity and female innocence' in the act of the crucifixion.[93] While she does indeed emphasise that 'spightfull men with torments did oppresse / Th'afflicted body of this innocent Dove' (993–4), it is not entirely true that this 'interpretation is independent of church tradition'.[94] The Gospels themselves call attention to the way in which Christ is systematically abandoned by all those who should help him, and persecuted by those who should recognise his glory. '[I]t is no maruell', Calvin wrote in his commentary on the synoptic Gospels, 'if the sluggishnes of them whō he had chosen for his felowes added a great & heauy burden to his sorow.'[95] For the English Calvinist commentators, it was important to emphasise that all human beings contributed to Christ's pain, even those who tried to help him.[96] 'His Disciples, alas: they forsooke him, one of them forsweares him; another runs away naked, rather than hee will stay and confesse him. His mother and other friends: they looke on indeed, and sorrow with him, but to his discomfort', Joseph Hall wrote.[97] The point was that cruelty and violence were endemic in sinful humanity, and separated it from a loving God. 'My Disciples are men, weake and fearefull; No maruell, if they forsake mee', Hall's Christ reasons. 'The Iewes are themselues, cruell and obstinate. Men are men, gracelesse, and vnthankefull. Diuels are according to their nature, spightfull and malitious. All these doe but their kind; and let them doe it[.]'[98]

It would thus be inaccurate to argue that *Salve deus rex judæorum* is unusual because 'the male Disciples, too, are criticized for their lack of

[91] 'To the Vertuous Reader', p. 48. As Ann Baynes Coiro and Lisa Schnell have pointed out, such passages in Lanyer's poetry betray more anxiety about the power of women over one another's reputation than about the power of men. Coiro, 'Writing in Service', pp. 365–6; Schnell, '"So Great a Difference"', pp. 29–35, and 'Breaking "the rule of *Cortezia*"', pp. 94–6.
[92] 'To the Vertuous Reader', p. 50.
[93] Clarke, *The Politics of Early Modern Women's Writing*, p. 160; Guibbory, 'The Gospel According to Aemilia', p. 200; Susanne Woods, 'Women at the Margins in Spenser and Lanyer', in *Worldmaking Spenser: Explorations in the Early Modern Age*, ed. Patrick Cheney and Lauren Silberman (Lexington, Kentucky: The University Press of Kentucky, 2000), p. 108; Phillippy, 'Sisters of Magdalen', p. 102.
[94] Guibbory, 'The Gospel According to Aemilia', p. 201.
[95] Calvin, *A harmonie*, p. 707, on Matthew 26:40.   [96] Shuger, *The Renaissance Bible*, pp. 91–2.
[97] Hall, *The passion sermon*, pp. 45–6.   [98] *Ibid.*, pp. 47–8.

constancy' in addition to the traditional male villains of the trial and crucifixion.[99] Lanyer's poem does draw attention to the distinction between the
women who sympathise with Christ – the Virgin Mary, the Daughters of
Jerusalem, and Pilate's wife – and the men who persecute him, particularly
in the apology from Eve, who argues that woman's original sin appears less
next to the male violence of the passion. Lanyer constructs this gendered
distinction by exaggerating elements of traditional passion narratives, in
which most of the actors are male and villainous, while the few women are
presented more ambiguously, and even positively. In Catholic passions, for
example, the Virgin Mary models the grief and devotion that should be
the reader's response, and Lanyer alludes to these texts by including a long
address to 'His woefull Mother wayting on her Sonne' (1009) at the centre
of her poem.[100]

The Daughters of Jerusalem play a much more ambiguous role in the
passion narratives. In the Gospels, these women weep at the sight of Christ
on his way to crucifixion, and he responds, vehemently and strangely, that
they should weep not for him but for themselves, because their suffering
will make them long for barrenness and even death. Some Calvinist writers
built on Christ's response and cast the Daughters of Jerusalem as those who
respond inappropriately to Christ's crucifixion, weeping for his pain rather
than their own complicity.[101] But for some the Daughters of Jerusalem
represented those of little faith whose understanding might grow through
Christ's self-sacrificing intervention: 'And though the faith of these women
was weake', wrote Calvin, 'yet it is to be supposed that the seed of piety
was hiddē in them, which afterwards in time conuenient sprang forth.'[102]
Given the traditional vehement condemnation of almost every other figure
in the story, Calvin's mildly expressed hope for these women is striking. He
also notes that the episode is a sign of Christ's courage, because he pauses
in his suffering to rebuke and warn these women. Lanyer embellishes these
elements of the passage, calling the Daughters 'Thrice happy women' (969)
because Christ had returned their gaze and stopped '[t]o comfort' (973)
them.[103]

Perhaps most significantly for Lanyer's poem, Calvin argues that the
immediate purpose of the Daughters' tears was 'the condēnation of
the wicked & vnspeakable cruelty of those men' who were complicit in

[99] Phillippy, 'Sisters of Magdalen', p. 102.
[100] The address to the Virgin is lines 1009–136. The Virgin rarely appears in Calvinist passion sermons;
see Shuger, *The Renaissance Bible*, pp. 92, 99.
[101] Shuger, *The Renaissance Bible*, p. 100.   [102] Calvin, *A harmonie*, p. 742.
[103] On Lanyer's use of the Daughters of Jerusalem see Phillippy, 'Sisters of Magdalen', p. 104.

the crucifixion.[104] The suggestion that only men are responsible for the sin of the crucifixion may well be accidental, but Calvin's reading of the passage does draw on the tradition of the mourning woman, and specifically the Biblical women who mourn for Christ after his death.[105] Lanyer exploits this tradition of sorrowful, blameless women and cruel men in order to draw the gender lines more explicitly, embellishing the Gospel story by having the women 'By teares, by sighes, by cries intreat' (996) the 'spightfull men' (993) to stop torturing Christ.

For Lanyer the figure of Pilate's wife adds to this construct, not only pleading with her husband not to crucify Christ, as she does in the Gospel (Matthew 27:19), but also voicing 'Eves Apologie', in which she suggests that men's torture of Christ 'makes our former fault much lesse appeare' (762) because Eve's sin was merely ignorance, not wilful cruelty. Although Lanyer's arguments in defence of Eve are not original, the placement of the apology in the midst of Christ's passion, in the voice of Pilate's wife, is one of the unique elements of the poem, drawing together women's great sin with the sin for which men seem more clearly responsible.[106] Lanyer may have been inspired by late medieval passion plays and poems, in which Pilate's wife's dream comes not from God but from Satan, who realises at the last minute that the crucifixion is God's plan and will not serve his own evil ends. Satan decides to persuade Pilate's wife to prevent the death of Jesus because 'He þou[y]te þat wy*m*men to ouer*c*ome esy [&] Mylde were.'[107] The language is reminiscent of Satan's first successful attempt to overcome a woman, and the scene serves as a foil to that earlier, catastrophic temptation.[108] Satan visits Pilate's wife in a dream, persuading her to do his bidding with lies and half-truths, telling her she will come to harm if she does not warn her husband. This time, however, Satan's success is hollow; Pilate's wife is unable to persuade her husband to do anything other than wash his hands of the affair, and Satan's original plan – which had always been God's will – succeeds. The scene thus serves as a reminder that the violence of the crucifixion is the direct result of the first sin in the Garden of Eden. Lanyer may have placed 'Eves Apologie' in the mouth of Pilate's wife

---

[104] Calvin, *A harmonie*, p. 742, on Luke 23:27–8.

[105] See Phillippy, 'Sisters of Magdalen', throughout.

[106] On Lanyer's sources for her defence of Eve, see Clarke, *The Politics of Early Modern Women's Writing*, p. 159.

[107] Beatrice Daw Brown, ed., *The Southern Passion* (London: Early English Text Society, 1927), line 1268. See also Stephen Spector, ed. *The N-Town Play* (Oxford: Early English Text Society, 1991), I. 314–17; and Wilhelm Heuser and Frances A. Foster, eds., *The Northern Passion* (London: Early English Text Society, 1930), lines 1409–68.

[108] On the connection between Eve and Pilate's wife in medieval passion narratives, see Rosemary Woolf, *The English Mystery Plays* (London: Routledge, 1972), p. 245.

in order to point to this tradition and underline the connection between the woman who initially succumbed to Satan and the men who are his servants in the crucifixion.

That Lanyer uses these female figures to demonstrate women's relative virtue has become a critical commonplace, and the basis for the argument that Lanyer is a feminist whose primary purpose is opposition to patriarchy. While it is clear that these figures do emphasise that it is possible for a woman to be a virtuous follower of Christ, the argument is not made in historical isolation, and appears paradoxically more creative and radical when considered alongside the established tradition. Rather than inventing a discourse to vindicate women, Lanyer makes use of the existing discourse, drawing out episodes that witness to women's virtue. She thus answers the slanders of both 'evill disposed men' and the women who forget their own sex by using the very texts and language that elsewhere justify such misogyny.

Ultimately, however, although Lanyer argues that Eve's sin should be for-given in light of the persecution of Christ, her poem acknowledges that not all women are supporters of Christ, nor all men his persecutors. As we have seen, women, too, sometimes fail to have true vision in the poem, particu-larly Cleopatra and her English counterpart Rosamond. Male virtue, on the other hand, is represented in the eulogy to the 'noble Actes' (1814) of male martyrs that closes the poem (1745–1824). In Lanyer's vision these men – Stephen, Laurence, Andrew, Peter and John the Baptist – model Christ's radical virtue, refusing all earthly glory and embracing even death for the sake of his love. Lanyer here may recall Hall, who ends his passion sermon with the example of female martyrs to spur his hearers to self-sacrificing faith: 'I see there euen women (the feebler sexe) running with their little ones in their armes, for the preferment of martyrdome, and ambitiously striuing for the next blow. I see holy and tender virgins, chusing rather a sore and shamefull death, then honourable Espousals.'[109] Significantly, in *Salve deus rex judæorum* the 'holy zeale and love most pure and chaste' (1797) of the martyrs is the same virtue which Lanyer continually exhorts Margaret Clifford to embrace, and in the last stanzas of the poem Lanyer deposits the example of these men along with Christ's in the breast of her patron:

> Loe Madame, heere you take a view of those,
> Whose worthy steps you doe desire to tread,
> Deckt in those colours which our Saviour chose;

---

[109] Hall, *The passion sermon*, p. 80.

> The purest colours both of White and Red,
> Their freshest beauties would I faine disclose,
> By which our Saviour most was honoured:
>   But my weake Muse desireth now to rest,
>   Folding up all their Beauties in your breast.
>   (1825–32)

In these closing lines Lanyer significantly paints martyred men in the same language of beautiful suffering with which she has presented Christ to her patrons. She implies in this portrait that the virtue of these men is as desirable as the heavenly lover himself. Not surprisingly, the implications of this conciliatory ending to such a challenging poem have proved troubling for some of Lanyer's critics. 'Lanyer seems to have finally caved in to the pressures of patriarchy when she concludes her poem with a list of male martyrs – a strange tactic if indeed she means to defend women', argues Su Fang Ng. 'Apparently, in the end, the standard for virtuous behavior is still man, despite Lanyer's heroic efforts to praise women throughout the poem.'[110] Ng's own language is cautious about the essentialism inherent in the assumption that praise of women must automatically exclude praise of men. It is the inverse of the hierarchical paradigms that have traditionally been used to demean women. Rather than embracing such essentialism, Lanyer herself seems to be struggling towards a model of ungendered virtue: a fluidly gendered Christ, whose paradoxically powerful silence and passivity present a challenge to the models of manhood that victimise women (and Christ himself), and the models of authority that disenfranchise the poor and powerless. Thus in praising male martyrs at the end of her poem, and in encouraging Margaret Clifford to 'take a view of those, / Whose worthy steps you doe desire to tread', Lanyer is presenting a much more radical vision than a binary opposition between good women and bad men. She elevates the elements of Christ's life that both men and women are enjoined to follow, in the process suggesting that the call to be Christ-like may supersede any gendered distinctions of virtue. Women like Margaret Clifford and Aemilia Lanyer herself should be judged not by their gender but alongside men by the universal standard of Christ's life.

---

[110] Ng, 'Aemilia Lanyer and the Politics of Praise', p. 439.

CHAPTER 3

Serpents and doves: Lady Anne Southwell and the new Adam

In recent years scholars have begun to realise that it is not only misogynist perceptions that make it difficult for us to recover early modern women writers. As the example of Aemilia Lanyer demonstrates, we must also be wary of feminist ideals of the woman writer. As Margaret Ezell first argued, the earliest attempts to understand early modern women writers were hampered by narrow definitions of both femininity and writing.[1] A critical stance that privileged outspoken 'public' print writers – a modern feminist ideal – slighted or ignored a wide variety of voices from the early modern period which did not display such proto-feminist characteristics. The fault was, of course, not in the texts but in the criticism: 'If these texts refuse to yield up feminism,' Danielle Clarke writes in a recent essay, 'it may also be the case that feminism, as it has been applied, does not yield up the texts.'[2]

The work of Lady Anne Southwell (1574–1636) stands between the two critical poles. Her verse is unabashedly outspoken and even radical in its gender politics, anatomising the constraints placed on both women and men when some early modern gender ideals were taken to their extreme. On the other hand, her manuscript religious verse – itself among the most difficult of genres to reconcile with modern feminist ambitions – never strays from conventional Biblical orthodoxies, and appears to have been 'corrected' by her husband. In a single œuvre Southwell embodies the plurality and contradiction among all early modern women writers, a diversity that should no longer surprise us in a group of writers united only by their gender. What does surprise – although again, perhaps, it should not – is that Southwell's combination of pointed wit and solemn piety is not as extraordinary as it may seem. A study of Southwell's biography and the

---

[1] Margaret Ezell, *Writing Women's Literary History* (Baltimore: Johns Hopkins University Press, 1993).
[2] Danielle Clarke, Introduction to *'This Double Voice': Gendered Writing in Early Modern England*, ed. Danielle Clarke and Elizabeth Clarke (Basingstoke: Macmillan, 2000), p. 7.

evidence of her manuscripts, together with a reading of her poetry, suggests that while writing like Southwell's may not have been common, it was a recognised type. A woman whose accomplished writing was seen as a marker of status, part of a complex campaign for patronage, Lady Anne Southwell is less of an exception than she is a paradigm of one early modern ideal of the woman writer.[3]

The first section of this chapter explores the construction of that ideal in Southwell's life and works. The documentary evidence of Southwell and her husbands reveals that both men had suffered financial losses that made their need for patronage acute. Like her social inferior Aemilia Lanyer, Southwell shared in her husbands' ambitions, and used her writing as part of their joint social capital to advance those ambitions. The evidence of her manuscripts bears out this conclusion, demonstrating collaboration between husband and wife in the process of creating her as an ideal gentlewoman of letters. Considered alongside other examples of collaboration, Southwell's manuscripts add to the evidence that a husband's participation in a woman's manuscript writing was as often a shared promotion of the family as it was an act of suppression.

The complex power relationships that characterised Southwell's own marriages are also apparent in her verse meditations on Christian matrimony. The final section of this chapter posits that Southwell exploits her own exemplary image to create a space for a different reading of women's experience of marriage and Christ. In Southwell's work the metaphor of mystical marriage opens a window on to both gendered religious formation and gendered experience of marriage. Southwell uses the multifaceted metaphor to reveal the mutability of gender in an individual's relationship to God. She maintains, somewhat playfully, that women enjoy a privileged understanding of the sacrificial love of Christ, the perfect husband, but simultaneously uncovers the arbitrariness of conventional constructions of masculine and feminine virtues. Southwell's verse demonstrates that early modern women were aware of the conflicts in contemporary gender norms

---

[3] Both of Lady Anne Southwell's manuscripts are edited by Jean Klene in *The Southwell-Sibthorpe Commonplace Book: Folger MS. V.b.198* (Tempe, Arizona: Renaissance English Text Society, 1997). All references to the manuscripts in this chapter use the original folio numbers, which are included in Klene's edition. Many of the poems are heavily corrected; I have silently omitted most deletions. For physical descriptions of the manuscripts see Klene's Introduction, pp. xxxiii–xxxviii and xlii–xliii; and Victoria Burke, 'Medium and Meaning in the Manuscripts of Anne, Lady Southwell', in *Women's Writing and the Circulation of Ideas: Manuscript Publication in England, 1550–1800*, ed. George L. Justice and Nathan P. Tinker (Cambridge: Cambridge University Press, 2002), pp. 94–120; also Burke's 'Women and Early Seventeenth-Century Manuscript Culture: Four Miscellanies', *The Seventeenth Century* 12.2 (1997): 141–4. See also Klene's article, '"Monument of an Endless affection": Folger MS V.b.198 and Lady Anne Southwell', *English Manuscript Studies 1100–1700* 9 (2000): 165–86.

and capable of using scripture to craft an intelligent criticism of men who would abuse those conflicts for their own ends.

The nuances of birth, fortune and connections that determined all social relationships in this period would also have affected the relative status of early modern husbands and wives, and the archival traces of Lady Anne Southwell and both of her husbands suggest that their married lives must have been shaped by such subtle distinctions in status. Lady Anne Southwell's own birth and connections were reputable, but not among the most influential in the kingdom. She was born in 1573 into a well-respected West Country family with connections in London. Her father was Sir Thomas Harris of Cornworthy, Devon, both an MP and sergeant-at-law of the Middle Temple; he may have been acquainted with Sir Walter Ralegh, also a member of the Middle Temple and owner of land a few miles from Cornworthy. Her mother was Elizabeth Pomeroy, of the prominent Devon family of Berry Pomeroy.[4] The Pomeroy pedigree extended back to the time of William the Conqueror, and thus was considerably more impressive than the Harris family tree, which includes only two generations before Sir Thomas. That a daughter of an old family would marry the son of such a new one might be explained by the fact that the couple were already closely connected through family marriages: Elizabeth's mother was also Sir Thomas's stepmother, and Sir Thomas's mother was Elizabeth's father's cousin.[5]

Anne Harris's first marriage connected her to a landed family older and more illustrious than her own. Her first husband was Thomas Southwell of Spixworth, Norfolk (d. 1626), whom she married on 24 June 1594.[6] The Southwells were from a large Norfolk family that had enjoyed favour under Elizabeth; his cousin Sir Robert Southwell of Woodrising was Rear-Admiral in 1588 and Sir Robert's wife, Lady Elizabeth Southwell (occasionally confused with Lady Anne), was the daughter of the Earl of Nottingham, Lord High Admiral of England.[7] Sir Thomas's mother was Alice Cornwallis, daughter of Sir Thomas Cornwallis, Comptroller of

---

[4] Klene, Introduction, *The Southwell-Sibthorpe Commonplace Book*, pp. xii–xiii.

[5] J. L. Vivian, ed., *The Visitations of the County of Devon* (Exeter: Henry S. Eland, 1895), pp. 452 (Harris), 607 (Pomeroy).

[6] Klene, Introduction, *The Southwell-Sibthorpe Commonplace Book*, pp. xii–xiii. For Sir Thomas Southwell's pedigree see Walter Rye, ed., *The Visitacion of Norfolk* (London: Harleian Society, 1891), pp. 258–61.

[7] See the family tree in Sir Francis W. Steer, *Woodrising Church, Norfolk: Notes on the Southwell and Other Families Connected with the Parish* (Norwich: The Diocese of Norwich, 1959).

Queen Mary's household and a noted recusant.[8] The most famous member of the family was another Catholic, Thomas's uncle Robert Southwell, the Jesuit poet whose martyrdom must have brought unwelcome notoriety to the politic conformists in the rest of the immediate family. Their financial situation would have made the Southwells keen to avoid the taint of recusancy: Thomas's grandfather Richard Southwell of Horsham St Faith's was an illegitimate heir who had seen the main Southwell estate pass to his Woodrising cousins, then accumulated massive debts on his own inheritance. He eventually died a prisoner for his debts in the Fleet.[9]

The intricacies of the family finances are apparent in a Chancery case recording a dispute between Richard's second wife, Margaret, and his heirs by his first wife, including Thomas Southwell. The quarrel is over an annuity of eighty pounds per annum from the rents of several manors promised to Margaret, and a recognisance of five thousand pounds established so that she and her children might pay the debts and clear the estates. The case is evidence not only of the difficult financial circumstances of Anne Harris's new family, but also of the lifestyle to which they were accustomed. Despite having lost the main estate, the family still enjoyed income from a number of Norfolk manors, and the amounts of money stipulated in the case were by no means small.[10] The annuity of eighty pounds compares starkly with the rent of five pounds per annum Anne and her second husband would pay at the end of her life.[11]

Anne Harris's first husband was, it seems, the sole heir of a large fortune that was encumbered by old debts and the responsibility of supporting various female relatives, including his mother Alice Cornwallis and his step-grandmother Margaret Southwell.[12] The family financial situation may explain the younger Southwells' decamping to Poulnelong Castle, County Cork sometime early in the seventeenth century, perhaps after he was knighted in 1603.[13] The exact date is unknown; the first references to Sir Thomas Southwell in the records of Munster, where he became a member of the Council, appear in April 1620.[14] He may have served in Ireland

---

[8] According to the DNB, Cornwallis officially submitted to the Elizabethan settlement in 1567, but had a lifelong reputation as a staunch Catholic who never attended Church of England services.

[9] Christopher Devlin, *The Life of Robert Southwell Poet and Martyr* (London: Longmans, Green and Co., 1956), pp. 5, 11–12, 202–3.

[10] The case is PRO C2/Eliz/S14/58; see also PRO C3/249/10.

[11] Receipts for payment of rent are in the Folger manuscript, ff. 71^{r-v}, 72^v.

[12] Alice Cornwallis is named in PRO C3/249/10.

[13] Klene, Introduction, *The Southwell-Sibthorpe Commonplace Book*, p. xvi; see also Sir Thomas Southwell's funeral certificate in British Library Additional MS 4820, f. 98v.

[14] British Library Harl. MS 697, ff. 104 and 106v. The Earl of Cork's diaries refer to Sir Thomas Southwell in June 1621: Alexander B. Grosart, ed., *The Lismore Papers (First Series)*, 5 vols. ([London]: For private circulation, 1886), II. 18.

as early as the 1590s: there is a 'Mr Southwell' and a 'Captain Thomas Southwell' listed in Munster in the service of Sir Walter Ralegh, who may have been introduced to Thomas Southwell by Anne Harris's family. In addition, the Chancery Rolls of Ireland record an indenture in 1598 from Ralegh to a Thomas Southwell of land in counties Waterford and Cork, where the Southwells eventually settled.[15] While it is not certain that this Thomas Southwell was Anne Harris's husband, it would not have been at all unusual for the heir of a landed but debt-encumbered family to serve abroad as a means to preferment, like many other young men of his time, including Sir Philip Sidney and, less illustriously, Aemilia Lanyer's husband Alphonso. If he did distinguish himself in the campaign enough to earn the notice of Ralegh, such service may explain how Thomas Southwell earned a knighthood, an honour new to his illegitimate branch of the Southwell family. If Thomas Southwell was in Ireland in the 1590s, however, it is unlikely that he brought his new wife with him to the rebellion-torn province.

From early in their marriage Anne Southwell also played her part in advancing the family fortunes. Two letters written to Robert Cecil in 1603 reveal that the Southwells had hoped that Anne might gain favour with the new queen.[16] Their plans appear to have backfired dramatically: the first letter is from a captain who was ordered to escort the very reluctant Anne Southwell back to London from Berwick, where James's queen was resting on her journey from Scotland. According to the captain's letter Anne Southwell struggled violently against her removal, feigning illness and complaining about her treatment. The captain planned to remove her forcibly to a house in the country, where 'I will keep her close prisoner without suffering her to write or receive any letters but what I may see, to stop her importuning those she should not, and clamouring', although he admits 'I am sent to from her Majesty to use her civilly, who otherwise renounceth her.' His letter provides a picture of a woman grown hysterical

---

[15] *CSPI, 1598–1599*, pp. 172, 398; John Caillard Erck, ed., *A Repertory of the Inrollments on the Patent Rolls of Chancery, in Ireland: Commencing with the Reign of King James I*, vol. 1 part 1 (Dublin: James M'glashan, 1846), p. 82 n. 13. See also Klene, who quotes different sources for this information, Introduction, *The Southwell-Sibthorpe Commonplace Book*, p. xiv and note 10.

[16] *HMC Salisbury*, XV. 74–5, 90–1, 105, 124 and 388. I concur with Klene (Introduction, *The Southwell-Sibthorpe Commonplace Book*, p. xv) and Burke ('Medium and Meaning', pp. 97, 114 n. 12), who both assert that this Mrs Southwell is Anne Harris. No other Thomas Southwell of this period was married and of sufficient social status to aspire to associate with the Queen. His uncle, Thomas Southwell, would have been an obscure old man; Sir Thomas Southwell of Woodrising was only seven years old in 1603. See the family tree in Steer, *Woodrising Church*; also entries for the Southwell family in Francis Blomefield, *An Essay Towards a Topographical History of the County of Norfolk*, 10 vols. (London: for William Miller by W. Bulmer, 1805–9), especially VII. 8, 11; VIII. 236; X. 275, 277, 287, 300, 302, 455.

from fear of travelling so far alone (she 'fears she shall be murthered')
and perhaps also from her acute disappointment at being dismissed by the
queen, who had already formed a close association with Lucy, Countess of
Bedford, and had chosen her royal attendants from among the countess's
circle.[17]

A very different view of events is painted in a response from Thomas
Southwell, who wrote to Cecil to clear his wife's name. Southwell asserts 'it
was ye quenes mai^{tes} gracious Letters y^t moued my wifes iorney', acknowledging that 'if we had pretended wthout suche a cause ther had been ye lesse
regarde dewe vnto vs'. He begs Cecil to redress the many wrongs suffered by
the Southwells, particularly due to the 'malytiou[s] slanderers' who sought
the queen's favour, especially 'ffowler[e]s wife'.[18] Since the slanders are never
specified, nor the queen's reason for dismissing Mrs Southwell, it is difficult
to discern precisely what happened in Berwick. But the letters hint at the
intense rivalry among the women who sought the favour of the queen, and
also the vital role of reputation – 'regarde' – in sealing a woman's fate at
court. The fact that it is Thomas Southwell who writes to clear his wife's
name also demonstrates that for a struggling couple like the Southwells
co-operation in advancing the family name was absolutely essential: it was
his ambition, as well as hers, that might have been materially damaged
through the harm to her reputation.

The most intriguing passage in these letters is Thomas Southwell's assertion that the queen's letters had moved his wife's journey, for it suggests
that, whatever her reception at Berwick, Anne Southwell was somehow
connected to the queen's household. There is no evidence that Southwell
ever had an official place at court, but she may have been associated with
the queen's circle through her religious affiliations: her booklist includes
many of the divines popular in the households of the queen and Prince
Henry, such as Lewis Bayly, Bishops Joseph Hall and John King, and Daniel
Featley, whose curate, Roger Cox, would write poetry for Anne Southwell's
memorial more than thirty years later.[19] In addition to her possible religious

[17] *HMC Salisbury*, xv. 90–1. Leeds Barroll, 'The Court of the First Stuart Queen', in *The Mental World of the Jacobean Court*, ed. Linda Levy Peck (Cambridge: Cambridge University Press, 1991), pp. 200–4.

[18] *HMC Salisbury*, xv. 388. My transcriptions are from the British Library microfilm of the original, Cecil Papers, vol. 103, f. 57.

[19] Klene asserts that Southwell was not a member of Elizabeth's court, Introduction, *The Southwell-Sibthorpe Commonplace Book*, p. xxii, n. 33; Helen Payne in a personal communication has confirmed that Southwell is not listed among women serving Queen Anne. The booklist is Folger MS V.b.198, ff. 64^v–66^r. See the chapter on Queen Anne and Prince Henry in Peter McCullough, *Sermons at Court: Politics and Religion in Elizabethan and Jacobean Preaching* (Cambridge: Cambridge University Press, 1998), pp. 169–94.

connections, Southwell used her literary skill as a means of establishing networks of influence, participating in the court writing games that attracted John Donne, Sir Thomas Overbury and a number of minor court ladies. Two of Southwell's contributions were printed in the 1614 and 1615 editions of *The wife now the widdow of Sir Thomas Overburye*: a response to Donne's 'Newes from the very Country' and one to Overbury's 'Newes from Court'. The existence of these brief pieces as works by Lady Anne Southwell suggests the extent of her interaction with individuals in court circles, particularly if she were receiving and responding to the pieces while in Ireland. In addition, Southwell's 'Newes' pieces demonstrate her abilities to play along in the courtly game of versifying, which frequently employed misogynist commonplaces. In 'Answere to the Court Newes' she playfully asserts 'That Man, Woman, and the Diuell, are the three degrees of comparison': although Southwell's own status may have allowed her more freedom to write, the world she lived in was nevertheless one in which the role of women was hotly contested. The 'Newes' pieces, along with the numerous considerations of gender in her manuscript poetry, demonstrate her own ability to participate in the debate.[20]

Further evidence of Lady Anne Southwell's social standing in the 1620s is apparent in letters she wrote to the Earl of Cork and Sir Thomas Browne on behalf of Sir Richard Edgecombe; in marriage negotiations she made on behalf of the daughter of the Countess of Somerset; and in letters to Henry Cary, Lord Falkland and Cicely MacWilliams, Countess of Londonderry, lovingly preserved in the Folger manuscript of her works.[21] This list of names suggests that Lady Anne Southwell enjoyed some influence, but also that its reach was limited: the Earl of Cork and the Countess of Londonderry may

[20] Klene's evidence for the attribution of these pieces to Southwell is convincing, Introduction, *The Southwell-Sibthorpe Commonplace Book*, pp. xxix–xxx. The Overbury works are edited by James Edwin Savage, as *The 'Conceited Newes' of Sir Thomas Overbury and his Friends* (Gainesville, Florida: Scholars' Facsimilies & Reprints, 1968), pp. 218–22, 225–7, 233–4; the passage quoted above is on p. 226. Southwell may have been connected to the Overbury circle through her acquaintance with Frances Howard; see Sarah Ross, 'Women and Religious Verse in English Manuscript Culture, c. 1600–1668: Lady Anne Southwell, Lady Hester Pulter and Katherine Austen' (unpublished D. Phil. thesis, University of Oxford, 2000), pp. 47, 49. John Considine disagrees with the attribution of these pieces to Southwell, and also argues that the news pieces may not have originated in a coterie: 'The Invention of the Literary Circle of Sir Thomas Overbury', in *Literary Circles and Cultural Communities in Renaissance England*, ed. Claude J. Summers and Ted-Larry Pebworth (Columbia, Missouri: University of Missouri Press, 2000), pp. 59–74, especially p. 69.

[21] The letters to the Earl of Cork and Sir Thomas Browne are Lismore MSS XIV, ff. 160 and 174, in the Devonshire Collections at Chatsworth in Derbyshire; I am grateful to Peter Day, Keeper of Collections at Chatsworth, for kindly providing me with photocopies of these letters. Sarah Ross discusses the marriage motion episode, 'Women and Religious Verse', pp. 47, 49. The letter to Falkland is copied in Folger MS V.b.198, f. 4^r; those to Cicely MacWilliams on ff. 3^r and 19^v–20^v. The second is a mock elegy; it is followed by a genuine epitaph on f. 21^r.

have been important in Ireland, but the Countess of Somerset and Lord Falkland suffered serious political upsets.[22] Southwell's manuscript religious poetry may have been aimed at a coterie audience of similar figures on the fringes of the court or influential in Ireland, and her second husband's attempt to memorialise her as an ideal woman should be read in this social context.

Sir Thomas Southwell died in June 1626, and his widow was soon married again, to a Captain Henry Sibthorpe, before the end of the year.[23] Henry Sibthorpe also pursued fortune and preferment in Ireland, but unlike his wife's first husband he did not have the benefit of a knighthood or an ancient landed family. The handicap of his status is apparent in lists of payments to Sibthorpe and other officers in Ireland: while Sibthorpe's payments are consistently on the high end, men with titles receive considerably higher rewards.[24] Like many who served the Stuarts, Sibthorpe also found that his faithful service was overlooked: in October 1627 Lord Falkland supported Sibthorpe's petition to the king for promotion to the captainship of a substitute company, testifying Sibthorpe had a company in the Cadiz expedition which he kept faithfully for two years in Ireland, watching others being promoted over his head.[25] Similar references in the domestic state papers suggest that Henry Sibthorpe sought favour in London directly: on 25 June 1625 John Chamberlain offered the gratitude of Captain Sibthorpe to Sir Dudley Carleton, presumably for a place in the Cadiz expedition, while on 22 October 1631 John West, an official of the Exchequer and Sibthorpe's uncle, wrote to Carleton, then Secretary of State, thanking him for favours to Captain Sibthorpe and begging him to 'further the latter with the King'.[26] Such royal recognition seems never to have materialised, as by this time Sibthorpe had left service in Ireland for London, moving first with his wife to fashionable Clerkenwell and then, in 1631, to Acton.[27] By

[22] The countess lived in retirement after she was pardoned for her part in the conspiracy to murder Sir Thomas Overbury; see the DNB for Falkland's troubles as Lord Deputy of Ireland.
[23] See Sibthorpe's epitaph for his wife, Folger MS V.b.198, f. 74ʳ; see also Sir Thomas Southwell's funeral certificate in British Library Additional MS 4820, f. 98v.
[24] Payments and other references to Henry Sibthorpe are in the *CSPI 1625–1632*, pp. 145, 158, 165, 172, 173, 194, 261 and 273.
[25] *CSPI 1625–1632*, pp. 145, 172, 273.
[26] *CSPD 1625–26*, p. 48; *CSPD 1629–31*, p. 364. Klene (Introduction, *The Southwell-Sibthorpe Commonplace Book*, pp. xix-xx and n. 22) also notes references to Sibthorpe in Chamberlain's letters, both petitions from his uncle John West, in 1618 and 1625. See Norman Egbert McClure, ed., *The Letters of John Chamberlain*, 2 vols. (Philadelphia: American Philosophical Society, 1939), II. 166, 624.
[27] The Folger manuscript includes inventories of goods moved from Clerkenwell to Acton in 1631: see ff. 59ʳ, 60ᵛ, 61ʳ. T. F. T. Baker, *A History of Middlesex*, The Victoria History of the Counties of England, ed. C. R. Elrington, vol. VII. (Oxford: Oxford University Press, 1982), pp. 7, 35–6; Klene, Introduction, *The Southwell-Sibthorpe Commonplace Book*, p. xxi.

1635, shortly before Lady Anne Southwell's death, Sibthorpe had turned to other ventures, waging an unsuccessful fight for a royal patent 'for making ovens after a new way by him found out'.[28]

If she had moved up the social hierarchy through her first marriage, marrying Henry Sibthorpe must have meant a step down for Anne Southwell, since he was considerably less well connected than either Lady Anne herself or Sir Thomas Southwell. The difference was not merely in social standing but also in age, as Henry Sibthorpe was almost certainly younger than Lady Anne Southwell. He outlived his wife by many years; as Burke points out, 'A List of my Bookes' in the Folger manuscript, which probably catalogues the Southwell-Sibthorpe family library, contains items published as late as 1650. Burke also asserts that 'he is probably the Henry Sibthorpe of St Dunstan-in-the-West, London, whose will was proved on 16 December 1672'.[29] If Sibthorpe died as late as 1672, he was probably considerably younger than his wife, who had been born almost a century earlier.

The distinction between them is sharply demonstrated in her use of her title from her first marriage: it was more illustrious to be Lady Anne Southwell than Mrs Sibthorpe.[30] The title 'Lady Anne Southwell' itself hints at the couple's ambitions, as it is not even the correct appellation for a woman who was the widow of a knight with no title in her own right. But although she is occasionally referred to as 'Lady Southwell', she is never called by her full correct title 'Anne, Lady Southwell'.[31] On the other hand, she is called 'Lady Anne Southwell' on the title page of the Folger manuscript, in letters and receipts and in the memorial to her in St Mary's, Acton.[32] Inaccurate or not, this is clearly the title she was known by in her own circles, and its use suggests the hopes of greater things held by both Anne Southwell and Henry Sibthorpe.

Financially, the Southwell-Sibthorpe household was by no means poor, but their small business transactions do not match the large sums of money and land the Southwells squabbled over. The inventories of their goods moved from Clerkenwell to Acton in 1631 include furniture for several rooms, five velvet and satin gowns and three petticoats for Lady Anne. The

---

[28] *CSPD 1635*, p. 404, and *CSPD 1637*, p. 17. I am grateful to Jean Klene for pointing me toward these references.

[29] Burke, 'Medium and Meaning', p. 98. The book list is on ff. 64^v–66^r.

[30] This was not uncommon practice; Lady Anne Clifford, for example, continued to use her maiden name throughout her life. 'Lady Southwell', the poet's correct title, was of course less impressive than the incorrect 'Lady Anne Southwell', which implied that she was the daughter of a peer.

[31] See, for example, the second receipt on Folger MS V.b.198, f. 72^v.

[32] Ff. 1^r, 4^r, 21^r, 22^r, 59^r, 72^v, 74^r. Because this chapter is concerned with the poet's self-presentation and the social function of her writing, I refer to her throughout by the title by which she wished to be known whenever I refer to her by her full name.

couple could also afford to employ secretaries to look after their accounts and transcribe Lady Anne's poetry. For their house in Acton they paid five pounds rent a year to Anne Johnson, widow of court musician Robert Johnson.[33] In the 1630s, five pounds per annum was probably on the high end of rents for hamlets like Acton, but constituted a small amount compared to the ten pounds or more paid for the prosperous merchants' houses in the desirable district of Tower Wharf.[34] The rent is in any case a stark contrast to the sums of five thousand or even eighty pounds mentioned in Southwell family chancery cases.

The fact that the couple chose to reside in Acton is in itself suggestive. In the 1630s Acton was little more than a hamlet at the five-mile post on the road from London. It was 'a summer retreat for courtiers and lawyers', and the retirement home of Lady Conway, widow of Charles I's Secretary of State, and Lady Dudley, widow of Robert Dudley, but it was hardly a centre of politics or a likely place for advancement.[35] In such small communities the best measure of an individual's importance was their position among those who governed the parish.[36] The rector of St Mary's, Acton, in the 1630s was the prolific and influential Daniel Featley, but he spent little time in Acton, leaving the running of the parish to his curate, Roger Cox.[37] Cox was acquainted with Lady Anne Southwell and wrote poetry for her memorial plaque in the chancel of the church, facts which demonstrate that she at least was of some standing in the parish. The surviving parish records suggest that her husband, on the other hand, did not distinguish himself in parish affairs. Although the churchwarden's accounts for this period have been lost, all important material was transcribed into the 1674–99 accounts. In the lists of men who held church offices from 1628–40, Henry Sibthorpe's name never appears. In addition, in a list of influential and noteworthy inhabitants culled from the assessment books, including Dr Featley, Roger Cox and Robert Johnson, neither Lady Anne nor her husband is mentioned, perhaps because they were not landowners. Whatever the reason for their

[33] Inventories of their goods are on Folger MS V.b.198, ff. 59ʳ, 60ᵛ–61ʳ; receipts for rent are on ff. 71ʳ⁻ᵛ, 72ᵛ.

[34] M. J. Power, 'East London Housing in the Seventeenth Century', in *Crisis and Order in English Towns 1500–1700: Essays in Urban History*, ed. Peter Clark and Paul Slack (London: Routledge, 1972), pp. 254–5.

[35] Baker, *A History of Middlesex*, pp. 7, 35–36; Klene, Introduction, *The Southwell-Sibthorpe Commonplace Book*, p. xxi.

[36] Susan Dwyer Amussen, *An Ordered Society: Gender and Class in Early Modern England* (Oxford: Basil Blackwell, 1988), p. 28.

[37] Roger Cox was also the author of a book of verse on the nativity, STC 5467 *Hebdomada sacra* (London: Felix Kyngston for Henry Seile, 1630).

absence, it seems their standing in the parish was not significant enough to rate notice by a later resident.[38]

Far from seeking to be part of the royal retinue, as Lady Anne Southwell and her first husband had in 1603, the Southwell-Sibthorpes lived a retired life in Acton, where she exerted a minor influence on local affairs through an acquaintance with the curate. Viewed from their modest house in Acton, the image of Lady Anne Southwell as an ideal of her status takes on a different hue. Was Henry Sibthorpe – and possibly Lady Anne herself – aiming for some financial or political gain when her poetry was collected? Certainly we have ample evidence that Lady Anne and both her husbands used every other means in their power to secure honour and fortune. If Lady Anne Southwell could write a witty lyric, why not use that talent too?

This hypothesis is supported by material and literary evidence from the two manuscripts of Southwell's poetry: Folger MS V.b.198 and Lansdowne MS 740. Both manuscripts seem to have been prepared with those family ambitions in mind: the Folger manuscript repeatedly foregrounds Lady Anne's court connections through verse and prose letters to the good and the great of her circle, while the Lansdowne manuscript is dedicated to the king himself. Both manuscripts contain framing material – memorial poetry by Henry Sibthorpe and their curate Roger Cox in the Folger manuscript, and a praise poem by Sibthorpe in the Lansdowne manuscript – constructing Lady Anne Southwell as a model gentlewoman. But how much was the poet involved in creating this image of herself in manuscript and verse? A detailed analysis of the composition of the two manuscripts suggests that she took an active part in overseeing the scribal publication of her work.

Folger MS V.b.198 is a motley collection of lyrics, meditations, verse and prose letters and household accounts, all bound into the manuscript in a variety of ways. Its eclecticism defies categorisation: it is a miscellany only in the broadest sense, and, despite the title of Jean Klene's recent scholarly edition, *The Southwell-Sibthorpe Commonplace Book*, only a few entries resemble the collection of excerpts in a commonplace book. I would argue that the apparent chaos of the volume is the result of at least two different types of scribal publication bound together when the author died, leaving the fair copy of her works unfinished.

The multiple purposes of the Folger manuscript become apparent in an analysis of the paper, which can be divided into two distinct sections: the leaves bound into a paper book, and loose papers pasted or tipped on to guards. The paper bound into the manuscript appears – for the most part – to have come from the same stock: fourteen of thirty-eight folios

---

[38] Greater London Record Office MS DR052/133, pp. 211–12, 203.

bear the same Nicholas Lebe watermark, and most of the others bear no watermark at all.[39] The folios I identify as belonging to the stock bound into the volume are folios 1–11, 16–17, 24–5, 30 and 59–72.[40] The bound folios contain scribal copies of Southwell's lyrics and her verse and prose letters, and include only a few occurrences of Southwell's hand signing or correcting the scribe's work. With their bold heading 'The workes of the Lady Ann Sothwell:.~ / Decemb: 2° 1626°:.', these folios present the appearance of a fine scribal copy of original poetry, perhaps intended for a coterie audience.

The papers tipped or pasted into the manuscript, on the other hand, seem to belong to an entirely different manuscript publication project. The majority of these folios, numbered 31–58 in the manuscript, came from a second stock of Nicholas Lebe paper with a distinct watermark. This paper was used for autograph and scribal drafts of Southwell's lengthy meditations on the ten commandments, liberally corrected in her own hand, which is evident on all but three of folios 31–58.[41] These are clearly works in progress, containing multiple cancellations and corrections of corrections, and including nearly illegible autograph drafts scrawled in both portrait and landscape orientation.

Why were these works-in-progress bound into a fair copy of complete works? The presence of a memorial to Lady Anne at the end of the manuscript may provide a clue. Henry Sibthorpe must have decided to complete 'The workes of the Lady Ann Sothwell' after his wife's death, gathering together her loose papers and tipping them into the manuscript, then finishing the project with his own poetic monument. The manuscript thus becomes something more than the sum of its parts; it is a material record of the life and work of Lady Anne Southwell, meant to be read as much as a monument to her as for its literary or theological merit. Like the prayers and meditations of Elizabeth Cavendish Egerton, or the memorial to Anne Ley in her husband Roger's commonplace book, the Folger manuscript uses the combination of a variety of genres – poems, letters, devotional verse – and biographical context to provide evidence of a life

---

[39] Klene has compiled a chart of the watermarks, *The Southwell-Sibthorpe Commonplace Book*, pp. 117–23. See also her description of the manuscript, p. xxxiv. Probably more than thirty-eight folios of this stock of paper were bound into the book originally, but in many cases where a new sheet has been tipped into the manuscript the backing folio has been cut away along with the identifying watermark.

[40] Although bound into the volume, folios 12–15 contain sheets with a second Nicholas Lebe watermark, while 18–23 include a dog watermark found nowhere else in the volume. Their content is also distinct.

[41] Folios 12–15, although bound into the volume, seem to belong to this group as they bear the same watermark and contain scribal drafts of a poem on the fifth commandment, corrected by Southwell.

lived as well as of a finished artistic product.[42] Both the Egerton and Ley manuscripts offer evidence of a widower's use of his wife's literary remains for political or personal advantage. Elizabeth Egerton's prayers and lengthy scriptural meditations were collected and transcribed by her grieving husband, John Egerton, Earl of Bridgewater, who had been imprisoned for fighting a duel shortly before her death and may have hoped to gain by her pious reputation.[43] Roger Ley, on the other hand, was curate of the embattled Laudian stronghold of St Leonard's, Shoreditch, and included a memorial of his wife's pious letters and poems as the centrepiece of a manuscript that celebrates Laudian heroes.[44]

The manuscripts of Elizabeth Egerton and Anne Ley thus suggest women whose life and work was exploited by their husbands after they had died.[45] Southwell's manuscripts, on the other hand, offer strong evidence of politic co-operation between husbands and wives in early modern literary production.[46] The date on the opening page, ten years before her death, and the liberal presence of her hand, correcting and signing throughout the manuscript, demonstrate that Lady Anne was active and involved in the project of publishing her work. The memorial poetry, on the other hand, together with corrections in Sibthorpe's hand and his physical assembly of the manuscript, reveal that he also had an influence over the final state of the text, an influence that continued after his wife's death. The couple's financial and social struggles offer a compelling reason for this collaboration, especially as the Folger manuscript eventually found its way back to the family of Anne Harris's first husband sometime before 1834 when it was sold by Thomas Thorpe as part of the Southwell family papers.[47] Was Henry Sibthorpe attempting to curry favour with his wife's in-laws by capitalising on her poetic reputation?

[42] Elizabeth Egerton's prayers and meditations are in British Library MS Egerton 607 and Huntington Library MS EL 8376 (35/B/35) (a facsimile; the original is in the possession of the Duke of Sutherland). The memorial to Anne Ley is in the commonplace book of her husband Roger Ley, Clark Library MS L6815M3 C734 [16–/50?] Bound, ff. 90ʳ–111ʳ. See Sarah Ross, 'Women and Religious Verse', pp. 85–7, for a more detailed comparison of Folger MS V.b.198 with these works.

[43] DNB, s.v. John Egerton, second Earl of Bridgewater. See also Betty Travitsky, *Subordination and Authorship in Early Modern England: The Case of Elizabeth Cavendish Egerton and her Loose Papers* (Tempe, Arizona: Arizona Center for Medieval and Renaissance Studies, 1999), p. 115.

[44] The poetry may not be by Anne Ley: the letters are signed with her name by the scribe, but the attribution of the poetry is less clear. Roger Ley's own memorial poems to Laudian churchmen follow the memorial to his wife on ff. 167ʳ–195ᵛ.

[45] Using an individual's literary remains was not necessarily a gendered activity; both Lancelot Andrewes and Richard Sibbes are examples of men whose writings were politically recast after their deaths. Peter McCullough, 'Making Dead Men Speak: Laudianism, Print, and the Works of Lancelot Andrewes, 1626–1642', *The Historical Journal* 41.2 (1998): 401–24. On Richard Sibbes see chapter 1 above.

[46] Jean Klene offers a somewhat more romantic version of the couple's collaboration: '"Monument of an Endless affection"', pp. 165–86.

[47] Burke, 'Medium and Meaning', p. 94.

The second manuscript of Lady Anne Southwell's verse supports the conclusion that, as in so many households, the gathering of her poetry was part of a larger family bid for preferment. British Library Lansdowne MS 740 contains scribal copies of Lady Anne's meditations on the third and fourth commandments, with a poetic dedication to the king.[48] The manuscript is in an intermediate stage between draft and fair copy; it includes numerous corrections, none in the author's hand. But despite the absence of her hand, there is good evidence that Lady Anne was alive when the manuscript was prepared: the praise poem at the end of the manuscript, signed 'H' and probably by Henry Sibthorpe, refers to her several times in the present tense, unlike the epitaph in the Folger manuscript. Certainly there is no reason to assume that the dedication to the king is not by Southwell: a stanza transcribed upside-down on the verso, seemingly for inclusion in the final fair copy of the poem, is a version of lines from Southwell's poem on the first commandment in the Folger manuscript, with the address redirected from God to the king.[49] If the rest of the poem, 'signed' by the scribe with Southwell's name, was also written by her, its presence demonstrates that she was preparing these poems to be read by a wider audience, even if the final touches to the transcription were not her own. The Lansdowne manuscript thus establishes that Southwell was active in the scribal publication of her own work, with ambitions that it might reach as high as the monarch.

If Southwell was living when the praise poem at the end of the Lansdowne manuscript was written, it seems probable that she was aware of, and possibly collusive in, its construction of herself as an exemplary gentlewoman. Significantly, although the Lady Anne of the poem is 'as gracefull as shee [is] full of fauour', such stereotypical praise of women is woven into praise of her superior ability in the courtly arts of 'rimes' and 'wit':

> Ther's nothing art or nature doth descrye
> but shee can draw it through her needles eye
> when yf she chaunce to worke by imitation
> shee goes beyond her patternes commendation
> all to the life is soe exactly done
> as nature doth by pencill of the sunne[.]

[48] Ultimately the manuscript was most likely intended for Charles, unless we speculate that Sibthorpe was editing his wife's poetry before their marriage in 1626. Internal evidence suggests that the dedication and the meditations may have been written before 1625 for James, particularly the line 'to pray him bee a rose was borne a thistle' (f. 163ᵛ, l. 450), which (as Elizabeth Clarke has suggested to me) depends on iconography associated with James, not Charles. See also Burke, 'Medium and Meaning', pp. 104–6.

[49] Lansdowne MS 740, f. 142ᵛ, lines 1–6; and Folger MS V.b.198, f. 28ᵛ, lines 49–54.

Although ostensibly these lines praise Southwell's skill in needlework, their presence immediately after two long verse meditations, as well as the unfortunately now incomplete references to 'rimes' and 'wit' in the preceding lines, suggest that Southwell's writing is intended as much as any other feminine 'worke'. The metaphorical language of 'imitation', 'patternes', 'nature' and 'pencill' implies a precise literary context: Sidneian poetic imitation, through which poets could rival nature in their imaginative creativity. Southwell's talents as a writer are thus situated as a distinct marker of status and refinement with a particular social function, to improve and inspire her peers. This, Sibthorpe asserts, is what 'a Lady can or ought to doe': not only to be beautiful, devoted and chaste, but to write.[50]

The epitaph in the Folger manuscript confirms the importance of both status and intellectual activity to Sibthorpe's notion of 'the compleate Character of ffemale perfection'. Alongside traditionally feminine virtues of 'Charity', 'affibility' and 'beautie', the epitaph praises Lady Anne Southwell for her

> Zealous constancy in Religion,
> Exemplary vertue in life,
> Pious frequency in devotion,

and, most significantly, her 'Profound knowledge in learning'. Her pious study and devotion (and presumably the poetry in the Folger manuscript that provides evidence of both) are signs of status as visible as any physical beauty. 'She was a Lady by the generall verdict of all that knew her', Sibthorpe asserts on the monument. The appearance of gentility was a vital tool for ambition, and at the end of her life, the two manuscripts of her poetry served as important evidence for those who would pass a verdict on her final reputation.[51]

If the manuscripts were part of the couple's bid for preferment, the emphasis on the exemplarity of Lady Anne Southwell's character is not surprising, and perhaps it should also be unsurprising that writing is the key to her exemplarity. The ideal of Sibthorpe's poems hearkens back to the versifying gentry daughters of the Tudor period, adorned with abilities in Latin and Greek to help smooth their families' paths to preferment at court. Like Jane Lumley, Ann Cooke Bacon, Elizabeth Cary and the Countess of Pembroke, Lady Anne Southwell is capable of both instructing and pleasing

---

[50] Lansdowne MS 740, f. 167ᵛ, lines 12, 6, 8, 13–18, 19.
[51] Folger MS V.b.198, f.74ʳ, lines 18, 14, 15, 17, 11–13, 16, 7.

a powerful audience, even potentially the king himself.[52] Their literary work was not merely tolerated because of their social position, but in fact served as an intrinsic marker of status: Sibthorpe's poems cry out for recognition of his wife's natural right – displayed in her writing and the life that lay behind it – to her title, Lady Anne Southwell: 'What is't a Lady can or ought to doe / but shee both knowes & doth excell in to.'[53]

Sibthorpe was also not the only early modern husband to encourage his wife's writing in a joint bid for advancement. In addition to Anne Ley and Elizabeth Egerton, Aemilia Lanyer's *Salve deus rex judæorum* (1611) may well have been promoted by her husband's more illustrious connections, while Lady Anne Southwell's contemporaries Alice and John Sutcliffe used her writing and his position at court to fashion an otherwise conventional volume of patronage poetry.[54] Alongside these examples Lady Anne Southwell's work offers important evidence that, for women of certain social ambitions, writing was neither unusual nor straightforwardly transgressive, but one of many acceptable means of advancing family fortunes. Jean Klene has asserted that '[i]deas about early modern women need to be expanded to include' Lady Anne Southwell, a woman writer seemingly neither chaste, silent, nor obedient.[55] I would argue further that rather than fitting Southwell into existing normative concepts as a proto-feminist exception, we should entertain the notion that she herself may be the norm for socially ambitious early modern gentlewomen.

ADAM, EVE AND CHRIST

The construction of Lady Anne Southwell the poet as a paradigm of femininity rather than an exception is particularly suggestive when compared to her own account of gender relations in her poetry. As much as any modern feminist, Southwell was aware of the constructed nature of gender, and her writing both exposes and exploits this truth. But, biting as her critique of gender relations may be, it is never out of harmony with her 'compleate Character of ffemale perfection'. In fact, witty lyrics by Southwell that

[52] Diane Purkiss argues that the education of Tudor gentlewomen was counted as a family asset; see the Introduction to her edition of the plays of Lumley, Sidney and Cary: *Three Tragedies by Renaissance Women* (London: Penguin, 1998), pp. xiii–xv, xx–xxi.
[53] British Library Lansdowne MS 740, f. 167[v], lines 19–20.
[54] The Lanyers and the Sutcliffes are discussed in chapter 2 above; see also Leeds Barroll, 'Looking for Patrons', in *Aemilia Lanyer: Gender, Genre, and the Canon*, ed. Marshall Grossman (Lexington, Kentucky: University Press of Kentucky, 1998), pp. 36–41; and STC 23447, Alice Sutcliffe, *Meditations of man's mortalitie* (London: by B. Alsop and T. Fawcet for Henry Seyle, 1634).
[55] '"Monument of an Endless affection"', p. 183.

disparage 'blockish Adam' are entirely in keeping with the persona of a courtly gentlewoman. These lyrics use the same repertoire of wit as the courtly games she participated in with the likes of Donne and Overbury, and one might argue that it is in fact her wit that enables her to speak, no matter how boldly. It is not a sign of Southwell's audacity that some of her most radical statements on gender occur in the manuscript dedicated to the king, but rather a sign of how the persona of a gentlewoman poet maintained in the manuscripts serves to authorise what might otherwise be objectionable.

As well as using witty language to authorise her comments on gender, Lady Anne Southwell also draws on scripture and Puritan theology to the same end. Revolutionary as they may seem, Southwell's perceptions of gender are in fact derived from the Biblical principle that, in spite of different moral standards for men and women, ultimately both sexes are the same before God, and must face the same judgement. This is a contradiction inherent in the teachings of a Church that emphasises the equality of all believers but maintains a hierarchy of gender: St Paul, for example, asserts both that women must submit to their husbands (Ephesians 5:22), and that in Christ there is no male or female (Galatians 3:28). Southwell was certainly not the only woman writer to exploit this inconsistency, but she is one of the most sophisticated. Her extensive Biblical knowledge enables her to construct a critique that is both radical in its defence of women and exemplary in its adherence to traditional sources of authority, the Bible and Puritan marriage commentaries.

It is the Biblical figures of Adam, Eve and Christ who provide Southwell with fuel for her critique of early modern gender stereotypes. These three appear repeatedly in her poetry, playing out the drama of the Fall and Redemption as a slightly ludicrous tragicomedy of early modern social relations. Southwell utilises the story of Adam and Eve to promote a form of active virtue which is the only proper human response to the consequences of the Fall. She urges Adam, playfully imagined as literally 'tumbled from the nest', to 'rise', virtue consists in action', echoing her own paraphrase of Seneca:

> Vertue consists in Action: and the wise
> Hould all Afflictions, vertues exercise
> To shake the Lazy rust from off their mynd
> For ease & welth makes ignorant & blynd[.][56]

---

[56] Folger MS V.b.198, f. 20ᵛ, line 112; f. 18ᵛ, line 86; f. 8ᵛ, lines 41–44.

In the 'Letter to Doctor Adam', Southwell divides 'vertues exercise' into the three cardinal virtues of 1 Corinthians 13, faith, hope and love, and each of these virtues is evident in the action it provokes. It is only in the active exercise of these virtues that the 'foggye vapours' of sin can be dispersed, and Adam can work to regain some of his lost understanding of God.[57] Action leads to better contemplation and knowledge of God, a hypothesis that is significant in Southwell's critique of married men who make perverse use of their intellect, twisting God's Word to accommodate their own sin, but whose actions fall far short of the mark.

This definition of 'virtue', equating piety with action and apostasy with idleness, draws on the language of popular devotional manuals. The Southwell-Sibthorpe library catalogue includes a number of widely read devotional works that construct a form of piety that is both private and active.[58] In a dedicatory epistle, for example, Joseph Hall imagines his *Arte of divine meditation* (first edition 1606) as a remedy for a crisis of idleness:

> Sir, euer since I began to bestow my selfe vpon the co[m]mon good, studying wherein my labours might bee most seruiceable; I still found they could bee no way so well improued, as in that part which concerneth deuotion, and the practice of true piety . . . respecting the Reader, I sawe the braines of men neuer more stuffed, their to[n]gues neuer more stirring, their hearts neuer more emptie, nor their handes more idle.[59]

Like Southwell, Hall considers the idleness of Christians to be the result of intellectual confusion. Hall's solution, and that of other writers of devotional manuals, is to set aside doctrine and polemics for practical instruction in 'the practice of true piety'. Devotion, the private communication between the individual and God, becomes an active means of righting the social ills of tongues that are stirring and hands that are idle.

Daniel Featley draws on a specific social crisis in the preface to his immensely popular *Ancilla pietatis: or, the hand-maid to priuate devotion* (1626), describing his book arising out of the 'most vrgent necessity of PRIVATE DEVOTION' following 'the late dreadfull Visitation' of the plague. Private devotion is the remedy for the spiritual idleness and apathy

---

[57] Folger MS V.b.198, f. 19ʳ, line 96.

[58] See Sister Jean Carmel Cavanaugh, 'The Library of Lady Southwell and Captain Sibthorpe', *Studies in Bibliography* 20 (1967): 243–54, nos. 99, 100, 101 and 106. Their popularity is suggested by their appearance in the manuscript library catalogue of Frances Egerton, Countess of Bridgewater, in the possession of the Duke of Sutherland but available in facsimile at the Huntington Library, MS EL 6495.

[59] STC 12643 (London: H. Lownes for Samuel Macham, 1607), sig. A3ʳ–A4ʳ. This title is not on the Southwell-Sibthorpe booklist, but Hall's *Meditations and vowes* is number 101; see Cavanaugh, 'Library', p. 253.

caused by such fearful visitations, because devotion leads to public religious practice, specifically the Eucharist. Featley constructs his book as a 'hand-maid' to the figure of private devotion, described as a retiring woman: 'I haue furnished and replenished this *Manuel*, which I name THE HAND-MAID TO PRIVATE DEVOTION, to waite on her in her Chamber, or Oratorie. The purtraying of her Mistresse I leaue to the pensill of some Diuine Apelles, whose taske will be the harder, because she neuer commeth abroad.'[60] Because the figure of devotion is a woman, and the book is dedicated to a woman, the Duchess of Buckingham, it is easily assumed that *Ancilla pietatis* was intended as a handbook for Christian women only.[61] But Featley's gendering of devotion is not so firmly fixed. In *The svmme of saving knowledge* (1626), a catechism appended to *Ancilla pietatis*, Featley attributes an active role to devotion that slips across gender lines:

Wherefore I haue thought fit not to confine *Deuotion* to her chamber, but to giue her the liberty of her house, and so not onely fasting, and praying with, but examining also, and *Catechizing* of those that are vnder her roofe, come within her walke. Euery godly Parent, Tutor, and Master of a Family, resoluing with *Iosua, that He and his house will serue the Lord*, calleth those that are vnder his charge sometimes to an account[.][62]

The actions of the feminine figure of devotion teaching her family are equated with those of a male tutor or 'Master of a Family' ruling his charges. The fact that Featley chooses to construct the private activity of devotion using the traditional figure of the retired female does not necessarily mean that the practice of private devotion was confined to women. And, given the active element of piety assumed by these manuals, we must be cautious in reading any kind of retirement or retreat from public life into such constructions of piety. Although devotion may enter her closet in order to know her God, her knowledge brings her into the public sphere to act upon her faith.[63]

   Lady Anne Southwell herself represents one who has put this code of active devotion into practice, her private piety leading to the work of her poetry, shared in a discourse with readers like Bishop Adams and Roger

[60] STC 10726 Daniel Featley, *Ancilla Pietatis* (London: for Nicholas Bourne, 1626), sig. A4[r-v], p. 1, sig. A7[v]. Cavanaugh speculates that number 99 on the booklist may refer to this title, 'Library', p. 253.
[61] With little evidence, Suzanne W. Hull speculates that the book was 'probably used largely by women', although she concedes that it 'gave devotional instructions for both men and women', *Chaste Silent & Obedient. English Books for Women 1475–1640* (San Marino, California: Huntington Library, 1982), pp. 168, 99.
[62] STC 10739 Daniel Featley, *The svmme of saving knowledge* (London: George Miller for Nicholas Bourne, 1626), sig. A2[v].
[63] The public implications of private devotion are discussed further in chapters 4 and 5 below.

Cox. Significantly, Southwell also applies her definition of active virtue to both men and women. Her poetry challenges Eve to action, but recognises that the obstacles to Eve's piety are even more impenetrable than Adam's sinfulness, since Eve herself is subject to Adam's headship. Like Adam, Eve has also lost qualities of godliness in the Fall. But Southwell, in the tradition of defences of Eve, playfully absolves her 'Grandam' of sole responsibility for the Fall. Because Adam and Eve are one flesh, Southwell argues, both must be blamed equally for the first sin.[64]

But the Adam of Southwell's poetry does not always recognise the true role of gender in relation to Christian virtue. At times, the Adam and Eve of her poetry represent not fallen humanity but misogynist husbands and oppressed wives. This Adam most decidedly has a gender, and he uses it to his full advantage, manipulating his traditional superiority in order to justify his own ill-treatment of women. Southwell cautions other women to beware such Adams, who will lead them into temptation:

> 66. Are you denyed soules then, you shelles of men,
> are they but hatched in you & flye away
> noe maruell though theyr wisedomes doe contemne
> your sex, since you are only formall clay.
> > but trust them not that would perswade you soe
> > such serpents but advise you to more woe.

> 67. Goe search the sacred writt, where you shall find
> what your creation was & to what end
> Lett not theyr envious folly make you blind
> who pittyes him that is not his own frend.
> > Adam did sleepe whilst [god] built your fayre frame:
> > & hee still sleepes that would haue you thus lame.[65]

In Southwell's rewriting of the drama Adam is not cast asleep by God but is responsible for his own drowsiness. His sleep is a sign that Adam does not really know what is going on around him, but it is also proof of a deeper culpability. In Southwell's verse such images of idleness, sleep and death are commonly linked to fallen ignorance, which becomes tantamount to a denial of God. For example she opens a poem on the commandment 'Thou shalt haue noe other gods before mee' by exhorting herself to 'Raise vp thy ffacultyes my Soule ti's time / to Wake ffrom Idleness the Childe of death'.[66] The sin against this, the first commandment is, significantly, the only sin that leads to death. It is, in a very real sense, this sin that men

---

[64] Folger MS V.b.198, f. 26 ᵛ, line 1.   [65] Lansdowne MS 740, ff. 163ʳ, lines 397–408.
[66] Folger MS V.b.198, f. 28ʳ, lines 1–2.

commit when they deny women souls and thus lead them, like the original serpent, into idleness and sin (for those without souls have no need for moral action): 'Adam did sleepe whilst [god] built your fayre frame: / & hee still sleepes that would haue you thus lame.' Such sleeping men wilfully misread the 'sacred writte' when they assume that women's gender makes them less before God, and this assumption is a form of apostasy because it denies God's power to form women in his image. Southwell's poem thus boldly suggests that manipulating gender for malicious means is an offence against God himself.

The fact that Southwell inserts these lines in her poem on the fourth commandment ('Remember the Sabbath day') also suggests that such behaviour hampers women's ability to honour God and obey his commandments. Southwell does not deny that a wife is required to be subject to her husband, but elsewhere she recognises how difficult it is for the misgoverned wife to be virtuous:

> for since that Adam is the slaue to evill'
> and shee \<is\> commanded to obey his will'
> how fares that state thats governd by the devill
> shewerly theyre woorship is for feare of ill.
> then thinck what ever seeming face wee carry
> tis betor dy a vergin then to marry[.]

These are very harsh words indeed, and not entirely in keeping with the rest of Southwell's poetry. The lines occur in her meditation entitled 'Thou shalt not commit Adooltery'; and someone, whether the scribe or Southwell herself, has even crossed out the stanza's final damning line: 'wee hould youre sex oure soule and bodyes foe'.[67] Yet even if this bitter resentment of men is more extreme than in other poems, the principle is consistent with Southwell's argument that some men's assertion of power can cripple a woman's attempt to carry out her Christian duties.

Southwell is vehement in this poem about such moral crippling of women who are 'governd by the devill', forced to obey a man who is himself 'the slaue to evill'. At the heart of his evil is manipulation of gender expectations: the 'feminine' qualities that men desire in women are often directly opposed to the Christian virtues. 'Remember the Sabbath day' includes a catalogue of such unattractive virtues: a melancholy woman, 'although her deedes bee good & thoughts bee holy', nevertheless is censured as a madwoman because she is too grave. By contrast, 'A sanguin

[67] Folger MS V.b.198, f. 48^r, lines 37–42.

woman is of all accurst' because 'shee must bee merry though her neck were burst' and is almost literally hounded by spaniel-like men who assume that her cheerfulness means that she is sexually lax. And women who write receive the strongest censure of all, particularly if they fail to flatter men:

> 74. Dare you but write, you are Mineruaes bird
> the owle at wch these battes & crowes must wonder,
> they'l crittickize vppon the smallest word
> this wanteth number case, that tense & gender
> then must you frame a pittifull epistle
> to pray him bee a rose was borne a thistle.

Although Southwell's own circumstances may demonstrate that a woman's writing skills could be not only tolerated but encouraged and even promoted by her husband, it appears that a woman's writing was nevertheless particularly open to criticism from other men who did not feel sufficiently flattered by it. The whole tenor of these stanzas implies that writing is one of the virtuous qualities that good men should promote in women, but some men find insufficiently feminine and therefore threatening to their masculinity. Pious women, solemn women, thoughtful women simply cannot be pleasing women, it seems: 'for it cannott bee / goodnes & mirth should hold a simpathye.'[68] And mirth is what attracts men. Gender stereotypes therefore force women into a moral conundrum: needing to please the men who have power over them, but in pleasing incapable of carrying out their duty to God.

Southwell counters such unfair treatment by doing some gender manipulation of her own. She advises women to 'chuse the wise for fathers frends & mirrors', borrowing Christ's instructions to his disciples before sending them out into the wilderness: 'Behold, I send you forth as sheep in the midst of wolves: be ye therefore wise as serpents, and harmless as doves' (Matthew 10:16).

> 82. Bee wise as serpents, innocent as Doues
> you are borne subiects & you must obey
> that death, wch all you feare all clogges remoues
> tis god you honour in it let them bray
> hee will reward you, at theyr bountyes spurne
> naked they came, & naked shall returne.[69]

---

[68] Lansdowne MS 740, f. 164^r, lines 476, 469; f. 163^v, lines 445–50; f. 164^r, lines 473–4.
[69] Lansdowne MS 740, f. 164^v, lines 489, 493–8.

For readers who know their scripture, the implication is clear: early modern Adams who do not respect their wives are as despicable as the Israelites (the wolves of the Biblical text) who rejected the messengers of Christ himself. The same readers might recall Christ's next words, 'But beware of men: for they will deliver you up to the councils, and they will scourge you in their synagogues' (Matthew 10:18). Southwell cleverly re-genders the Authorised Version's ungendered pronoun 'men', suggesting that it is truly the depraved members of the male sex that women must beware of, and ultimately disdain, just as Christ's disciples shake off the dust of the towns that reject them. The warning is not just for women: if Adam cannot reform, his cheap 'bountyes' will mean nothing in the next life, when obedient servants of both genders will be lifted up above those who denied Christ by mistreating his servants:

> 83. & when you both are stript out of this clay
> there will not bee a difference in your sex
> you haue one Iudge & must goe both one way
> the good wth good & bad wth bad soules mix[.]

'there will not bee a difference': a bold statement indeed, and yet one that is unquestionably scriptural. Southwell calls on the ultimate irrelevance of gender to moral accountability to encourage women who are wronged because of their gender on this earth. In the final judgement, both men and women will be rewarded or punished according to how well they have lived up to the universal standard of the 'one Iudge', how well they have walked with Christ. And in light of this final judgement, women must prepare themselves, even if it means disobeying men, for, as Southwell concludes the stanza, 'twill bee to late when you in hell shall grone / to curse those so[u]les that taught you, you had none.'[70]

Southwell thus exploits the universalism of Christianity, arguing that when gendered morals are in conflict with universal truths, women have no choice but to behave like Christians rather than women. She recognises, however, that not all women are innocent victims of gender manipulation:

> Now feamale be not you so madd to thincke
> for sexes sake your faltes shall hydden lye
> hee is noe frende that at oure follyes winck
> nor must you looke for my connyvencye[.][71]

Although she herself is female, Southwell will not admit solidarity with women who exploit the common assumption that women are the weaker

---

[70] Lansdowne MS 740, f. 164^v, lines 499–504.   [71] Folger MS V.b.198, f. 51^r, lines 215–18.

gender. Women, like men, must take responsibility for their actions, and recognise that gender, whether male or female, is no excuse for sinful behaviour. These four short lines thus neatly demonstrate how Southwell makes use of the multiplicity of gender attributes; in her vision of the kingdom of heaven, whatever their earthly weaknesses women will still face God's judgement alone, as his children.

In addition to calling on the ungendered aspects of Christian virtue, Southwell also makes use of the fact that the Christian godhead most definitely took on a human gender. Christ for her represents a possibility for difference: a new man, an ideal husband who does not use his masculinity to oppress women. Southwell would have been the last to say that Christ himself was actually a woman, or even that he was primarily feminine. What she does note, however, is that Christ's virtues are the opposite of what is termed masculine by the world. She points out that a man who refuses to break the commandments by killing, swearing, lying or stealing 'is scornde and calde a femynine'. Femininity – gender attributes that are associated with women – becomes an insult, a means for unreformed men to slander virtuous men and women. But to use their gender as a curse is not merely to offend against women, but also to insult Christ himself: 'well, you that dare abuse youre maker thus / well gyue you leaue to scorne and rayle at vs'. Christ, the poet argues, typifies just these 'femynine' virtues so scorned by men:

> Was christ a swaggerer in deede or woord
> or did his life contemne at modestye
> he sayes whoe stricks shall perish with the swoord
> his doctrine houlds with yours noe sympathye
> what is yours iendors honour or renowne
> is it in strength, to pull all honoure downe[.][72]

As Lady Anne Southwell imagines him, Christ is a different kind of man. He is modest, non-violent and most importantly uses his strength not to tear down but to build up. These are the very virtues frequently decried as 'feminine' weaknesses in other men: but, as Southwell asserts, 'his doctrine houlds with yours noe sympathye'. Southwell's verse exposes the existence of competing standards of masculinity, and demonstrates that the standard which oppresses women is out of sync with the foundation of Christian morals and Christian masculinity. How can behaviour be masculine if it contradicts the example of Christ himself?

---

[72] Folger MS V.b.198, f. 48^r, lines 46, 47–8, 49–54.

Southwell's Christ thus represents masculinity with a difference. But he is also a very hard act for any human man to follow. Perhaps in keeping with her witty, knowing persona, Southwell constructs Christ as an ironic challenge to men, one she knows they are doomed to fail. In some ways, this Christ can be seen as an answer to the ideal husbands imagined by Puritan marriage writers. Like Southwell, many of these writers utilise the model of marriage found in Ephesians: wives should 'submit your selues vnto your own husbands, as vnto the Lord' while husbands should 'loue your wiues, euen as Christ also loued the Church, and gaue himselfe for it' (5:22, 25). Husbands are equivalent to Christ, the loving, dominant partner, while wives are equivalent to the Church, submissive and indebted to her spouse for his sacrifice. For the most prescriptive of these writers, the transfer of power inherent in this analogy was absolute. William Gouge, for example, insists that for women to disobey their husbands is the same as disobeying God:

Wiues in subiecting themselues aright to their husbands are subiect to the Lord. And on the contrary side,

Wiues in refusing to be subiect to their husbands, refuse to be subiect to the Lord.[73]

Lady Anne Southwell's poetry demonstrates that writers like Gouge are only looking at half the picture. If women must submit like the Church, then men must rule like Christ, who sets a dauntingly high standard of wisdom and self-sacrifice. Southwell makes her case for the reformation of men by building on the very prescriptive literature that her poetry seems to deconstruct. Rather than challenging such men's insistence on women's submission directly, Southwell takes the model of a Christ-like husband to its logical extreme, incorporating all the characteristics of an archetypal Puritan husband, but also adding the element of sacrifice. Just as William Gouge asserts of the husband that 'loue must shew it selfe in his commandements, in his reproofes, in his instructions, in his admonitions, in his authoritie, in his familiaritie', Southwell's Christ corrects the Church's faults gently, and his own behaviour is an example of godliness:

> Christ doth not curse, sweare, rayle, at spouses error
> but with softe voyce, with humble woords and teares
> and his good life, becomes hir gratious myrror
> his loue and patience with hir weakenesse beares[.][74]

---

[73] STC 12119 William Gouge, *Of domesticall dvties* (London: John Haviland for William Bladen, 1622), p. 29.
[74] *Ibid.*, p. 351; Folger MS V.b.198, f. 49ᵛ, lines 133–6.

He also gives generously, even of his blood and life, a theme which is repeated in marriage guidebooks such as Daniel Rogers's *Matrimoniall honovr*, printed in 1642 after Southwell's death:

So that the manner of this imparting love must be orderly: the husband is to offer, to bestow, and communicate himselfe first to his wife; in a free, bountifull, full love; she is not so much bound to vie upon his love, or to love bountifully and actively, as to reflect and returne upon himselfe his owne love, and that in a reverent, amiable and modest maner[.][75]

Because men are closer to the godhead, their love should come first, like the love of Christ, and should not be dependent on their wives' response. In Southwell's poem on adultery the figure of Christ demonstrates his love by sacrificing himself for his spouse's honour. Unlike the adulterous husband, whose own behaviour brings infamy upon his wife, Christ offers his own life's blood to avenge his spouse even when she is in the wrong:

> Nor will hee suffer every slaunderous breath
> to wrongg her fame and whisper him with lyes
> but doth revenge her infamy with death
> and tenders her renowne as his owne eyes[.]

Southwell draws her concept of the mutuality of wives' and husbands' honour directly from Ephesians 5, using Paul, the advocate of men's authority over women, to demonstrate that men are also responsible in that authority: 'She is thy honour therfore houde her deere / she is thy flesh: Whoe will his owne flesh hate?'[76]

The ideal husband Southwell imagines is forgiving, generous, kind and sacrificially loving to the point of death, but he is also his wife's superior. Despite those scorned 'femynine' traits he possesses, Christ retains the traditional male prerogative of headship over his spouse, drawn from Ephesians 5 and reiterated in all the prescriptive literature of Southwell's time. But headship comes at a price. Almost with a wink, Southwell dares men to emulate Christ's example of sacrificial love:

> Christ is the churches powerfull head you knowe
> lyke tytle hath the man over his wife
> you finde what loue christ to his spouse did showe
> that gaue for her his pretious blood and life
> woolde you commande; then learne for to obey
> woolde you bee payde your debt; youre owne debt paye?[77]

[75] Wing R1797 Daniel Rogers, *Matrimoniall honovr* (London: Th. Harper for Philip Nevil, 1642), pp. 152–3.
[76] Folger MS V.b.198, f. 49ᵛ, lines 148–51; f. 50ʳ, lines 179–80.
[77] Folger MS V.b.198, f. 49ᵛ, lines 127–32.

Southwell takes the metaphor to its extreme, forcing men to accept grave responsibility along with the authority they often exploit. If men cannot learn to be obedient as Christ was obedient – an obedience that ultimately led to the cross – then they have no hope of ever commanding their wives' obedience. Southwell makes deliberate use of legal language in this stanza – the man has 'tytle' over his wife, he commands, she obeys, they both must pay debts – language drawn from parables describing Christ's freeing of sinners from judgement, but which here emphasises the contractual nature of the relationship between husband and wife. The husband is the head over his wife, but he must fulfil his rather daunting contractual responsibilities if he wants to retain all the powers of headship.

Even this seemingly radical notion has its counterpart in the marriage literature – with the exception of William Gouge's unusually strict *Of domesticall dvties*.[78] For other Puritan male writers, husbands must come to understand their subordinate relationship to Christ and his headship over all Christians before they can exercise authority over their wives. Daniel Rogers asserts, for example: 'How evident is it, by mens practice, that although all confesse they ought to be religious (and who now adayes is otherwise?) yet few will admit the yoake of God upon their necke, in the wise undergoing of those relations wherein they stand obliged? Among which this of marriage is a rooted and fundamentall one[.]'[79] Other scholars have demonstrated how marriage writers like Rogers and Gouge tend to inscribe marriage into a larger hierarchy of power relations, so that relations between man and wife become a subset of relations between subjects and magistrates, and ultimately of the human relations with the divine.[80] Significantly, however, Rogers, unlike Gouge, emphasises that human wives and husbands are equally subject to Christ, and equally empowered through that submission to become like Christ to one another. Their submission earns them 'the fellowship with Christs holy nature, by which the soule partakes the properties of Christ, qualifying it with wisedome, influence, strength, meeknesse, patience, holinesse, cheerfulnesse, long-suffering and compassion; which graces, as they make him a meet head and husband for the Church, so they make married couples meet heads and helpers for each other'.

Rogers envisions both partners in the human marriage taking the roles of the partners in the divine marriage: 'This is a short description of a

---

[78] See chapter 1 above.   [79] Rogers, *Matrimoniall honovr*, sig. A2v.

[80] See Sylvia Brown, 'Godly Household Government from Perkins to Milton: The Rhetoric and Politics of *oeconomia*, 1600–1645', (unpublished PhD thesis, Princeton University, 1994); Amussen, *An Ordered Society*.

spouse of Christ,' he concludes, 'and a sonne or daughter of *Abraham*: and such an one (in measure more or lesse) is each soule married to Christ[.]'[81] In this idealised image, both husband and wife are equal before the ultimate authority, Christ.

Southwell's meditations therefore manipulate a seemingly misogynist tradition in order to expose men who misuse their authority as husbands. There is an element of playfulness, almost spitefulness, in all of these passages; one gets the sense that male excess arises out of ignorance and laziness rather than pure malevolence. Southwell's poetry also insinuates that women know rather more about gender and mystical marriage than men do, since women have been forced to negotiate through a maze of inhibiting stereotypes. They know what it is to be subject to the devil himself, and like the Church they yearn for a truly loving husband whose authority will be a blessing, not a curse.

Such playful use of stereotypes, even in serious meditations like these, recalls the misogynist and anti-misogynist commonplaces bandied about in other of Southwell's writings, particularly her contributions to the writing games of the Overbury circle and the secular lyrics of the Folger manuscript.[82] Read alongside Donne's *Songs and sonnets* or the Inns of Court wits, it becomes apparent that Southwell's verse is in a sense baiting men with their own language as well as their own theology. This is most apparent in one of the lyrics from the Folger manuscript, which combines many of Southwell's favourite themes into a witty manifesto:

> All.maried.men.desire.to.haue good wifes:
> but.few.giue good example. by thir liues
> They are owr head they wodd haue vs thir heles.
> this makes the good wife kick the good man reles.
> When god brought Eue to Adam for a bride
> the text sayes she was taene from out mans side
> A simbole of that side, whose sacred bloud.
> flowed for his spowse, the Churches sauinge good.
> This is a misterie, perhaps too deepe.
> for blockish Adam that was falen a sleepe[.][83]

Leaving poor Adam quite literally in the dust, Southwell combines the concepts of Adam's sleep signifying Christ's death, Eve's creation signifying the birth of the Church in the blood that flowed from Christ's side and

[81] Rogers, *Matrimoniall honovr*, pp. 25, 23.
[82] See, for example, Southwell's version of the popular manuscript lyric 'The Lie', f. 2[r].
[83] Folger MS V.b.198, f. 16[r].

Eve's position as a companion to Adam, taken from his side not his head or heels. These were commonplaces of early modern marriage treatises, used to urge women's submission to their husbands.[84] Thomas Becon's popular Tudor marriage handbook asserts that women are dependent upon men for everything because Eve was made out of Adam's rib, and that this act of creation foreshadows and parallels the dependence of the Church on Christ's sacrifice. Becon also declares that a wife should be reminded 'that she was not made of the ma[n]s head, because she should not be maister, nor yet of the feete that she should be altogether an vnderling or a slaue, but of the mans side that she should be his helper and comfortour'.[85] As she did with the example of Christ as a husband, Southwell again turns potentially misogynist metaphors on their heads, combining these images not to encourage women to submission but to show up the 'blockish Adam[s]' who have misunderstood their role as husbands and heads of their wives. Men, she suggests, must learn how to rule in love over their own wives before they can understand the sacrifice of Christ; if not, Adam remains asleep, ignorant of the sacred mystery that only Eve can witness.

This is almost the stuff of caricature: 'blockish Adam', the kicking wife and reeling husband are hardly the noble figures of conventional marriage literature. It is also somewhat suspect reasoning: after all, in Genesis it is God who *casts* Adam into a sleep, not Adam who becomes drowsy of his own accord, or out of his own stupidity. Caricature and suspect reasoning are conventions frequently used against women in popular manuscript lyrics, such as Donne's seduction poem 'The Flea'. Read within this tradition, 'All.maried.men' becomes a display of Lady Anne Southwell's proficiency in this kind of courtly wit, and her ability to manipulate a potentially misogynist poetic form to her own ends.

In the last few years, since the first wave of early modern feminist criticism in the 1980s, readings of early modern women have expanded beyond the initial notion that all women were constrained to be chaste, silent and obedient, and that any woman who did write was somehow a lonely exception who was lucky to miss the fate of Judith Shakespeare. Lady Anne Southwell's poetry is, in a sense, yet another nail in Judith Shakespeare's coffin: it demonstrates that the relationship between gender and power in this period was in fact complex and contradictory, and that women did possess agency in negotiating such power relationships. While Southwell is neither silent

---

[84] The concepts originate in the writings of St Augustine and Peter Lombard; see Marcia L. Colish, *Peter Lombard*, 2 vols. (Leiden: E. J. Brill, 1994), I. 365.

[85] STC 1710 Thomas Becon, *The worckes of thomas becon* (London: John Day, 1564), vol. I, f. DClxxiiii^v. See also STC 13014 William Heale, *An apologie for women* (Oxford: Joseph Barnes, 1609), p. 54.

nor unquestioningly obedient, she explicitly does not contradict Puritan morals for wives and husbands, but rather manipulates them to her own ends, just as she manipulates the misogynist traditions of manuscript lyrics. She imagines Christ as a new man, and Adam as a blockhead, but nevertheless her model of a husband seldom departs from conventional Puritan literature.

Such playfulness is perhaps unusual in women's religious poetry, but it is important not to allow Southwell's wit to blind us to the fact that she is writing as part of a tradition. If feminist criticism has moved beyond chaste, silent and obedient, there is still an understandable tendency to view women writers as trapped in gendered concepts of authorship. The fact that Lady Anne Southwell the critic of men is the same Lady Anne Southwell whom Henry Sibthorpe called 'the compleate Character of ffemale perfection' ought to alert us that negotiating gender might be as much a sign of a woman's skill as of necessity. Feminist criticism has tended to assume that conscious theorising of gender is a privilege enjoyed only at this end of history. When Lady Anne Southwell the ideal and Lady Anne Southwell the critic are read together, and alongside other gentry and noble women of the period, it becomes apparent that early modern women were capable of being participants in, rather than victims of, the gender politics of their times.

CHAPTER 4

Public worship and private thanks in Eliza's babes

On 25 July 1652, George Thomason, owner of a collection of tracts now in the British Library, purchased a slim duodecimo volume titled *Eliza's babes: or, the virgins-offering*. Like *The countess of lincolns nurserie* (1622), *Eliza's babes* is often mistaken for a children's book; but in fact the 'babes' are poems and prose meditations, brought forth through the 'marriage' of the author to Christ. 'Looke on these Babes as none of mine', she cautions in the prefatory poem 'TO MY SISTERS':

> For they were but brought forth by me;
> But look on them, as they are Divine,
> Proceeding from Divinity[.][1]

As even that brief epigraph suggests, the metaphor of marriage to Christ serves as a primary vehicle of poetic authority in this small but remarkable volume. It consists of ninety-five devotional poems (seventeen of four lines or shorter) followed by thirty-two prose meditations (ranging in length from a few lines to a few pages) and closed by a statement beginning 'Wings my Doves you have now obtain'd' that is obviously derivative of Herbert's 'Easter Wings'. The mere existence of such a *printed* collection of devotions from a woman not associated with a radical sect is unusual in itself. Even more exciting for scholars of early modern women is the controlling presence of marriage and birth metaphors that justify the author's 'publique thankes', as she calls the act of sending her 'babes' out into the world.

Despite these striking qualities, *Eliza's babes* has, until very recently, received little academic attention, even from scholars of early modern

---

[1] Wing E535C *Eliza's babes* (London: M. S. for Laurence Blaiklock, 1652), sig. Aᵛ, ll. 1–4. There are two extant copies, one in the University of Illinois library and one in the Thomason Tracts collection in the British Library (number E 1289). All subsequent references are from the edition by L. E. Semler, *Eliza's Babes: or The Virgin's Offering (1652): A Critical Edition* (Madison, Wisconsin: Fairleigh Dickinson University Press, 2001). I have used the page numbers of the original, which Semler's edition includes in brackets.

women. The book's obscurity seems due to a combination of its scarcity, a mistaken assumption that it is intended for children and the preference of many feminist scholars for texts that are either religiously or politically radical or of high literary quality, of which *Eliza's babes* is neither.[2]

Eliza, it must be said, is no thwarted Judith Shakespeare, nor a lost Katherine Philips or Lucy Hutchinson.[3] Her poetry is conventional in much of its imagery, unimaginative in its word choice and occasionally sacrifices sense to preserve metre by adding or omitting monosyllables. What is fascinating about *Eliza's babes* is not, for the most part, its aesthetic qualities, but the author's attempt to negotiate her entrance into print in terms that are not always straightforwardly gendered. In her preface 'To the Reader', and in the poems and meditations themselves, Eliza continually foregrounds her reasons for making these initially 'private' devotions 'public' by having them printed. For feminist scholars interested in how the power negotiations of public and private speech were inflected by gender, such a clear awareness of these issues on the part of an early modern woman is a treasured find, a chance to explore a woman's own entry into printed authorship beyond the limitations of prescriptive literature or 'reading' silences within women's texts.

As with all such early modern texts, feminist critics must be careful not to project their own gender politics onto *Eliza's babes*. Helen Wilcox suggests that the devotional subject position of the book 'offers a freedom to the speaker that is all the more notable when the voice is female'.[4] This proposition opens up a number of questions that deserve further exploration. How aware is Eliza herself of the gendering of her voice? Does

---

[2] Helen Wilcox treats *Eliza's babes* alongside other early modern women's devotions in '"My soule in silence"? Devotional Representations of Renaissance Englishwomen', in *Representing Women in Renaissance England*, ed. Claude J. Summers and Ted-Larry Pebworth (Columbia, Missouri: University of Missouri Press, 1997), pp. 9–23; as does Elizabeth Clarke in 'Ejaculation or Virgin Birth? The Gendering of the Religious Lyric in the Interregnum', in *'This Double Voice': Gendered Writing in Early Modern England*, ed. Danielle Clarke and Elizabeth Clarke (Basingstoke: Macmillan, 2000), pp. 208–29. Liam E. Semler has written several scholarly studies of the book's theology: 'Who is the Mother of *Eliza's Babes* (1652)? "Eliza," George Wither, and Elizabeth Emerson', *Journal of English and Germanic Philology* 99.4 (2000): 513–36; 'The Protestant Birth Ethic: Aesthetic, Political and Religious Contexts for *Eliza's Babes* (1652)', *ELR* 30.3 (2000): 432–56; and 'The Creed of *Eliza's Babes* (1652): Nakedness, Adam and Divinity', *Albion* 33 (2001): 185–217. The author kindly sent me copies of the last two articles before they were available in print. Eliza is also mentioned in Elaine Hobby, *Virtue of Necessity: English Women's Writing 1649–1688* (Ann Arbor, Michigan: University of Michigan Press, 1989), pp. 55–9; and a few of her poems are anthologised in Germaine Greer *et al.*, eds., *Kissing the Rod: An Anthology of Seventeenth-Century Women's Verse* (London: Virago, 1988), pp. 141–7.

[3] For the sake of simplicity I refer throughout this chapter to the author of *Eliza's babes* as 'Eliza', although I recognise that it is important to distinguish between the author-persona and the author herself.

[4] Wilcox, '"My soule in silence?"', p. 14.

she register a sense of transgression with regard to her writing? How closely is this transgression linked with gender?

Underlying all of these questions are the unstable categories of public and private that underpin so many judgements about the 'freedom' of women writers. There is still a tendency to assume, as Wilcox's statement suggests, that women were more free to write in private forms, such as devotional meditation, and that the perceived privacy of these forms justified their entrance into the public medium of print. Such assumptions may suggest more about our post-Lockean notions of the relationship between privacy and gender than they do about any seventeenth-century woman's experience of writing. The following chapter seeks to define these terms in the specific devotional context of *Eliza's babes*, revealing how one woman writer created a new paradigm of public and private that justified both her entrance into print and a radical theology of marriage.

LIFE AND INFLUENCES

But who was the 'mother' of these 'babes'? Eliza's identity and politico-religious affiliation have been a point of contention, and it is worth pausing to consider these issues, as they have a direct effect on the religious and literary influences for which I will argue. She gives no clues to her family name in the text, and the few identifying characteristics – the initials of two sisters (or possibly one married sister), the deaths of her father and brother, her own visit to Elizabeth of Bohemia at the Hague – are suggestive but insufficient for any firm identification.[5] It seems apparent that she was a gentlewoman: the title page of *Eliza's babes* attests that it was '[w]ritten by a LADY', and her visit to the exiled court at the Hague also suggests at least gentry status. Her social position may have limited the severity of opposition she faced; although her writing was criticised, she seems never to have been threatened with the spectre of violence that haunted Anna Trapnel, the daughter of a shipwright who could take no refuge in her class.[6]

Beyond these bare facts, however, Eliza remains tantalisingly anonymous. Liam Semler attempts to pinpoint her identity in 'Who is the Mother of *Eliza's Babes* (1652)?', but acknowledges that there is as yet no hard evidence for his claim that she is Elizabeth Emerson, the wife of George Wither. Semler's argument hinges not on the few identifying characteristics in the book itself but on religious and political affinities he discerns between Wither and the author of *Eliza's babes*.

---

[5] See *Eliza's babes*, pp. 8, 27, 38, 79, 23–24.   [6] See chapter 5 for Anna Trapnel.

Along with others who have tried to identify her, Semler's scholarship runs against the obstacle of Eliza's clever concealment of her true position. *Eliza's babes* is poised between the crisis of the regicide in 1649 and the erosion of Parliamentarian ideals that led to the formation of the Protectorate in the end of 1653. Like so many texts in this volatile period, *Eliza's babes* adopts a tone of deliberate obscurity to avoid the persecution that was the fate of those with beliefs at either extreme of the politico-religious spectrum. Such obscurity was typical of poets politically disenfranchised after 1649, both dispirited royalists and disaffected republicans. Lucy Hutchinson's oblique references to political events in *Order and disorder* are one example; and the continuing critical confusion over the loyalties of Marvell's 'An Horatian Ode' proves that such slipperiness was an effective way of disguising potentially dangerous views.[7] Adding to this obscurity is the fact that, as Lois Potter has argued, royalist and sectarian literary styles were often similar, as both drew on Biblical models of history, albeit for different purposes.[8]

The combination of obscure style and literary and theological cross-fertilisation make it extremely difficult to define Eliza's religion or politics. Liam Semler, for example, marshals considerable evidence that Eliza, like Wither, was familiar with Baptist, Presbyterian and Independent theology. *Eliza's babes*, in Semler's reading, is an enthusiast 'book of experiments', similar to those by 'experimental' Calvinists who examined their own life experiences for evidence of election.[9] In spite of the evidence for these influences, however, Semler's conclusion that Eliza was on the radical end of the religious spectrum remains suspect because it ignores the frequent parallels of doctrine among seemingly opposing factions during the Caroline period. Semler makes much, for example, of the influence of Richard Sibbes, one of the best examples of a moderate who underwent a radical makeover. In his own time, Sibbes was fiercely critical of Laud but loyal to Charles I, and it was only after his death that his sermons were appropriated for radical causes.[10] As the later sections of this chapter demonstrate, Eliza's concept of experiential, practical piety does not necessarily indicate religious dissent or radicalism. Her experimentalism might as easily have originated

---

[7] See chapter 6 for Lucy Hutchinson. For the critical debate over 'An Horatian Ode', see Nigel Smith, *Literature and Revolution in England, 1640–1660* (New Haven, Connecticut: Yale University Press, 1994), pp. 277–8; David Norbrook, *Writing the English Republic: Poetry, Rhetoric and Politics, 1627–1660* (Cambridge: Cambridge University Press, 1999), pp. 243–71.

[8] Lois Potter, *Secret Rites and Secret Writing: Royalist Literature, 1641–1660* (Cambridge: Cambridge University Press, 1989), especially pp. 208–10.

[9] Semler, 'The Protestant Birth Ethic', p. 444; Introduction, pp. 20–1.

[10] See chapter 1 above, and Mark E. Dever, *Richard Sibbes: Puritanism and Calvinism in Late Elizabethan and Early Stuart England* (Macon, Georgia: Mercer University Press, 2000), pp. 27–48, 71–95.

in loyalist, moderate and Puritan divines such as Joseph Hall and Daniel Featley.

If Eliza's religious affiliation is difficult to define, her political sympathies are even more suggestively obscure. Elaine Hobby and the editors of *Kissing the Rod* assert that Eliza was a royalist. Liam Semler contradicts this assumption, offering as evidence a reading of the poem 'To the King, writ, 1644': 'something of an informal petition to Charles I' that came 'sometime between the royalist defeat at Marston Moor in 1644 and the end of the Uxbridge negotiations of winter 1644–45'. Semler argues that this poem is in line with Parliamentary proposals to Charles, the *Solemn league and covenant* (1643), and especially Wither's *Vox pacifica* (1645) and *Prosopopoeia britannica* (1648), all urging the king to surrender for the greater good of the nation.[11]

While it would certainly be a mistake to read 'To the King' as evidence of fanatical support of the monarch, I would argue that it would also be a mistake to read the poem as a sign of Parliamentarian or anti-royalist alliances.[12] As Elizabeth Clarke points out, 'To the King' could easily demonstrate Eliza's royalist sympathies; for many loyal to Charles I were also urging a settlement in 1644.[13] Given its date, the fact that the poem advocates peace proves little about the author's politics.

There are, however, other elements of the poem that suggest a royalist inclination. 'To the King' retains an explicit parallel of Charles I to Christ: 'My Prince by yeelding won the field, / Be not too rigid, dear King yeeld[.]'[14] Although this comparison is not notable in itself – Eliza considers any elect individual ultimately comparable to Christ – it is suggestive when read alongside her prose meditation 'The Royal Gods':

And shall not wee, who know from whom and by whom Kings reigne, think our Princes to be as they are stil'd by that great King, who set them to reigne for him? God forbid, but that we should so think of them, and they of themselves. He is the great God of the world, and hath set them as lesser Gods under him, to governe and protect that people over which he hath plac'st them. The people must then honor their King, as a God under him, not observe or adore him above him; and hee must esteem himselfe as a God tool; if he be of that great immortall race he

---

[11] Greer, *et al.*, eds., *Kissing the Rod*, pp. 141–7; Hobby, *Virtue of Necessity*, p. 55; Semler, 'The Protestant Birth Ethic', p. 437, and 'Who is the Mother of *Eliza's Babes* (1652)?', pp. 525–7.
[12] Semler himself agrees that the poem is 'by no means in essence antimonarchal', Introduction to *Eliza's Babes*, p. 16.
[13] Clarke, 'Ejaculation or Virgin Birth?', p. 219. See also J. S. Morrill, *The Revolt of the Provinces: Conservatives and Radicals in the English Civil War 1630–1650* (London: Longman, 1980), pp. 97–114 and the petitions from Clubmen in royalist counties excerpted on pp. 196–200.
[14] *Eliza's Babes*, p. 23, lines 9–10.

will not degenerate, but will be like to him: He will be like a fiery pillar in the night of ignorance and darknesse, to direct them which way they shall walk; and as a cloud in the day of persecution, to keep them from the pursuing adversary[.]¹⁵

In imagery and its use of Biblical language, this meditation closely echoes the absolutist rhetoric in sermons and royal writings of the 1620s and 1630s. Most telling are the references to Psalm 82:6, 'I have said, ye are gods' and Proverbs 8:15, 'By me kings reign', two of the principle proof-texts of the notorious Maynwaring sermons on *Religion and allegiance* (1627).¹⁶ In the 1640s and 1650s, the use of such proof-texts was refuted by republicans like Milton, who in *The tenure of kings and magistrates* (1649) warns against the danger of assuming that the king is accountable only to God: 'for if the King feare not God, as how many of them doe not? we hold then our lives and estates, by the tenure of his meer grace and mercy, as from a God, not a mortal Magistrate'.¹⁷ Eliza's use of scripture is the opposite of Milton's; she argues that not only should the people admit that the king is 'a God under' God, but that if the king himself would acknowledge his divine heritage then he would understand his divine responsibility. This is a subtle critique of Charles I, far from the iconoclasm of Milton but in line with disaffected royalists who did not find Charles's behaviour sufficiently kingly or divine.¹⁸

In keeping with its indirect criticism of Charles, 'The Royal Gods' ends on an ambiguous note: '[Kings] thus imitating thee, their great patterne, shall be blessed by thee with eternall renown, and crowned by thee in immortal glory: but first thou hast said, *They must dye like men*.'¹⁹ Ostensibly, the italics of the final phrase indicate that this is a quotation from scripture (Psalm 82:7, a stern warning to unjust judges), but here the

---

¹⁵ *Ibid.*, p. 71.
¹⁶ STC 17751 Roger Maynwaring, *Religion and alegiance: in two sermons preached before the kings maiestie* (London: I[ohn] H[aviland] for Richard Badger, 1627), pp. 3–4, 11–12. Donne also makes use of these texts in several sermons, *The Sermons of John Donne*, ed. George R. Potter and Evelyn M. Simpson, 10 vols. (Berkeley, California: University of California Press, 1953–62), I.233, 240; II.313; III.183, 290, 385; IV.135, 187, 246–7, 333; VI.194, 297; VIII.121. See also Kevin Sharpe, 'Private Conscience and Public Duty in the Writings of Charles I', *The Historical Journal* 40.3 (1997): 643–65, and 'Private Conscience and Public Duty in the Writings of James VI and I', in *Public Duty and Private Conscience in Seventeenth-Century England: Essay Presented to G. E. Aylmer*, ed. Paul Slack, John Morrill and Daniel Woolf (Oxford: Clarendon Press, 1993), pp. 77–100.
¹⁷ Merritt Y. Hughes, ed., *Complete Prose Works of John Milton*, 8 vols. (New Haven, Connecticut: Yale University Press, 1962), III:204. On royalist and Parliamentarian polemic in the 1640s, see Smith, *Literature and Revolution*, pp. 98–114.
¹⁸ In keeping with his view of Eliza as a Parliamentarian, Semler reads 'The Royal Gods' as a denial of the divinity of the king, a reading which to me seems possible only if the grammar of the passage is distorted; Introduction, *Eliza's Babes*, p. 18.
¹⁹ *Eliza's Babes*, p. 72.

typography has the additional effect of making the sentence read like a
warning. It is possibly a warning to Charles (actual or posthumous, since
the meditation may have been drafted before 1649) or even a warning to his
successor, Cromwell, to remember that he as a mortal man may die as his
enemy did. The ambiguity is further advanced by the previous sentence in
the meditation, which reminds the 'Royal Gods' – kings or generals – that
death is the surest way to eternity and glory. Read through this lens, the
meditation might be seen to cast Charles I's death as martyrdom. All of these
political possibilities are wrapped up and concealed, in the unexceptionable
theological point that kings, like all the elect, are in fact mortal men who
must die to be taken up in glory. Such political sleight-of-hand is typical of
Eliza's babes, which makes veiled references to enemies and religious leaders
that must have been intelligible only to the author's immediate circle.[20]

Whatever her opinions of the king and kingship, that Eliza was no fan of
Cromwell is clear in her poem 'To Generall Cromwell'. Although merely
opposing Cromwell did not make one a royalist (witness John and Lucy
Hutchinson), the poem's accusation that 'thou'rt the rod that scourgeth
mee', coupled with the revised absolutism of 'The Royal Gods', suggests
that, like many other royalists, Eliza endured the loss of her property and
curtailment of her liberties in the 1650s. The second half of the poem to
Cromwell supports this reading:

> Sith Kings and Princes scourged be,
> Whip thou the Lawyer from his fee
> That is so great, when nought they doe,
> And we are put off from our due.[21]

To be 'put off from our due' suggests not religious persecution but unfair
seizure of goods, a hypothesis supported by the hints in 'To the Queen
of Bohemia' that hardship forced Eliza to make a longed-for visit to the
Hague.[22] Did the sequestration of their property compel Eliza and her
husband to plead with the exiled queen for assistance? Or was Eliza a
political exile? Both of these possibilities seem likely. Her true situation
may never be known, but what is apparent from these glimpses of her
politics is that although she felt let down by Charles I, she found Cromwell
a tyrant. There is more evidence of political scepticism than of political
conviction in *Eliza's babes*, a scepticism that suggests confused, post-1649
royalism more than it does radical or dissenting politics. That she was the

---

[20] See, for example, the prose meditations 'Security in Danger', pp. 99–100, and 'The secure Pavillion',
p. 101, in *Eliza's Babes*.
[21] *Eliza's Babes*, p. 54, lines 4, 9–12.   [22] *Ibid.*, pp. 23–4, especially lines 5–8.

wife of George Wither, a Parliamentarian (although a bit of a failure as a politician), seems highly unlikely.[23]

PUBLIC AND PRIVATE PRAYER

The format of *Eliza's babes*, self-consciously modelled upon Herbert and his imitators, provides further evidence of Eliza's moderate Protestant royalism. In style, subject matter, and even their brief titles ('The Invocation', 'The Rapture') her poems clearly partake of the tradition of Herbert imitation best exemplified by Henry Vaughan's *Silex scintillans* (1650; augmented 1655). Nigel Smith explains that Herbert's lyrics 'came to have an impeccable authority as a kind of manual or handbook on the godly parish, which was, of course, the most immediate and vital context for the religious politics of the Interregnum'. In invoking such a tradition, Eliza situates her verse as part of the same project of combining the courtly and the sacred, the simplicity of the word and the outward show of ceremony and furnishing, into a Protestant 'middle way'.[24]

Eliza's self-conscious invocation of the moderate ecclesiology of Herbert and Vaughan is in keeping with her devotional heritage. Vaughan described his poems as an attempt, with Herbert, to write '*A true Hymn*': a solemn but simple exercise of devotion in which the believer communicated directly with heaven.[25] Such devotional practice is consistent with the writings of moderate, peace-making divines like Daniel Featley, Isaac Ambrose and most especially Joseph Hall. As Peter Lake has recently demonstrated, men like Hall occupied a middle ground of conformist Stuart churchmanship, a vast and contentious space accommodating clergy of widely differing ecclesiastical policies.[26] Isaac Ambrose, although he ultimately supported Parliament and Presbyterians, nevertheless enjoyed royal favour in the 1630s.[27] Even after the polarising events of the 1640s, royalist politics did not necessarily go hand-in-hand with ceremonialist episcopacy. It should

---

[23] Semler is by no means certain of his identification, ending 'Who is the Mother of *Eliza's Babes* (1652)' with the admission, 'I do not regard the hypothesis I have presented as a closed case', p. 536.

[24] Smith, *Literature and Revolution*, p. 266. See also Helen Wilcox, 'Exploring the Language of Devotion in the English Revolution', in *Literature and the English Civil War*, ed. Thomas Healy and Jonathan Sawday (Cambridge: Cambridge University Press, 1990), pp. 80–3; and Clarke, 'Ejaculation or Virgin Birth?', p. 214.

[25] Louis L. Martz, ed., *George Herbert and Henry Vaughan* (Oxford: Oxford University Press, 1986), p. 347. See Smith, *Literature and Revolution*, pp. 265–72.

[26] Peter Lake, 'Joseph Hall, Robert Skinner and the Rhetoric of Moderation at the Early Stuart Court', in *The English Sermon Revised: Religion, Literature and History 1600–1750*, ed. Lori Anne Ferrell and Peter McCullough (Manchester: Manchester University Press, 2000), pp. 167–85.

[27] See DNB, s. v. Isaac Ambrose.

therefore come as no surprise to find a pious royalist such as Eliza drawing on godly Calvinists who were simultaneously loyal to Charles I and opposed to Archbishop Laud. Their guides to meditation influenced both Eliza's devotional experience and her concepts of private and public with regard to her own writing.

The first half of the seventeenth century saw the publication of numerous how-to guides to prayer, meditation and devotion, which together amounted to a kind of primer to practical Christianity that was particularly influential among 'experimental' Christians such as the author of *Eliza's babes*. These handbooks were extremely popular, and extend back at least as far as Lewis Bayly's *The practice of pietie*, first printed 1612 and in its twenty-fifth edition by 1630.[28] A paradigmatical example is Isaac Ambrose's *Media: the middle things* (1649/50), which attempts to compile from the vast corpus of English divinity 'The Means, Duties, Ordinances, B O T H Secret, Private and Publike, For continuance and increase of a Godly life, once begun, till we come to Heaven'. Although the programme *Media* prescribes may seem rigorous to a modern reader, the whole aim of the book is to make Christianity pragmatic, accessible and unambiguous to ordinary unscholarly Christians. While there is no direct evidence that Eliza used *Media*, as an 'experimental' Christian she would have reached for such 'wholesom Directions' from another exemplary believer to guide her own self-examination: 'that which issues from the heart of an experimental Christian, usually reacheth to the heart of such as labor after the like Experience', as John Waite writes in a commendatory epistle to Ambrose's book.[29]

Media and other guides like it emphasise the paramount importance of prayer, devotion and meditation in the Christian life. Although these three activities are recognised as separate, the boundaries between them are blurred. Meditation ('a deep and earnest musing upon some point of Christian instruction') leads to prayer ('that which seasoneth all other seruices which we offer vnto God') which yields a life of devotion ('a constant intertainment of our selves here below with the God of spirits, in our sanctifyed thoughts, and affections'). Together these three bring to the believer an infusion of the heavenly into the earthly, so that he or she is constantly reminded of the presence of God, 'so walking on earth, that he

---

[28] STC 1601.5 Lewis Bayly, *The practice of pietie* (London: W. H. for John Hodgets, 1612) and STC 1609 *The practice of pietie* (London: for Robert Allot, 1630). See also Richard McCabe, *Joseph Hall: A Study in Satire and Meditation* (Oxford: Clarendon Press, 1982), pp. 146–7.

[29] Wing A2958 Isaac Ambrose, *Media: the middle things* (London: John Field for Nathaniel Webb and William Grantham, 1649/50), sig. A^r, b^r.

doth in a sort carry his heaven with him'.[30] Such an apprehension of the divine was at the core of what it meant to be 'Godly', and was the primary duty of every believer.

Yet even if these duties were essential to the Christian faith, they were not easily practised or understood, as the existence of so many handbooks with titles like *A helpe vnto deuotion* (1608) suggests.[31] 'Meditation' in this period could refer to spontaneous thoughts on a religious subject; Ambrose terms this '*Occasional* or *Extemporal Meditation*', and lay Christians such as Anne, Lady Halkett often used this term to describe their own devotional jottings in spiritual journals. More specifically it signified a form of intense methodical contemplation – '*Deliberate, set*, or *solemn Meditation*' – that was ultimately derived from Catholic devotional practice.[32] Chapter VII of Ambrose's book, for example, 'Of the nature and kindes of Meditation', borrows a 'Scale of Meditation' from Bishop Joseph Hall's oft-reprinted *The arte of divine meditation* (1606). The 'Scale' itself is a translation of the *Scala Meditatoria* in the *Rosetum exercitorum spiritualium et sacrarum meditationum* of Joannes Mauburnus (1494). This highly influential book popularised directed meditation in Continental circles and ultimately dictated the shape of the *Spiritual Exercises* of St Ignatius Loyola, to whom, as Louis Martz has demonstrated, all roads of meditation in seventeenth-century England ultimately lead. Hall's version of the 'Scale' guides the meditator in 'Degrees of Preparation', 'Degrees of proceeding in the vnderstanding', 'degrees of affection', and a conclusion, each with intermediate steps.[33] For his lay readers, the Presbyterian Ambrose simplifies 'the understandings' as he calls them, to aspects of the object of meditation ('In its Causes', 'In its Properties' etc.) rather than the abstruse scholastic thought processes prescribed by Mauburnus and Bishop Hall ('Tractation', 'Dijudication'),

---

[30] *Ibid.*, p. 136; STC 13406.3 Samuel Hieron, *A helpe vnto deuotion* (London: H. L. for Samuel Macham, 1608), sig. A3ᵛ; Wing H422 Joseph Hall, 'The devout soul', in *Three tractates* (London: M. Flesher for Nathaniel Butter, 1646), pp. 8, 104. See also STC 10726 Daniel Featley, *Ancilla pietatis* (London: for Nicholas Bourne, 1626), especially pp. 2–3.

[31] See previous note.

[32] Ambrose, *Media: the middle things*, p. 136. The spiritual diaries of Anne, Lady Halkett are in the National Library of Scotland, MSS 6489–6502. See also McCabe, *Joseph Hall*, pp. 152–3, 182.

[33] Chapter VII of *Media* begins on p. 136. Louis L. Martz, *The Poetry of Meditation: A Study in English Religious Literature of the Seventeenth Century* (New Haven, Connecticut: Yale University Press, 1954). Appendix 1: 'Mauburnus, Hall, and Crashaw: the "scale of Meditation"', pp. 331–7, offers a schematic comparison of *The arte of divine meditation* and the *Rosetum*. Chapter 4, 'Problems in Puritan Meditation: Richard Baxter', pp. 153–75, describes the use of the 'Scale' and Ignatian meditation in Baxter's *The saints everlasting rest* (1649/50). Hall initially rejected the 'Scale' in favour of a simpler method, but nevertheless incorporated much of it into his work; see McCabe, *Joseph Hall*, p. 182.

but despite such adaptations the method remains essentially the same for practitioners of meditation from all breeds of Christianity.[34]

While Eliza's meditations do not follow precisely the steps prescribed by Ambrose and his predecessor Joseph Hall, it is apparent that she experienced the devotional state that was the goal of such meditation, a kind of enthusiastic union with God. Many of her prose passages, in particular, read like the conclusions to Ignatian meditations, the 'colloquies' in which the soul speaks ecstatically to God and is answered in turn.[35] 'My Lord!' she often begins, addressing God directly rather than contemplating him as an object of meditation. Her phrases flow out in a kind of joyful excess, and if she expresses doubts they are quickly overcome by assurance of her election.[36]

Such passages in *Eliza's babes* most resemble Joseph Hall's devotional works of the 1640s, small books (octavo or less) such as *The devout soul* (1646) and *Christ mysticall; or, the blessed union of Christ and his members* (1647). In his final years Hall became increasingly mystical, his lifelong practice of Continental forms of devotion culminating in a near-ecstatic outpouring of holy love.[37] 'With much labour therefore,' Hall contends, 'and agitation of a mind illuminated from above, we must find our selves wrought to an high, awfull, adorative, and constant conceit of that incomprehensible Majesty, in whom we live, and move, and are[.]' These works urge the believer to a 'kinde of ecstaticall amazement' in perceiving 'the infinite goodnesse of thy God, that hath exalted thy wretchednesse to no lesse then a blessed and indivisible Union with the Lord of glory'.[38] This awe is primarily an emotional response: 'it is better felt than vnderstood', averred Daniel Featley in his influential guidebook *Ancilla pietatis*. Featley, Hall and others emphasise that the most important function of meditation and devotion is not to understand God, but to love him: 'the end of this *Duty* is not to practise Logick, but to exercise Religion, and to kindle Piety and Devotion', for, 'if there bee some that haue much zeale, little knowledge, there are more that haue much knoweledge without zeale'.[39]

[34] Ambrose, *Media: the middle things*, p. 141.
[35] For Ignatian 'colloquy', see Martz, *The Poetry of Meditation*, pp. 27, 36–7; McCabe, *Joseph Hall*, p. 314.
[36] See, for example, 'On Eccles. 9.7. *Goe eat thy bread with joy, &c*', *Eliza's Babes*, pp. 80–2.
[37] McCabe, *Joseph Hall*, pp. 313–15, also p. 178.
[38] Joseph Hall, *The devout soul*, pp. 10–11; Wing H374 *Christ mysticall* (London: M. Flesher for William Hope, Gabriel Beadle and Nathaniel Webbe, 1647), p. 6.
[39] Featley, *Ancilla pietatis*, p. 2; Ambrose, *Media: the middle things*, pp. 141; STC 12643 Hall, *The arte of divine meditation* (London: H. Lownes for Samuel Macham, 1607), p. 9. On the role of affective piety in Hall, see McCabe, *Joseph Hall*, p. 175.

Eliza's babes serves as a record of achievement of such zeal for heaven, as she testifies in her 'Invocation':

> Aspire, aspire, my minde, aspire,
> From earthly things unto the higher.
> Set not thy minde on base desires,
> But thinke upon the heavenly Quires,
> Of Angels sweet, that singing be,
> And still the face of God doe see.[40]

In poem after poem Eliza moves '[f]rom earthly things unto the higher', explicitly rejecting the priorities of this world for the sake of her devotional goal:

> *Eliza* for, aske now not here,
> She's gone to heaven, to meet her Peer.
>
> This earthly state's, too meane for mee,
> Ile flee where the bright Angels bee[.][41]

The 'flee from the world' theme is common enough in religious poetry of this period; after all, St Paul warns all Christians not to be conformed to this world, but to be transformed by the renewing of their minds.[42] But renewal of the mind is a flexible and subjective concept, as Eliza herself suggests in the meditation 'Upon the Temptation of the doubting of Heaven', in which she debates whether the afterlife 'is a fancy of a studious braine, and writ to keep people in awe to human obedience'. The truth of such beliefs can only be judged through '[r]eason and experience', but since the experiential evidence for heaven is paltry, ultimately Eliza must rely on the fact that the belief itself is profitable: 'it is so just and pleasing to my soul' that she ought to live as if it were true regardless of whether it actually is.[43]

Such reasoning opens the possibility for Eliza to justify almost any extreme she can reach in her devotional zeal. All of the 'flights' to heaven recorded in her poetry and meditations are open to the same accusation as her belief in heaven: that they arise only out of her own fancy, and have nothing to do with reason and knowledge. But they can also be justified with the same reasoning: that if they *feel* 'just and pleasing', it does not matter if they are true. Her apprehension of heaven must always be right, even if it contradicts orthodox 'truths'. As the discussion later in this chapter

---

[40] *Eliza's Babes*, p. 2, lines 9–14.
[41] 'The Flight', p. 11, lines 1–2; 'The Rapture', p. 10, lines 5–6, in *ibid.*
[42] Romans 12:2.   [43] *Eliza's Babes*, pp. 90–1.

demonstrates, her view of both human and heavenly marriage undoubtedly crosses the line of orthodoxy but remains justified by her recourse to
emotional piety.

For all of its potential unorthodoxy, Eliza's position is only a logical extension of the Calvinist devotional guides. Although Featley and Hall undoubtedly possessed much knowledge themselves, their focus on 'affection' in
devotion is potentially profoundly anti-intellectual; taken to its greatest
extreme it allows a believer like Eliza to justify her experience not intellectually but solely through intensity of emotion. Hall attempted to guard
against these deviations by warning that meditation should 'be not either
too farre-fetcht, or fauouring of Superstition'; in other words, the imagination must not be allowed free rein, 'in which case our thoughts proue
loose & heartlesse; making no memorable impression in the mind', and the
believer must guard against beginning to worship the object of meditation.
But the line between the reasonable and the far-fetched is never clearly
drawn, and Hall's own prose often climbs to exorbitant heights.[44] Jeremy
Taylor, less sympathetic towards Puritan Christianity than Joseph Hall,
appended a catechism to his guide to daily devotion – 'a short Summary of
What is to be Believed, Practised, Desired' – in order to anchor meditative
practice firmly in orthodox doctrine.[45] *Eliza's babes* serves as proof that such
fears were not entirely unwarranted; her meditations on mystical marriage
in particular (discussed later in this chapter) challenge traditional gender
norms as she insists her position as bride of Christ precedes her status as an
earthly woman and wife.

Eliza gains power from more than the emotional excesses of devotional
literature; she also borrows the guides' emphasis on the privacy of devotion.
Such 'privacy' is a necessary corollary to union with God: in order to
achieve 'prepossession of heaven' the earthly believer must spurn all worldly
associations. This clearing of the mind, or 'Excussion', is an early and
essential part of the 'Scale of Meditation'.[46] It is meant to be accompanied
by a physical sequestration: 'priuate Deuotion', as Daniel Featley succinctly
puts it, 'alwaies shuts her selfe vp in her closet'. Isaac Ambrose states the
matter less poetically: 'We judge solitariness and solitary places, fittest for
Meditation[.]'[47] Such 'privacy' that is both physical and mental not only has

---

[44] Hall, *The arte of divine meditation*, pp. 17–18. See McCabe, *Joseph Hall*, pp. 178, 307, 313–15.

[45] Wing T336 Jeremy Taylor, *The golden grove* (London: J. F. for R. Royston, 1655), title page. Featley also added a catechism to *Ancilla pietatis*: STC 10739 *The svmme of saving knowledge* (London: George Miller for Nicholas Bourne, 1626).

[46] Hall, 'The devout soul', p. 1; Martz, *The Poetry of Meditation*, p. 334.

[47] Featley, *Ancilla pietatis*, p. 2; Ambrose, *Media: the middle things*, p. 137. Richard McCabe argues that Hall deliberately links his meditation technique to the personal devotion advocated by the Puritans, *Joseph Hall*, p. 153.

the practical effect of preventing distractions to the meditator, but more importantly allows for an attentive interiority in which the believer can converse directly with God. The resulting experience is one of profound intimacy: 'A mans own soul is not so intimate to himselfe, as God is to his soul; neither doe we move by him only, but in him: What a sweet conversation therefore, hath the holy soule with his God? What heavenly conferences have they two, which the world is not privy to[?]'[48]

It is this sense of privacy as withdrawal from the world which Eliza invokes in her epistle 'To the Reader' defending the printing of her works. In the early modern period, as now, 'privacy' was a multifaceted term that suggested multiple associations: individual, family, society, state and all of the complex and interconnecting relationships among these spheres. Eliza's writing plays with the possibilities of the term but anchors it in its specific devotional meaning from the beginning of the epistle, when she reminds the reader that the idea to publish was confirmed in her during the act of 'private' meditation: 'But rising one day, from my Devotions, it was suggested to my consideration, that those desires were not given me, to be kept in private, to my self, but for the good of others.' The words 'to be kept in private' do indeed have the connotation of modest withdrawal from society – and, in this case, a literary audience – a limitation which conventional wisdom still imposed upon women. But by linking that phrase with a very different kind of 'private' activity, and one which she would not regard as limiting or self-repressive, Eliza opens the possibility for a new paradigm of what is 'public' and 'private' with entirely different gender associations.[49]

Eliza builds this framework by associating her literary activity explicitly with devotional practice. It would, she contends, be a form of ingratitude to keep her devotions to herself: 'nor can I smother up those great and infinite blessings, that I have received from him, with private thankes', she writes, the word 'thankes' itself suggesting a devotional act. Eliza cleverly opposes the 'private thankes' she had previously rendered in her intimate devotions to the 'publique thankes' she now proposes to make by printing her works: 'And was so great a Prince, not ashamed to avow so great affection and love to mee, and shall I be ashamed to returne him publique thankes, for such infinite and publique favours?'.[50] As a kind of printed act of prayer, her volume participates in the long-standing debate about the efficacy of private versus public prayer and whether these should be prescribed or extemporaneous, exemplified by responses like Jeremy Taylor's *A discovrse concerning prayer extempore* (1646) to the Westminster *Directory for the*

---

[48] Hall, 'The devout soul', pp. 12–13.   [49] *Eliza's Babes*, sig. A2^r.   [50] *Ibid.*, sig. A2^v–A3^r.

publique worship (1645).[51] Like Herbert and his imitators, Eliza takes part in this debate by addressing a handful of poems to specific liturgical occasions: 'The Friday before Easter', 'On Easter day', 'On the day dedicated to the God of Heaven' and, most tellingly, 'Being taken with a sudden pain on the Day appointed for God's publick Service'. In 'On going to the Sacrament' in particular she declares her intention to go 'to some publick place' to partake of the Eucharist, which in the 1650s suggests prayer-book or possibly Presbyterian churchmanship.[52] Writing a poem on the experience is also a way of connecting a collective, liturgical act of worship to closeted personal devotion.

In doing so Eliza echoes Featley and others who set the private spiritual act of devotion against the public act of worship in a congregation. These two acts are not opposites but exist on a continuum, and feed one another, as Featley asserts in the opening paragraph of *Ancilla pietatis*:

Premeditation is the Preparation to priuate prayer; priuate to publike; priuate, and publike to the hearing of the Word; priuate, and publike prayer, together with the hearing of the word to the worthie participation of the holy Sacrament. For the Sacrament receiues strength and vigour from the word; the word preached from publik prayer; publike prayer from priuate Deuotion; and that from premeditation[.][53]

In essence 'private' and 'public' devotion is the same act with the same end; the difference is only a matter of degree. Viewed in such a framework, as she obviously intends it to be, Eliza's 'public' act of publishing her writing cannot earn her the charge of immodesty. She is not setting forth into the world where her virtue may be threatened; she is merely rendering an act of worship, albeit a 'public' one, that is the duty and privilege of all Christians, male or female. Her 'publique thankes' are also explicitly aligned with Christ's 'publique favours' and 'publique death', sacrificial acts that serve as the model for all Christians.

Equating one's own words with Christ's was, of course, a defence any Christian could use, and hundreds of preachers defended the printing of their sermons through similar conceits. What is fascinating about Eliza's framework is the added element of gender, or rather, perhaps, the absence of it. Hers is a very backhanded form of transgression, one that refuses to engage with the meanings of 'private' and 'public' that would open a

[51] Wing T312 Jeremy Taylor, *A discovrse concerning prayer extempore* ([London]: 1646); and Wing D1546 *A directory for the publique worship of God* (London: Evan Tyler, Alexander Fifield, Ralph Smith and John Field, 1645).
[52] *Eliza's Babes*, pp. 13, 31, 48, 58 l. 3.   [53] Featley, *Ancilla pietatis*, p. 1.

woman author to the persecutions feared by Anna Trapnel. Instead, Eliza effaces those gendered definitions of public and private, creating a new, internally consistent paradigm in which her book serves as an act of devotion and must be judged as such, regardless of the author's gender. Any attempt to misconstrue the book or its author's intentions is a misunderstanding of Christian devotion itself that casts doubt on the critic's own piety.

MYSTICAL MARRIAGE IN *ELIZA'S BABES*

Even as she attempts to establish a new paradigm in which she is judged for her piety before her gender, Eliza is aware that she is under threat from other competing standards of womanly behaviour. Her text repeatedly betrays anxieties that her work will be misread. 'Looke on these Babes as none of mine', she cautions in the epigraph quoted earlier in this chapter, and the title page itself declares the book '[w]ritten by a LADY, who onely desires to advance the glory of GOD, and not her own'. She clearly anticipates '[b]eing told, she was proud', as one of her poems is titled; and to defend herself she reaches for the protective metaphor of marriage to Christ, through which she cleverly connects her 'private' and 'public' activity under the unimpeachable authority of a divine husband.[54]

In the early modern period as now, the marriage ceremony served as a public acknowledgement of what was essentially a private relationship: 'Dearly beloved friends, we are gathered together here in the sight of God, and in the face of his congregation, to join together this man and this woman', or so the Elizabethan prayerbook marriage service began.[55] Marriage was 'of Publique interest in every Commonwealth', asserted the Westminster *Directory for the publique worship*: a way for the community to recognise the knitting together of two persons' social and economic capital, their emotional unity ('mutual society, help, and comfort'), and their sexual intimacy ('for a remedy against sin, and to avoid fornication').[56] Eliza makes use of the intersection of the private and the public in marriage by putting forth her 'marriage' to Christ as the public defence of her private intercourse with him. Like human children, her 'Babes' are born in an act of the utmost intimacy, but she is careful to make clear that these 'Babes' are

[54] *Eliza's Babes*, p. 39.
[55] John Booty, ed., *The Book of Common Prayer 1559: The Elizabethan Prayer Book* (Charlottesville, Virginia: University of Virginia Press, 1976), p. 290.
[56] *A directory for the publique worship of god*, p. 58; Booty, ed., *The Book of Common Prayer 1559*, p. 291, 290.

no bastards: 'for before I knew it, the Prince of eternall glory had affianced mee to himselfe', she confirms in the preface, 'and that is my glory'.[57]

This relationship amounts to a kind of divine *couverture*, the early modern legal principle whereby married women had no standing in civil courts. Wives were instead 'covered' by the legal identity of their husbands, who were meant to represent their wives' interests in all matters.[58] Eliza clearly regards herself as 'covered' in this fashion by her 'husband's' righteousness: 'I might now behold my selfe, as cloathed with thy self', she asserts, altering the Biblical image of the saints clothed in the white of Christ in order to demonstrate that her entire nature – and any accountability for her actions – has been swallowed up in the glory of Christ: 'that my mortall nature might be made immortall, by being joyned to thy divinity'. Like Anna Trapnel, Eliza thus positions herself so that any criticism of her devotional activity becomes a criticism of her 'husband', and an implication that the marriage is not legitimate: 'for such a strict union is there betwixt my deare God and mee, that his glory is mine, and mine is his'.[59]

But unlike Anna Trapnel, Eliza never claims that the spirit spoke directly through her, and so cannot rely too heavily on the principle of *couverture*, with its attendant implication that women should be silent while their husbands speak for them. In order to create a model of mystical marriage that authorises rather than silences her speech, Eliza develops an extended allegory of Christ as a 'Prince of Peace', who rescues her with 'publique favours':

That Great Prince of Heaven and Earth, proclaimed by Angels, that he was come into the world, to shew his good will and love to mee; was here content, to dye a publique death for me, to save me, from a Hell of misery; in which I lay, and should have layen, had not he, the Prince of Peace, and the fairest and chiefest among the sons of men, shed his most precious and royal blood, for mee; and before he dyed he left word, that I should not feare, for it was his great and glorious Fathers will, to bestow on us a Kingdome. And was so great a Prince, not ashamed to avow so great affection and love to mee, and shall I be ashamed to returne him publique thankes, for such infinite and publique favours?[60]

It is no coincidence that of Christ's many titles Eliza has chosen 'Prince of Peace': a prince is not only a royal figure but a public official. In fact, she

[57] *Eliza's babes*, sig. A2ʳ.
[58] See Susan Dwyer Amussen, *An Ordered Society: Gender and Class in Early Modern England* (Oxford: Basil Blackwell, 1988), p. 72.
[59] *Eliza's Babes*, p. 69; sig. A2ʳ.
[60] *Ibid.*, sigs. A2ʳ–A3ʳ. Similar passages are in the poem 'To a Lady unfaithfull', pp. 40–1, and the prose meditation 'The true Object of Love', pp. 94–6, in *ibid*.

seldom refers to her 'Prince' by any name other than this title, a tactic that
helps exclude other potential readings of her relationship with Christ just as
she effaces other implications of 'public' and 'private'. Like a good monarch
acting to preserve a subject, Eliza's 'Prince' intervenes for her in the public
'world' and then claims a private relationship with her, a relationship that
is his right by virtue of the 'publique favours' he has bestowed. 'He then
with his fierce enemy did fight, / To reingain you as his ancient right', the
author advises in 'To a Lady unfaithfull'.[61]

   In addition to his traditional role as the 'Prince of Peace', Eliza's 'Prince'
also takes on some of the characteristics of the medieval image of Christ
as a knight and lover. In 'To a Lady unfaithfull', for example, the narra-
tor admonishes an unnamed woman for abandoning the 'chast love, so
pleasing and so sweet' of her 'dear sweet Prince' for a 'wanton Paramour'.[62]
The use of courtly love epithets for Christ was part of a very long tradition of English allegory sprinkled liberally through sermons and devotional
works in the seventeenth century.[63] The most extended version of the lover-
knight tale is Francis Rous's *The mysticall marriage*, discussed in the first
chapter of this study. Rous subtitled the book 'Experimentall Discoveries of
the heavenly Mariage betweene a Soule and her Saviour'; in good Calvinist
tradition, it describes how the soul experiences doubt and sin and then
is ravished again by her lover, Christ. In keeping with this 'experimental'
focus on self-examination and the potential of falling away, Rous, as I have
argued, emphasises the great social difference between the soul and her
lover, so that in the final consummation her will is entirely swallowed up
in his greater righteousness.[64]

   Unlike Rous, Eliza does not focus on her own inferiority, but instead
makes Christ her model for superiority: Christ's 'publique favours' and
'publique death' become an imperative for her own 'publique thankes'.
'[L]ove cannot, will not be silent', she declares: 'If you him love you may be
bold[.]' Because her 'Prince' has rendered his services to her in the public
sphere, she must, in keeping with the social code, return those favours in a
public manner. Not to speak would be to deny his sacrifice: '*I being wedded
to Heavens King, / As his blest Spouse must his praise sing*' she concludes at
the end of a prose meditation aptly termed 'My Contract', the very title

[61] *Ibid.*, p. 40, lines 16–17.   [62] *Ibid.*, p. 40, lines 8, 12, 9.
[63] For the medieval tradition of knight-lover allegories, see Frances Beer, *Women and Mystical Experience in the Middle Ages* (Woodbridge, Suffolk: The Boydell Press, 1992), pp. 56–77.
[64] STC 21343 Francis Rous, *The mysticall marriage* (London: W. Jones and T. Paine for I. Emery, 1635). The book is 350 pages in 18mo.

of which reinforces her perspective of her own speech as a social and even legal obligation.[65]

As with Lucy Hutchinson's principle of conscience, Eliza's paradigm of public devotion as a contractual imperative ultimately enables her to override even the limitations of gender.[66] 'But shall my womanish fear make thee loose thy glory; My God it must not!' she cries in 'The Acknowledgement', cleverly invoking a gender stereotype in order to overturn a gender standard. Even if publishing her writing opens her to accusations of pride or immodesty unbecoming a woman, she is under an obligation to ignore such 'womanish fear': 'Thy glory must so dazle mine eyes, that I must not regard the censure of the world.' Although she acknowledges the 'weakness' of her sex, she views it as something to be despised and overcome, which must not hinder her duty to write for God: 'though I finde it a thing now adays done but by few; and so by doing it, may make my self a wonder, and ridiculous to the world, and some other womanish reasons', 'I dare not say, I am an ignorant woman, and unfit to write'.[67]

Eliza tackles the issue of gender and calling head-on in 'The Royall Priest-hood'. 'Peace!' she demands,

Present now no more to me (to take my spirit from the height of felicity) that I am a creature of a weaker sex, a woman. For my God! If I must live after the example of thy blessed Apostle, I must live by faith, and faith makes things to come, as present; and thou hast said by thy servant, that we shall be like thy blessed Son: then thou wilt make all thy people as Kings and Priests. Kings are men, and men are Kings; And Souls have no sex; the hidden man of the heart, makes us capable of being Kings; for I have heard it is that within makes the man; then are we by election capable of as great a dignity as any mortall man[.][68]

Eliza here highlights and exploits a fundamental conflict of early modern gender politics, between woman as the 'weaker sex' and the fact that in Christ there is neither male nor female (Galatians 3:28). Women were enjoined to be silent in public worship but were simultaneously expected to walk the same Christian path as any man. When public speech, whether oral or in writing, becomes a universal Christian duty, as it does in Eliza's writing, then women are faced with the necessity of choosing between their duty as believers and the gendered morals that would keep them silent.

---

[65] 'The true Object of Love', p. 95; 'The renowned King', p. 26, line 22; 'Hosea 2.19 My Contract', p. 67, in *Eliza's Babes*.

[66] See chapter 6 for Lucy Hutchinson.

[67] 'The Acknowledgement', p. 77; 'My Redemption acknowledged', p. 87; 'The Support', p. 75, in *Eliza's Babes*.

[68] *Ibid.*, p. 100.

Eliza confronts this choice by erasing the distinctions of gender. She seizes upon the supposed fact that in the afterlife there will be no gender, and since 'faith makes things to come, as present', she must live as if this revolutionary change has already occurred. This is not merely wishful thinking, but part of the Christian imperative to live heavenly values on earth: 'I will close the eyes of my Soul, to mortality', she declares, thereby suggesting that those who do have their eyes open to distinctions of gender are living in sinful mortality rather than in consciousness of heaven. Although she states her case with supremely assured logic, Eliza must be aware of the radical nature of her stance; as Liam Semler notes, she even misappropriates St Peter's phrase 'the hid man of the heart' which he uses to demonstrate that women should have 'a meek and quiet spirit' (1 Peter 3:4).[69] The end of her passage returns to the calling to speak that permeates her writing: 'And as a Royall Priest *must* I be to thee'. Eliza's phrasing here combines two grammatical connotations of the word 'must': the 'must of logical deduction' and the imperative. It is a trick that neatly encapsulates the way she elides the distinction between future equality and present inequality. She can logically conclude that in heaven she will be a 'Royall Priest', singing praises to God, because this is how all of the saints, gender unspecified, are depicted in Revelation 7:9–17; but serving as a priest by praising God also has the force of a command for her earthly life. That she 'must' sing 'public' praises by printing her devotions is both reasonable and necessary, and overrides any 'weakness' of gender in this life or the next.[70]

This complete denial of gender differences – in reality in heaven, and in apprehension of that reality on earth – is particularly startling because of Eliza's heavy reliance on gendered metaphors to authorise her text. For a writer so familiar with mystical marriage imagery to declare 'Souls have no sex' is striking: souls were traditionally feminine, particularly in mystical marriage allegories. Francis Rous ties himself in knots attempting to describe the relationship between a female soul, a male body and the male husband, Christ; and the gender of the soul is implicitly exploited by writers such as Lady Anne Southwell and Anna Trapnel, who imply that their gender makes them more fit for marriage with Christ. Eliza is in this way more radical than either of these women: although she insists on her marriage to the 'Prince', ultimately she does not legitimise her writing through her gender but rather in spite of it.[71]

---

[69] *Ibid.*; Semler, 'The Protestant Birth Ethic', p. 454.   [70] *Eliza's Babes*, p. 101, emphasis added.
[71] Rous, *The mysticall marriage*, pp. 31–3; see also chapters 3 and 5.

One gendered implication of mystical marriage in *Eliza's babes* does deserve further exploration. Although she does not claim a privileged access to her 'Prince' because of her gender, Eliza does contend that her marriage to him obviates the need for another gendered duty: human marriage. In her youth, Eliza tells us, she was so zealous in her devotion that she fled from the world not only metaphorically but literally:

> I did withdraw me from the stage
> Of this vain world, in my best age,
> Thinking for heaven thou hadst bedrest,
> So I retired for my rest.

So extreme was her 'retirement' from the world that the young Eliza fervently wished to die, preferably as a Protestant martyr, a wish she expressed in poems with appropriate titles like 'The Submission' and 'The worlds farewell'.[72] We must be careful, of course, of reading such confessional poems as expressing an objective autobiographical truth. Yet, given the emphasis on lived experience in Eliza's Calvinist spirituality, it is appropriate to treat the 'autobiographical' poems of *Eliza's babes* as constructions of a woman's experience much like those in the spiritual journals it emulates. Like a spiritual journal, *Eliza's babes* provides an exemplary version of lived religious truth, but the value of such examples was always perceived to be their basis in experience.[73] Regardless of whether the poems in *Eliza's babes* correspond to the author's actual experience, they were meant to be perceived as doing so.

In *Eliza's babes*, the author constructs her younger self as harbouring an unusual death wish in conjunction with a hope that was potentially even more radical: a wish to remain unmarried so that she might devote herself to God.[74]

---

[72] 'My Second Part', p. 51, lines 1–4; pp. 14, 16, and see 'The Support', p. 74, for her desire that she 'might have offered up my life in flames', *Eliza's Babes*.

[73] Elizabeth Clarke, 'Conflagration, Coincidence, Conscience: the Journal of Elizabeth Jekyll', paper given at the Trinity–Trent Colloquium, Nottingham Trent University, 4 November 1998.

[74] Eliza's desire for virgin autonomy draws on a long tradition of men and women shunning sexual relations to devote themselves to God, a choice still available in her own day to the Catholic women who joined Continental cloisters. For women in particular, the choice of virginity could mean liberation from family and kinship ties. See Heather Wolfe, ed. *Elizabeth Cary Lady Falkland: Life and Letters* (Cambridge: Cambridge University Press, 2001). Karen Armstrong, 'The Acts of Paul and Thecla', and Eleanor McLaughlin, 'Women, Power and the Pursuit of Holiness in Medieval Christianity', both in *Feminist Theology: A Reader*, ed. Ann Loades (London: SPCK, 1990), pp. 83–8, 99–120; and Barbara Newman, *From Virile Woman to WomanChrist: Studies in Medieval Religion and Literature* (Philadelphia: University of Pennsylvania Press, 1995), p. 4.

> Sith you me ask, Why borne was I?
> I'le tell you; twas to heaven to fly,
> Not here to live a slavish life,
> By being to the world a wife.[75]

Although it was a conventional aspect of mystical marriage that one who was not married to Christ was married to the world, and thus devoted to earthly values, it is clear from the previous poem that the young Eliza believed earthly marriage itself to be contrary to her desire to live in heaven. In this poem, 'The Heart', the speaker addresses a human lover who has offered his heart to his beloved. It is a gift she cannot accept, she explains, because her own heart

> . . . is in Heaven, and will admit no change,
> To leave my rest in heaven, on earth to range.
> I'de have it written in my happy story,
> None had my heart but heav'ns great prince of glory
> My youths affection, to him I did send,
> None can have any but what he will lend.
> From mortall thraldome deare Prince keep thou me
> So though on earth, I as in heaven shall bee.[76]

Strong words indeed: for Eliza, human love and human marriage are not merely undesirable, they are a 'mortall thraldome', a 'slavish life' that is potentially so worldly that it will prevent her from living out the devotional life she yearns for. She does have some practical reasons for preferring celibacy – most wives are 'troubled' and 'live in strife' – but for the most part her reasons are entirely theological, based on a surprising literalisation of the mystical marriage metaphor.[77]

Eliza simply cannot have two husbands, even one on earth and one in heaven, for how can she be intimate with a human husband and still enjoy the privileged intimacy she knows with Christ? In 'The Gift' she pleads with Christ not to give away her love to a human husband:

> To thee I onely gave my heart,
> Wouldst thou my Lord from that gift part?
> I know thou wouldst deliver me
> To none, but one belov'd by thee.

[75] 'The Bride', p. 31, lines 1–4, *Eliza's Babes*.   [76] 'The Heart', p. 30, lines 7–14, *ibid*.
[77] 'The change', p. 44, lines 3–4, *ibid*.

> But Lord my heart thou dost not give,
> Though here on earth, while I doe live
> My body here he may retain,
> My heart in heaven, with thee must reigne.[78]

This is a shocking belief for a supposedly Puritan young woman. To argue that a human husband should have only his wife's 'earthly part', her body, but her heart and love belong solely to God, contradicts all Puritan literature on marriage of the time, which placed a primary emphasis on the role of love and companionship – 'mutual society, help, and comfort' – in marriage. In a typical combination of orthodoxy and radically emotionalised devotion, Eliza arrives at this position not through an original unorthodoxy but by stretching orthodoxy to its extreme, playing upon the fact that Puritan wives were required to submit firstly to God and only secondly to their husbands. No Puritan divine would have agreed that a heart devoted to God was incompatible with a heart devoted to a human husband, or that a husband's right was only to the wife's body. The very suggestion hints that marriage is a kind of physical prostitution. For Eliza, the opposite is true: to be emotionally devoted to two husbands is a kind of adultery.

Eliza arrives at this unique position by actively implementing what is meant to be primarily metaphorical, or at least only spiritual. Her descriptions of Christ as a lover do not differ much in their enthusiasm from the tone of Rous:

Let thy spirit then looke and long, and lust for this Lord who is the spirit, the chiefest spirit; let it cleaue to him, let it hang about him, and never leave him till hee be brought into the chambers of thy soule.[79]

Or Hall:

Out of the sense of this happy union ariseth an unspeakable complacency and delight of the soul in that God and Saviour, who is thus inseparably ours, and by whose union we are blessed; and an high appreciation of him above all the world; and a contemptuous under-valuation of all earthly things, in comparison of him; And this is no other then an heavenly reflection of that sweet contentment, which the God of mercies takes in the faithfull soul; *Thou hast ravished my heart, my sister, my Spouse*[.][80]

Hall ends his passage with an extensive list of quotations from the Song of Songs, from which such expressions of ecstasy in Christ's love ultimately

---

[78] 'The Gift', p. 42, lines 5–12, *ibid.*   [79] Rous, *The mysticall marriage*, pp. 13–14.
[80] Hall, 'The devout soul', pp. 54–5. The passage goes on to quote the Song of Songs 4:9, 6:4–5, 5:10, 8:6, 2:5.

derive. But in all of their emotionalised paeans to divine love, neither of these writers could have imagined the extremes to which Eliza takes the notion of cleaving to Christ and being 'contemptuous' of all earthly things. By adhering strictly to the principle that her devotion should be 'felt rather than vnderstood', the young Eliza arrives at a unique and radical position in which her heights of love for Christ override any earthly duties.

Given Protestant societal pressures, this stance may be untenable for a gentlewoman, even one as devout as Eliza. Ultimately Eliza consents to marriage, as she explains in 'The change' and 'My Second Part': because God has given her a husband so good '[a]s if of heaven, he were elect', Eliza finds it is no struggle to submit to him. For Eliza, the experience becomes further evidence of her dependence on God – 'For thou alone that blisse canst send' of a devout husband who will not hinder his wife's devotion – while for twenty-first-century readers, Eliza's attitude to her marriage hints at the lack of control such gentlewomen had when choosing the man they would be required to obey. [81]

Even this cautious recantation of her commitment to virgin autonomy is limited, as is suggested merely by the title of the poem 'Not a Husband, though never so excelling in goodness to us, must detaine our desires from Heaven' – the very length of this title, compared with Eliza's usual pithiness, may be evidence that the idea was so radical that it was difficult to express in contemporary English. In 'The change', Eliza reveals that she was chiefly pleased in her husband because he did not attempt to take her heart from Christ, but instead worked

> To take all trouble quite from me,
> That earths possession here doth bring,
> And so doth leave me quite to thee,
> Thy praises here to sit and sing.[82]

In 'My Second Part', although she consents to marriage that '[w]e happy in that life may be', she goes on to reiterate that no earthly husband can be as devoted or caring as 'Heavens Prince', who emerges as the better husband by far.[83] In the end, although she is reconciled to human marriage, Eliza never agrees that her husband may have even a portion of her love:

> Great blessings from him I injoy,
> And with him I have no annoy,
> Yet these must not retaine my heart,
> Another of me claims his part.

---

[81] 'The change', p. 44, line 9; 'My Second Part', p. 52, line 18, *Eliza's Babes.*
[82] P. 45; 'The change', p. 44, lines 10–13, *ibid.*   [83] 'My Second Part', p. 52, lines 16, 21, *ibid.*

To heavens great prince I must away,
No love on earth here must me stay.
He lent me but awhile to you,
And now I must bid you adieu.[84]

Her human husband is good and does not distract her, but he can never be Christ, and she will never consent to share her love.

Such a position is particularly surprising in a woman of Eliza's status, who as a gentlewoman would have been expected to marry in order to enhance her family's property and connections. Just as she did when confronted about the propriety of a 'weak woman' printing her poems, Eliza prioritises her personal devotional imperative above all other gendered standards of behaviour. She is called to one marriage, a divine marriage, and the social and religious duty of women of her class to find a human husband must fall before this greater calling. It is, curiously, a fundamentally emotional calling. It is the possession of her heart, not her intellect, that concerns Eliza; and the only 'freedom' she desires is the freedom to be emotionally and spiritually united with Christ, and to express that union publicly.

In the beginning of this chapter I raised the question of whether it was possible to define the concept of 'freedom' in *Eliza's babes*. Does her devotional voice allow her 'freedom' as a writer, and is this a particularly gendered 'freedom'? Such questions require a carefully nuanced answer: although Eliza's commitment to emotionalised excesses does lead her to a number of surprising and even challenging positions, the 'freedom' she exercises operates chiefly on the devotional spectrum I discussed earlier in this chapter. Whether writing in 'private' or in 'public' Eliza always views her words as primarily a communication with God, and the implication of her work for other women's – or even her own – 'public' persona as a writer, as a twenty-first-century critic would understand that phrase, must be examined with great care.

One point I have sought to demonstrate in this chapter is that Eliza's challenge to gender hierarchies, although unusual, is always carefully constructed as orthodox. Along with many other women of her time, she does not challenge the prevailing norms of Christianity, but rather exploits the contradictions of the New Testament, which not only orders that women be silent in churches but simultaneously declares that in Christ 'there is neither male nor female'.[85] In modern feminist terms Eliza's might be considered

---

[84] 'Not a Husband . . .' p. 45, lines 9–16, *ibid*.
[85] Galatians 3:28. For prohibitions on women's speaking, see for example I Corinthians 14:34–35.

a conservative position, because it preserves the prime tenets of Calvinist Christianity, the supremacy of Christ and the necessity for every believer to test his or her experience for evidence of election. Along with the work of Lucy Hutchinson, Fanny Burney and Christina Rossetti, *Eliza's babes* challenges modern critics to accept the possibilities for female agency inherent in such moderate and even conservative religious and political positions.[86]

When reading *Eliza's babes*, therefore, we must be careful to define 'freedom' in the author's own terms, even if these are not as radical as our own. Although I have used the term 'radical' to describe Eliza's position, it is in fact only radical in its departure from the norm, in its surprising extremes and idiosyncratic moral standards. In seventeenth-century terms, Eliza is in fact no radical, politically or religiously: she displays little millenarianism, scant political vision, no concern with alerting her readers to the country's plight. Her single-minded devotion to Christ she clearly designates as her own calling, and although she does advise others to love and even marry Christ, nothing in the text hints that she saw her own extremes of celibacy as desirable for the world. Her gender politics are also highly personalised: she is concerned with defending herself and her own devotional project, and does not seem interested in defending other women or engaging in these debates beyond her own personal interest in printing her poems.[87]

And yet the fact remains that *Eliza's babes* had an audience, or at least was intended for one. Were *Eliza's babes* a manuscript (and missing its bold preface), like so many women's spiritual journals it would be difficult to label as 'public' or 'private': were these meditations genuinely composed in the author's closet, or did she always have an audience in mind? The façade of self-enclosure is, of course, deliberate, and is integral to the whole psychology of the Puritan spiritual exemplar of which Eliza partakes. Anyone who reads *Eliza's babes*, or any spiritual journal, is invited to share and emulate another's most intimate religious experience. A manuscript copy could even perpetuate the fiction that the reader was witnessing such

---

[86] On Lucy Hutchinson, see Christopher Hill, *The Experience of Defeat: Milton and Some Contemporaries* (London: Faber and Faber, 1984), p. 21; N. H. Keeble, '"The Colonel's Shadow": Lucy Hutchinson, Women's Writing and the civil war', in Healy and Sawday, eds., *Literature and the English civil war*, pp. 227–47; and David Norbrook's response to Keeble in 'Lucy Hutchinson's "Elegies" and the Situation of the Republican Woman Writer (with text)', *English Literary Renaissance* 27 (1997): 468–521. On Fanny Burney, see Julia Epstein, 'Burney Criticism: Family Romance, Psychobiography, and Social History', and Susan C. Greenfield, '"Oh Dear Resemblance of Thy Murdered Mother": Female Authorship in *Evelina*', both in *Eighteenth-Century Fiction* 3.4 (1991): 277–82, 301–20. On Christina Rossetti, see Jan Marsh, *Christina Rossetti: A Literary Biography* (London: Jonathan Cape, 1994).

[87] Semler takes the opposite position in 'The Protestant Birth Ethic', p. 454.

experiences at first hand, or at least as they were first recorded: the copy of Elizabeth Jekyll's spiritual journal made more than thirty years after her death is nevertheless 'signed' by her.[88] As a printed book *Eliza's babes* cannot maintain that illusion, but instead openly contributes to the efforts of Herbert, Vaughan and their followers to use personal piety as a way to model the ideal religious subject. I use the term 'subject' with deliberate awareness of both its possible meanings: Eliza clearly constructs for herself a powerful subject position, but crucial to this position is her role as a subject of both divine and human monarchs. The handful of political poems in her book may seem atypical among the mass of personal devotions, but in fact all of the poems and meditations together contribute to one of the vital political debates of the 1650s: how the Puritan person could also be a pious citizen.

To point out the political nature of her writing is not to dismiss Eliza's piety. On the contrary, it is the sincerity of her devotion that makes Eliza such a useful model of citizenry, at a time when the connection between theology and political philosophy was highly charged and continually changing. Religion is not merely a code, it is the message itself, and for us as twenty-first-century critics *Eliza's babes* serves as an example of how religious decisions were intrinsically – if not necessarily straightforwardly – political and social decisions.

But does this constitute 'freedom' for Eliza as a woman writer? *Eliza's babes* is an interesting case in point because it authorises itself almost entirely by denying distinctions of gender. This strategy, of course, in itself suggests how fraught gendered moral standards might be for a woman writer, particularly a pious woman writer. As a woman, Eliza cannot print her devotions without transgressing, yet she cannot view herself as a true Christian unless she does print them. Similarly, she cannot but face pressure and criticism if she chooses to remain unmarried, but she also cannot maintain her calling to be married to Christ if she loves a human husband. Negotiating gender, choosing among competing standards and defining her own notions of 'public' and 'private' were crucial choices for any woman writer, whatever her politics. The 'freedom' of *Eliza's babes* hardly constitutes a call to arms for all women who cannot speak, although it does provide an example of one who does. Rather it looks forward to a time when all women will be able to speak, when piety will be judged before gender.

---

[88] Beinecke Library Osborne MS b.221; Clarke, 'Conflagration, Coincidence, Conscience: the Journal of Elizabeth Jekyll'.

CHAPTER 5

Anna Trapnel 'sings of her Lover'

In December 1654, at the end of Anna Trapnel's *annus mirabilis* of visions, missionary journeys and imprisonment, a Londoner confided to a friend about the puzzling experience of meeting a prophetess in the flesh:

As for your desires concerneing Anna Trapnell, it is (to be playne) to me a very strange dispensation, yet I am perswaded she hath communion with God in it, but under what sort to ranke it, I am at some stand. The dispensation is strange, because rare, more strange, because to me there appeares no such amongst the Scripture Records, as to the manner of it, for I cannot reckon it among the vissions and Revelations of the Lord, because in the thinges she utters (whether in verse or prose) it's onely what she hath beene conversant in before, and had the knowledge of . . . If she did continue in it but for one or two dayes, I should be apt to thinke she might do it when she would, in the strength of parts, save for two thinges. 1st. she is so stifned in hir Body that were she not warme one would thinke hir dead. 2^{ly}. Because (she saith) she cannot make a verse when she is hir selfe . . . And on the last day of the weeke she declared in my heareing, that she would be the next morning at the young mens meeting, which I much doubted, seeing how she lay, and had layne; so I went that morneing on purpose, and found hir there, she takeing me by the hand ere I was aware; she came out without eating, or drinking save a little small Beere, yet did not experience hir selfe weake, or fainte . . . I tould hir it was the opinion of some, that what she delivered was from the strength of hir naturall memorie? She answered, no? but throwne in by the Spirit to hir.[1]

If we were to describe this account in modern terms, we might say that this witness is *reading* Anna Trapnel: examining her experience (like a good Calvinist), considering the words she speaks and even the signs of her body, and comparing them to his own knowledge of human nature and

---

[1] Bodleian Library Rawlinson MS A 21, p. 325. MS A 21 is one of the files of John Thurloe, Cromwell's master of spies. The letter is signed 'B. T.' and headed 'Coppy of Another letter from London, Dated 21° – 10th – 54'. The addressee is not recorded and the letter was most likely intercepted by Thurloe, as the writer seems to sympathise in the second half of the letter with both the Fifth Monarchists and the Anabaptists, and distrusts the Protector (p. 324 – the letter is recorded backwards). The author is listed as an 'Anabaptist Leveller' in the Rawlinson catalogue.

the scriptures. The norm is nothing less than true inspiration: 'she hath communion with God in it', he concludes. Other witnesses who had seen her first highly publicised trance, a year earlier in the political heart of Whitehall, were less forgiving: 'some say what she doth is by a mighty inspiration, others say they suppose her to be of a troubled mind, and people flocking to her so as they doe, causeth her to continue this way, and some say worse, so every one gives their opinions as they please'. Yet even this sceptical newsbook account concludes with a list of evidence of inspiration that 'is visible to those that see and hear her'.[2]

Like all charismatic religious leaders, or even modern-day celebrities, Anna Trapnel and other women prophets of the 1640s and 1650s depended upon their visibility. If they were to be believed among the Calvinist masses of London, it was important that others be able to test their experiences. Yet at the same time they must carry themselves as 'sweet, meek, sober' and 'unblameable' women, chosen by the Lord as his instrument – not, like Quaker women, preaching boldly on street-corners.[3] As a result, there is a curious mixture of the passive and the active in the behaviour and writings of non-Quaker women prophets. At one moment Anna Trapnel is in a trance, under the scrutiny of a witness with whom she seemingly cannot communicate; at another she modestly seeks him out when he has come to test her – 'she takeing me by the hand ere I was aware', he reports – to defend her prophetic dispensation.

This tension between the agency of the woman who speaks for herself, and the passivity of the 'Empty Nothing Creature' who is a vessel for inspiration cuts across women's prophetic writings in this period.[4] It creates a difficulty for the feminist critic: such women open themselves to being read as signs, but at the same time are themselves manipulators – or, to use a more recent term, theorists – of gender. When Anna Trapnel herself says she speaks only what is 'throwne in by the Spirit to hir', it is difficult to balance a desire to respect her experience of inspiration with a need to explore the agency of an outspoken early modern woman.[5]

---

[2] *Severall proceedings of state affaires*, no. 225 (London: Robert Ibbitson, 12–19 January 1653/54), pp. 3562–3. The same report is in *The faithful scout*, no. 161 (London: [no printer], 13–20 January 1654), pp. 1274, 1276.

[3] Letter from John Proud and Caleb Ingold, lay leaders of Trapnel's congregation, Wing T2032 Anna Trapnel, *A legacy for saints* (London: for Thomas Brewster, 1654), sig. A3ᵛ. On Quaker prophecy see Phyllis Mack, *Visionary Women: Ecstatic Prophecy in Seventeenth-Century England* (Los Angeles: University of California Press, 1992), especially pp. 166–7.

[4] Wing J688, Henry Jessey, *The exceeding riches of grace advanced* (London: by Matthew Simmons for Henry Overton and Hannah Allen, 1647). The quotation is from the title.

[5] Significant feminist scholarship on Trapnel and other women prophets includes: Phyllis Mack, *Visionary Women*; Jane Shaw, 'Fasting Women: The Significance of Gender and Bodies in Radical Religion

This chapter balances an awareness of the woman prophet's 'nothingness' with an analysis of the discourses that enabled her to speak with the voice of authority. For many women prophets of this period, these two poles were not as far apart as they might appear to a twenty-first-century critic. As the previous chapter demonstrated, careful examination of the theology of public and private religious action reveals that private godliness existed on a continuum with public devotion and speech, and that, for men at least, each was expected to feed the other. For women, the connections between public and private meant that it was possible to negotiate a space which occupied both realms at once: a paradigm most clearly visible in the experiences of women such as Anna Trapnel and Sarah Wight, attracting attention while lying prone on their beds. In order to contextualise Trapnel's experience alongside that of other women who spoke, wrote and printed widely and freely, the first half of this chapter looks closely at their prophesyings within the context of public and private spaces in the debate on women's religious speech in the 1640s and 1650s.

James Holstun has argued that such women 'created a sort of inter-private publicness' by ministering from within households, and his convoluted phrase indicates yet again the difficulties of imposing modern concepts of public, private and gender on early modern individuals.[6] As David Cressy wrote in 1994, studies of such women ought 'to question the coherence of the categories, and to wonder how long it would take for them to collapse'.[7] This is a difficult task – even the *Oxford English Dictionary* confesses that '[t]he varieties of sense [of the word public] are numerous and pass into each other

and Politics, 1650–1813' and Charlotte Sussman, 'Women's Private Reading and Political Action, 1649–1838', both in *Radicalism in British Literary Culture, 1650–1830: From Revolution to Revolution*, ed. Timothy Morton and Nigel Smith (Cambridge: Cambridge University Press, 2002), pp. 101–15 and 133–50. Diane Purkiss, 'Gender, Power and the Body: Some Figurations of Femininity in Milton and Seventeenth-Century Women's Writing' (unpublished DPhil thesis, University of Oxford, 1991), pp. 279–319, and 'Producing the Voice, Consuming the Body: Women Prophets of the Seventeenth Century', in *Women, Writing, History 1640–1740*, ed. Isobel Grundy and Susan Wiseman (Athens, Georgia: University of Georgia Press, 1992), pp. 139–58; Susan Wiseman, 'Unsilent Instruments and the Devil's Cushions: Authority in Seventeenth-Century Women's Prophetic Discourse', in *New Feminist Discourses: Critical Essays on Theories and Texts*, ed. Isobel Armstrong (London: Routledge, 1992), pp. 176–96; and Hilary Hinds, *God's Englishwomen: Seventeenth-century Radical Sectarian Writing and Feminist Criticism* (Manchester: Manchester University Press, 1996), also her introduction to her edition of *The cry of a stone* (Tempe, Arizona: Arizona Center for Medieval and Renaissance Studies, 2000). Because this edition modifies spelling, punctuation, typeface and other textual attributes, I have given page numbers from the edition in brackets but quotations from the original, Wing T2031 (London: 1654).
[6] James Holstun, *Ehud's Dagger: Class Struggle in the English Revolution* (London: Verso, 2000), p. 273.
[7] David Cressy, 'Response: Private Lives, Public Performance, and Rites of Passage', in *Attending to Women in Early Modern England*, ed. Betty S. Travitsky and Adele F. Seeff (Newark: University of Delaware Press, 1994), p. 187.

by many intermediate shades of meaning'. To add to the confusion, the word 'private' is very often a negative category (that which 'is not open to the public, or not publicly done or performed').[8] If designations of what is public are often relative and shift according to perspective, then what is private is often discernible only in context. By paying close attention to early modern contexts, this chapter aims to add to existing scholarship on Anna Trapnel and other women prophets by delimiting some of the shifting lines drawn around public and private spaces where women's speech is concerned.

In the second half of the chapter I use the results of this exploration to consider the role of mystical marriage in Trapnel's prophetic writing. Trapnel is notable among women prophets because of the length of her career and the voluminous quantity of her prophecies, but more significantly for her remarkable political agency. In April of 1654, a few months after her Whitehall 'debut', she was sent as a missionary of the Fifth Monarchist cause to Cornwall, and in 1658 ten months' worth of her prophecies were collected in a new Fifth Monarchist scripture.[9] She posed such a threat that those in power did not treat her as an unruly woman to be suppressed by a woman's punishment, but as 'a dangerous seditious Person' to be silenced for the safety of the Commonwealth.[10] The second half of this chapter considers how the manipulation of the discourses of public and private through the metaphor of mystical marriage may have enabled Trapnel to reach such a remarkable position in her own sect, and to avoid the gendered persecution inflicted on other women prophets. Trapnel's prophecy develops the notion of her privileged relationship with God as his 'married Wife', ultimately establishing the female speaker of the Song of Songs as a prophetic forerunner who, like the early modern women prophets, entered the public sphere only to 'sing[] of her Lover', Christ.[11]

PROPHETIC HERITAGE

Before considering what it meant for Anna Trapnel and other women prophets to negotiate a public voice, it is worth acknowledging the contrasts

---

[8] *Oxford English Dictionary Online* (Oxford: Oxford Unversity Press, 2000), 'public', A; 'private', A.5.c. Other relevant entries include B.3.a. 'in public' and B.6.b. 'in private'. On the 'residual character' of the private in eighteenth-century thought, see John Brewer, 'This, That, and the Other: Public, Social and Private in the Seventeenth and Eighteenth Centuries', in *Shifting the Boundaries: Transformation of the Languages of Public and Private in the Eighteenth Century*, ed. Dario Castiglione and Lesley Sharpe (Exeter: Exeter University Press, 1995), p. 8.

[9] Only one copy of this volume remains as Bodleian Library shelfmark S 1.42 Theology. There is no extant title page.

[10] Wing T2033 Anna Trapnel, *Anna trapnel's report and plea* (London: for Thomas Brewster, 1654), p. 52.

[11] Trapnel, S 1.42 Theology, p. 1.

these women encountered because of their differences in economic and social status. A glance at Trapnel's own accounts of her life as a spinster in London suggests that her dwindling economic means had a significant impact on her prophetic experience.

Anna Trapnell was baptised in the parish church of St Dunstan's, Stepney on 10 September 1620, the daughter of William Trapnel, a shipwright, and his wife Anne.[12] She grew up in the hamlet of Poplar, in the parish of Stepney to the East of London. Her father died when she was young (no will or burial records have been located) and her mother died around 1640, when Anna Trapnel was twenty. A shipwright in this period would likely have been a craftsman of respectable income; although nothing is known of William Trapnel's finances his daughter seems to have been well enough provided for. After her trial in Cornwall in 1654 she was at pains to establish her respectability and financial solvency, and particularly to defend herself against the charge of vagrancy. She reports that when orphaned she 'kept house with the means my Mother left me' and paid her taxes to support the army 'freely and willingly'. She also 'freely gave for the Armies use' from her legacy, sold her 'Plate and Rings, and gave the mony to the Publick use' and 'wrought many nights hard to get mony, the which I chearfully bestowed, not on my own back nor belly chear, but fared hard, that so I might minister towards the relief of the Nation'.[13]

James Holstun situates Trapnel among '[w]idows or maids of means' who maintained their independence by refusing to marry, but Trapnel's own account suggests that, however comfortably she began, along with many others the civil wars had reduced her to more strained circumstances.[14] At some unspecified time she left Poplar to live with various women friends and kin in neighbourhoods near the Tower and in Hackney, perhaps because she was no longer able to support herself.[15] During her imprisonment in Bridewell she relied on the goodness of her friends to pay her keep of five shillings a week, although she also reports that she had 'some means of my own' to help pay the cost.[16]

Trapnel's financial and social status bears significantly on her reception as a prophetess. She defends her moral respectability by pointing to the ministers who can attest to her reputation – among them the important figures of Henry Jessey and John Simpson – but does not claim any social intimacy with them. She is merely 'known' to them, but is not part of their

---

[12] Baptismal register of St Dunstan's, now Greater London Record Office X024/066.

[13] Trapnel, *Report and plea*, p. 50. It is not clear what kind of work Trapnel did when she 'wrought many nights', but there is surely no suggestion of prostitution or any other ungodly occupation.

[14] Holstun, *Ehud's Dagger*, p. 268. [15] Trapnel, *Report and plea*, p. 50. [16] *Ibid.*, p. 44.

circle.[17] Unlike the noblewoman Lady Eleanor Davies or Trapnel's fellow
Fifth Monarchist Mary Cary Rande, a 'Gentlewoman' whose learning
attests to her status, Anna Trapnel could not expect support or an open-
minded audience based on her social intimacy with the men in power.[18]
Cary Rande's texts make it clear that her exegesis of millenarian scriptures
is based on study, not direct inspiration. In fact, she specifically denies any
such mystical revelation: 'Here let me not be mistaken, as though I made
any comparison with the Prophets, or with those women in the Gospel, I
say not that I have any immediate revelation that the Witnesses are risen,
or that I have been told it by an Angel, or the like.'[19] Significantly, the
comparisons Cary Rande disavows are precisely those that Trapnel makes
for herself: the prophets and Biblical women. For a poorly educated woman
of the middling sort, it was more effective to claim to be inspired than to
speak for herself.

The sense of Trapnel's marginality is borne out by the language used
to describe her in prefaces written by the men of her congregation at
Allhallows. Trapnel is characterised as a 'handmaid', a 'Maid' and a 'simple
and unlikely hand'.[20] Although these epithets are laden with Biblical significance that is part of Trapnel's own complex authorising vocabulary, they are
also indicative of her class and marital status. Mary Cary Rande could not
be described as a 'handmaid', a title drawn from scripture which indicates
that a woman is a servant and in most cases unmarried. In the Authorised Version, the term 'handmaid' is used for Jacob's concubines, who are
the servants of his wives Rachel and Leah. It is also used by women who
wish to emphasise their apparent subservience to a man in power, much
as a contemporary of Trapnel's might describe himself as 'your servant' to
a social superior: Ruth, Hannah, Abigail, the witch of Endor, Bathsheba
and Judith all use the term of themselves as part of their persuasion and
manipulation of men.[21] Even the Virgin's use of the term in the Magnificat
(Luke 2:46–55) underlines the grace of God in deigning to notice such a
lowly servant. Many of these women appear in Trapnel's later prophecies
as examples of virtuous womanhood and analogues to her own prophetic

---

[17] Trapnel, *The cry of a stone*, p. 3 [6].
[18] Epistle by Christopher Feake in Wing C737 Mary Cary, *The little horns doom & downfall* (London: [W. H.] for the author, 1651), sig. a7[r].
[19] Wing C738 Mary Cary, *The resurrection of the witnesses* (London: H. Hills for R. C. and Thomas Brewster, 1653), sig. C4[v].
[20] Unsigned epistle 'To the little Remnant that are followers of the Lamb in this day, where ever it shal meet you' in Wing T2035 Anna Trapnel, *Voice for the king of saints and nations* (London: 1658), sig. A2[r]; unsigned epistle 'To all the wise Virgins in Sion', in Trapnel, *The cry of a stone*, sig. a2[r-v] [2].
[21] Genesis 30; Ruth 2:13; 3:9; 1 Samuel 1:16, 18; 25:24–5, 27; 28:22; 1 Kings 1:13, 17; Judith 11:5–6.

enterprise.[22] Although the primary nuance of the term as Trapnel herself uses it is metaphorical – her 'service' is to the Lord, like that of the Virgin Mary, the most famous 'handmaid' – when used by men in authority it also shows Trapnel's place within the community, and emphasises the miraculous nature of authoritative vision issuing from a person of lowly status. The exhortation 'let us not despise it, ecause [*sic*] it comes through a handmaid' points to both her gender and her social status as unlikely – and potentially despicable – vessels for the inspired message of God.[23]

An incident recorded in the state papers suggests that the tradition of inspiration for women of lower status had a longer history than is generally acknowledged. In March of 1629, when the assassination of Buckingham and the recent dissolution of Parliament made Charles I particularly anxious about popular unrest, a woman from the Cambridgeshire village of St Ives experienced trances that were an early (unsuccessful) application of the model of prophecy that would provide Trapnel and her contemporaries with a public voice. For a symbolically significant three days and nights, Jane Hawkins lay on her bed 'to preach in verse' and was attended by 'an Auditorye of very nere two hundred people, the most beinge of the weaker Sex'. As with Anna Trapnel, Jane Hawkins was supported and encouraged by women, but it was the men who provided the authority for her prophecy. In February 1654, the informer Marchamont Nedham would observe the leaders of Allhallows planning to print Anna Trapnel's verse just weeks after her first well-publicised trance in Whitehall; twenty-five years earlier, in April 1629, John Williams, Bishop of Lincoln, discovered the vicar, Job Tokey, his curate, Mr Wise and the local schoolmaster transcribing fair copies of Hawkins's verse with the intent to have it printed. Unlike Nedham, Williams was successful in quashing the little rebellion, confiscating both originals and copies of the verses, dismissing the curate and schoolmaster from the diocese, and forcing the vicar to recant in public.[24]

In letters recording the events, Williams justifies his actions with reasoning closely parallel to the accusations Anna Trapnel feared a quarter century later. Both women's economic and social value was in question: Trapnel was accused of vagrancy, while Jane Hawkins was 'of very badd fame' and 'but a pedlar'.[25] These factors clearly reflected on the credibility of their

---

[22] Trapnel, S 1.42 Theology, pp. 706–7, 928–31.   [23] Trapnel, *Voice for the king of saints*, sig. A2ʳ.
[24] Letter from Marchamont Nedham to Cromwell, 7 February 1653/4, PRO SP 18/66 no. 20. Letter from Williams to Secretary Dorchester, 28 April 1629, PRO SP 16/141 no. 63. Williams records that the trance began on 24 March. Phyllis Mack makes a somewhat garbled account of the events in *Visionary Women*, p. 77.
[25] PRo SP 16/141 no. 63. *Report and plea*, pp. 50–1. See also PRO SP 18/66 no. 20.

prophecy; as Nedham put it, 'the vulgar is a superstitious Animal', both more gullible and more likely to deceive.[26] The ignorance and theological simplicity of such women could make their sudden inspiration more believable, but it was also a potential Achilles heel. Just as the witness to Trapnel's trances believed her inspiration 'Because (she saith) she cannot make a verse when she is hir selfe', John Williams reported of the events in St Ives: 'The Miracle (stifly maynetayned by the Churchmen) is this. That she never could make verse befor, nor can nowe.'[27] But although the spectacle of an ignorant woman preaching in verse was enough to convince many that the inspiration was true, men in power such as John Williams and Marchamont Nedham used the women's ignorance to suggest that they were cunning, manipulative and ungodly. Nedham called Trapnel's congregation 'a Confluence of silly wretches', while Williams dismissed Jane Hawkins as 'a wittye and a craftie Baggage', and her verses as more mad than inspired, 'dotages and Reveries of a franticke weoman'.[28]

Whatever their personal opinion of the truth of such prophecies, both Nedham and Williams knew that once believed, these women could be dangerous. Both men reported to those higher up; Nedham's account went straight to the Protector, and Williams's two letters to Secretary Dorchester. Williams was particularly concerned that the king would have heard of the unruly events occurring in the diocese of Lincoln, and wrote to Dorchester to explain 'what I conceyue the truth of the Buysines'. He is at pains to emphasise that there is nothing overtly political in the verses, nothing 'concerninge the state or the Governmᵗ of the Church'. In other words, the king need not worry about Jane Hawkins; she may have disrupted the order of a Cambridgeshire community, but her prophecies will not inspire any to rebellion.[29] Intriguingly, Williams's biographer, John Hacket, records precisely the opposite: that Hawkins's prophecies were 'full of Detraction and Injury to the Authority of the Bishops, to the Church-way of *England* in the Liturgy, and not sparing some Occurrences of the Civil Government'. Hacket may be exaggerating his hero's role – the whole account reads like a sensational romance as Williams dons a disguise and leaps up to surprise the culprits – but the fact that Williams felt it necessary to write to Dorchester in 1629 reveals an underlying anxiety about the power of the spirit in lay, Puritan (and perhaps particularly female) believers.[30] Had

---

[26] PRO SP 18/66 no. 20.   [27] Bodleian Library Rawlinson MS A 21, p. 325; PRO SP 16/141 no. 63.
[28] PRO SP 18/66 no. 20; PRO SP 16/141 no. 63.   [29] PRO SP 16/141 no. 63.
[30] Wing H171 John Hacket, *Scrinia reserata: a memorial* (London: Edward Jones, for Samuel Lowndes, 1693), II.47.

Jane Hawkins spoken more of king and Church she might have been threatening indeed.[31]

Despite their similarities, it is of course highly unlikely that Anna Trapnel knew of Jane Hawkins of St Ives. Trapnel was a child living in London in 1629, and the localised scandal was quickly hushed by Bishop Williams, who destroyed all but sixteen lines of Jane Hawkins's prophecy. No contemporary records remain save the letters in the state papers.[32] The women almost certainly acted independently, but this very fact may suggest something more exciting than a direct relationship: that a tradition of the 'Riminge precheresse' existed even before the civil wars, a tradition for which the records have been lost or destroyed, as they very nearly were in the case of Jane Hawkins of St Ives.[33] By 1654 Anna Trapnel must have known that inspired 'Riminge' was one of the few ways a woman might become a 'precheresse'.[34]

One major difference between Trapnel's experience in 1654 and Jane Hawkins's in 1629 was that by the time of the Commonwealth Trapnel could expect her inspiration to be taken seriously by those in power. In 1629, Bishop Williams dampened the ardour of the congregation in St Ives by preaching a sermon denouncing the validity of *all* such forms of spontaneous inspiration:

[31] In PRO SP 16/142 no. 19, Williams appends a transcription of sixteen lines of Jane Hawkins's verse, 'All that, may haue any reflection vpon the state':

> O lett it bee for euer told
>   to ages that succeed,
> That they may lay it vp in store
>   for then will bee most need
> When that you see these fearefull times
>   W^{ch} now in p[ar]te you feare,
> for they are sure to come to vs,
>   o they draw wondrous neare.
> And then (good truth) you may beleiue
>   I take it still for graunt,
> that punishment will follow sinn
>   & euer will it haunte.
> And therefore now in shortest speech
>   o labour to beleiue
> Least afterwards it bee too late,
>   when you so sore shall greiue.

[32] Lincolnshire Archives have no records relating to the event among Williams's correspondence or the ecclesiastical court books.

[33] PRO SP 16/141 no. 63.

[34] Diane Watt considers the evidence for a tradition of women prophets in *Secretaries of God: Women Prophets in Late Medieval and Early Modern England* (Woodbridge: D. S. Brewer, 1997).

I tooke occasion to speake (vpon my text) of the scandale wch the papists put vpon our Church, that we mayntayne private Spirits, and infusions by Extasies, and raptures. wch I shewed to be false, and that we clayme noe Inspiration, of the holy Ghost, otherwise then what is given vs, by hearinge, readinge, meditatinge the word of God, & the devout receivinge of the Blessed Sacram^ts. And that the spirit of god, never doth, nor did, vnder the Gospel, speake in Raptures & extasies.[35]

It is interesting to note the use of the word 'private' – as a sober Caroline churchman, John Williams refuses to believe that the Gospel allows for any individual to receive a sudden message from the spirit. Just as Charles and Laud would attempt to establish that church authority existed only in the episcopal hierarchy, so Williams asserts that communication from God comes only through the regular (public) channels of scripture and sacraments. In the feverish atmosphere of Commonwealth London, on the other hand, increasing concern for individual religious conscience meant that every revelation had the potential to be true, and must be closely examined to determine if it were divine or demonic.

Anna Trapnel, therefore, may have had an opportunity to speak that Jane Hawkins was denied. In order to seize that opportunity she needed to demonstrate that her speech was indeed prophetic, not merely a woman's 'infirmitie of the Tongue' or the distracted ramblings of a vagrant.[36] As the letter quoted at the beginning of this chapter demonstrates, however, there was no definitive model of true prophecy even in 1650s London. As a 'Riminge precheresse', 'singing' quietly in a trance, Trapnel participates in a form of prophecy that she can construct as private devotion, the praying in her chamber that was acceptable for a woman where preaching in public was not. In doing so she is able to answer both the charges levied against Jane Hawkins, and which she herself feared: 'They will say the spirit of madness and distraction is upon her, and that it is immodesty[.]'[37]

By the time of Trapnel's fame a generation after Jane Hawkins, women's role in the church had become a fiercely contested issue. Women were crucial to the establishment of many independent and gathered congregations, and as a result male leaders were forced to reconsider women's role.[38] The

---

[35] PRO SP 16/141 no. 63. Hackett asserts that Williams preached on 29 April (*Scrinia reserata*, II.47), but Williams's own letter describes it as 'Sundaye last' or 22 April, the first Sunday after Easter. Peter McCullough has informed me that it was unusual for preachers in the 1620s to preach on the assigned text, which further suggests Williams's anxiety about the event and the king's response. The texts for that Sunday are 1 John 5:4–13, which describes the testimony of God as greater than the testimony of men (v. 9), and John 20:19–24, the 'doubting Thomas' episode in which Jesus confers the Holy Spirit on his disciples (v. 22).

[36] Bodleian Library Rawlinson MS D 828, p. 31; see below for a discussion of this manuscript.

[37] Trapnel, *The cry of a stone*, p. 67 [71].

[38] Keith Thomas, 'Women and the Civil War Sects', *Past and Present* 13 (1958): 42–62.

unusually liberal John Rogers, for example, devoted an entire chapter of his treatise on church government to defending the right of women to speak in church affairs because, as he himself put it, 'it is so much opposed'.[39] The contentiousness of this issue is apparent in the records of one godly gathered church that resembled Trapnel's congregation of Allhallows, Upper Thames Street. The account book of this unnamed London congregation for 1652–4 records the debate caused by a woman's refusal to attend a meeting:

Brother Naudin by y[e] desire (as he saith) of Sister Anne >Harriman< declard that she was not free to come to the meeting because that Bro: Naudin said He would not well wth such as gave libertie to woemen to speak in y[e] Church ffor she could not walk where she had not libertie to speak. And therefore rather than Brother Naudin should withdraw, shee would withdraw.[40]

A Christian's 'walk' encompassed all realms of life in which she acted out her faith: in the home, in the marketplace, in church, in prayer. It was part of the 'process of collective growth in grace' through which an individual's gifts and graces could enhance the spiritual capital of the entire community.[41] Anne Harriman's declaration thus highlights the faultline between the duties expected of all Christians – which must sometimes be carried out in public, open to view – and the restrictions placed upon women by St Paul's command: 'Let your women keep silence in the churches: for it is not permitted unto them to speak' (1 Corinthians 14:34). The Calvinist emphasis on the examination of experience meant that all Christians, men and women, were meant to test their faith in action, to question and to debate.[42] Theodore Naudin's – and St Paul's – attempts to silence Anne Harriman in public restrict her ability to learn and experience God in private. Her 'withdraw[al]' into privacy where she will not be able to learn and serve makes this connection clear.

---

[39] Wing R1813 John Rogers, *Ohel, or beth-shemesh* (London: for R. I. and G. and H. Eversden, 1651), p. 294 and chapter 8, pp. 563–[5]77.

[40] Bodleian Library Rawlinson MS D 828, p. 28. The congregation is identified only as the 'church'. The volume contains numerous letters recording a contentious debate between the leaders and Peter Chamberlen, a London doctor whom the DNB credits with inventing the short forceps. The manuscript is mentioned by Diane Purkiss, 'Gender, Power, and the Body', p. 315, and Anne Laurence, 'A Priesthood of She-Believers: Women and Congregations in Mid-Seventeenth Century England', in *Women in the Church: Papers Read at the 1989 Summer Meeting and the 1990 Winter Meeting of the Ecclesiastical Historical Society*, ed. W. J. Sheils and Diana Wood (Oxford: Basil Blackwell, 1990), p. 351.

[41] Peter Lake, 'Feminine Piety and Personal Potency: The "Emancipation" of Mrs Jane Ratcliffe', *The Seventeenth Century* 2.2 (1987): 144.

[42] Nigel Smith, *Perfection Proclaimed: Language and Literature in English Radical Religion, 1640–1660* (Oxford: Clarendon Press, 1989), pp. 33–4.

Like the witness to Trapnel's trances quoted at the beginning of this chapter, the men of Anne Harriman's congregation did not pass judgement immediately, but felt obliged to examine the scriptures. They faced a difficult task: in 1 Corinthians alone they had to reconcile the verses in chapter 14 that insisted on women's silence in church with those in chapter 11 that implied that women praying or prophesying was an occurrence common enough to require some regulation.[43] The men eventually came down on the side of chapter 14, as well as 1 Peter 3, determining that ordinary wives were prohibited from speaking for three reasons:

1 lest boldnes should make them presumptuous ag[ain]st their Husbands (vs: 34) the. 2^d. Reason is because they may ask their husbands at home, & have husbands to aske (if beleevers) & the. 3^d. is because it is a shame for a Married Woeman (who hath no necessitie for conscience sake to ask in ye Church[)], to shew before all their infirmitie of the Tongue.[44]

One significant result of their reliance on St Paul is the fact that meetings of the congregation were considered public ('before all'), despite the fact that many independent churches resembled extended families and their gatherings were elsewhere termed 'privat meeting[s]'.[45] In comparison with the marital home the church is deemed a public place, unfit for women to display the weakness and inferiority they might reveal to their husbands.

The men of the congregation extended this limitation to 'in general comprehend *All Widdowes & Maydes*' because 'the Male hath naturally Dominion over the Female. & ye Femal hath naturally Weaknes & Subjection to ye Male'; in other words, public speech by any woman would offend against male authority.[46] Underlying their reasoning is the assumption that ordinary women have nothing of merit to add to the discussion. Anne Harriman's assertion that 'she could not walk where she had not libertie to speak' is therefore categorically denied; the men's argument implies that her speech would have no moral value, and therefore add nothing to her walk with Christ. Interestingly, John Rogers, one of the few non-Quaker men to defend a limited right for women to speak, does so on the basis of the

---

[43] Rawlinson MS D 828, pp. 28, 30–1. 1 Corinthians 14:34–5: 'Let your women keep silence in the churches: for it is not permitted unto them to speak; but they are commanded to be under obedience as also saith the law. And if they will learn any thing, let them ask their husbands at home: for it is a shame for women to speak in the church'; 1 Corinthians 11:5: 'But every woman that prayeth or prophesieth with her head uncovered dishonoureth her head: for that is even all one as if she were shaven.'

[44] Rawlinson MS D 828, p. 31.

[45] See for example the title page of Wing L425B John Lanseter, *Lanseter's lance* (London: 1646).

[46] Rawlinson MS D 828, p. 31.

Independent principle that Church decisions should be made collectively, and makes no mention of the benefit of women's speech to the women themselves.[47]

In the London debate, the notable exception to the rule are 'Prophetesses', who unfortunately are not defined in this debate, nor is the reason for their exception recorded. At the end of the debate the scribe wrote, 'The Conclusion is a Woeman, (Mayd, Wife, or Widdow) being a Prophetess (1 Cor: 11.[)] may speake, Prophesie, Pray, wth a Vayl. Others may not.' 1 Corinthians 11:5 remained a sticking point that required the men to accept that the spirit could rest on a woman as well as a man. Such an extraordinary event would occasion special dispensations from the usual dictates of public decorum, although the fact that even a prophetess is required to wear a veil when speaking suggests that some form of modesty was still necessary. The spirit could speak through anyone, and when the spirit spoke, the normal order was suspended, and the 'Weaknes & Subjection' of a woman's speech were subsumed in the (male) authority of the spirit speaking through her.[48] Such a view disallows the connection between public speech and private devotion made by Anne Harriman and, at times, Anna Trapnel, because the public voice of the woman is in some sense not her self.[49]

The views of this London congregation are not unusual: although such radical Churches allowed women more scope than the Catholic Church or conformist Church of England, women's ability to speak, lead or even hold their own meetings was strictly limited even among sectarians.[50] Yet, while there were continued attempts to control women's public behaviour, we must also remember that women were not always passive in the face of such obstacles. Although the question about women's speaking should have prevented her from airing her opinions, Anne Harriman nevertheless makes a stand in her very absence by asking her male opponent to declare her objections. A note in the margin that 'Sist[r] Anne came in y[e] Afternoon denyed y[e] cercumestance' further suggests that she engineered the conflict in order to make her case against the traditional gendering of public and private speech without weakening her position by actively transgressing

---

[47] Rogers, *Ohel, or beth-shemesh*, pp. 563–[5]77.

[48] Rawlinson MS D 828, pp. 31, 32. Paul's position on the matter is contradictory; despite the forcefulness of 11:5, the section ends with the ambiguous statement, 'But if any man seem to be contentious, we have no such custom, neither the churches of God' (verse 16), and includes the extraordinary verse, 'For this cause ought the woman to have power on her head because of the angels' (verse 10).

[49] See the letter quoted at the beginning of this chapter.

[50] Laurence, 'A Priesthood of She-Believers', pp. 362–3.

those traditional boundaries.[51] Trapnel's writing similarly exploits the contradictions inherent in early modern gendered morals, using the seemingly limiting model of the prophetess who was not herself when she spoke in order to emphasise the divine origins of her speech: 'thy servant knows there is no selfe in this thing' as she put it in one tract.[52] The paradigm enabled her and other women prophets to deflect attacks against themselves onto God himself: 'I have *no wit, no wisdom, no understanding, no will* of *my own*', Anne Wentworth declared a generation later. 'And if this be to be *mad*, I confess my self to be *beside my self to God*[.]'[53]

The experiences of Anne Harriman and Jane Hawkins suggest that women such as Anna Trapnel knew that the prophetic trance would grant them – or rather the spirit within them – a chance to speak in the public congregation that they would otherwise be denied. Knowingly or not, Anna Trapnel's prophesyings exploit this paradigm of a 'Riminge precheresse'. But Trapnel was also aware that, as the newspaper accounts suggest, observers might doubt her inspiration, or believe her 'of a troubled mind', or, ominously, 'worse'.[54] As a result, much of her defence of herself resides not in claims to great inspiration but in evidence of ordinary godliness that exploits the connections between private prayer and public worship.

In their preface to *A legacy for saints*, the leaders of Trapnel's congregation testify to her 'love to the truth, holiness, authority, and pretious usefulness of the Scriptures' and her regular attendance at 'the ordinances of God' at Allhallows, as well as her respect for non-episcopally ordained clergy.[55] When she was arrested and examined during her prophetic tour of Cornwall, Trapnel tried to emphasise this image of her self as 'a woman like others that were modest and civill':

[Justice] Launse said, *Pray Mistress tell us, what moved you to come such a journey?*

A.T. *The Lord gave me leave to come, asking of him leave, whitherever I went: I used still to pray for his direction in all I do: and so I suppose ought you,* I said.

Justice Launse. *But pray tell us, what moved you to come such a journey?*

A.T. *The Lord moved me, and gave me leave.*

Launse. *But had you not some of extraordinary impulses [of] Spirit, that brought you down? pray tell us what those were.*

---

[51] Rawlinson MS D 828, p. 28. It is possible that Theodore Naudin misunderstood his conversation with Anne Harriman, but his own firm stance against women's speech and the way he conveys her wishes as modest and devout make it unlikely that he deliberately misrepresented her position.

[52] Trapnel, *The cry of a stone*, p. 42 [45]. See Phyllis Mack, *Visionary Women*, p. 106.

[53] Wing W1356, Anne Wentworth, *A vindication of anne wentworth* ([London]: 1677), p. 8.

[54] *Severall proceedings* no. 225, p. 3563.

[55] Trapnel, *A legacy for saints*, sig. A3[r–v]; see also Trapnel, *Report and plea*, p. 46.

A.T. *When you are capable extraordinary of* [sic] *impulse of Spirit, I will tell you; but I suppose you are not in a capacity now:* for I saw how deridingly he spoke[.][56]

Conformist pamphleteers commonly argued that Puritans merely pretended to be moved by the spirit in order to further their aims, and this accusation was especially common against women, characterised as 'Holy Whore[s]' whose aims were frequently sexual.[57] When Justice Launce attempts to force Trapnel to admit that she believes herself moved by the spirit to travel to Cornwall, it is not surprising that Trapnel, who elsewhere declared her inspiration boldly, here avoids the question like a trap. Her answers evade reference to gender and thus typically gendered accusations such as witchcraft or whoredom: she suggests that her relationship with God is no more than any other believer can enjoy, and chides the judge for not asking God's permission as she does. She later explains herself by referring to the accounts of prayer in the Psalms and Isaiah, and Justice Launce agrees, perhaps irritably, that '*[s]uch impulse was common, they hoped they had that*'.[58] But Trapnel refuses to acknowledge that her own dispensation is 'uncommon', only implying that perhaps Justice Launce himself is not spiritually ready to comprehend it. Ironically, denying her inspiration in this situation may in fact make it more difficult for the men in authority to dismiss her; to disprove her claims of authority would only be an attack on Anna Trapnel, but to deny the power of prayer for an ordinary Christian woman would be an attack on the spirit itself.

The scene also demonstrates the interconnections between public and private in a society that places a premium on 'godliness', as Trapnel hints that any 'extraordinary impulses [of] Spirit' that might urge her to public action come as she prays alone for direction. Even the most personal prayer has a public dimension as a proof of godliness; the countless spiritual autobiographies of this period, Trapnel's included, sought to place a public stamp of approval on an individual's private wrestling with God.[59] For Trapnel, private spirituality was especially important because it served as a defence for her public speech as a woman and a prophetess, as when she was called back to the Assizes in Cornwall to be accused of making '*a disturbance in the town*':

---

[56] Trapnel, *Report and plea*, pp. 49, 26[1] (the numbers 25–8 are each used twice).

[57] Wing H50 I. H., *A strange wonder or a wonder in a woman* (London: for I. T., 1642), p. 4; see also Wing S4990 *A spirit moving in the women-preachers* (London: for Henry Shepheard and William Ley, 1646), p. 2. On the debate about women preaching and prophesying, see Holstun, *Ehud's Dagger*, pp. 258–61; and Anne Laurence, 'A Priesthood of She-Believers', especially 362–3.

[58] Trapnel, *Report and plea*, p. 28[1].

[59] Smith, *Perfection Proclaimed*, pp. 33–45. Trapnel, *A legacy for saints*, pp. 1–20.

I asked, *Wherein?* he said, *[b]y drawing so many people after me:* I said, *How did I draw them?* he said, *I set open my Chamber-doors and my windows for people to hear.* A.T. *Tha.'s a very unlikely thing, that I should do so; for I prayed the maid to lock my chamber-door when I went to bed, and I did not rise in the night sure to open it:* I said, *why may not I pray with many people in the room, as well as your professing wom[a]n that prays before men and women, she knowing them to be there; but I know not that there is any body in the room when I pray: and if you indite one for praying, why not another? why are you so partial in your doings?* Justice *Lobb. But you don't pray so as others.* A. T. *I pray in my chamber.* Justice *Travel. Your chamber!* A. T. *Yea, that it's my chamber while I am there, through the pleasure of my friends.*[60]

Given the reports of hundreds who flocked to her bedside in Whitehall, there is probably more than a little exaggeration in Trapnel's testimony. But more significant than whether she had locked her door is the way in which she describes her prophetic activity as prayer, not preaching. St Paul may have forbidden women to speak in church, but as Trapnel points out, even in public it is not wrong for a woman to pray, and her own prayer is even more modest as she is unaware of any audience. Henry Jessey similarly emphasised that his protégé Sarah Wight 'knew not that others listened, and heard her, (and wrote it downe, as here followeth:)' 'much lesse that there is any intent of publishing to the world'.[61] The point was not so much the presence or absence of an audience but the rather the privileged nature of prayer. Communicating with God is such an intimate activity that it is always in a sense private: 'And may not I speak in my Chamber, and sing on my Bed, and pray on my Knees?' Trapnel argues in *A legacy for saints*.[62]

Jessey and Trapnel exploit the connections between public and private prayer to create a liminal space in which a woman could speak almost by accident, in a sense redefining the public sphere by bringing it into a woman's bedchamber.[63] Their experiences are worth comparing with the very different public actions of Quaker women, who shouted on street-corners and defied ministers mid-sermon.[64] Unlike more conventional Independent women such as Trapnel and Wight, the Quakers did not subscribe to traditional distinctions between the sexes in spiritual matters; in fact, when the spirit spoke, all human distinctions, including gender, disappeared. '[I]f Christ be in the female as well as in the Male,' insisted George Fox, 'is not he the same?'[65] If indeed he is the same, then Quaker

---

[60] Trapnel, *Report and plea*, p. 28[1].   [61] Jessey, *The exceeding riches*, sig. A6[r].
[62] Trapnel, *A legacy for saints*, p. 59.   [63] See Holstun, *Ehud's Dagger*, pp. 279–80.
[64] Mack, *Visionary Women*, pp. 166–7.
[65] Wing F1991 George Fox, *The woman learning in silence* (London: for Thomas Simonds, 1655/6), p. 5. See also Wing F514 Richard Farneworth, *A woman forbidden to speak in the church* (London: for Giles Calvert, 1654); Elaine Hobby, 'Handmaids of the Lord and Mothers in Israel: Early Vindications of Quaker Women's Prophecy', *Prose Studies* 17.3 (1994): 88–98.

women did not need to be 'Empty Nothing Creature[s]' in their bed-chambers, because when they went into public it was Christ himself who spoke.

The experiences of Quaker women are a powerful reminder that neither gender nor misogyny was monolithic in this period. There were competing standards for both men and women, which differed depending upon religious allegiance, status and circumstance. In light of these potential gender confusions, it is interesting to look back at Trapnel's trial and notice that it is she, not the justices, who raises the issue of gender. To the general accusation that she was causing a public disturbance, Trapnel suggests the gendered implications by comparing her prayer with that of other devout women and by insisting repeatedly that her own prayer is in her private chamber and thus complicit with Pauline restrictions and cultural norms of feminine modesty.

In fact, although Trapnel regularly defends herself against perceived gendered accusation, in all of the surviving news reports, trial records and eye-witness accounts there is rarely a misogynist slur of the sort frequent in the pamphlet literature about women preachers.[66] She is 'a dangerous seditious Person', and possibly an imposter, but not a whore.[67] In Cornwall the charges against her were vagrancy, unlawful meeting and treason, not scolding, gadding or any other female crime.[68] Trapnel herself describes the mob ascending to her chamber with the cry '*A witch, a witch*', but the charge was never mentioned in court or in any other account.[69] Similarly, none of the 'reproachfull, scandalous, base, horrid, defaming speeches . . . published in scurrilous Pamphlets' that Trapnel claimed had called her a witch and a whore have survived.[70] The hostile accounts that do survive attack Trapnel for reasons that are not clearly gendered: because she 'withdraws from Ordinances' and is 'Non-sensical', or because she is part of a dangerous 'ffanatick Crew' of both men and women.[71] Why, then, did Trapnel herself feel the need to print a ten-page self-defence against such 'defaming speeches' at the end of her *Report and plea*?[72]

---

[66] In addition to her own account of her trial and sources already quoted, Trapnel is mentioned in 1654 in *CSPD 1654*, pp. 86, 89, 134, 197, 436, 438; *The grand politique post*, no. 127 (London: for George Horton, 10–17 January 1653/4), p. 1236; *The moderate publisher*, no. 1 (London: 13–20 January 1653/4), pp. 1, 5; *Mercurius politicus*, no. 201 (London: Thomas Newcomb, 13–20 April 1654), pp. 3429–430, also in *Certain passages*, *The weekly intelligencer* and *The moderate intelligencer* for the same week. On misogynist stereotypes of women preachers, see Holstun, *Ehud's Dagger*, pp. 258–9.

[67] Trapnel, *Report and plea*, p. 52. [68] *Mercurius politicus*, no. 201, p. 3430.

[69] Trapnel, *Report and plea*, p. 21. Several scholars emphasise the connection between prophecy and witchcraft; see Purkiss, 'Producing the Voice', p. 140; Mack, *Visionary Women*, p. 80.

[70] Trapnel, *Report and plea*, p. 49. [71] *Mercurius politicus*, no. 201, p. 3430; PRO SP 18/66 no 20.

[72] Trapnel, *Report and plea*, pp. 49–59.

Trapnel was probably not overestimating any potential gendered threat: there was an abundance of misogynist literature against women preachers, and her Quaker contemporaries endured the scold's bridle, the traditional punishment for a shrewish woman.[73] The fact that Trapnel's fears were justified only makes it the more curious that the men in charge seem to have viewed Trapnel first as a political danger and only secondarily, if at all, as an unruly woman. It may be the fact that Trapnel caused political unrest that shielded her from such accusations – if people did believe her to be inspired, misogynist charges might only have strengthened the image of a humble godly woman persecuted by ungodly authorities. Whatever their reasons, the reaction of those authorities provides yet more evidence that extreme care is needed when evaluating what might be called the practice of misogyny in this period. If the justices and hostile journalists and even the Council of State chose not to use the misogynist arguments that were undoubtedly available, it suggests that those arguments were perhaps not as monolithic and absolute as critics have previously argued. In certain cases – perhaps more frequently than we realise – women might be treated as political or religious individuals rather than as females. If public and private spaces could not always be clearly defined, the gendering of those spaces was equally open to shifts and changes according to circumstance.

PROPHETIC VOCABULARIES: THE 1654 TRACTS

It may have been the ability to take control of definitions of public, private and gender that enabled Anna Trapnel to avoid the threats facing a woman prophet. Just as she had lain in bed in order to emphasise that her prayer – and her body itself – were private no matter who was in the room, in her prophecy Trapnel exploits the shifts in public and private spaces by constructing a liminal space in which her private communication with God is broadcast to the public. Trapnel creates this liminal space through the metaphor of mystical marriage: because the early modern marriage ceremony served as a public acknowledgement of private intimacy, taking Christ as a husband allowed women such as Trapnel to put a public face on their personal relationship with God.[74]

Trapnel draws her imagery of divine marriage from the Psalms, Hosea, Revelation and particularly the Song of Songs. These images form only part of a complex metaphorical vocabulary that evolves throughout Trapnel's

---

[73] See note 57. Sussman, 'Women's Private Reading', p. 139.   [74] See chapter 4 above.

prophecies, but they deserve attention because they bring into focus the issues of public and private speech that were so crucial for a woman prophet. Marriage imagery is less prominent in the 1654 tracts that feature in most studies of her work, but even in these texts mystical marriage defines both Trapnel's public calling and her private intimacy with God.

Trapnel's spiritual autobiography *A legacy for saints* uses images of marriage to Christ to define her experience of conversion. Her account employs the conventions of the genre to underline that her calling is both personally felt and outwardly confirmed, and thus crosses the divide between public and private. The narrative begins as she repeatedly hears herself called by God in words echoing the Song of Songs, such as '*Christ is thine, and thou art his*'. The voice of the spirit is only in her own mind, and yet the fact that it 'followed me where ever I went', even 'going along the streets', is a reminder that Trapnel is almost literally learning to walk with Christ in the public places of London.[75] The next step in the process of conversion is for Trapnel to pray to accept her calling in the public context of a sermon, where she again hears, 'Christ is thy wel-beloved, and thou art his'. Significantly, it is in this context, while she is still in the congregation as the sermon 'was almost ended', that she first connects her calling with a need to speak publicly about Christ: 'I could not keep love in, it would flame forth into a declaration, I must now tell Saints what I had now received from the spirits testimony[.]'[76] Although it is not clear whether she did actually speak in the meeting or only in a more private household setting, the fact is that it is in a public space where her speech was explicitly forbidden that she hears the call to bear witness.

The call is soon confirmed when Trapnel visits an aunt in Stepney who advises her: 'Cosen, the Lord hath taken your mother from you, now labour to be married to Christ, you have nothing to take up your time, but to labour for Christ[.]' As a sign of her new conviction Trapnel answers, 'I hope I am married to Christ[.]'[77] Instead of the traditional transfer of a woman from her parents' authority to that of an earthly husband, Trapnel depicts herself as free to choose a divine husband now that her parents have died. She thus creates for herself a publicly recognised spiritual freedom in her unmarried state, since she is ruled by no man but directly by divine authority.[78] The exchange also completes the external authorisation of Trapnel's calling,

[75] Trapnel, *A legacy for saints*, p. 7. Song of Songs 2:16, 'My beloved is mine, and I am his.'
[76] Trapnel, *A legacy for saints*, p. 9.   [77] *Ibid.*, p. 10.
[78] Diane Purkiss discusses virginity and authority among women prophets in 'Producing the Voice', pp. 157–8. See also her 'Gender, Power and the Body', pp. 279–319, and Holstun, *Ehud's Dagger*, pp. 270–2.

declared in front of a witness almost like a contract of marriage. She even records that she was rebuked by the spirit for not declaring her position more strongly: 'why didst thou say thou hopest, and didst not rather tell that thy God had assured thee that Christ was thine, thou having such a clear testimony of the spirit . . . that thou couldst not but assent to it, thou shouldst now have declared it?'[79] Like the author of *Eliza's babes*, Anna Trapnel's experience of religious conversion leads her to conclude that speaking publicly of her commitment to Christ is not only possible, but an inescapable duty.

Having established her duty to speak publicly, Trapnel employs the language of mystical marriage to describe her private relationship with God. In her *Report and plea*, for example, she describes how 'the Lord greatly ravished my soul with his smiling looks on me' and 'my heart was heat also with the flame of love, which many waters cannot quench, as the spouse saith in the Canticles'.[80] Her emotional phrases echo the conventions of Song of Songs commentators and the writers on devotion discussed in the previous chapter, all of whom let forth surprising excesses of emotion in praising the 'mysterious rapts of Divine Love'.[81] For Trapnel, the experience of mystical marriage is both an ordinary experience of conversion such as any godly individual might enjoy, and a precursor to her later individual calling as a prophetess. When crowds come to jeer her at Foy she defends herself as 'a simple creature' yet speaks of 'how the Church set him out in the *Canticles*', a favourite sermon topic throughout the century. The incident demonstrates the liminality of her pose of modesty, poised between self-deprecation and emboldened speech, private faith and public preaching. The phrase 'how the Church set him out' also anticipates her future pose as a universal bride of Christ whose speech is authorised because 'she sings of her Lover'.[82]

In her *Report and plea* Trapnel also develops the image of the garden as a place of liberating self-enclosure, in which she can escape from human intercourse for personal conversation with God. Of a difficult discussion with her friends in Cornwall, she writes, 'I not relishing the discourse, had a minde to walk in the Garden by my self, and so I did a while; wherein the Lord gave me much of his loving-welcome, and kinde salutations[.]' Trapnel's portrayal of the garden evokes both the garden of Eden where Adam and

---

[79] Trapnel, *A legacy for saints*, p. 10.   [80] Trapnel, *Report and plea*, pp. 9, 14.

[81] Wing D2802 James Durham, *Clavis cantici* (Edinburgh: George Swintoun and James Glen, 1668), p. 1. See chapters 1 and 4 above.

[82] Trapnel, *Report and plea*, p. 28[2], and S 1.42 Theology, p. 1.

Eve walked alone with God, and the locked garden used to describe the female speaker in the Song of Songs, open only to her lover (4:12–16). It thus serves as an image of both privileged, Edenic communication with God, and the inviolable privacy of such spiritual communion with a lover. In the garden Trapnel, like Adam, is able to speak to God directly: 'I had at that time such cordials from the Lord, that I could have walked many hours in that Garden[.]' When she is asked to rejoin the human conversation, Trapnel is unwilling, 'for my communion in the Garden was so delightful to me'.[83]

Although the garden in this passage is real it also has a mystical counterpart in a place where the soul is alone with God and separated from the human world. Trapnel uses similar language in *The cry of a stone* when she declares that she does not choose to declare her visions to the world:

Thy Servant knew that she was beloved of thee, and that she lay in thy bosome from a child, and there she might have lived without the condemnings or reproaches of men, or of this Generation; but since Father thou wilt have it so, thy Will be done. If the body suffer never so much, if it be for thy Selfe, thy Saints, thy Kingdome, it is better for her then to be in her own Habitation, and in pleasant Gardens; and when thy Servant has done thy work, she shall be willing to lock up her selfe in her Closet againe, and not to be seen of men[.][84]

Trapnel hints at the joys of the mystical garden when she asserts that it is better to suffer for God than to be 'in pleasant Gardens' on earth. This conventional differentiation between mystical communion and earthly pleasure is significant in light of the fact that this passage has been cited as evidence of Trapnel's apparent denial of agency in her prophecy. Particularly her determination 'to lock up her selfe in her Closet' has problematic resonances for feminist critics, since it suggests that Trapnel subscribed to the view that women should not be heard or even seen in public, even if only as a clever device for thwarting the 'condemnings or reproaches of men'.[85] But Trapnel's invocation of 'pleasant Gardens' in this passage suggests that there is more than just rhetorical ingenuity at work here; her desire for communion with God outside the world of men is real and urgent, and in no sense a punishment or retreat. As with her desire to remain virginal but married to Christ, there is a paradoxical element of spiritual freedom in Trapnel's self-confinement: 'not to be seen of men' is to see God. Like Julian of Norwich before her, or Emily Dickinson after, Anna Trapnel finds

---

[83] Trapnel, *Report and plea*, pp. 11–12, 13.   [84] Trapnel, *The cry of a stone*, p. 42 [45].
[85] Hinds, *God's Englishwomen*, pp. 90, 100–2.

a voice in drawing the boundaries of her own self-enclosure, in the process manipulating those shifting divisions between public and private space.[86]

THE 1658 FOLIO

In the early tracts mystical marriage plays a relatively small part in the stock of images Anna Trapnel uses to portray her prophetic calling. By 1658 when her later tracts were printed, these images had become central to Trapnel's presentation of herself as a prophet. In the later works, Trapnel develops a uniquely detailed picture of the Spouse – the female speaker of the Song of Songs – as a prophetic forerunner, particularly akin to Trapnel because of her gendered relationship to Christ.

Trapnel's 1658 publications arise seemingly out of nowhere; after her year of notoriety in 1654, she reappears briefly in Cornwall in 1655 and 1656, and then is unheard of until her months of prophesying in 1657, near the end of Cromwell's life and rule.[87] The first of the 1658 publications, *Voice for the king of saints and nations*, is a ninety-one page quarto pamphlet containing dated transcriptions of Trapnel's prophecies, mostly in verse, with brief 'Notes of true Vision' included at the end. In the unsigned epistle to the reader, one of Trapnel's witnesses sets out the group's purposes in printing again: 'I do beleeve it to be the testimony of Jesus, the Spirit of prophesy; for these ends it is published, that those in the Country, which cannot attend it so frequently, might partake of it in some kind[.]'[88]

The need to disseminate Trapnel's prophecies to those who could not come to London to hear them may help explain the existence of the other 1658 collection, a 990-page folio volume of which only one copy still exists.[89] This volume unfortunately has no extant title page or prefatory material, so we can only infer its purpose. The book is much too large to have been sent out to the believers in the country; nor is it plausible to believe that it was destined to spread the truth to the public through London bookshops. It seems to have been produced as cheaply as possible; the print quality is poor and the binding is inexpensive sheep. Nevertheless, the cost of setting

[86] Frederick Christian Bauerschmidt, *Julian of Norwich and the Mystical Body Politic of Christ* (Notre Dame, Indiana: University of Notre Dame Press, 1999), pp. 73–8. Joanne Dobson, *Dickinson and the Strategies of Reticence: The Woman Writer in Nineteenth-Century America* (Bloomington, Indiana: Indiana University Press, 1989), pp. 99 127. Beth Maclay Doriani, *Emily Dickinson: Daughter of Prophecy* (Amherst, Massachusetts: University of Massachusetts Press, 1996), pp. 153–84.

[87] *The publick intelligencer* no. 13 (London: Henry Hills, 24–31 December 1655), pp. 193–4; *Mercurius politicus* no. 312 (London: 29 May–5 June 1656), pp. 6997–8.

[88] Unsigned epistle, Trapnel, *Voice for the king of saints*, sig. A2^r.

[89] Trapnel, S 1.42 Theology. Page numbers of quotations are hereafter cited in the text.

up the presses for such a large volume would have been prohibitively high. The book's very existence thus suggests that someone in Trapnel's circle had more money than the poor 'handmaid' herself.[90]

The first fifty pages of the volume duplicate the prophecies (from 11 October to 12 November 1657) in the first seventy-six pages of *Voice for the king of saints*; the rest of the volume contains further dated prophecies, ending on 7 August 1658.[91] These dates bracket significant events in the history of the Protectorate. In September 1657 the most radical Fifth Monarchists split from the now more mainstream group; James Holstun speculates that Trapnel accompanied the radicals as their spokeswoman and oracle.[92] Nearly a year later, on 6 August 1658, the Protector's favourite daughter died, and shortly afterwards Cromwell fell into his last illness and died on 3 September, causing confusion among those who had opposed him.[93] The assertion in the preface to *Voice for the king of saints* that Trapnel's prophecies are 'the testimony of Jesus' suggests that the larger volume may be preserved as a record of a new revelation for the radical offshoot, a reading that is in keeping with the large, monumental format of the book. In other words, the volume is a new Fifth Monarchist Bible.

Both texts begin, in a sense, *in medias res*, since the first recorded prophecy from 11 October employs much of Trapnel's distinctive word usage – 'Spouse', 'song', 'spicknard', 'Emblem', 'King' – with no explanation of meaning. The sense of interrupting an already established personal vocabulary implies that there had been unrecorded prophecies before this date that helped establish the vocabulary and its meaning for the community. In the preface to *Voice for the king of saints* Trapnel's witness replicates some of her word usage, describing her prophecies as 'this glorious Revelation from Jesus Christ, which is let down in singing from *David* our King', one of Trapnel's favourite analogues.[94] The writer, as well as the title of the volume, also refers to Trapnel as a 'voice', a term that Trapnel uses frequently to characterise her role as prophet in the 1657–8 prophecies and in the earlier tract *The cry of a stone*. He also calls her prophecies 'Psalms', another favourite description.[95] The witness's verbal echoing of her prophecies implies that Trapnel's personalised vocabulary had been taken up by

---

[90] I am grateful to the Bodleian Library for allowing me access to the fragile original.
[91] There are numerous changes in orthography but no substantial variants in the passages I have compared.
[92] Holstun, *Ehud's Dagger*, p. 298.
[93] P. G. Rogers, *The Fifth Monarchy Men* (Oxford: Oxford University Press, 1966), p. 96.
[94] Unsigned epistle, Trapnel, *Voice for the king of saints*, sig. A2ʳ.
[95] *Ibid.*; *Cry of a stone*, p. 42 [45].

the community as a way to discuss the unique role of their prophet's – and by implication their own – relationship to God.

The key to the establishment of authority in these prophecies is the connection drawn between Trapnel's own 'Singing' and the Biblical Psalms. It is clear from the titles of her tracts and 'ear witness' accounts that Trapnel did in fact sing her verse prophecies.[96] Like the witnesses who edited *Voice for the king of saints*, Trapnel's prophecies several times identify her own verse as '*Davids* Psalm'.[97] Like so many of her images, 'Psalm' in Trapnel's prophecy carries multiple connotations. It is variously a song of praise, instruction, a polemical statement of doctrine and prophecy of forthcoming events. In Christian readings the Psalms do perform all of these tasks.[98] It is less usual to view the entire genre of the Psalm as prophetic: 'the Psalmist declares his works and word / By a Spirit of Prophecie' (p. 866), which also implicitly rests upon Trapnel herself. In this unique reading, the 'Psalm' is divine revelation itself, likened in power to the persons of the Trinity:

> There God, Christ, Spirit, and the Psalm,
> O they are all to be found:
> They come together, and they all
> Have a most blessed Crown.   (p. 665)

Because it comes directly from God, the Psalm, and implicitly Trapnel as its speaker, share in the crown of divine authority.

Trapnel's verse also aligns itself with the divine authority of the Psalms through a formal resemblance to English Psalm translations. Like the ubiquitous 'Sternhold and Hopkins' translation that was used for worship in most congregations, Trapnel's verse consists of rhymed fourteener couplets that are printed as four lines of an 8 6 8 6 metrical pattern. Like the Psalm translators, she also favours simple words, especially monosyllables.[99] Even the format of her later works, especially the monumental 1658 folio, recalls the physical appearance of the Psalms in a large Bible, with two columns of verse per page. Trapnel shares the formal characteristics of her verse with Jane Hawkins, a fact which suggests the usefulness of such a simple formula for 'ignorant' women wishing to emphasise their direct connection with the spirit, who speaks to them according to a well-known scriptural model.[100]

[96] Unsigned epistle, *Voice for the king of saints*, sig. A2^r; *Cry of a stone*, p. 1 [4].

[97] See for example S 1.42 Theology, pp. 637, 644, 859; italics original.

[98] Rivkah Zim, *English Metrical Psalms: Poetry as Praise and Prayer 1535–1601* (Cambridge: Cambridge University Press, 1987), pp. 27–34.

[99] *Ibid.*, pp. 114–18.   [100] For Hawkins's verse see note 31 above.

The similarity to English Psalm traditions also places both women within the sectarian debate about the role of liturgy within the community, and particularly the role of individual inspiration in worship. Like the songs of George Wither and Morgan Llywd, Anna Trapnel's prophecies participate in the invention of the English hymn to supplement the Psalms as the only form of singing allowed in orthodox worship.[101] Trapnel's prophecies also share with the Psalms the continuum between public and private devotion: although a vital part of the daily public prayer in most English churches, in their intimate expressions of human emotion the Psalms were ideal for private devotion. Individual Psalms were believed to have originated as private prayers; the Authorised Version describes Psalm 102, for example, as 'A Prayer of the afflicted, when he is overwhelmed, and poureth out his complaint before the LORD'.[102] There was, of course, considerable debate in Commonwealth London over whether it was appropriate to use 'prescribed' forms, including the Psalms, for private prayer; and Trapnel's description of her prophecies as Psalms may implicitly participate in this debate by supplementing the prescribed genre. Even if, as all the evidence suggests, she preferred spontaneous prayer, Trapnel's invocation of the Psalms nevertheless figures her prophecy as speech which originates in private devotion but is suitable for public worship.

Within this context, the imagery of singing and Psalms establishes a series of analogues for Trapnel in Biblical figures that 'sang' for and of Christ. The chief figures are David, the author of the Psalms and an archetypal king who was an important symbol for the Fifth Monarchists; and the Spouse of the Song of Songs, whose gendered marital relationship with Christ makes her an apt prototype for a woman prophet. By refiguring such Biblical characters as prophets inspired by God, Trapnel in her later prophecies provides sceptical witnesses with the Biblical analogues they sought. Like Trapnel, such figures could be said to speak only what they are already aware of through their 'naturall memorie' and piety, rather than extraordinary 'vissions and Revelations of the Lord'.[103]

[101] Nigel Smith, *Literature and Revolution in England, 1640–1660* (New Haven, Connecticut: Yale University Press, 1994), pp. 260–75. See also Danielle Clarke's discussion of the use of Psalm texts by members of the Sidney circle as a shorthand for politically sensitive devotional debates, *The Politics of Early Modern Women's Writing* (London: Longman, 2001), pp. 138–9.

[102] STC 13406.3, Samuel Hieron's *A helpe vnto deuotion* (London: H. L. for Samuel Macham, 1608), cites Psalm 102 as evidence that formal prayers were legal for private use in times of trouble, sig. A10ʳ. See also Psalm 142: 'Maschil of David; A Prayer when he was in the cave', and Wing D1238 Christopher Hatton's *Devotions for the helpe and assistance of all christian people* ([Oxford]: 1644) to which is appended a Psalter for assistance in private devotion.

[103] See the letter quoted at the beginning of this chapter.

Trapnel's verse attempts to prove that such 'common' devotion is in fact true inspiration.

Appropriately, the inaugural vision of both *Voice for the king of saints* and the untitled folio volume opens with the example of the Spouse. The passage continues for several pages and uses much of Trapnel's complex vocabulary, linking together the concepts of spiritual inspiration, singing, marriage to Christ and the privilege to speak of 'Emblems' of Christ. The first lines obliquely establish the connection between the Spouse and the spirit inspiring Trapnel's prophecy:

> The Spirit doth come in the way
> That the Spouse did before,
> The spouse she doth declare of him,
> So doth the Spirit, and more[.]
>
> (p. 1)

'The spouse she doth declare of him' refers to the rhapsodising, erotic paeans to love and the lover, Christ, spoken by the female speaker in the Song of Songs. In Trapnel's rewriting, these ecstatic expressions of love are necessary, even obligatory responses to Christ's sacrificial love,

> Which made the spouse come forth with song
> Of her beloved pure,
> Which must be sung to him alway,
> It ever shall indure.   (p. 1)

The song is not only authorised by the Spouse's relationship with Christ, but in fact 'must' be sung as part of her duties as a faithful wife. It is in this way, with the impetus of obligation as well as of privilege, that 'The Spirit doth come' to Trapnel to inspire her to sing of Christ's beauty. The Spouse, and by implication Trapnel, will not be silenced because her Lord commands that she speak.

It may seem obvious that such passages describe Trapnel's own experience, but despite the parallels between their callings, the connection between Trapnel and the Spouse remains an oblique one. Although otherwise often ambiguous in her use of pronouns, in one passage Trapnel's verse carefully distinguishes between herself and the Spouse:

> Christ was bright to the spouses view,
> And she did fear no harm,
> And my strength it is much renew'd
> From the same glorious arm:

> I have been laid within his breast,
> O how lovely is he!
> I must declare he is my rest;
> So did the spouse him see[.]   (p. 2)

In a rare use of the first person to speak of herself, Trapnel likens her own experience to that of the Spouse, both receiving rest 'From the same glorious arm'. But although the unusually explicit connection emphasises their parallel callings, it also establishes the two as different individuals: Trapnel is not the Spouse, but a distinct 'I'.

Yet aside from these brief lines, the words of the Spouse often seem interchangeable with what Trapnel says of herself in her non-prophetic prose. Although Trapnel's lexis is often very close to the text of the Song of Songs, she embellishes this vocabulary with episodes from her own experience. Thus she uses the vegetative imagery in the Song of Songs to justify her own use of 'Emblems' to portray Christ:

> O dost thou Christ compare, say they,
> To Pomgranate? dost thou
> Liken him unto such things?
> We cannot it allow.
> I, that I do, answers the spouse,
> It is an Emblem sweet;
> I will describe him throughout,
> Even from his head to feet[.]   (p. 1)

The Spouse of the Song of Songs is never accused of faulty comparisons in the original text, so the 'I' that speaks here articulates not scripture but what is probably Trapnel's experience.[104] The term 'Emblem' is certainly her own and does not occur in the Song of Songs. This interpolation of her own experience into that of the Biblical analogue is typical of the strategies of authorisation in Trapnel's prophecies, furthering the link between herself and those who were unquestionably authorised to speak, and suggesting that any impropriety was the fault of the reader. Sceptics who would criticise Trapnel's emblematic vocabulary should look to the sensual but canonical metaphors of the Song of Songs, in which the unusual depiction

---

[104] Contemporary commentators did find the figurative language of the ancient text puzzling, and a sign that it must not be read literally. As Church of Scotland minister James Durham (1622–58) argued, 'If properly understood, [the similes] would be monstrous, blasphemous, and ridiculous; such as *to have teeth like a flock of sheep, an head like Carmel*, &c. and so in many other things'; *Clavis cantici*, p. 7. See also Wing C 6410 John Cotton, *A brief exposition of the whole book of Canticles* (London: for Philip Nevil, 1642), p. 5. See chapter 1 above.

of Christ could only be understood by 'a most spiritual and divine frame of heart'.[105]

The justification of the Spouse's – and Trapnel's – public speech is also intimately linked with the privacy and privilege of her married relationship to Christ. As a faithful wife, the Spouse sings of Christ with the inspired familiarity of marriage, which Christ himself condones: 'O spouse my love, saith he, still sing, / Thou art the married Wife' (p. 1). Later in the folio volume Trapnel likens this close contact to walking in a vineyard, in language reminiscent of the garden imagery in her earlier tracts:

> And this the spouse in the Vineyard
> Of her love is sure to meet.
> O saith she, Here's the blood of the Vine,
> Here is the juyce of the Grape choice;
> Here the Pomgranates they do bud,
> Here's my Beloveds voice.
> O in the Vineyard it's very sweet,
> Saith the Spouse; it is most rare
> When I and my Beloved are
> Delighting our selves there.
> The Spouse with her Beloved had
> With Christ a very sweet walk
> In the vineyard, and together they
> Loved to sit down and talk.   (p. 535)

The imagery here becomes romantic, if not erotic; the vineyard is a trysting-place, where the Spouse can hear her beloved's voice, walk with him and taste of his wine, knowing him as only a wife can know her husband. As in the earlier tracts, the vineyard is a metaphor for the privacy of vision, in which the individual experiences Christ with an intimacy known only to lovers. Anne Harriman's congregation had demonstrated that for such sectarian groups it was only in private communication with her (human) husband that a woman could be completely free to display her 'infirmitie of the Tongue' on religious matters.[106] The implication of Trapnel's verse is that observers and even readers are in fact eavesdropping on such an intimate conversation between a woman and her (divine) husband.

---

[105] Dedicatory epistle by Margaret Durham in the second edition of *Clavis cantici*, Wing D2803 (London: J. W. for Dorman Newman, 1669), sig. A3ʳ.
[106] Rawlinson MS D 828, p. 31.

If anyone is to be thought immodest in this exchange, it is the listener, not the Spouse or Trapnel, for whom the presence of an audience is almost incidental. Despite her conviction during her conversion that she 'must now tell Saints' of Christ's love, rarely does Trapnel actively seek an audience for her prophecies. Instead she is passive before her audience, who might themselves be accused of immodesty if they do not hear her in the right spirit:

> The spouse comes forth with lovely song,
> And it was envied,
> What note is this that thou bringest forth?
> Was to her often said.
> What spirit is this? O it is strange,
> It differeth from other,
> They did against the song complain;
> But she sings of her Lover,
> And maketh unto him complaint,
> That they at her do strike.
> For they did tear and rent the vail
> Of Christs beloved Wife[.]   (p. 1)

These accounts of ridicule and abuse are drawn directly from the Song of Songs, in which the woman is attacked as she searches the city for her lover (5: 6–7). The passage describes both verbal abuse and physical assault akin to rape because it involves tearing the woman's protective veil, suggesting a violation of her modesty and the specific command that a prophetess should be veiled (1 Corinthians 11:5). The imagery glances at the charges of immodesty that Trapnel herself feared, and may provide a clue as to why such charges never materialised: vehemently attacking an apparently passive woman prophet could in itself be seen as a violation of her modesty. The lines recall the spectacle of Cornish officials attempting to drag the prone Trapnel from the privacy of her bedchamber: '[t]hese Justices that came to fetch me out of my bed, they made a great tumult'. The incident led the authorities to suspect that Trapnel could fall into a trance at will, and a similar accusation is implied in a newsbook report that 'she hath been in a Trance ever since' a second encounter with the Cornish authorities in December 1655.[107]

The passivity of Trapnel and the Spouse not only makes misogynist men seem like rampaging oafs, but also underlines the implication that their real target is a much more significant one: Christ himself.

[107] Trapnel, *Report and plea*, p. 21. *The publick intelligencer*, no. 13, p. 194.

> Many do strike at thee, my spouse,
> But I will take thy part,
> They scourge, and do thee so revile,
> Come spouse to *Solomons* porch.
> The shines of glory makes thee sing,
> And speak of love so much:
> O they do not know what it is,
> To have from Christ a touch:
> She goes, and sets him rarely out,
> Though many do scorn her,
> They at the spouse do for it flout,
> But she describes her Lord.   (p. 1)

Christ not only encourages the Spouse to sing her prophecies, but promises to succour and defend her with his almighty power. The whole passage serves as a manifesto of a woman's call to prophecy; because she herself does 'know what it is, / To have from Christ a touch', she will not be quelled by mockery or even physical violence. When attacked, she can take refuge in '*Solomons* porch', where private shelter with Christ is offered. The promised protection of Christ serves also as an implicit threat to those who would challenge his authority in her; those who would prevent her from speaking cannot touch her in '*Solomons* porch', and those who try to attack her are in a sense attacking Christ himself.

The shift from the prophet to Christ is consistent with the strategy throughout Trapnel's texts to deflect responsibilities on to others. From her trial in Cornwall in 1654 when she implied that her judges were ungodly if they could not understand her 'extraordinary impulses [of] spirit', to her final prone prophesyings in 1658, Trapnel continually refuses to take an active role that might be perceived as transgressive or unruly. It is the spirit who makes her speak, and the men who pursue and criticise her who violate gendered norms of modesty. Although there was considerable flexibility and flux in early modern understandings of public and private and how those spaces were gendered, Anna Trapnel ironically creates a space for herself to speak by applying these rules quite rigidly, using them to construct an inviolable *private* space for communicating with God in which it is immodest for any human male authority to criticise her. Rather than, as Anne Harriman had, insisting on her right and duty to speak in a *public* place, Trapnel chooses to define the frequently unstable *private* spaces where a woman undoubtedly was free to speak. By prophesying from her bedchamber and speaking only of – and to – her 'husband', Christ, Trapnel creates as modest behaviour that which might otherwise have earned her the scold's bridle or witch-trier's pin. In fact, her anticipation of such misogynist attacks in her earlier tracts and later through the figure of the spouse may be the reason why those attacks never materialised, and the absence of misogynist criticism may be the strongest evidence of Trapnel's agency as a woman prophet.

Crucially, this is an argument that is in keeping with Trapnel's own denial of agency in her prophecy. Like Fanny Burney's youthful journal addressed to 'nobody' or Christina Rossetti's secrets, the seventeenth-century woman prophet's 'nothingness' was, paradoxically, a source of self-definition and self-expression.[108] In refusing to stand up to speak as Quaker women did, Anna Trapnel entered her body and voice into the gender debates of the period, demonstrating that it was possible for women to participate in those debates not by defying restrictive standards of public and private behaviour but by exploiting their instability.

---

[108] Susan C. Greenfield, '"Oh Dear Resemblance of Thy Murdered Mother": Female Authorship in *Evelina*', *Eighteenth-Century Fiction* 3.4 (1991): 304–5. *The Early Journals and Letters of Fanny Burney*, ed. Lars E. Troide (Oxford: Clarendon Press, 1988), 1.2. For a reading of Rossetti's 'Winter: My Secret', see Tom Furniss and Michael Bath, *Reading Poetry: An Introduction* (London: Prentice Hall, 1996), pp. 98–101.

CHAPTER 6

The transfiguration of Colonel Hutchinson in
Lucy Hutchinson's elegies

Lucy Hutchinson would disagree heartily with the title of this chapter. 'I that am under a command not to grieve at the common rate of desolate women', as she insists in her biography of her husband, would never allow herself to be grouped with those 'who dote on mortal excellencies' and view their loved ones as 'adored idols'. Lucy, a devout and scholarly Puritan, knew the difference between human objects of desire and the God that had formed them: 'What shall I write of him is but a copy of [him]', she asserts of her husband. 'The original of all excellence is God him[self] and God alone'.[1]

This sentence creates a hierarchy with God himself at the apex, John Hutchinson below and Lucy Hutchinson decidedly near the bottom, creating a copy of a copy. Not surprisingly, such language of copies and originals, mirrors and reflections has caused difficulties for feminist critics. A woman who wrote that her husband 'soon made her more equal to him than he found her, for she was a very faithful mirror, reflecting truly, though but dimly, his own glories upon him' would seem to fit easily into the category of victimised, submissive wives.[2] The previous chapters of this book have demonstrated that it was possible for women to conform to such conventional models of wifely inferiority and submission and yet still develop an outspoken voice. Lucy Hutchinson is a particularly compelling example of this seeming conundrum. Far from confining her to a limiting role, her language of copies, reflections and shadows in fact enabled Lucy Hutchinson to speak seamlessly, and unapologetically, about both personal and political tragedy.

---

[1] N. H. Keeble, ed., *Memoirs of the Life of Colonel Hutchinson with a Fragment of Autobiography* (London: Everyman, 1995), pp. 16, 17. All subsequent references to the *Memoirs* are to this edition. I use the usually pejorative term 'Puritan' to describe Lucy Hutchinson because she used it proudly herself, along with the more neutral 'godly': in the *Memoirs* she writes that her husband's godliness 'branded him with the reproach of the world, though the glory of good men – Puritanism', p. 33.

[2] *Ibid.*, p. 51.

My admission that Hutchinson herself would not agree with the title of this chapter was not a mere opening gambit, for it is this distinction between idolatry and immortality that is a key to understanding both Lucy Hutchinson's theo-political vision and her private relationship with her husband. Alive and on earth, neither John Hutchinson nor the author herself, nor even the English republic they fought so hard to establish, could claim to be anything more than shadows of divine light, but dead they transcend all things earthly and human. And through Lucy Hutchinson's nimble pen, their mutual transcendence in turn rewrites our categories of public and private, and the traditional gender scheme we apply to them. This chapter offers a reading of the theology of transcendence in Lucy Hutchinson's writing, considering particularly how her categories are gendered – or gender-neutral – and attempting to discern her own complex notion of what is public and private in her writing. The final section challenges modern criticism of Hutchinson, using her writing to posit a way around the traditional categories of public and private in which we confine early modern women writers.[3]

---

[3] More than any of the women writers of this study, Lucy Hutchinson's work has been well contextualised in recent studies. David Norbrook is completing a study of Hutchinson's life and œuvre and a multi-volume edition of her works, and has elsewhere offered careful analysis of a wide variety of archival and bibliographic evidence. David Norbrook, 'Lucy Hutchinson's "Elegies" and the Situation of the Republican Woman Writer (with text)', *English Literary Renaissance* 27 (1997): 468–521; all texts of the elegies are taken from this edition, pp. 487–521. Norbrook has also edited the creation epic *Order and Disorder* (Oxford: Blackwell, 2001), which he first reattributed to Lucy Hutchinson in 'A devine Originall: Lucy Hutchinson and the "woman's version"', *Times Literary Supplement* 19 March 1999: 13–15. The evidence for reattribution is considered in more detail in his article 'Lucy Hutchinson and *Order and Disorder*: The Manuscript Evidence', *English Manuscript Studies 1100–1700* 9 (2000): 257–91. Because the spelling in the edition is modernised, quotations in this chapter are from the original printed text and manuscript. The first five cantos of the poem were printed in 1679 under the long title *Order and disorder: or, the world made and undone. Being meditations upon the creation and the fall; as it is recorded in the beginning of genesis*, Wing A3594 (London: Margaret White for Henry Mortlake); twenty cantos (the last unfinished) are preserved in Osborne MS fb. 100, in the Beinecke Library at Yale University. The poem was printed anonymously but long attributed to Hutchinson's brother, Sir Allen Apsley. Norbrook has also published a study and edition of 'To Mʳ: Waller upon his Panegirique to the Lord Protector': 'Lucy Hutchinson versus Edmund Waller: An Unpublished Reply to Waller's *A Panegyrick to My Lord Protector*', *The Seventeenth Century* 11 (1996): 61–86. N. H. Keeble's work has drawn out Lucy and John Hutchinson's political affiliations and their place within the tradition of nonconformist writing. See the Introduction to his edition of the *Memoirs*, pp. xix–xxix, and '"The Colonel's Shadow": Lucy Hutchinson, Women's Writing and the civil war', in *Literature and the English civil war*, ed. Thomas Healy and Jonathan Sawday (Cambridge: Cambridge University Press, 1990), pp. 227–47. He also makes frequent references to Hutchinson in *The Literary Culture of Nonconformity in Later Seventeenth-Century England* (Leicester: Leicester University Press, 1987). Rather than retrace these competent footsteps, I wish here to draw attention to the role of gender and intellectual ability in two specific episodes in Lucy Hutchinson's life as she herself narrated it.

After her husband's death in 1664 as an imprisoned regicide, Lucy Hutchinson wrote a manuscript account of *The Life of John Hutchinson of Owthorpe, in the County of Nottingham, Esquire*, in order to defend his actions to both his royalist enemies and his fellow Parliamentarians, who may have resented the pardon he received at the Restoration.[4] She also left behind an unfinished autobiography which partakes of the traditions of spiritual autobiography and also situates her as a woman of a certain class, the daughter of Lucy St John and Sir Allen Apsley, then Lieutenant of the Tower of London. Both the *Life* and the autobiography idealise Lucy Hutchinson, her husband and her marriage, a strategy that is hardly surprising given her need to vindicate their reputations.[5] What is surprising, perhaps, is the image of herself that she chooses to put forward as part of this idealisation, an image which offers some correction to the conventional model of a meek, godly woman, or even Milton's Eve, asking questions only of her husband and demurely refusing to take part in male intellectual exchange. The Lucy Hutchinson of the *Life* is a pious woman, but one not afraid to act on her own behalf or for her family, at one point undertaking to conceal her husband's identity before a royalist captain. She is also a markedly intellectual woman, who excels in classical as well as Biblical scholarship, with a studiousness that is above and beyond the usual exhortations to pious reading.[6]

The description she offers of her early education in the autobiography illustrates the importance of intellectual accomplishment to her self-fashioning. Just before giving birth in 1619/20, Lucy St John Apsley had a dream that 'she should have a daughter of some extraordinary eminency'. The expectant parents assumed that such a daughter would be a woman of great intellectual ability rather than a woman of beauty, gentleness or piety; and as a result Lucy Hutchinson received a lavish education, with eight tutors to teach her 'languages, music, dancing, writing and needlework'. From the age of four she could speak French and 'read English perfectly'. She excelled particularly at Latin, in which she boasts she 'was so apt that I outstripped my brothers who were at school, although my father's chaplain, that was my tutor, was a pitiful dull fellow'. She loved reading so much that

---

[4] On the purpose of the *Life* see Keeble, Introduction, *Memoirs*, pp. xix–xxviii.

[5] Julius Hutchinson, the first editor of the *Life*, included a transcription of the autobiography in *Memoirs of the Life of Colonel Hutchinson* (London: Longman, 1806). The manuscript of the autobiography is now lost. The manuscript of the *Life* is Nottinghamshire Archives DD/HU 4. Fragments of a previous draft are in British Library Additional MSS 25,901, 39,799, and 46,172N.

[6] *Memoirs*, pp. 89–91, 46–8.

her mother hid her books for fear that it would endanger her health, but it is not entirely clear from the narrative whether her mother felt this was a particular danger for a daughter, rather than a son, or if she simply hoped to force exercise on a child who at every spare moment 'would steal into some hole or other to read'.[7] What is significant is that Lucy Hutchinson's own account of herself does not hide or apologise for these accomplishments, but foregrounds them as demonstrations of her seriousness and piety.

The same element of intellectualism is apparent in Hutchinson's narrative of her courtship and marriage. In her *Life of John Hutchinson* she herself does not enter the scene until the age of eighteen. Here, in keeping with her purpose of vindicating her husband, her own character initially takes on a romance role, as the exemplary woman who through a fateful encounter wins the love of the hero.[8] In 1638 the author's younger sister Barbara lodged at the same house as one John Hutchinson, the son of Sir Thomas Hutchinson and Margaret Biron, and chanced to mention to Mr Hutchinson that some Latin books lying about belonged to her elder sister. On the basis of this evidence of her erudition, John Hutchinson fell in love with the absent elder sister, much to the disappointment of the women of the house, who 'used to talk much to him of her, telling how reserved and studious she was, and other things which they esteemed no advantage'.[9]

Nevertheless, the hero was not daunted in his affections. A few days later he heard a sonnet by 'a woman in the neighbourhood', and, 'fancying something of rationality in the sonnet beyond the customary reach of a she-wit', was enraptured to discover that it was by none other than his beloved, but as yet unseen, Lucy Apsley. Eventually, after some agonising fears that she had married someone else, he contrived to meet her, and many years later his wife recounted the scene with cool, coy irony: 'his heart, being prepossessed with his own fancy, was not free to discern how little there was in her to answer so great an expectation. She was not ugly; in a careless riding-habit, she had a melancholy negligence both of herself and others, as if she neither affected to please others, nor took notice of anything before her.' The women of the neighbourhood, frustrated that their attempts to dissuade him had failed, 'with witty spite represented all her faults to him, which chiefly terminated in the negligence of her dress and habit and all womanish ornaments, giving herself wholly up to study

[7] *Ibid.*, pp. 14–15.
[8] Romance conventions in the *Life* are mentioned in Norbrook, 'Lucy Hutchinson's "Elegies"', p. 483; and Keeble, *The Literary Culture of Nonconformity*, p. 155.
[9] *Memoirs*, pp. 46, 47.

and writing'. At length, in spite of Lucy Apsley's indifference and lack of 'womanish' charms, John Hutchinson persuaded her to marry him.[10]

Boy meets girl, boy loves girl, boy marries girl: but beneath the conventions of romance lurk some not-so-familiar elements. As a biographer Lucy Hutchinson declined to tell the whole story: 'I shall pass by all the little amorous relations which, if I would take the pains to relate, would make a true history of a more handsome management of love than the best romances describe[.]'[11] What she has left us is a tale of uncommon intellectual desire. Reading and writing play a significant part in John Hutchinson's initial attraction, much to the consternation of the women of the party, who 'esteemed no advantage' her pastimes of 'study and writing'. The gendering here is crucial: although John Hutchinson himself believes it unusual for a woman to write well, he does not find such an accomplishment unfeminine or monstrous, but rather that it attracts him to her as a potential wife. It is the women, on the other hand, who scorn the scholarly dedication that prevented a woman from being physically desirable and pleasing in conversation. These events that began her relationship with her husband bear remembering as we consider how Lucy Hutchinson, from her widowhood, characterises her role as a wife: like most women of the period, she was forced to negotiate among competing standards of 'womanish' behaviour.

HUMAN AND DIVINE: THE THEOLOGICAL WRITINGS

One of the seemingly 'unwomanish' elements of Lucy Hutchinson's œuvre is the well-developed philosophical and theological system that underlies all of her writing. As a republican who believed that '[t]rue religion was now almost lost' in the 1650s, Hutchinson, like Milton, sought comfort in discerning the complementary roles of God and human beings in human history.[12] Although, again like Milton, her interest in cosmic history is most profoundly expressed in a retelling of the creation story, all of Lucy Hutchinson's writings demonstrate a concern with 'the original of things', the divine order that governed the universe and established a connection between God and Adam, heaven and earth.[13] In the elegies and *Life* these images come to fruition in the posthumous union of both John Hutchinson and the republican cause with 'the original of all excellence', God himself.[14] These memorial texts thus serve as a climax of Lucy Hutchinson's personal

---

[10] *Ibid.*, pp. 47, 49, 51.   [11] *Ibid.*, p. 51.   [12] *Ibid.*, p. 257.

[13] From the preface to the 1679 printed edition of *Order and disorder*, sig. [A^r]; for a fuller discussion of her treatment of history in the poem see Norbrook, 'A devine Originall'.

[14] *Memoirs*, p. 17.

and political grief, of her vision of human beings and human history refined together in the perfecting fire of an all-encompassing God.

Before considering the culmination of her cosmology, however, it is useful to examine the theological underpinning of these images of union found in Lucy Hutchinson's other writings. The treatise for her daughter, *On the Principles of the Christian Religion*, together with *Order and disorder* and statements of faith in her theological commonplace book, offer evidence of Lucy Hutchinson's vision of a divinely ordered world. As David Norbrook has noted, her philosophy draws on a Neoplatonic cosmology that has been given a Christian gloss.[15] Like Aemilia Lanyer's, Hutchinson's cosmology has much in common with Spenser's vision in the *Foure hymnes*, although Hutchinson tends to use more philosophical terms than either Spenser or Lanyer.[16] The Triune God is the 'first uncaused cause' in whom all elements of the created universe begin and end.[17] Human beings, and human history, issue forth like streams or reflections, bearing with them an element of the divine within their corrupt forms. It is this element of the divine that enables human beings to know God, who is otherwise invisible.

But even the devout have but limited vision of God's divine nature, made visible only in imperfect copies. To clarify if not pierce through the 'Misterious Clouds', Lucy Hutchinson turns to imagery of divine love and union, bridging the Platonic gap between creator and created.[18] Cleaving, hungering, devotion, ecstasy, desire: all of these terms occur in her attempt to describe the divine love that unites mortal and immortal. Drawing on the affective language of the Psalms and Song of Songs, she describes love of God as 'the vitall heate of a true believer' that leads to displays of desire strikingly akin to human loves: 'Desire of enjoying him only', 'spiritual heate, and fervency in all the worship', 'strong aspirings towards God, and longings after a blessed com[m]union with him'.[19]

Lucy Hutchinson, of course, is not alone in using emotional and even erotic language to describe the relationship between the believer and God; as this study demonstrates, she draws on a rich tradition of literature and Biblical scholarship that likened divine love to human love. Hutchinson is particularly indebted to John Owen and other Independent and Presbyterian thinkers of the 1640s and 1650s; she translated Owen's *Theologumena*

---

[15] Norbrook explores Hutchinson's use of Neoplatonic mirrors and reflections in 'Lucy Hutchinson's "Elegies"', p. 471.

[16] See chapter 2 above.   [17] *Order and disorder*, 1679, p. 3.

[18] Osborne MS fb. 100, f. [2r]. The line is not in the 1679 edition.

[19] *On the Principles of the Christian Religion, and On Theology*, ed. Julius Hutchinson (London: Longman, 1817), pp. 83, 94, 97, 100.

pantodapa, a treatise against natural religion, and was probably attending his London conventicle in the 1670s.[20] During the interregnum Owen and his contemporaries developed the metaphor of union with God as the basis of their Calvinist doctrine of salvation. For these men, the purpose of Christ's sacrifice was to restore the communion between humans and God that had been lost in the Fall. 'But now in Christ, we have *bold-nesse and accesse* with *confidence*', wrote John Owen in his seminal work of popular divinity, *Of communion with god the father, sonne, and holy ghost* (1657). 'And truely for *sinners* to have *fellowship* with God, the infinitely *holy* God, is an astonishing dispensation.'[21] This assertion itself may not be especially controversial, but the consequent excessive use of affective and metaphorical language to describe human relations with God opened men like Owen, Samuel Annesley and Thomas Jacomb to the ridicule of Latitudinarians after the Restoration. As the first chapter of this study explores, William Sherlock and others used such statements as evidence that the nonconformist faith was based solely on emotion rather than reason.

Lucy Hutchinson for the most part avoids such linguistic excess by grounding her theology and cosmology in the vocabulary of classical philosophy and Neoplatonism.[22] Curiously, though, she does not use either the Christian or Platonic concepts of mystical union to invoke the metaphor of marriage, unlike all the other women of this study. Although *Order and disorder*, like *Paradise lost*, extols at length the joys of companionate marriage, in only a few instances does the marital union become a model of the divine union.[23] Hutchinson does glance at marriage repeatedly as one of the possible roles that Christ can play – he is 'head, husband, elder brother' in the treatise to her daughter, and 'father, brother, husband, son' in *Order and disorder*'s gloss on Genesis 3:15 – but with the exception of one crucial passage on the creation of Adam and Eve, she chooses instead to use a more generalised vocabulary of love.[24] Yet although she seldom describes Christ as a husband, her God is often implicitly a lover; like the God of Lanyer, Spenser and Donne, he is one whom human beings seek with a restless desire for fiery, self-immolating union.

---

[20] On Hutchinson's relationship to Owen, see Norbrook, Introduction to *Order and Disorder*, pp. xix–xx. Her manuscript translation of *Theologumena pantodapa* was printed in 1817 under the title *On Theology* with her treatise to her daughter, *On the Principles of the Christian Religion*.

[21] Wing O777 John Owen, *of communion with god the father, sonne, and holy ghost* (Oxford: A. Lichfield for Philemon Stephens, 1657), p. 3.

[22] On Hutchinson's classicism see Norbrook, Introduction to *Order and Disorder*, p. xxvi.

[23] See Norbrook, 'A devine Originall', pp. 14–15.

[24] *On the Principles*, p. 49; *Order and disorder*, 1679, p. 64.

The connection between her Platonic imagery of love and her theology of marriage is apparent in *Order and disorder*, in which Hutchinson uses the relationship between Adam and Eve as a way of revealing the hierarchy of desire between God and human beings. In an interesting parallel to *Paradise lost*, these passages use paradisal human sexuality as a metaphor for the union between God and his people made possible through Christ's sacrifice. Yet unlike *Paradise lost*, *Order and disorder* underlines the similarity of Adam and Eve, their relative equality in comparison with their inferiority to God. In the garden of Eden, God offers the lonely Adam, yearning for communion with the divine, an earthly partner in the shape of Eve. As another mortal human, Eve cannot 'Fill the more comprehensive soul of Man', but she is the closest and most satisfying match because she is the most like him, neither too high nor too low, like God or the 'bruitish' animals. Even the angels are not appropriate companions for Adam:

> No; for though man partake intelligence,
> Yet that being joyn'd to an inferiour sense,
> Dull'd by corporeal vapours, cannot be
> Refin'd enough for angels company:
> As strings screw'd up too high, as bows still bent
> Or break themselves, or crack the instrument;
> So drops neglected flesh into the grave,
> If it no share in the souls pleasures have.
> Man like himself needs an associate,
> Who doth both soul and sense participate.[25]

Not only can humans not fully communicate with the angels (or God, who is above them), but the very effort of communication is in itself destructive to human bodies, which strain and break under the stress of doing what they were not designed for. No, Adam and Eve must have each other, for if neither can fully satisfy the other, their physical and spiritual bond is the closest to divine union that either can reach.

But if the first marriage is a record of human frailty, in Lucy Hutchinson's account it also hints at the possibilities of union to come. In a passage drawing on the same tradition as Lady Anne Southwell's lyric 'All.maried.men', Hutchinson compares the creation of Eve from Adam's rib to the birth of the Church from Christ's wounds:

---

[25] *Order and disorder*, 1679, pp. 25, 33. 'Or break themselves, or crack the instrument;' in MS reads: 'Doe breake themselves, or crack the Instrument', f. [21ʳ].

> So from the second *Adams* bleeding side
> God form'd the Gospel Church, his mystique Bride,
> Whose strength was only of his firmness made,
> His blood, quick spirits into ours convey'd:
> His wasted flesh our wasted flesh supplied,
> And we were then revived when he died.[26]

Like John Owen and other nonconformist theologians, Hutchinson segues easily from the third person singular to the first person plural. What is the Bride's is also 'ours'; the 'mystique Bride' is not merely the institution but each individual before God. Their 'marriage' to Christ is essentially a healing process: the poet alludes to the passion tradition that informed Aemilia Lanyer's *Salve deus rex judæorum*, underlining that it is Christ's wasted body that enables him to heal and revive.

For Hutchinson, the healing power of Christ's sacrifice allows the Church to join with him in a union of equals, mirroring the ideal of a marriage of equals she imagined for Adam and Eve. Her Christ echoes the words of Adam, viewing his new-formed perfect bride:

> My spouse, my sister, said he, thou art mine;
> I and my death, I and my life are thine;
> For thee I did my heavenly Father quit
> That thou with me on my high throne mayst sit,
> My mothers humane flesh in death did leave
> For thee, that I to thee might only cleave,
>
> . . .
>
> Henceforth no longer two but one we are,
> Thou dost my merit, life, grace, glory share[.][27]

Weaving together the creation account in Genesis (particularly Adam's welcome to Eve in 2:23), the love lyrics of the Song of Songs and prophecies in the Psalms and Isaiah, Hutchinson unites the old Adam, still perfect before the Fall, and the new, made perfect in sacrifice. Hutchinson's language also blurs the distinction between the Church and Eve, both 'The Virgin fair', both presented by the grace of God to a lover's warm embrace.

This is proper, ordered desire, directed at an equal object that can be enjoyed, intellectually and sexually, without shame:

> The Bride with these caresses entertain'd
> In naked beauty doth before him stand,
> And knows no shame purg'd from all foul desire

---

[26] *Order and disorder*, 1679, p. 38.   [27] *Ibid.*

Whose secret guilt kindles the blushing fire.
Her glorious Lord is naked too, no more
Conceal'd in types and shadows as before.
So our first parents innocently did
Behold that nakedness which since is hid,
That lust may not catch fire from beauties flame
Engendring thoughts which die the cheeks with shame[.][28]

The nakedness of Adam and Eve, Christ and the Church signals their ability to see one another entire; when sin comes into the world it brings not only the 'foul desire' of sexual lust but also the darkening of the human vision of God, who can only be witnessed in 'types and shadows'. But the reverse of this separation is a fusion of sexual knowledge with spiritual knowledge that echoes *Paradise lost*: just as Adam cannot join with the angels because the lack of physical converse would destroy him, so Christ and the Church, like Adam and Eve, must know each other in entirety in order for their union to be complete. The vulnerable intimacy of human sexuality – or the purer, paradisal version of it – comes to represent the breaking of all barriers between Christ and his people in the Church that will be realised in the last days.

It is worth comparing Hutchinson's lines with Milton's description of Adam and Eve's first evening together:

> So spake our general mother, and with eyes
> Of conjugal attraction unreproved,
> And meek surrender, half embracing leaned
> On our first father, half her swelling breast
> Naked met his under the flowing gold
> Of her loose tresses hid: he in delight
> Both of her beauty and submissive charms
> Smiled with superior love, as Jupiter
> On Juno smiles, when he impregns the clouds
> That shed May flowers; and pressed her matron lip
> With kisses pure[.][29]

Milton's sexual politics differ subtly and significantly from Lucy Hutchinson's. Although in both *Paradise lost* and *Order and disorder* 'conjugal attraction' is 'unreproved' before the Fall, Milton's Eve nevertheless encounters sexual union with 'meek surrender' and 'submissive charms',

---

[28] *Ibid.*, 1679, p. 39.
[29] *Paradise Lost* IV.492–502, in John Carey and Alastair Fowler, eds., *The Poems of John Milton* (London: Longman, 1980).

implying that even before the Fall her inferiority is apparent in her experience of sexuality.[30] Hutchinson's description, on the contrary, contains
no such language of superior and inferior love. Eve and the Church triumphant know no shame, suggesting that in paradise, at least, the open
knowledge of sexuality is enjoyed by both men and women.

Hutchinson's concept of the relationships between body and soul, human
and divine, is in many ways entirely orthodox and conventional. Her escha-
tology has much in common with the Cambridge Platonists and, before
them, Spenserian images of divine love; and the interiority and mysticism of Platonism also had its attractions for some of her nonconformist
contemporaries.[31] Yet it is precisely the fact that she operates within an
intellectual tradition that makes Lucy Hutchinson intriguing as a woman
writer. The scholarly erudition of her theology is unequalled by any of
her female contemporaries, none of whom crafted such a coherent philosophical system. Superior even to Lady Anne Southwell's two generations
before, Hutchinson's reading ranges over a broad selection of classical and
contemporary sources, and she does not stop at nonconformist sermons or
the traditional humanist canon. Hutchinson's commonplace book includes
thoughtful paraphrases of Hermes Trismegistus and Ficino, both potentially heretical writers who would not have appeared on recommended
reading lists for Puritan gentlewomen: Hutchinson's favourite John Owen
had certainly professed a strong distrust of Ficino's brand of Platonic Christianity.[32] Along with her translation of Lucretius, her reading of occult texts
demonstrates that Lucy Hutchinson was willing to indulge curiosity about
unorthodox ideas for the sake of expanding her knowledge of God.[33] Such
liberal thinking may have been acceptable practice for university theologians, but it is unprecedented in a Puritan woman writer, and suggests that
in certain circumstances gender norms did not limit a woman's intellectual
experience.

[30] Not all critics agree. James Grantham Turner, for example, argues that Adam's superiority is subsumed
in moments of consummation: *One Flesh: Paradisal Marriage and Sexual Relations in the Age of Milton*
(Oxford: Clarendon Press, 1993), especially pp. 239, 286.

[31] On seventeenth-century Platonists see Sarah Hutton, 'Introduction to the Renaissance and Seven-
teenth Century', in *Platonism and the English Imagination*, ed. Anna Baldwin and Sarah Hutton
(Cambridge: Cambridge University Press, 1994), pp. 67–75. See also Keeble, *The Literary Culture of
Nonconformity*, pp. 166–70.

[32] Nottinghamshire Archives MS DD/HU 1, pp. 147–8. On the response of English Protestants to
the Continental occult, see Nigel Smith, *Perfection Proclaimed: Language and Literature in English
Radical Religion, 1640–1660* (Oxford: Clarendon Press, 1989), pp. 107–9; Hutton, 'Introduction to
the Renaissance and Seventeenth Century', p. 75.

[33] Hugh de Quehen, ed., *Lucy Hutchinson's Translation of Lucretius: De rerum natura* (London:
Duckworth, 1996).

THE ELEGIES: JOHN HUTCHINSON IN DEATH

As well as contradicting the early modern norms that emphasise women's intellectual weakness, Lucy Hutchinson also contradicts some twenty-first-century feminist models of the early modern woman writer. For example, given the cultural traditions that located woman's inferiority in her weaker, more polluted body, it is intriguing to find a woman writer so concerned with the perfectibility of human flesh after death. But the gender politics implied in such a statement are not Hutchinson's own: she makes little effort to apologise for Eve, and her notion of resurrected bodies applies equally to men and women. Unlike all of the other women of this study, her writing is without a gendered polemical edge; perhaps because she herself experienced little intellectual constraint as a woman writing, she makes no attempt to vindicate women. Her concern for higher, ungendered truths is precisely that, with little or no implication for relationships between human men and women. And yet it is this absence of interest in gender politics that makes Lucy Hutchinson so crucial to this study. She is the exception that disproves the rule, once again reminding us that early modern debates were not our own, and that we need to read women's writing in particular with careful attention to its own political concerns. While she may not champion her own rights or those of any other woman, Lucy Hutchinson's use of ungendered moral paradigms to authorise her highly politicised voice is a fascinating manifestation of a woman's power within what we might traditionally consider masculine domains.

In her elegies on the death of her husband and her account of his *Life*, Hutchinson uses that power to further the republican cause both she and her husband had fought for. Mystical union imagery is a crucial strategy in her demonstration that John Hutchinson's cause is in fact God's cause. Appropriating imagery used in her other writings, the poet envisions her husband in physical as well as spiritual union with God in heaven, his dead body transformed through a series of alchemical processes that reunite him with his divine source; but she describes herself, left behind on the impure earth, living a kind of spiritual half-life after she loses her earthly communion with her husband. As in *Order and disorder*, the pitch of her loss slides easily from the personal to the cosmic, for as she mourns her husband so she mourns the wreck of '. . . ye league of God himselfe dissould / W:^{ch} a whole Nation in one cvrse Involud[.]'[34] John Hutchinson has been taken from her, and the republican triumph they had hoped

---

[34] 'Elegies', 3.27–8.

for has passed into the night of the Restoration. Throughout the elegies and the *Life*, Lucy Hutchinson uses parallel imagery to connect these two poles of grief, almost literally immortalising both her husband and his politics.

Nigel Smith argues that elegies in the 1650s were almost entirely devoted to grief for the king and other royalist martyrs; the elegies to Cromwell, Essex and other Parliamentarians 'are really panegyrical and they had to be so'.[35] The elegies for John Hutchinson are part of an effort to reclaim the genre from royalism; in form and imagery they bear some resemblance to the poetry of Katherine Philips, but refit the romance elements of 'Orinda's' verse for republican political aims. The manuscript, in an unidentified late seventeenth-century hand, contains fourteen elegies, an inserted passage from *Order and disorder*, eight epitaphs, and two 'songs'. Like Philips, Hester Pulter and other royalist writers, Lucy Hutchinson frames several of her elegies according to real or imagined occasions: 'To the Sun Shineing into her Cham:ʳ', 'On the Spring 1668'.[36] She recapitulates and contrasts her own imagery; the poem to the sun is balanced by two on the night, and two poems use the conceit of the Hutchinson estate of Owthorpe mourning for its master. The epitaphs also reuse language and imagery, although each is unique enough to stand as an individual poem, rather than repeated drafts of the same. There is a sense within these poems of a circling around grief in an attempt to understand the process and keep hold of that which was lost.

Pivotal to Lucy Hutchinson's effort to console herself and her loved ones is her use of conventional Christian consolations for political ends. All Christians could hope for bodily resurrection and union with God at the end of time, but the transformation of the dead seldom receives the repeated and detailed descriptions Lucy Hutchinson offers in her elegies. When combined with her characterisation of her husband as a republican hero, her focus on his apotheosis has overtly political tones, the treasonous suggestion that not only he but the republic will be perfected and rise again. In the meditation appended to the manuscript of the *Life*, for example, Hutchinson hints that her husband was particularly favoured by God in his death: 'It is true the fiery chariot of a fever was sent to fetch him out [of] the double prison, that of his oppressors and that of his flesh which the [ ] soul was more oppressed with than the other while he remained in

---

[35] Nigel Smith, *Literature and Revolution in England, 1640–1660* (New Haven, Connecticut: Yale University Press, 1994), pp. 291 and 396 n. 92.

[36] 'Elegies', 2 and 14. On the relationship to Katherine Philips, see 'Elegies', p. 480. Hester Pulter's poems are in Leeds University Library, Brotherton Collection MS Lt.q.32.

it, [and] was translated out of this world into the Father's glory[.]'[37] The 'fiery chariot' points back to the end of the prophet Elijah, who did not die but was taken in his body into heaven by 'a chariot of fire and horses of fire' (2 Kings 3:11); the verb 'translated' (from the Latin 'carried over') also suggests that John Hutchinson was claimed physically by God. Thus John Hutchinson's republican martyrdom is compared to the death of a prophet of God, and both are granted the privilege of immediate union with God.

Crucially, the transformation of John Hutchinson's flesh begins before his death, so that when he reaches the moment of death, like Elijah he is already close to his creator. In the *Life* Lucy Hutchinson describes his last months in prison in language similar to Owen's *Of communion with god*, as a process of sublimation bringing the believer closer and closer to union with God. The immediate cause of John Hutchinson's transformations is his study of scripture while in prison, enhancing his knowledge of God above all other things. Having 'conversed in' the word of God he approaches the threshold of union with God himself: 'This continual study of the Scriptures did infinitely ravish his soul and refine it and take it off from all lower exercise[.]'[38] In the elegies, Lucy Hutchinson uses images of light, fire and even alchemical transformation to describe the change her husband undergoes. His reading in prison

> in his darkist sollitude shot rayes
> That shamd ye splendor of ye brightest days
> Each admirable leafe ye rich seene Varies
> And euery Seane a stock of glorie Carries
> This booke his soule wth God & heauen acquants[.]

The Bible is so powerful that it bathes John Hutchinson in a heavenly light, allowing him in his prison to see truths 'W:^{ch} no glad mortall in The free world meets'. Reversing the images of darkness that predominate after the Fall in *Order and disorder*, Lucy Hutchinson here imagines her husband almost literally enlightened by brighter and brighter rays of truth.[39]

Like Adam, John Hutchinson's body is too low and earthly, and cannot be taken up at once without being destroyed by consummation with what is wholly spiritual. The Colonel must ascend by degrees, learning not only to see God but slowly becoming like him physically and spiritually, even one with him. As Lucy Hutchinson writes in 'The Recovery', the centrepiece of her elegies,

---

[37] *Memoirs*, p. 337.   [38] *Ibid.*, p. 328.   [39] 'Elegies', 6.21–5, 18.

Here earth aduanct to heauen its frailty ends
For the pure Nature taking in The Crosse
By its powerfull touch to Gold conuerts ye Drosse
And as it Through ye fleshly medium shines
That body transubstantiates and refines[.]⁴⁰

Significantly, she reaches here for the paradigm that she elsewhere rejects for the Eucharist: transubstantiation, in which the earthly is mystically changed to the heavenly. The lines become a bold assertion of the Hutchinsons' faith in the power of Word-centred piety: never mind the Eucharist, John Hutchinson needs only the Word to become like God in his death.

In narrating her husband's death, Lucy Hutchinson brings her language to a mystical climax, envisioning her husband, like Elijah, almost flying to the arms of God:

Now had he reacht to Pieties high top
And Their Stood exstasied w:^th Joy & hope
While faith w:^ch led him all along did wate
Till death it Selfe vnlockt Heauens splendid gate
While open seene departing swift he Cries
Tis what tis wher I would so smiling dies[.]⁴¹

This passage echoes her prose account in the *Life* but transforms it into an apotheosis, culminating in her husband's last words. The euphemism 'departing' here loses its overtones of passive resignation and is transformed into an active, 'swift' movement. The dying man embraces death and is in turn embraced by his God, becoming inseparable from God himself.

Describing the dead as united with God is of course a convention of Christian piety, but Lucy Hutchinson's imagery is more apocalyptic and extreme than most. Richard Crashaw's elegy 'Vpon Bishop Andrewes his Picture before his Sermons' (1631) uses similar language of vision, light and divine communion but with an emphasis on rationality and learning:

This reverend shadow cast that setting Sun,
Whose glorious course through our Horizon run,
Left the dimme face of this dull Hemisphœre,
All one great eye, all drown'd in one great Teare.
Whose faire illustrious soule, led his free thought
Through Learnings Vniverse, and (vainely) sought
Roome for her spatious self, untill at length
Shee found the way home, with an holy strength

---

⁴⁰ *Ibid.*, 10.14–18.   ⁴¹ *Ibid.*, 6.49–54; cf. *Memoirs*, p. 330.

Snatch't her self hence, to Heaven: fill'd a bright place,
Mongst those immortall fires, and on the face
Of her great maker fixt her flaming eye,
There still to read true pure divinity.[42]

Significantly, Crashaw imagines Lancelot Andrewes as always godlike, a 'spatious self' that finds room for his intellect only in heaven. To Lucy Hutchinson this would have seemed like the idolatry she forswore at the beginning of the *Life*. By contrast, she introduces a Puritan element of human perfectibility into the picture: her husband must undergo the trials of prison and rigorous study of the scriptures before he can become like God. Although there is no way of knowing whether she had read Crashaw's poem, Hutchinson's elegies in a sense are a response to the royalist, conformist tradition that his hero Andrewes represented. In reclaiming the imagery of transfiguration, she makes her husband a hero of a very different kind of ecclesiology, one which viewed true piety not as an adherence to one true Church but as an individual's continual examination of his or her conscience. For John Hutchinson and for those he left behind, their commitment to the process of reaching heaven is what sets them apart: 'There let us seek them,' Lucy Hutchinson advises her children, 'thither let us hasten after him; there having found him, let us cease to bewail among the dead that which is risen, or rather was immortal.'[43]

The use of the past tense in the last clause is particularly suggestive: just when did John Hutchinson become immortal? In the final meditation at the end of the *Life*, Lucy Hutchinson implies that, as with his physical transformation, her husband's immortality was a fact before his death: 'poor blinded people believe him dead, but virtue and grace had so immortalized him that death hath very little of him; his soul living in God was secured from death'. While all of this is the conventional language of Christian grief, perhaps more striking are two direct allusions to the death of Christ, the man who truly was immortal even in life. In that same meditation, she imagines John Hutchinson consoling his friends and family in the words of Christ, 'Methinks when I see the poor virgins weeping I hear this member of Christ applying that Scripture, "Daughters of Jerusalem, weep not for me but weep for your selves"', echoing Luke 23:28, in which Jesus admonishes the bereaved women following him to the place of execution. In a like tone Lucy Hutchinson admonishes herself in the elegies, 'Why seeke wee y:ⁿ

---

[42] L. C. Martin, ed., *The Poems, English, Latin, and Greek, of Richard Crashaw*, 2nd edn (Oxford: Clarendon Press, 1957), pp. 163–4, lines 1–12.
[43] *Memoirs*, p. 17.

amoung y:ᵉ dead', quoting the angels who stand outside Christ's empty tomb (Luke 24:5).[44]

Because Christ's resurrection foreshadows human resurrection, it was not necessarily unusual or heretical to compare grief for a mortal human to grief for Christ. Within the context of framing her husband as a hero, however, Lucy Hutchinson's pointed comparisons of her husband to Christ elevate John Hutchinson's death to the level of martyrdom. The parallels between John Hutchinson and Christ are evident throughout the memoirs: as she narrates them, the events of his life, or at least of his death, bear a striking resemblance to the Messiah's. Like Christ, John Hutchinson dies innocent, 'Deaths Spotlesse victime'. Like Christ he goes willingly to 'Prison exile death for his deare sake'. Like Christ he is crowned in 'deathlesse glory'. Most importantly, like Christ he seeks to usher in the Kingdom of God on earth.[45] Along with her allusion to Elijah, such connections run perilously close to the idolatry that Lucy Hutchinson abjures in the beginning of the *Life*.

These parallels between John Hutchinson and Christ have a distinctly political edge; Lucy Hutchinson may have lost a husband, but England had also lost a champion who fell '. . . a Sacrifice / For his Greate Kings Supreame pure pᵣfect Laws[.]'[46] David Norbrook's study of the elegies explores in detail the political implications of Lucy Hutchinson's idealisation of her husband the republican hero: in extolling his virtues she defends and immortalises his political and moral vision.[47] I would complement this reading by arguing that she also creates a connection between her husband and his republicanism by placing both in the realm of the divine, above normal human conversation. In the elegies and the *Life* Lucy Hutchinson imagines a John Hutchinson so transformed by divine conversation that in death he becomes continuous with God himself. The republican cause, likewise, is envisioned as a reflection of divine government, even an attempt to transform the earthly into the heavenly, to usher in the Kingdom of God on earth.

In the Hutchinsons' political vision, the Kingdom of God and the hoped-for Kingdom of England were continuous, united in the triplet of 'Parliament, Gospel ministry, and English liberty'. In terms of details, Lucy Hutchinson is cagey about what this Kingdom might look like: as the Commonwealth was formed in 1649, she admits 'at that time every man almost was fancying [a] form of government, and angry, when this came

---

[44] *Ibid.*, pp. 337, 338; 'Elegies', 8.46.   [45] 'Elegies', 17.8, cf. also 20.7; 15.13; 15.18.
[46] *Ibid.*, 16.12–13.   [47] Norbrook, 'Lucy Hutchinson's "Elegies"', throughout.

forth, that his invention took not place', but she does not record what her own design might have been. The term 'republic' itself took on a variety of different meanings during the Commonwealth, and the vagueness of John and Lucy Hutchinson's politics is not unusual. The Hutchinsons were not part of the classical republican wing, but were among those, like Milton, 'more concerned with the virtue of those in power than with the precise model', and Puritans 'for whom the heavenly kingdom in the end mattered more than secular freedom'.[48] The Hutchinsons believed any model of government should be based on scripture: John Hutchinson argued that he could not reject the king's death warrant without 'giving up the people of God' whom he had led 'by the oath of God'.[49]

After Cromwell suspended Parliament, the Hutchinsons lamented the loss of this unique combination of religious and political values – 'all faith, honesty, religion and English liberty' – in which many had hoped that the will of God would become the will of the Parliament. John Hutchinson had always been convinced that he was acting according to God's plan. In the wreck of republicanism at the Restoration, he became almost millenarian in his sense of the cosmic implications of English political development. He re-examined the principles of republicanism and his own role in attempting to establish them, and became convinced that theirs had indeed been the cause of God:

he discovered the doctrine of the kingdom of Christ to be set up in visibility and glory over all the nations as well as over his saints in the Church and in their consciences. And he much admired at himself that he had so long overlooked what seemed to him now so plain in the word of God, which every day gave him new glorious discoveries of the mysteries of Christ and Antichrist, and made him rejoice in all he had done in the Lord's cause.[50]

Christ ruling 'in visibility and glory': this, the Hutchinsons now believed, was what the radicals had hoped and fought for, the rule of God's kingdom on earth.

In fact, the Hutchinsons and other republicans never did witness the rule of God on earth; they were dissatisfied with Cromwell's management of government from the beginning of the new order in 1649. But despite the long series of setbacks and disappointments, for Lucy Hutchinson the final devastating blow came with her husband's death in 1664. Towards the end of her biography, when John Hutchinson is imprisoned in Sandown

---

[48] *Memoirs*, pp. 301, 236. David Norbrook, *Writing the English Republic: Poetry, Rhetoric and Politics, 1627–1660* (Cambridge: Cambridge University Press, 1999), p. 18, see also pp. 16–17.
[49] *Memoirs*, p. 235.   [50] *Ibid.*, pp. 259, 286–7.

Castle, Kent, Lucy Hutchinson narrates a scene in which they discuss the connection between his approaching death and that of the republic:

One day when she was weeping, after he had said many things to comfort her, he gave her reasons why she should hope and be assured that this cause would revive, because the interest of God was so much involved in it that he was entitled to it. She told him she did not doubt but the cause would revive. 'But,' said she, 'notwithstanding all your resolution, I know this will conquer the weakness of your constitution, and you will die in prison.' He replied, 'I think I shall not, but if I do, my blood will be so innocent I shall advance the cause more by my death, hasting the vengeance of God upon my unjust enemies, than I could do by all the actions of my life.'[51]

One of the curious things about this scene is that it is unclear, as it opens, what Lucy Hutchinson is weeping for: is it her husband's ill health, as her answer to him suggests, or the failure of the republican cause about which he tries to comfort her? The tide of their conversation moves easily between the two forms of loss, scarcely acknowledging a boundary. It is as if John Hutchinson, already undergoing the process of transfiguration, has become continuous with the cause in which 'the interest of God was so much involved', both part of a divine reality that can only be copied on earth.

The entire *Life* is, in a sense, an attempt to grapple with this twin loss. In the preface to her children she writes that she seeks to do justice to her husband and console herself by preserving his memory, but the detailed history she narrates preserves the memory not only of his actions but of the cause he fought for. One of the reasons why it is easy for husband and wife to move from hope for the republic to hope for his life and back again is that both of these beloved objects have an element of the divine: John Hutchinson, because he is 'one of the fairest copies' of God's image; and the republic, because it too is a copy, of the heavenly Kingdom. If the failed republican faction was in fact 'ye league of God himselfe', then like the transformed John Hutchinson it is in some sense immortal, even if it has lost its last champion on earth.[52]

The dual immortality of John Hutchinson and his political vision, both emanating from and returning to the Creator, enables Lucy Hutchinson to construct a memorial to both that is also a covert call to arms. If, like John Hutchinson, the cause cannot die, then 'Why seeke wee y:^n amoung y:^e dead'? Such a manifesto is far bolder than most of Hutchinson's nonconformist associates, who turned to an inner, spiritual victory to demonstrate

---

[51] *Ibid.*, pp. 321–2.   [52] *Ibid.*, p. 337, 'Elegies', 3.27.

that individual dissenters were not beaten even when their political hopes were dashed.[53] Although Hutchinson's glorification of her husband is likewise a sign of such a personal triumph, in the elegies she also promotes a politics that is revolutionary, not defeatist. The many epitaphs she drafted, the only poems among the elegies written with a wider audience in mind, most poignantly illustrate this impossible hope for joint resurrection:

> Ye sons of England whose vnquenched flame
> Of Pious loue may yet y^t title Clayme
> Let not y:^{r} rash feete on y:^{t} Marble tread
> Before you haue its Sade Inscription read
> Beholde it weepes doe not These tears presage
> Decending Showers on This prodigious age
> Where only Rocks for Innocent bloodshed mourne
> While humane hearts to flintie quarries turne
> Now read, This stone doth Close vp ye darke Cave
> Where Liberty sleepes in her Champions grave[.]

The images of darkness and sleep that close the epitaph are deceptive: while apparently the opposite of the light and vision that accompanied a transformed John Hutchinson, the images thinly disguise a hope in the 'vnquenched flame' of future Englishmen who may revive the cause of Liberty. Even the grave that encloses John Hutchinson and dormant Liberty is a 'darke Cave' closed with a stone, which surely must remind the onlooker of another tomb, one that stood triumphantly empty after a darkness of three days. Like Christ, Liberty will rise again to rule in light and glory, extinguishing the Royalist sun:

> Then Shall our King his Shining host display
> At whose approach our mists shall fly away
> And wee Illuminated by his Sight
> No more shall neede Thy everquenched Light[.][54]

But despite this brave (and treasonous) display of apocalyptic hope, for those remaining on earth after the defeat, the wait seems unending and the darkness impenetrable. Like John Hutchinson, the Republican vision was but an earthly version of a transcendent reality; it, too, needed to experience a period of transmutation before it could triumph. In a sense, all of England needed to undergo the same process of purification that

[53] Keeble, *The Literary Culture of Nonconformity*, pp. 23–4.
[54] 'Elegies', 20; 3.51–4; for Lucy Hutchinson's use of the sun as a royalist symbol, see Norbrook, 'Lucy Hutchinson's "Elegies"', p. 475.

refined John Hutchinson. Lucy Hutchinson knew that such true restoration might be a long time in coming. In the meantime she was left to cope with lonely defeat, and the elegies are filled with images of darkness and shadows that characterise both the lost republic and the poet's own desolate widowhood, in sharp contrast to the divine light pouring out on her husband. In 'The Night', for example, the poet contrasts the 'artificiall heate and light' of 'other roomes', presumably royalist palaces, with the darkness that 'ouer all ye low world reignd'. Similarly, 'On The Spring 1668' warns the newly wakened countryside that the glories of the season are merely 'As The triumphant Sounds & Showes / Of Conquerers to their Captiues be[.]' and that these beauties will soon be betrayed by the sun that bestows them, which will 'Scorch you w:th his burning rayes' until it is extinguished. Although England may rejoice temporarily in Restoration prosperity, ultimately the sham will be revealed and the darkness will return:

> And you faire Skies growne Calme & bright
> Againe y:^{r} Clowdy veiles must weare
> And weepe black Showers for y^r lost Light
> When battles in y:^{r} bowells are[.]^{55}

Such images of 'Clowdy veiles' and ensuing conflict echo Lucy Hutchinson's description of the withdrawal of God from earth after the Fall:

> Love, tho' immutable, its smiles did shrowd
> Under the dark veil of an angry cloud.
> And while he seem'd withdrawn, whose grace upheld
> The order of all things, confusion fill'd
> The Universe. The air became impure,
> And frequent dreadful conflicts did endure[.]^{56}

Since the republicans had hoped to bring the earth closer to the heavenly vision, their failure, even if temporary, was like a second Fall, ushering in darkness and dissent among those who were now even further separated from God and incapable of knowing him fully. They had glimpsed a second paradise, a way closer to God, but had lost it through human folly.

The connection between the elegies and Lucy Hutchinson's impression of the Fall is not merely a coincidence of repeated images. Inserted between the second and third elegies in the manuscript are forty-two lines of lament that begin 'ah! why doth death its latest stroke delay'. They were included

---

^{55} 'Elegies', 8.5–6, 11; 14.1–2, 28, 37–40.
^{56} *Order and disorder*, 1679, p. 66; 'whose grace upheld' reads 'his grace vpheld' in the MS f. [44r].

in the manuscript presumably at the request of Julius Hutchinson, the son of John Hutchinson's half-brother, who notes at the top of the page 'These verses transcribed out of my other Book J: H:' and at the bottom, 'Mem^dm these verses were writ by Mrs Hutchinson on ye occasion of ye Coll: her Husbands being then a prisoner in ye Tower: 1664'. The lines are in fact a passage from *Order and disorder* in which Eve laments her own part in the Fall and the expulsion from Paradise.[57] It is possible that Julius Hutchinson, unaware of the longer poem, simply hazarded a guess as to what occasion produced the verses. We do not know how much of the poem was contained in his 'other Book'; it was certainly not the surviving manuscript of *Order and disorder* or the 1679 printed version, which are both missing two lines transcribed in the elegies manuscript.[58] Given the fact that the imagery is consistent with the surrounding passages in *Order and disorder*, it does seem unlikely that Lucy Hutchinson wrote the lines independently. But this does not mean that Julius Hutchinson's note is wrong. Like the Henry King elegy reattributed to a mourning neighbour in Lady Anne Southwell's commonplace book, or the continual reapplication of occasional poetry to new occasions by the poets of the Sidney circle, Lucy Hutchinson might have reappropriated her own work to record fresh emotions.[59] It may be this reappropriation, known to him through family tradition, that Julius Hutchinson records.

Regardless of whether Lucy Hutchinson intended the lines to be read in her own voice, they offer a useful example of the overlap between personal and public grief that is apparent in the elegies. Like Lucy Hutchinson's sorrow, Eve's grief is a mixture of lament for 'our nere, to be reenterd paradice' and 'ye man I Love by me betrayd'. Echoing the thirteenth elegy ('Vnwellcome life why dost Thou Stay'), the opening of Eve's lament wishes for death to end her prolonged sufferings:

> ah! why doth death its latest stroke delay
> if we must Leaue ye light, why do we stay?
> by slow degrees, more paynefully to die,
> & languish in a Long calamitye.

Life outside of paradise – or following Cromwell's rule and the Restoration – is lived in a kind of half-light, a parody of the divine that is nevertheless

[57] 'Elegies', 2A. The presence of these lines led to Norbrook's reattribution of *Order and disorder* to Lucy Hutchinson; see 'A devine Originall', and 'Lucy Hutchinson and *Order and Disorder*', pp. 259–60.
[58] Beinecke Library Osborne MS fb. 100, f.46^r, and Nottinghamshire Archives DD/HU 2, pp. vi–vii, respectively; the missing lines are 31–2 in 'Elegies'. In the printed edition the lament is on pp. 69–70.
[59] Arthur F. Marotti, *Manuscript, Print, and the English Renaissance Lyric* (Ithaca, New York: Cornell University Press, 1995), pp. 135–47.

not quite the dark of night. But their separation from divine light is not merely a matter of the flaming sword at the garden gate or the king upon the throne, distinguishing one socio-political existence from another, but also the personal divide that prevents human beings from knowing one another fully as they had in paradise. Eve steals a 'private glance' at Adam and laments the sin that has come between them:

> oh! yᵗ I had but sind' & dyed alone,
> Then had my torture, & my woe been lesse
> I yet had Florishd in thy happyness[.][60]

Read through the theology of marriage so carefully constructed in *Order and disorder*, the shared happiness that Eve laments is not merely earthly conversation and comfort, but the knowledge of God through one another that was possible when they were both naked and unashamed. Thus by losing paradise and her true communion with Adam she has been doubly bereft of God's light.

The context of Eve's lament also provides a lens for reading the language of darkness and shadow that pervades Lucy Hutchinson's descriptions of her life as a widow. Like Eve, some of the poet's darkness derives from being shut out of paradise; her England grows ever darker as republican light fades. But some of her darkness also stems from the lost communion with her husband. It is a language that need not be read as entirely submissive, but rather in keeping with her theology of companionate marriage. When she writes that her beauty is 'like y:ᵉ shadow w:ᵗʰ its substance fled', this is not necessarily an expression of her own inferiority but rather of the communication, the link with the divine that she has lost: 'Yet after all this he is gone hence and I remain, an airy phantasm walking about his sepulchre and waiting for the harbinger of day to summon me out of these midnight shades to my desired rest.' What Lucy Hutchinson has most significantly lost is her husband's body, not the sinful flesh but the human self that made him a perfect match for her, as Adam was for Eve. Without that communication she feels herself almost dead:

> For, 'twas not he; twas only I That died
> In that Cold Graue which his deare reliques keepes
> My light is quite extinct where he but sleepes
> My substance into yᵉ darke vault was laide
> And now I am my owne pale Empty Shade[.][61]

---

[60] 'Elegies', 2A.28, 35, 1–4, 33, 40–2.   [61] *Ibid.*, 7.34; *Memoirs*, p. 337; 'Elegies', 1.4–8.

It is important to read these repeated images of darkness and shad-ows alongside the images of light and glory the poet uses to describe her husband's transformation. John Hutchinson, as he progresses further and further on the ladder toward heaven, glows brighter and brighter with transfiguring light. He has gained union with the divine; in a sense he is experiencing the divine marriage between Christ and the Church that Lucy Hutchinson imagined in *Order and disorder*. She, on the other hand, must remain behind, in a politically darkened world and bereft even of her husband's companionship. In the equation of mystical marriage, she is the jilted lover who is cast aside; in losing John Hutchinson she has lost her primary link with the divine. In 'The Recovery', she witnesses her husband's transformation in a vision of God's transcendent love, and prays 'O rocke of Life O [quickning] power of loue / Here lett me fix; nor ~~from~~ hence againe remooue[.]' But such a vision can never be fully satisfying, because of course Lucy Hutchinson can never be fixed on the heavenly rock until she is dead; she is shut out of the very communion that she has now witnessed her husband enjoying. Not surprisingly, after this glimpse of hope the elegies return to the same longing for closure and death with which they began. In losing her husband and their republican vision, Lucy Hutchinson has lost both of her chances for closer communion with God on earth. Thus she can assert of herself in the *Life*, 'all that she is now at best is but his pale shade'.[62]

WOMEN'S WRITING AND POLITICAL PIETY

In his study of the elegies, David Norbrook asserts that 'the personal and the political are never clearly separable for Lucy Hutchinson'.[63] On the face of it, my reading would agree with this statement: what we would call personal and political – or perhaps private and public – are inextricably intertwined in Lucy Hutchinson's memorial texts. But, having established how Hutchinson's writing confuses and even breaks down these categories, I would like to go one step further and question why critics apply them to her in the first place. It is too often easy to fall into the trap that public/political means masculine and private/personal means feminine. For this reason scholars of early modern women have often dismissed the *Life of John Hutchinson* because they have taken Lucy Hutchinson's claims of private, wifely submission at face value, forgetting that the *Life* itself is an outspoken public text. Christopher Hill admits that 'Lucy Hutchinson should have

[62] 'Elegies', 10.65–6; *Memoirs*, p. 26.   [63] Norbrook, 'Lucy Hutchinson's "Elegies"', p. 470.

been a candidate' for his book on defeated radicals, 'but in her *Memoirs* of her husband she is far too concerned to cover up the Colonel's weaknesses to allow her own views to come through. We get the impression that she was the stronger character of the two, but she would have repudiated such an idea.' N. H. Keeble argues with more subtlety that the *Life* betrays an internal conflict between Lucy Hutchinson's 'creatively independent, defiant and opinionated' narrative voice and her 'conformity with the ideal of feminine reticence'.[64] Both of these positions assume that there is a single definition of femininity, and that it necessarily excludes participation in public or political debate.

The truth is that our gendered assumptions about public and private behaviour – based in large part on outdated scholarship of Victorian 'separate spheres' ideology – hold true only some of the time and for only some early modern texts. For Lucy Hutchinson, gender separation along the lines of public and private behaviour seems not to exist. This is not to suggest that she did not acknowledge differences between women and men and genuinely believe herself to be inferior to her husband. She believed that John Hutchinson had raised her 'aboue vulgar Girles' by his superior wisdom, knowledge and virtue. But that difference in degree did not necessarily yield a difference in spheres of influence. In writing the *Life* Lucy Hutchinson registers no conflict or unease in recording her own very public behaviour during the national conflict, particularly in transacting her husband's business in London when his case was before Parliament.[65]

The same could be said of her writing. Not only does it unconcernedly mix public issues with private (and one wonders if the reading I have offered would be necessary if the writer were a man) but it is also unconcerned about the public or private nature of the writing itself, at least in terms of the author's gendered voice. Lucy Hutchinson does use traditional apology tropes in the prefaces to many of her writings, but on careful inspection very few of these turn out to be gendered apologies. When she tells her children, for example, that in her account her husband's life will 'shine as under a very thick cloud', her self-deprecation must be read in the complex of light and darkness images used throughout the text to distinguish the earthly and living from the dead and immortalised, regardless of gender: in the same paragraph she contends that 'there is need of this medium to this world's weak eyes'. Similarly, when she acknowledges herself 'a trifling schollar' in her treatise to her daughter, her concern seems to be for the

[64] Christopher Hill, *The Experience of Defeat: Milton and Some Contemporaries* (London: Faber and Faber, 1984), p. 21; Keeble, '"The Colonel's Shadow"', pp. 240, 237.
[65] 'Elegies', 7.13; *Memoirs*, pp. 289–90.

loss of 'many blessed oppertunities' through a lack of seriousness that is not necessarily – and certainly not explicitly – linked to her gender. Similar protests of inability in the 1679 preface to *Order and disorder* ('elevations of stile' and 'charms of language' 'are gifts I have not') did not prevent Anthony Wood and subsequent generations of readers from attributing the poem to a man.[66]

The fact is that there were competing strands of discourse about women's writing in the early modern period, a multiplicity which Lucy Hutchinson's writing registers and with which she engages. She is aware of, and even subscribes to, the notion that 'our sex, through ignorance and weakenesse of iudgement (which in the most knowing weoman is inferior to the masculine understanding of men), are apt to entertaine fancies, and pertinacious in them'. But the sheer size and scholarly rigor of her canon demonstrate that such a belief did not limit her own venture into writing. In the dedication of her translation of Lucretius, most often cited as evidence of her anxiety about being a woman writing, Lucy Hutchinson cleverly balances a number of available discourses on writing. She apologises to her patron, the Earl of Anglesey, for not having offered him a copy of the translation before he requested it: 'Had it bene a worke that had merited glory, or could my sex (whose more becoming vertue is silence) derive honor from writing, my aspiring Muse would not have sought any other Patrone then your Lordship[.]'[67] Our 'more becoming vertue is silence', or so some might say. One wonders, rather, if Lucy Hutchinson believes it, given that the assertion is embedded in a lengthy, outspoken preface to a six-book translation. What is apparent is that Lucy Hutchinson recognises that, in the eyes of at least some of the world, women are not accorded honour for their writing. Such an acknowledgement is prudent: we might cast our minds back to the scene in the *Life* in which John Hutchinson, enamoured of Lucy Apsley's ability to read Latin and write verse, is warned by jealous women that she is too dull and scholarly to merit his attention. For some, not always men, the notion that a woman could write was not to her public credit. Keenly aware of this strand of opinion, Lucy Hutchinson in the Lucretius dedication leaves open the possibility that *her* muse, at least, is not aspiring. But even this potential modesty is mitigated by the fact that she is seeking patronage by writing the dedication at all. Is this a public or a private work? It is almost impossible to say.[68]

[66] *Memoirs*, p. 16; *On the Principles*, pp. 89–90; *Order and disorder*, 1679, sig. [A2ʳ].

[67] *On the Principles*, p. 6; de Quehen, ed., *Lucy Hutchinson's Translation*, p. 23.

[68] For a fuller reading of this dedication and parallels between it and the 1679 preface to *Order and disorder*, see Norbrook, 'A devine Originall', pp. 14–15, and 'Lucy Hutchinson's "Elegies"', p. 484.

Even within the work of one writer, then, we can discern several possible discourses about the role of writing in public and private intercourse. Not all of these discourses are gendered, as John Hutchinson's attraction to his scholarly bride so sharply illustrates. In fact, it is a discourse she shares with her husband through which Lucy Hutchinson understands her position as author and scholar: the concept of Christian conscience. Throughout her account of his life Lucy Hutchinson offers evidence of her husband acting only according to his conscience, to the exclusion of all other motives, particularly the political. The primacy of conscience in an individual Christian's decision-making was developed by Independent theologians in the 1640s to limit state authority over religious practice: each individual must have the liberty to determine, through prayer, the most God-pleasing form of worship. In practice the principle extended to far more than worship, however. Lucy Hutchinson repeatedly records John Hutchinson rendering all of his personal and political decisions to his conscience, praying to know the will of God before taking any major action. For this reason he often acted independently, without the support of a party or faction, even to the point of criticising those ostensibly on his own side, like Cromwell, whose power he thought was not in keeping with God's will. As his wife attests in the *Life*:

they very little knew him that could say he was of any faction; for he had a strength of judgment able to consider things himself and propound them to his conscience, which was so upright that the veneration of no man's person alive, nor the love of the dearest friend in the world, could not make him do the least thing without a full persuasion of conscience that it was his duty so to act[.][69]

For women, the duty to be fully persuaded in their own consciences contained within it the possibility of a different kind of independence: independence from gender stereotypes. That Lucy Hutchinson subscribed to the principle of conscience is apparent not merely in her praise of her husband's conviction but also in the few accounts of her own actions that creep into the *Life*. Early in their marriage, for example, she stumbles across treatises against infant baptism and privately becomes persuaded that the practice was not justified, 'but being then young and modest, thought it a kind of virtue to submit to the judgment and practice of most churches rather than to defend a singular opinion of her own, she not being then

[69] Gary S. de Krey, 'Rethinking the Restoration: Dissenting Cases for Conscience, 1667–1672,' *The Historical Journal* 38.1 (1995): 53–83; see also Nicholas Tyacke, *Aspects of English Protestantism c. 1530–1700* (Manchester: Manchester University Press, 2001), pp. 68–71; Keeble, *The Literary Culture of Nonconformity*, p. 33. *Memoirs*, p. 207.

enlightened concerning that great mistake of the national churches'. In her own mature opinion, Lucy Hutchinson regards her youthful suppression of her 'singular opinion' as a pale 'kind of virtue' that is only justified because she was not yet enlightened in her conscience about Church hypocrisy. Later in life, however, she feels compelled to take a stand on the issue before giving birth to one of her children. She 'communicated her doubts to her husband', not that she might submit to his will (although undoubtedly she would have), but that he might 'endeavour her satisfaction' by considering the problem intellectually and answering her arguments if he disagreed.[70] Clearly in her later life Lucy Hutchinson felt that it was not merely her right but her duty to determine such issues for herself.

In her writing, the principle of conscience is most apparent in the prefaces to *Order and disorder* and the translation of Lucretius. Both of these apologies arose out of Lucy Hutchinson's profound guilt at having chosen to translate the 'Atheismes and impieties' of *De rerum natura*, then fashionable among the royalist poets and scientists of the Newcastle circle. She tells us that she translated the poem out of curiosity, but later must have felt her principles wavering under the 'vain, foolish, atheistical Poesie' of Lucretius' version of creation.[71] This conviction led her to repudiate the translation, insisting that she would have thrown it into the fire if she had not already lost control of the text 'by misfortune' 'gone out of my hands in one lost copie'. But conscience also led her to write the long preface to the translation, professing in detail her true religious convictions, and offering vehement criticism of those who 'make it a specious pretext within themselves, to thinke religion is nothing at all but an invention to reduce the ignorant vulgar into order and Government'. Conscience thus allows Lucy Hutchinson to take control of her texts, choosing what to publicise and what to retract, without recourse to a gendered, and thus potentially limiting, concept of authorship.[72]

The same principles are evident in the preface to the 1679 printing of *Order and disorder*. 'These Meditations were not at first design'd for publick view,' the poet confesses, 'but fix'd upon to reclaim a busie roving thought from wandring in the pernicious and perplexed maze of humane inventions', presumably the translation of Lucretius that she had so regretted. In the ensuing years, however, the value of the poem itself has led Lucy Hutchinson to print it for the sake of 'every one that hath need of it'. Her

[70] *Memoirs*, p. 210. The child was not baptised.
[71] De Quehen, ed., *Lucy Hutchinson's Translation*, p. 23; *Order and disorder*, 1679, sig. [A^v]
[72] De Quehen, ed., *Lucy Hutchinson's Translation*, pp. 23, 26.

chief aim is to join with other believers in glorifying God, assisting them 'to admire the glories and excellencies of our great Creator':

if I have weakly compos'd, yet 'tis a consenting testimony with the whole Church, to the mighty and glorious truths of God which is not altogether impertinent, in this atheistical age; and how imperfect soever the hand be, that copies it out, Truth loses not its perfection, and the plainest as well as the elegant, the elegant as well as the plain, make up a harmony in confession and celebration of that all-creating, all-sustaining God, to whom be all honour and glory for ever and ever.[73]

No matter the abilities of the writer, no matter if her text is imperfect, if it is written in imitation of a higher truth then it deserves to take its place in the wider religious community. The writer must determine in her conscience if her text is true to its divine original; all other standards, whether of aesthetics or gender, are subordinate.

Lucy Hutchinson may, to some extent, be unusual. The paradigm of conscience was not available to every early modern woman writer. But what Lucy Hutchinson's situation suggests to us, as twenty-first-century critics of these writers, is that not all was chastity, silence and obedience. Other paradigms for women's writing, and women's 'public' activity, did exist, and could operate side-by-side even in the work of a single woman writer. Lucy Hutchinson's 'private' grief for her husband and her 'public' mourning for the republic cannot be easily disentangled, and must be read within the larger context of her vision of the relationships between God, humans and human history. In this cosmic kingdom, her own position is complicated: subordinate to her husband but yet subject to the dictates of her own conscience. Where duty to God is concerned, distinctions between public and private, and the way those categories may or may not be gendered, collapse into the higher order of conscience. Rather than continue to wonder at the confusion of public and private in the work of an early modern woman writer, perhaps it is time we interrogate our own investment in those categories, and question whether we understand their historical resonance in the early modern period.

[73] *Order and disorder*, 1679, sigs. [A^r], [A2^r], [A2^{r-v}].

Conclusion

Among the numerous seventeenth-century verse paraphrases of the Song of Songs is one by Barbara Mackay, Lady Scourie (fl. 1657), a Highland Scotswoman. Her translation is prefaced with the following poem:

O Song off Songs o Song most pretious rare
To speak off the let no song elss compare
O Song that Superlatively exceed
All can be said o sweet song that feed
With Heavnly raptures with inchanted Stoūnds
Off love-sick flames, it both charmes and wounds
The soul that reads it, fixing all its darts
Within the centre off all Heavnly hearts
For majesty, let non with it compare
For melodie it is exceeding rare
For harmonie it is all one intire
For puritie it is the truth most pure
It ravisheth, it captivates, it charmes
All sound affections in the beloveds armes
This sweet dealgoue[1] that point out the Love
Betwixt the creature and his Lord above
No wonder though the wisest off all men
Were chois'd to dip in the his sacred pen
No wonder though his name to this accord
[For][2] he was born beloved off the Lord
Come then sweet singer with thy heavnly Song
For I intend to heare you all a Long[.][3]

---

[1] Perhaps 'dialogue'?
[2] The line begins 'Or' but 'For' is written below in the margin with an arrow to the word 'Or', and seems to fit the sense of the line.
[3] National Library of Scotland MS Wodrow Qu. xxvii, f. 10ᵣ. I am grateful to Peter Davidson for sharing this reference and a photocopy of the manuscript. An excerpt of Lady Scourie's paraphrase is in his *Early Modern Women Poets (1520–1700): An Anthology*, edited with Jane Stevenson (Oxford: Oxford University Press, 2001), pp. 471–3. Davidson and Stevenson do not note that the manuscript

Like many other translators and commentators, Barbara Mackay's poem plays on the Hebrew title of the Song of Songs, which can be read 'song above all other songs' or, as she puts it, 'Song most pretious rare'. Such literalism was common among Calvinists like Lady Scourie, and applied frequently to all scriptures, not only the Song of Songs. But the question remains how the Song of Songs would 'superlatively exceed' all other songs in the Bible: what is so astounding about this particular text?

One answer lies in Barbara Mackay's poem: the Song both 'charmes and wounds', it 'point[s] out the Love/ Betwixt the creature and his Lord above'. In other words, the 'creature' can both speak *about* the love of God and speak *to* God directly, through the 'darts' of love contained in the scripture verses. The Song thus offers a way to express the inexpressible: the intensely personal relationship of an individual to his or her God.

One of the conclusions of this book is that such language matters, or rather, the piety that it enables matters to the way we read early modern religious poetry. The model of mystical marriage scriptures and the interpretative tradition surrounding them provided the women writers of this study with a way to speak of divine and human love simultaneously. Such relationships had, as we have seen, political and social implications, whether in the government of wives or the government of the nation. But in each case one of the crucial elements that authorises these women's political and social commentary is a deeply personal relationship with Christ. Anna Trapnel parallels herself to Christ's Spouse, Aemilia Lanyer writes lyrically of the beauty of Christ's beloved body, Lucy Hutchinson crafts a persona of a devoted wife who struggles through study to know Christ. The sincerity of their personal piety is not at all incidental. As women who faced the possibility of being told they could not speak, it was vital to establish that their communication was not contrary to God's word, if it did not come from him directly. They could not claim religious authority if they themselves did not partake of 'All sound affections in the beloved arms'.

Barbara Mackay's poem thus brings us, inadvertently, to the crux of the relationship between public, private and religious devotion for women in the early modern period. As a metaphor, mystical marriage effectively illustrates this crux: the ceremony of marriage is a public act that authorises

---

originates from powerful Scottish royalists: it is signed 'Barbara Macky' (f. 28^r), probably the daughter of Colonel Hugh Mackay and sister of General Hugh Mackay (1640–92), both of Scourie. According to the DNB she married a distant cousin, John Mackay, second Baron Reay (fl. 1657). The manuscript is dedicated to the Countess of Caithness, most likely Mary, daughter of Archibald Campbell, Marquis of Argyll, who in 1657 married George Sinclair, sixth Earl of Caithness (d. 1672).

private intimacy, just as women's 'private' intimacy with Christ allowed them to speak publicly of him. As we have seen in the chapter on *Eliza's babes*, what was called 'private' prayer had 'public' implications as a preparative for communal worship and a model for other Christians. The works of Lady Anne Southwell and Lucy Hutchinson likewise demonstrate that a gentlewoman who displayed exemplary intellectual piety could write boldly, even radically, of gender relations and political reform. What these examples suggest is that 'private' and 'public' existed for these women not as opposites but on a continuum, at least as far as religious speech was concerned. 'Private' piety enables 'public' speech, and thereby upsets all conventional gendering of those categories.

I would not suggest that private devotion was the *same* as public speech; that would be a generalisation as unwieldy and inaccurate as any 'separate spheres' paradigm. Nor would I argue that their public, political implications justify our scholarly interest in private devotions. To do so would require assuming that the public and political is necessarily more valuable than the private or religious, a principle that frequently has been used to marginalise women's writing, and which in any case – as this study demonstrates – does not always hold true for the early modern period. Rather I would suggest that the relationship between piety and speech ought to make us rethink our definitions of public action in the early modern period.

In recent years feminist historians and literary critics have begun the process of redefining politics in order to register women's participation in events previously viewed chiefly through the interactions of powerful men. It is now acknowledged that, even if they could not vote or hold political office, women's patronage, their aesthetic accomplishments, their social networks and their exchange of news all influenced political culture.[4] I would add another category to this list: women's pious, politicised, simultaneously public *and* private religious polemic. When the role of religion in early modern political and social structures is taken seriously, women's voices emerge louder, stronger and more engaged in the most important debates of the time.

---

[4] See, for example, Margaret P. Hannay, *Philip's Phoenix: Mary Sidney, Countess of Pembroke* (Oxford: Oxford University Press, 1990); Diane Purkiss, Introduction, in *Three Tragedies by Renaissance Women* (London: Penguin, 1998), pp. xi–xliii; Margaret J. M. Ezell, *The Patriarch's Wife: Literary Evidence and the History of the Family* (Chapel Hill, North Carolina: University of North Carolina Press, 1987); Jane Donawerth, 'Women's Poetry and the Tudor–Stuart System of Gift Exchange', in *Women, Writing, and the Reproduction of Culture in Tudor and Stuart Britain*, ed. Mary E. Burke *et al.* (Syracuse, New York: Syracuse University Press, 2000), pp. 3–18; Dagmar Freist, *Governed by Opinion: Politics, Religion, and the Dynamics of Communication in Stuart London, 1637–1645* (London: I. B. Tauris Publishers, 1997), especially pp. 278–98.

One other general conclusion can be drawn from these case studies: gender influenced concepts of religious virtue, concepts which in turn authorised writing. There was a moral double bind in Christianity in the early modern period, a double bind which some women writers exploited in order to authorise their own speech. St Peter and St Paul ordered women not to speak in public services, but St Paul also made vocal evangelism and witness an imperative for both genders, as Christ had in the Gospels. For some women, it became impossible to follow both of these models of Christian behaviour.

Like the relationship between public and private piety, the double bind for women's speech is also encapsulated in the metaphor of mystical marriage. Was the bride of Christ a specifically female example, or could she represent all Christians? These confusions were a source of creativity for many women writers: far from confining them to a limited role in religious and social spheres, the double bind gave them an opportunity to negotiate among competing definitions of femininity and Christian duty. The gendering of the mystical marriage enabled some, like Anna Trapnel and Lady Anne Southwell, to claim that their gender offered them a privileged relationship with Christ, as women who could understand what it meant to be his bride better than any man. Aemilia Lanyer, Eliza and Lucy Hutchinson, on the other hand, reached with varying degrees of success for a paradigm of ungendered virtue, in which a woman's piety and especially her writing was authorised not because of but in spite of her gender.

This book thus makes the bold claim that women participated in defining what it meant to be a woman and how a woman ought to behave. They were not victims but agents in a continual process of changing gender relations. And while it is exciting to find women exerting power over their own status, ultimately this was a process that had implications beyond gender politics. Negotiating Christian standards of femininity meant examining the manhood represented by Christ, and, as the work of the writers examined here demonstrates, rethinking Christ had profound implications for the way both women and men were expected to behave. Their poetry thus demonstrates that both women's writing and the categories of gender were not incidental but crucial to the formation of Christian piety and Christian virtue in the early modern period.

Finally, whatever their impact on the past, it is a pity these works should remain confined to the early modern period, or at least to early modern studies departments. For the attempt to define what it is to be female and a disciple of Christ is as crucial to feminists seeking to reform modern Christianity as it was to Aemilia Lanyer, Anna Trapnel and other early modern women who sought a voice for their religious experiences. A brief survey of their modern feminist counterparts reveals surprising parallels between early modern women's use of scripture and modern feminist Biblical criticism.

Like Phyllis Trible, Elisabeth Schüssler Fiorenza and Rosemary Radford Ruether, the early modern women of this study also searched for the liberating elements of scripture: 'the recognition', as Schüssler Fiorenza writes, 'that God's gracious goodness establishes equality among all of us, righteous and sinner, rich and poor, men and women, Pharisees and Jesus' disciples'.[5] For early modern women, of course, the radical challenging of hierarchical systems was more difficult, and all of these women accept some degree of women's essential weakness and subordination to men as God-given truths. Their hope, frequently, is in eschatological equality – that 'there will not bee a difference in your sex' after death, as Lady Anne Southwell claimed – but as Southwell's poetry or *Eliza's babes* or Anna Trapnel's writings testify, the hope for equality in the afterlife frequently resulted in a woman's writing as if she were equal in this life.[6] 'If I must live after the example of thy blessed Apostle, I must live by faith, and faith makes things to come, as present' asserted the author of *Eliza's babes* in the meditation in which she claimed 'The Royall Priest-hood'. Her logic is, as always, somewhat slippery, and yet in declaring 'I will no more now see my self as mortall' she had sound Biblical precedent in Jesus's statement that the apostles do not belong to the world (John 17:16).[7]

For modern feminists the distinction between present hierarchy and future equality is also key. The Catholic theologian Rosemary Radford Ruether, for example, works 'to do something about the intolerable disjunction between talk of redemptive community and actual lived experience', while Elisabeth Schüssler Fiorenza demonstrates that modern attempts to confine the effects of Pauline statements of equality such as Galatians 3:28 to the afterlife do serious violence to the text: 'Such commentaries are prepared to state the opposite of what Paul actually says in order to preserve a "purely religious" interpretation.'[8]

[5] Elisabeth Schüssler Fiorenza, *In Memory of Her: A Feminist Theological Reconstruction of Christian Origins*, 2nd edn (London: SCM, 1994), p. 132. Phyllis Trible, *God and the Rhetoric of Sexuality* (London: SCM, 1978).
[6] British Library Lansdowne MS 740, f. 164ᵛ, l. 500, edited by Jean Klene in *The Southwell-Sibthorpe Commonplace Book: Folger MS. V.b.198* (Tempe, Arizona: Renaissance English Text Society, 1997).
[7] Wing E535C, *Eliza's babes* (London: M. S. for Laurence Blaiklock, 1652), pp. 100–1. Edited by L. E. Semler, *Eliza's Babes: or The Virgin's Offering (1652): A Critical Edition* (Madison, Wisconsin: Fairleigh Dickinson University Press, 2001).
[8] Ann Loades, ed. and commentary, *Feminist Theology: A Reader* (London: SPCK, 1990), p. 136; Schüssler Fiorenza, *In Memory of Her*, p. 207.

Galatians 3:28 and the 'last shall be first' ethos apparent in the Gospels have always offered the possibility for an equality that was seldom realised in the institutional Church. The presence of such liberationist texts in scripture has remained a touchstone for women throughout history who sought a voice for themselves. 'Paul's ringing liberationist manifesto did profoundly change the way Christians, if they so chose, could understand the most basic social categories', argues Barbara Newman in her study of medieval women. And 'despite the chasm between theory and practice, the theory had been perpetually inscribed in Holy Writ, where it lay in a state of dormancy and could be reactivated at any time'.[9] For modern feminists these texts provide a scriptural basis for challenging oppressive hierarchial traditions, but for early modern women they often formed a rationale for living out a vocation that was not necessarily conceived as subversive.

The women of this study, for the most part, did not regard themselves as 'nurtur[ing] hopes for the liberation of humanity into a just and equitable political order', but as living out a duty to Christ that was incumbent upon all human beings.[10] And yet, in practice, women's fulfilment of their calling did at times bring them into conflict with gendered norms of behaviour, as Sister Anne Harriman discovered when she attempted to gain the right to speak in her London congregation.[11] At those times, the liberationist elements of scripture offered a means to negotiate the strictures of the social world. As Schüssler Fiorenza has argued of early Christian women, and Eleanor McLaughlin of medieval women, for early modern women an 'empowering prior obedience to God' at times enabled them to transcend the expectations of gender.[12] The importance of serving and obeying Christ before all worldly commitments played a significant role in the work of each of the women studied here: from Lady Anne Southwell's complex indictment of men who limit women's spiritual development through gender stereotyping, to Eliza's unorthodox response to her human marriage, to Lucy Hutchinson's call on the principle of conscience to justify her outspoken and potentially unfeminine speech.

Although feminist theologians share with their early modern counterparts a desire to live as if the equality to come is present, at the same time,

[9] Barbara Newman, *From Virile Woman to WomanChrist: Studies in Medieval Religion and Literature* (Philadelphia: University of Pennsylvania Press, 1995), p. 4.

[10] Susan Frank Parsons, ed., *The Cambridge Companion to Feminist Theology* (Cambridge: Cambridge University Press, 2002), p. xiv.

[11] See chapter 5 above.

[12] Schüssler Fiorenza, *In Memory of Her*, p. 211; the quotation is from Eleanor McLaughlin, 'Women, Power, and the Pursuit of Holiness in Medieval Christianity', in *Feminist Theology: A Reader*, ed. Loades, p. 100.

in their critique of the Bible many modern theologians might be said to do the opposite of realising future hope. As Ann Loades writes of Schüssler Fiorenza, 'Those like her who want to reclaim biblical material, may of course be expressing, despite themselves, not so much recovery of what has been lost from the original community around Jesus, as *hope* for new possibilities in a still-alive tradition.'[13] Aemilia Lanyer's connection of the story of the crucifixion to the lives of her women patrons (and male readers) partakes of the same tradition. Lanyer draws on the existing scriptural and exegetical tradition which emphasised the violence and weakness of men while using the patient grief of the women in Jesus's circle as a model of Christian devotion.[14] She might have recognised her own arguments in those of Schüssler Fiorenza:

Whereas according to Mark the leading male disciples do not understand the suffering messiahship of Jesus, reject it, and finally abandon him, the women disciples who have followed Jesus from Galilee to Jerusalem suddenly emerge as the true disciples in the passion narrative. They are Jesus' true followers (*akolouthein*) who have understood that his ministry was not rule and kingly glory but *diakonia*, 'service' (Mark 15:41). Thus the women emerge as the true Christian ministers and witnesses.[15]

As Bridget Gilfillan Upton has demonstrated, Schüssler Fiorenza's reading of Mark's gospel is 'a little utopian'. Upton points out that the women who go to Jesus' tomb at the end of Mark's gospel perform little better than the male disciples: 'they are confused and bewildered, go completely to pieces and tell "nothing to anyone, for they were afraid"'.[16] Lanyer's sources, too, are probably less interested in promoting women's virtue as equal to men's than she herself is. Both Schüssler Fiorenza and Lanyer use the scripture to imagine a historical model that is perhaps more egalitarian than historical evidence will allow. Their purpose is to find a way in which women can walk with all liberties in Christ, unrestricted by gender expectations, to paraphrase Sister Anne Harriman. Or to quote Schüssler Fiorenza: 'The history and theology of women's oppression perpetuated by patriarchal biblical texts and by a clerical patriarchy must not be allowed to cancel out the history and theology of the struggle, life, and leadership of Christian women who spoke and acted in the power of the Spirit.'[17]

---

[13] *Feminist Theology*, ed. Loades, p. 49. [14] See chapter 2 above.
[15] Schüssler Fiorenza, *In Memory of Her*, p. xliv.
[16] Bridget Gilfillan Upton, 'Feminist Theology as Biblical Hermeneutics', in *The Cambridge Companion to Feminist Theology*, ed. Parsons, p. 106. The scripture quotation is from Mark 16:8, which is the last verse in Mark's Gospel in many of the earliest manuscript witnesses.
[17] Schüssler Fiorenza, *In Memory of Her*, p. 36.

Schüssler Fiorenza is writing of early Christian women, but her comment could equally apply to the speech and actions of their early modern counterparts. These women deserve to be heard, and reading them alters not only our perceptions of early modern history but our perceptions of Biblical criticism. I have no interest in arguing that these early modern women were feminist theologians; their goals and methods are their own, and they remain essentialist in a way that has contributed to their marginalisation among even feminist scholars. Yet there is an irony in the fact that the recovery of early modern women's impact on theology and religious activity in their own time parallels modern feminist theologians' recovery of Biblical women's activity: if only these texts had been available, perhaps modern feminist theologians would not have had to work so hard.[18]

---

[18] This argument is itself not new. See Schüssler Fiorenza, 'Introduction: Transforming the Legacy of *The Woman's Bible*', in *Searching the Scriptures. Volume 1: A Feminist Introduction*, ed. Elisabeth Schüssler Fiorenza (London: SCM, 1993), p. 1, where she draws on the insights of Gerda Lerner and Dale Spender that women's intellectual work is frequently forgotten from generation to generation.

Bibliography

For early printed books, the place of publication is London unless otherwise specified.

MANUSCRIPTS

All Souls' College, Oxford
  MS 117. Booklist of Humphrey Dyson. Early seventeenth century.
British Library
  Additional MS 4820, f. 98ᵛ. Sir Thomas Southwell's funeral certificate. June 1626.
  Additional MSS 25,901, 39,779 and 46,172N. Draft fragments of Lucy Hutchinson's *Life* of her husband. 1640s.
  Egerton MS 607. Prayers and meditations by Elizabeth Egerton, Countess of Bridgewater. After 1663.
  Harleian MS 697. Records of Munster, Ireland. Seventeenth century.
  Lansdowne MS 740, ff. 142–67. An intermediate copy of Lady Anne Southwell's meditations on the third and fourth commandments. *c.* 1630.
  Microfilms of the Cecil Papers, vols. 100 ff. 11, 12, 16; 103, f. 57. Letters relating to the visit of 'Mrs Southwell' to Berwick. 1603.
Devonshire Collections, Chatsworth House
  Lismore MSS xiv, ff. 160, 174. Letters from Lady Anne Southwell on behalf of Sir Richard Edgecombe. 1623.
Folger Shakespeare Library
  MS V.b.198. Poetic miscellany of Lady Anne Southwell. 1626–36.
Greater London Record Office
  MS DR052/133. Churchwardens' accounts of St Mary's, Acton, late seventeenth century, with transcriptions of important early seventeenth century entries.
  MS X024/066. Baptismal register of St Dunstan's, Stepney. Seventeenth Century.
Huntington Library
  MS Z Early X Eng. 1620 LF 297343 (EL 8/G/8) and EL 8376 (35/B/35). The Biblical meditations and a facsimile of the 'Loose Papers' of Elizabeth Egerton, Countess of Bridgewater. *c.* 1663.

MS EL 6495. A facsimile of the catalogue of the library of Francis Egerton, Countess of Bridgewater. 1627–32.
Leeds University Library, Brotherton Collection
MS Lt.q.32. Poetry by Hester Pulter. *c.* 1645–65.
National Library of Scotland
MSS 6489–6502. The spiritual diaries of Anne, Lady Halkett. Second half of seventeenth century.
MS Wodrow Qu. xxvII, ff. 9ᵛ–28ʳ. Barbara Mackay, Lady Scourie's verse paraphrase of the Song of Solomon. *c.* 1660.
Nottinghamshire Archives
MS DD/HU 1. Lucy Hutchinson's commonplace book. *c.* 1660.
MS DD/HU 2. A transcription of Lucy Hutchinson's elegies. Late seventeenth century.
MS DD/HU 3. Lucy Hutchinson's religious commonplace book. *c.* 1660.
MS DD/HU 4. Lucy Hutchinson's *Life* of her husband. Late 1660s.
Oxford University, Bodleian Library
Rawlinson MS A 21, p. 325. Copy of a letter signed 'B T' dated 21.10.54, giving an account of the author's meeting with Anna Trapnel. 1654.
Rawlinson MS D 828. Account book of a London gathered church. *c.* 1652–4.
Tanner MSS 74, 265, 278 and 283. Contain transcriptions of Sir Walter Cope's dialogue or character of the Earl of Salisbury. Early seventeenth century.
Public Record Office
C3/249/10 and C2/Eliz/S14/58. Chancery cases concerning the estates of Sir Thomas Southwell. 1592 and 1600/1.
SP 16/141 no. 63 and SP 16/142 no. 19. Letters from Bishop John Williams to Secretary Dorchester. 1629.
SP 18/66 no. 20. Letter from Marchamont Nedham to Oliver Cromwell. 1654.
William Andrews Clark Memorial Library MS L6815M3 C734 [16–/50?] Bound Commonplace book of Roger Ley containing a memorial to his wife Anne. *c.* 1641.
Yale University, Beinecke Rare Book and Manuscript Library
Osborne MS b.221. Copy of Elizabeth Jeckyll's spiritual journal. *c.* 1685.
Osborne MS fb.100. *Order and Disorder. c.* 1664.

EARLY PRINTED BOOKS

Ainsworth, Henry. *Annotations vpon the five bookes of moses.* For John Bellamie, 1627. STC 219.
Alsop, Vincent. *Anti-sozzo, sive sherlocismus enervatus.* For Nathanael Ponder, 1676. Wing A2905.
Ambrose, Isaac. *Media: the middle things.* John Field for Nathanaell Webb and William Grantham, 1649/50. Wing A2958.

Andrewes, Lancelot. *xcvi sermons*. George Miller for Richard Badger, 1629. STC 606.

Annesley, Samuel. *Communion with god. In two sermons*. Evan Tyler for Nathanael Web and William Grantham, 1655. Wing A3227.

Annotations upon all the books of the old and new testament. John Legatt and John Raworth, 1645. Wing D2062.

Annotations upon all the books of the old and new testament. Evan Tyler, 1657. Wing D2064.

Aylett, Robert. *The song of songs, which was salomons*. William Stansby, 1621. STC 2774.

Bayly, Lewis. *The practice of pietie*. W. H. for John Hodgets, 1612. STC 1601.5.
  The practice of pietie. For Robert Allot, 1630. STC 1609.

Becon, Thomas. *The worckes of thomas becon*. John Day, 1564. STC 1710.

Brayne, John. *An exposition upon the canticles*. Robert Austin, 1651. Wing B4324.

Brightman, Thomas. *A commentary on the canticles*. In *Workes*. John Field for Samuel Cartwright, 1644. Wing B4679.

Brooks, Thomas. *The unsearchable riches of christ*. Mary Simmons for John Hancock, 1657. Wing B4919.

Calvin, John. *A harmonie vpon the three euangelists*. Translated by Eusebius Paget. George Bishop, 1584. STC 2962.

Collinges, John. *The intercourses of divine love*. A. Maxwel for Thomas Parkhurst, 1676. Wing C5323.

Cary, Mary. *The little horns doom & downfall*. [W. H.] for the author, 1651. Wing C737.
  The resvrrection of the witnesses. H. Hills for R. C. and Thomas Brewster, 1653. Wing C738.

Certain passages. No. 114. 14–21 April 1654.

Chamberlaine, Bartholomew. *The passion of christ, and the benefits thereby*. For Thomas Pauier, 1612. STC 4946.9.

Cleaver, Robert, and John Dod. *A godlie forme of hovseholde government*. Felix Kingston for Thomas Man, 1600. STC 5384.

Cotton, John. *A brief exposition of the whole book of canticles*. For Philip Nevil, 1642. Wing C6410.

Cox, Roger. *Hebdomada sacra*. Felix Kyngston for Henry Seile, 1630. STC 5467.

Crofts, Robert. *The lover*. B. Alsop and T. F. for Richard Meighen, 1638. STC 6042.

A directory for the publique worship of God. Evan Tyler, Alexander Fifield, Ralph Smith and John Field, 1645. Wing D1546.

Dove, John. *The conversion of salomon*. W. Stansby for John Smethwick, 1613. STC 7080.

Durham, James. *Clavis cantici*. Edinburgh: George Swintoun and James Glen, 1668. Wing D2802.
  Clavis cantici. 2nd edition. London: J. W. for Dorman Newman, 1669. Wing D2803.

Eliza's babes. M. S. for Laurence Blaiklock, 1652. Wing E535C.

The faithful scout. No. 161. 13–20 January 1654.

Farneworth, Richard. *A woman forbidden to speak in the church.* For Giles Calvert, 1654. Wing F514.

Featley, Daniel. *Ancilla pietatis.* For Nicholas Bourne, 1626. STC 10726.

The svmme of saving knowledge. George Miller for Nicholas Bourne, 1626. STC 10739.

Ferguson, Robert. *The interest of reason in religion.* For Dorman Newman, 1675. Wing F740.

Fergusson, James. *A brief exposition of the epistles of paul to the galatians and ephesians.* Edinburgh: Christopher Higgins, 1659. Wing F773.

[Finch, Henry]. *An exposition of the song of solomon.* Ed. William Gouge. London: John Beale, 1615. STC 12113.

Fletcher, Giles. *Christs victorie, and triumph.* Cambridge: C. Legge, 1610. STC 11058.

Fox, George. *The woman learning in silence.* For Thomas Simonds, 1655/56. Wing F1991.

Fraunce, Abraham. *The countesse of pembrokes emanuel.* Thomas Orwyn for William Ponsonby, 1591. STC 11339.

Gearing, William. *The love-sick spouse.* For Nevill Simmons, 1665. Wing G436.

Gouge, William. *Of domesticall dvties.* John Haviland for William Bladen, 1622. STC 12119.

The grand politique post. No. 127. For George Horton, 10–17 January 1653/4.

H., I. *A strange wonder or a wonder in a woman.* For I. T., 1642. Wing H50.

Hacket, John. *Scrinia reserata: a memorial.* Edward Jones, for Samuel Lowndes, 1693. Wing H171.

Hall, Joseph. *The arte of divine meditation.* H. Lownes for Samuel Macham, 1607. STC 12643.

The passion sermon, preached at pavles crosse on good-friday. (London: W. S. for Samuell Macham, 1609. STC 12694.

Salomons diuine arts. H. L. for Eleazar Edgar, 1609. STC 12712.

Three tractates. M. Flesher for Nathaniel Butter, 1646. Wing H422.

Christ mysticall. M. Flesher for William Hope, Gabriel Beadle and Nathaniel Webbe, 1647. Wing H374.

Hatton, Christopher. *Devotions for the helpe and assistance of all christian people.* [Oxford]: 1644. Wing D1238.

Heale, William. *An apologie for women.* Oxford: Joseph Barnes, 1609. STC 13014.

Heinsius, Daniel. *The mirrovr of hvmilitie.* Translated by John Harmar. Bernard Alsop, 1618. STC 13039.

Hieron, Samuel. *A helpe vnto deuotion.* H. L. for Samuel Macham, 1608. STC 13406.3.

The bridegroome. For Samuel Macham, 1613. STC 13392.

Homes, Nathanael. *A commentary literal or historical, and mystical or spiritual.* In *Works.* Printed for the author, 1652. Wing H2559.

Hugo, Herman. *Pia desideria.* For Henry Bonwick, 1686. Wing H3350.

[Hutchinson, Lucy]. *Order and disorder.* London: Margaret White for Henry Mortlock, 1679. Wing A3594.

Guild, William. *Loves entercourse*. W. Wilson for Ralph Smith, 1657. Wing G2206.

Jacomb, Thomas. *Several sermons preach'd on the whole eighth chapter of the epistle to the romans*. W. Godbid for M. Pitt, R. Chiswel and J. Robinson, 1672. Wing J119.

Jellinger, Christopher. *The excellency of christ*. I. L. for Thomas Nichols, 1641. Wing J542A.

Jessey, Henry. *The exceeding riches of grace advanced*. By Matthew Simmons for Henry Overton and Hannah Allen, 1647. Wing J688.

Knollys, Hanserd. *An exposition of the first chapter of the song of solomon*. W. Godbid for Livewel Chapman, 1656. Wing K709.

Lanseter, John. *Lanseter's lance*. 1646. Wing L425B.

Lanyer, Aemilia. *Salve devs rex ivdæorvm*. Valentine Simmes for Richard Bonian, 1611. STC 15227.

   Salve devs rex ivdæorvm. Valentine Simmes for Richard Bonian, 1611. STC 15227.5.

Lock, Ann. *Sermons of john calvin*. John Day, 1560. STC 4450.

Mallery, Thomas. *The inseperable communion of a believer with god*. For R. D., 1674. Wing M337.

Mayer, John. *A commentary upon the holy writings of job, david, and salomon*. For Robert Ibbitson and Thomas Roycroft, 1653. Wing M1423.

Maynwaring, Roger. *Religion and alegiance: in two sermons preached before the kings maiestie*. I[ohn] H[aviland] for Richard Badger, 1627. STC 17751.

Mercurius politicus. No. 201. Thomas Newcomb, 13–20 April 1654.

Mercurius politicus. No. 312. 29 May–5 June 1656.

The moderate intelligencer. No. 175. Robert Wood, 19–26 April 1654.

The moderate publisher. No. 1. 13–20 January 1653/54.

More, Gertrude. *The holy practises*. Paris: Lewis de la Fosse, 1657. Wing M2631A.

   The spiritval exercises. Paris: Lewis de la Fosse, 1658. Wing M2632.

Myriell, Thomas. *Christs suite to his church*. For Nathaniel Butter, 1613. STC 18322.

Owen, John. *Of communion with god the father, sonne, and holy ghost*. Oxford: A. Lichfield for Philemon Stephens, 1657. Wing O777.

   A vindication of some passages in a discourse concerning communion with god. For N. Ponder, 1674. Wing O821.

Parker, Samuel. *A Discourse of ecclesiastical politie*. For John Martyn, 1670. Wing P459.

Polhill, Edward. *An answer to the discourse of mr william sherlock*. For Ben. Foster, 1675. Wing P2749.

The publick intelligencer. No. 13. Henry Hills, 24–31 December 1655.

Quarles, Francis. *Sions sonets*. W. Stansby for Thomas Dewe, 1625. STC 2776.

   Emblemes. J. Dawson for Francis Eglesfield, 1639. STC 20542.

Rogers, Daniel. *Matrimoniall honovr*. Th. Harper for Philip Nevil, 1642. Wing R1797.

Rogers, John. *Ohel, or beth-shemesh*. For R. I. and G. and H. Eversden, 1651. Wing R1813.

Rous, Francis. *The mysticall marriage.* W. Jones and T. Paine for I. Emery, 1635. STC 21343.

Saltmarsh, John. *Poemata sacra.* Cambridge: Ex Academia celeberrimæ typographeo, 1636. STC 21638.

Sandys, George. *A paraphrase vpon the song of solomon.* John Legatt, 1641. Wing B2629A.

Severall proceedings of state affaires. No. 225. Robert Ibbitson, 12–19 January 1653/4.

Shepard, Thomas. *The sincere convert.* T. P. and M. S. for Humphrey Blunden, 1641. Wing S3118.

The sound beleever. For R. Dawlman, 1645. Wing S3133.

The saints jewel, printed with *The sincere convert.* E. Cotes for John Sweeting, 1652. Wing S3123A.

Sherlock, William. *A discourse concerning the knowledge of jesus christ, and our union and communion with him.* J. M. for Walter Kettilby, 1674. Wing S3288.

A defence and continuation of the discourse concerning the knowledge of jesus christ. A. C. for Walter Kettilby, 1675. Wing S3281.

Sibbes, Richard. *A fountain sealed.* Thomas Harper for Lawrence Chapman, 1637. STC 22495.

The brides longing. E. Purslowe for G. Edwards, 1638. STC 22478.

Two sermons. T. Cotes for Andrew Kembe, 1638. STC 22519.

Bowels opened. G. M. for George Edwards, 1639. STC 22476.

A spirit moving in the women-preachers. For Henry Shepheard and William Ley, 1646. Wing S4990.

Sutcliffe, Alice. *Meditations of man's mortalitie.* B. Alsop and T. Fawcet for H. Seyle, 1634. STC 23447.

Taylor, Jeremy. *A discovrse concerning prayer extempore.* 1646. Wing T312.

Taylor, Jeremy. *The golden grove.* J. F. for R. Royston, 1655. Wing T336.

Trapnel, Anna. *Anna trapnel's report and plea.* For Thomas Brewster, 1654. Wing T2033.

The cry of a stone. 1654. Wing T2031.

A legacy for saints. For Thomas Brewster, 1654. Wing T2032.

Voice for the king of saints and nations. 1658. Wing T2035.

Untitled. 1659. Bodleian Library Shelfmark S 1.42 Theology.

Trapp, John. *Solomon's ΠΑΝΑΡΕΤΟΣ.* T. R. and E. M. for John Bellamie, 1650. Wing T2046.

Turner, Richard. *The song of solomon rendred in plain & familiar verse.* J. H. for J. Rothwell, 1659. Wing B2629E.

Verstegan, Richard. *Odes.* [Antwerp]: 1601. STC 21359.

Vincent, Thomas. *Christ the best husband.* For George Calvert and Samuel Sprint, 1672. Wing V428.

Walsall, Samuel. *The life and death of iesvs christ.* [Cambridge]: for I. Porter and L. Greene, 1607. STC 24996a.

Watson, Thomas. *Christs lovelinesse.* In *Three treatises.* For Ralph Smith, 1660. Wing W1145.

The weekly intelligencer. No. 328. F. Neile, 18–25 April 1654.

Wentworth, Anne. *A vindication of anne wentworth.* 1677. Wing W1356.

Whately, William. *A bride-bvsh: or, a direction for married persons.* Felix Kyngston for Thomas Man, 1619. STC 25297.

A care-cloth: or a treatise of the cvmbers and trovbles of marriage. Felix Kyngston for Thomas Man, 1624. STC 25299.

Whitney, Isabella. *The copy of a letter.* Richard Jones, 1567. STC 25439.

A sweet nosgay. Richard Jones, 1573. STC 25440.

Willet, Andrew. *A treatise of salomons mariage.* F[elix] K[ingston] for Thomas Man the elder and William Welby, 1612. STC 25705.

Wilson, Thomas. *A christian dictionarie.* W. Iaggard, 1612. STC 25786.

Wither, George. *The hymnes and songs of the chvrch.* For G. W., 1623. STC 25908.

EDITIONS AND TRANSLATIONS

Bjorvand, Einar, *et al.*, eds. *The Yale Edition of the Shorter Poems of Edmund Spenser.* New Haven, Connecticut: Yale University Press, 1989.

Booty, John, ed. *The Book of Common Prayer 1559: The Elizabethan Prayer Book.* Charlottesville, Virginia: University of Virginia Press, 1976.

Brown, Beatrice Daw, ed. *The Southern Passion.* London: Early English Text Society, 1927.

Carey, John, and Alastair Fowler, eds. *The Poems of John Milton.* London: Longman, 1980.

Clarke, Elizabeth, and Victoria Burke, eds. *The 'Centuries' of Julia Palmer.* Nottingham: Trent Editions, 2001.

Colledge, Edmund, O. S. A., and James Walsh, S. J., eds. *A Book of Showings to the Anchoress Julian of Norwich.* Studies and Texts 35. 2 vols. Toronto: Pontifical Institute of Mediaeval Studies, 1978.

Davidson, Peter, and Jane Stevenson, eds. *Early Modern Women Poets (1520–1700): An Anthology.* Oxford: Oxford University Press, 2001.

Ellis, Roger, ed. *The Liber Celestis of St Bridget of Sweden: The Middle English Version.* Early English Text Society Original Series 291. Oxford: Oxford University Press, 1987.

Felch, Susan M., ed. *The Collected Works of Anne Vaughan Lock.* Tempe, Arizona: Renaissance English Text Society, 1999.

Greer, Germaine, *et al.*, eds. *Kissing the Rod: An Anthology of Seventeenth-Century Women's Verse.* London: Virago, 1988.

Grosart, Alexander B, ed. *The Lismore Papers (First Series).* 5 vols. [London]: For private circulation, 1886. Vol. II.

Halligan, Theresa A., ed. *The Booke of Gostlye Grace of Mechtild of Hackeborn.* Studies and Texts 46. Toronto: Pontifical Institute of Mediaeval Studies, 1979.

Hannay, Margaret P., Noel J. Kinnamon, and Michael G. Brennan, eds. *The Collected Works of Mary Sidney Herbert Countess of Pembroke.* 2 vols. Oxford: Clarendon Press, 1998.

Hart, Columba, trans. *Hadewijch: The Complete Works.* New York: Paulist Press, 1980.

Heuser, Wilhelm, and Frances A. Foster, eds. *The Northern Passion*. London: Early English Text Society, 1930.

Hinds, Hilary, ed. *The Cry of a Stone*. Tempe, Arizona: Arizona Center for Medieval and Renaissance Studies, 2000.

Hughes, Merritt Y., ed. *Complete Prose Works of John Milton*. 8 vols. New Haven, Connecticut: Yale University Press, 1962. Vol. III.

Hutchinson, Julius, ed. *Memoirs of the Life of Colonel Hutchinson*. London: Longman, 1806.

   On the Principles of the Christian Religion, Addressed to Her Daughter; and On Theology. London: Longman, 1817.

Keeble, N. H., ed. *Memoirs of the Life of Colonel Hutchinson with a Fragment of Autobiography*. London: Everyman, 1995.

Klene, Jean, ed. *The Southwell-Sibthorpe Commonplace Book: Folger MS. V.b.198*. Tempe, Arizona: Renaissance English Text Society, 1997.

MacDonald, James H., and Nancy Pollard Brown, eds. *The Poems of Robert Southwell, S. J.* Oxford: Clarendon Press, 1967.

Martin, L. C., ed. *The Poems, English, Latin, and Greek, of Richard Crashaw*. 2nd edn Oxford: Clarendon Press, 1957.

Martz, Louis L., ed. *George Herbert and Henry Vaughan*. Oxford: Oxford University Press, 1986.

McClure, Norman Egbert, ed. *The Letters of John Chamberlain*. 2 vols. Philadelphia: American Philosophical Society, 1939.

Norbrook, David, ed. 'Lucy Hutchinson versus Edmund Waller: An Unpublished Reply to Waller's *A Panegyric to My Lord Protector*'. *The Seventeenth Century* 11 (1996): 61–86.

   'Lucy Hutchinson's "Elegies" and the Situation of the Republican Woman Writer (with text)'. *English Literary Renaissance* 27 (1997): 468–521.

   Order and Disorder. Oxford: Blackwell, 2001.

Parker, T. H. L., trans. *Calvin's Commentaries: The Epistles of Paul the Apostle to the Galatians, Ephesians, Philippians and Colossians*. Edinburgh: Oliver and Boyd, 1965.

Potter, George R., and Evelyn M. Simpson, eds. *The Sermons of John Donne*. 10 vols. Berkeley, California: University of California Press, 1953–62.

de Quehen, Hugh, ed. *Lucy Hutchinson's Translation of Lucretius: De rerum natura*. London: Duckworth, 1996.

Rickey, Mary Ellen, and Thomas B. Stroup, eds. *Certain Sermons or Homilies*. Gainesville, Florida: Scholars' Facsimiles and Reprints, 1968.

Rye, Walter, ed. *The Visitacion of Norfolk*. London: Harleian Society, 1891.

Savage, James Edwin, ed. *The 'Conceited Newes' of Sir Thomas Overbury And His Friends*. Gainesville, Florida: Scholars' Facsimilies & Reprints, 1968.

Semler, L. E. *Eliza's Babes: or The Virgin's Offering (1652): A Critical Edition*. Madison, Wisconsin: Fairleigh Dickinson University Press, 2001.

Spector, Stephen, ed. *The N-Town Play*. Oxford: Early English Text Society, 1991.

Troide, Lars E., ed. *The Early Journals and Letters of Fanny Burney. Volume I 1768–1773*. Oxford: Clarendon Press, 1988.

Vivian, J. L., ed. *The Visitations of the County of Devon*. Exeter: Henry S. Eland, 1895.

Windeatt, Barry, ed. *The Book of Margery Kempe*. London: Longman, 2000.

Woods, Susanne, ed. *The Poems of Aemilia Lanyer: Salve Deus Rex Judæorum*. Oxford: Oxford University Press, 1993.

SECONDARY SOURCES AND CRITICISM

Aers, David, and Lynn Staley. *The Powers of the Holy: Religion, Politics, and Gender in Late Medieval English Culture*. University Park, Pennsylvania: The Pennsylvania State University Press, 1996.

Amussen, Susan Dwyer. *An Ordered Society: Gender and Class in Early Modern England*. Oxford: Basil Blackwell, 1988.

Armstrong, Karen. 'The Acts of Paul and Thecla'. In *Feminist Theology: A Reader*. Ed. Ann Loades. London: SPCK, 1990. 83–8.

Astell, Ann W. *The Song of Songs in the Middle Ages*. Ithaca, New York: Cornell University Press, 1990.

Baker, T. F. T. *A History of Middlesex*. The Victoria History of the Counties of England. Ed. C. R. Elrington. Vol. VII. Oxford: Oxford University Press, 1982.

Barroll, Leeds. 'The Court of the First Stuart Queen'. In *The Mental World of the Jacobean Court*. Ed. Linda Levy Peck. Cambridge: Cambridge University Press, 1991. 191–208.

'Looking for Patrons'. In Grossman, ed., *Aemilia Lanyer: Gender, Genre, and the Canon*. 29–48.

Bauerschmidt, Frederick Christian. *Julian of Norwich and the Mystical Body Politic of Christ*. Notre Dame, Indiana: University of Notre Dame Press, 1999.

Beal, Peter. *In Praise of Scribes: Manuscripts and their Makers in Seventeenth-Century England*. Oxford: Oxford University Press, 1998.

Beer, Frances. *Women and Mystical Experience in the Middle Ages*. Woodbridge, Suffolk: The Boydell Press, 1992.

Beilin, Elaine. 'The Feminization of Praise: Aemilia Lanyer'. In *Redeeming Eve: Women Writers of the English Renaissance*. Princeton: Princeton University Press, 1987. 177–207.

Benson, Pamela. 'To Play the Man: Aemilia Lanyer and the Acquisition of Patronage'. In *Opening the Borders: Inclusivity in Early Modern Studies: Essays in Honor of James V. Mirollo*. Ed. Peter C. Herman. Newark, Delaware: University of Delaware Press, 1999. 243–64.

Blomefield, Francis. *An Essay Towards a Topographical History of the County of Norfolk*. 10 vols. London: for William Miller by W. Bulmer, 1805–9.

Brewer, John. 'This, That, and the Other: Public, Social and Private in the Seventeenth and Eighteenth Centuries'. In *Shifting the Boundaries: Transformation of the Languages of Public and Private in the Eighteenth Century*. Ed.

Dario Castiglione and Lesley Sharpe. Exeter: Exeter University Press, 1995. 1–21.

Brown, Sylvia. 'Godly Household Government from Perkins to Milton: The Rhetoric and Politics of *oeconomia*, 1600–1645'. Unpublished PhD thesis. Princeton University, 1994.

Burke, Mary E., *et al.*, eds. and Introduction. In *Women, Writing, and the Reproduction of Culture in Tudor and Stuart Britain*. Syracuse, New York: Syracuse University Press, 2000. xvii–xxx.

Burke, Victoria. 'Women and Early Seventeenth-Century Manuscript Culture: Four Miscellanies'. *The Seventeenth Century* 12.2 (1997): 135–50.

'Medium and Meaning in the Manuscripts of Anne, Lady Southwell'. In *Women's Writing and the Circulation of Ideas: Manuscript Publication in England, 1550–1800*. Ed. George L. Justice and Nathan P. Tinker. Cambridge: Cambridge University Press, 2002. 94–120.

Burke, Victoria, and Jonathan Gibson, eds. *Early Modern Women's Manuscript Writing: Selected Papers of the Trinity–Trent Colloquium*. London: Ashgate, 2004.

Bynum, Caroline Walker. *Holy Feast and Holy Fast*. Berkeley: University of California Press, 1987.

Fragmentation and Redemption: Essays on Gender and the Human Body in Medieval Religion. New York: Zone Books, 1991.

Cavanaugh, Sister Jean Carmel, S. L. 'The Library of Lady Southwell and Captain Sibthorpe'. *Studies in Bibliography* 20 (1967): 243–54.

Clark, Alice. *The Working Life of Women in the Seventeenth Century*. London: Routledge, 1919.

Clarke, Danielle. Introduction to *'This Double Voice': Gendered Writing in Early Modern England*. Ed. Danielle Clarke and Elizabeth Clarke. Basingstoke: Macmillan, 2000. 1–15.

The Politics of Early Modern Women's Writing. London: Longman, 2001.

Clarke, Elizabeth. 'Conflagration, Coincidence, Conscience: the Journal of Elizabeth Jekyll'. Trinity–Trent Colloquium. Nottingham Trent University. 4 November 1998.

'Ejaculation or Virgin Birth? The Gendering of the Religious Lyric in the Interregnum'. In *'This Double Voice': Gendered Writing in Early Modern England*. Ed. Danielle Clarke and Elizabeth Clarke. Basingstoke: Macmillan, 2000. 208–29.

'Re-writing the Bride': Politics, Authorship and the Song of Songs in Seventeenth Century England. London: Macmillan. Forthcoming.

Coiro, Ann Baynes. 'Writing in Service: Sexual Politics and Class Position in the Poetry of Aemilia Lanyer and Ben Jonson'. *Criticism* 35.3 (1993): 357–76.

Colish, Marcia L. *Peter Lombard*. 2 vols. Leiden: E. J. Brill, 1994.

Collinson, Patrick. *Godly People: Essays on English Protestantism and Puritanism*. London: Hambledon, 1983.

The Birthpangs of Protestant England: Religious and Cultural Change in the Sixteenth and Seventeenth Centuries. London: Macmillan, 1988.

'Ecclesiastical Vitriol: Religious Satire in the 1590s and the Invention of Puritanism'. In *The Reign of Elizabeth I: Court and Culture in the Last Decade*. Ed. John Guy. Cambridge: Cambridge University Press, 1995. 150–70.

Considine, John. 'The Invention of the Literary Circle of Sir Thomas Overbury'. In *Literary Circles and Cultural Communities in Renaissance England*. Ed. Claude J. Summers and Ted-Larry Pebworth. Columbia, Missouri: University of Missouri Press, 2000. 59–74.

Crawford, Patricia. 'Public Duty, Conscience, and Women in Early Modern England'. In *Public Duty and Private Conscience in Seventeenth-Century England: Essays Presented to G. E. Aylmer*. Ed. John Morrill, Paul Slack and Daniel Woolf. Oxford: Clarendon Press, 1993. 57–76.

Cressy, David. 'Foucault, Stone, Shakespeare and Social History'. *ELR* 21.1 (1991): 121–33.

'Response: Private Lives, Public Performance, and Rites of Passage'. In *Attending to Women in Early Modern England*. Ed. Betty S. Travitsky and Adele F. Seeff. Newark, Delaware: University of Delaware Press, 1994. 187–97.

Dever, Mark E. *Richard Sibbes: Puritanism and Calvinism in Late Elizabethan and Early Stuart England*. Macon, Georgia: Mercer University Press, 2000.

Devlin, Christopher. *The Life of Robert Southwell Poet and Martyr*. London: Longmans, Green and Co, 1956.

Dillon, Janette. 'Holy Women and their Confessors or Confessors and their Holy Women? Margery Kempe and Continental Tradition'. In *Prophets Abroad: The Reception of Continental Holy Women in Late-Medieval England*. Ed. Rosalynn Voaden. Cambridge: D. S. Brewer, 1996. 115–40.

DiPasquale, Theresa M. 'Woman's Desire for Man in Lanyer's *Salve Deus Rex Judaeorum*'. *Journal of English and Germanic Philology* 99.3 (2000): 356–78.

Dobson, Joanne. *Dickinson and the Strategies of Reticence: The Woman Writer in Nineteenth-Century America*. Bloomington, Indiana: Indiana University Press, 1989.

Donawerth, Jane. 'Women's Poetry and the Tudor–Stuart System of Gift Exchange'. In Mary E. Burke *et al.*, eds., *Women, Writing, and the Reproduction of Culture in Tudor and Stuart Britain*. 3–18.

Doriani, Beth Maclay. *Emily Dickinson: Daughter of Prophecy*. Amherst, Massachusetts: University of Massachusetts Press, 1996.

van Dorsten, Jan. 'Literary Patronage in Elizabethan England: The Early Phase'. In *Patronage in the Renaissance*. Ed. Guy Fitch Lytel and Stephen Orgel. Princeton, New Jersey: Princeton University Press, 1981. 191–206.

Duffy, Eamon. *The Stripping of the Altars: Traditional Religion in England c. 1400–c.1580*. New Haven, Connecticut: Yale University Press, 1992.

Dutton, Elisabeth Mary. 'Compiling Julian: The *Revelation of Love* and Late-Medieval Devotional Compilation'. Unpublished D. Phil. thesis. Oxford University, 2002.

Epstein, Julia. 'Burney Criticism: Family Romance, Psychobiography, and Social History'. *Eighteenth-Century Fiction* 3.4 (1991): 277–82.

Erck, John Caillard, ed. *A Repertory of the Inrollments on the Patent Rolls of Chancery, in Ireland: Commencing with the Reign of King James I.* Vol. 1 part 1. Dublin: James M'glashan, 1846.

Ezell, Margaret. *The Patriarch's Wife: Literary Evidence and the History of the Family.* Chapel Hill, North Carolina: The University of North Carolina Press, 1987.

'"To Be Your Daughter in Your Pen": The Social Functions of Literature in the Writings of Lady Elizabeth Brackley and Lady Jane Cavendish'. *Huntington Library Quarterly* 51.4 (1988): 281–96.

Writing Women's Literary History. Baltimore, Maryland: Johns Hopkins University Press, 1993.

Social Authorship and the Advent of Print. Baltimore, Maryland: Johns Hopkins University Press, 1999.

Fletcher, Anthony. *Gender, Sex & Subordination in England 1500–1800.* New Haven, Connecticut: Yale University Press, 1995.

Freist, Dagmar. *Governed by Opinion: Politics, Religion, and the Dynamics of Communication in Stuart London, 1637–1645.* London: I. B. Tauris Publishers, 1997.

Furniss, Tom, and Michael Bath. *Reading Poetry: An Introduction.* London: Prentice Hall, 1996.

Gilbert, Sandra M., and Susan Gubar, eds. *The Norton Anthology of Literature by Women: The Tradition in English.* London: W. W. Norton & Company, 1985.

Giuseppi, M. S., ed. *Calendar of the Manuscripts of the Most Hon. The Marquess of Salisbury, preserved at Hatfield House, Hertfordshire.* Part 15. London: His Majesty's Stationery Office, 1930.

Greenfield, Susan C. '"Oh Dear Resemblance of Thy Murdered Mother": Female Authorship in Evelina'. *Eighteenth-Century Fiction* 3.4 (1991): 301–20.

Grossman, Marshall, ed. and Introduction. *Aemilia Lanyer: Gender, Genre, and the Canon.* Lexington, Kentucky: University Press of Kentucky, 1998. 1–9.

Guibbory, Achsah. 'The Gospel According to Aemilia: Women and the Sacred'. In Grossman, ed., *Aemilia Lanyer: Gender, Genre, and the Canon.* 191–211.

Haliczer, Stephen. *Between Exaltation and Infamy: Female Mystics in the Golden Age of Spain.* Oxford: Oxford University Press, 2002.

Hannay, Margaret P., ed. *Silent But for the Word: Tudor Women as Patrons, Translators, and Writers of Religious Works.* Kent, Ohio: Ohio State University Press, 1985.

Philip's Phoenix: Mary Sidney, Countess of Pembroke. Oxford: Oxford University Press, 1990.

Haselkorn, Anne M., and Betty S. Travitsky, eds. *The Renaissance Englishwoman in Print: Counterbalancing the Canon.* Amherst, Massachusetts: The University of Massachusetts Press, 1990.

Herz, Judith Scherer. 'Aemilia Lanyer and the Pathos of Literary History'. In *Representing Women in Renaissance England.* Eds. Claude J. Summers and Ted-Larry Pebworth. Columbia, Missouri: University of Missouri Press, 1997. 121–35.

Hill, Christopher. *The Experience of Defeat: Milton and Some Contemporaries.* London: Faber and Faber, 1984.

Hinds, Hilary. *God's Englishwomen: Seventeenth-century Radical Sectarian Writing and Feminist Criticism.* Manchester: Manchester University Press, 1996.

Hobby, Elaine. *Virtue of Necessity: English Women's Writing 1649–1688.* Ann Arbor, Michigan: University of Michigan Press, 1989.

'Handmaids of the Lord and Mothers in Israel: Early Vindications of Quaker Women's Prophecy'. *Prose Studies* 17.3 (1994): 88–98.

Holmes, Michael Morgan. 'The Love of Other Women: Rich Chains and Sweet Kisses'. In Grossman, ed., *Aemilia Lanyer: Gender, Genre, and the Canon.* 167–90.

Holstun, James. *Ehud's Dagger: Class Struggle in the English Revolution.* London: Verso, 2000.

Hull, Suzanne W. *Chaste Silent & Obedient. English Books for Women 1475–1640.* San Marino, California: Huntington Library, 1982.

Hutson, Lorna. 'Why the Lady's Eyes are Nothing Like the Sun'. In *Women, Texts, and Histories 1575–1760.* Ed. Claire Brant and Diane Purkiss. London: Routledge, 1992. 13–38.

Hutton, Sarah. 'Introduction to the Renaissance and Seventeenth Century'. In *Platonism and the English Imagination.* Ed. Anna Baldwin and Sarah Hutton. Cambridge: Cambridge University Press, 1994. 67–75.

Johnson, Francis R. 'Notes on English Retail Book-prices, 1550–1640'. *The Library* 5.5 (1950): 83–112.

Keeble, N. H. *The Literary Culture of Nonconformity in Later Seventeenth-Century England.* Leicester: Leicester University Press, 1987.

'"The Colonel's Shadow": Lucy Hutchinson, Women's Writing and the Civil War'. In *Literature and the English Civil War.* Ed. Thomas Healy and Jonathan Sawday. Cambridge: Cambridge University Press, 1990. 227–47.

Kelly-Gadol, Joan. 'Did Women Have a Renaissance?'. In *Becoming Visible: Women in European History.* Ed. Renate Bridenthal, Claudia Koonz and Susan Stuard. 2nd edn. Boston: Houghton Mifflin, 1987. 175–202.

Keohane, Catherine. '"That blindest Weakenesse be not over-bold": Aemilia Lanyer's Radical Unfolding of the Passion'. *ELH* 64.2 (1997): 359–89.

Klein, Lawrence E. 'Gender and the Public/Private Distinction in the Eighteenth Century: Some Questions about Evidence and Analytic Procedure'. *Eighteenth-Century Studies* 29.1 (1995): 97–109.

Klene, Jean. '"Monument of an Endless affection": Folger MS V.b.198 and Lady Anne Southwell'. *English Manuscript Studies* 9 (2000): 165–86.

de Krey, Gary S. 'Rethinking the Restoration: Dissenting Cases for Conscience, 1667–1672'. *The Historical Journal* 38.1 (1995): 53–83.

Krontiris, Tina. *Oppositional Voices: Women as Writers and Translators of Literature in the English Renaissance.* London: Routledge, 1992.

Lake, Peter. *Anglicans and Puritans? Presbyterianism and English Conformist Thought from Whitgift to Hooker.* London: Unwind Hyman, 1988.

Lake, Peter. 'Feminine Piety and Personal Potency: The "Emancipation" of Mrs Jane Ratcliffe'. *The Seventeenth Century* 2.2 (1987): 143–65.

    'Joseph Hall, Robert Skinner and the Rhetoric of Moderation at the Early Stuart Court'. In *The English Sermon Revised: Religion, Literature and History 1600–1750*. Ed. Lori Anne Ferrell and Peter McCullough. Manchester: Manchester University Press, 2000. 167–85.

    The Boxmaker's Revenge: 'Orthodoxy', 'Heterodoxy', and the Politics of the Parish in Early Stuart London. Manchester: Manchester University Press, 2001.

Lamb, Mary Ellen. 'Patronage and Class in Aemilia Lanyer's *Salve Deus Rex Judaeorum*'. In Mary E. Burke *et al.*, eds., *Women, Writing, and the Reproduction of Culture in Tudor and Stuart Britain*. 38–57.

Laurence, Anne. 'A Priesthood of She-Believers: Women and Congregations in Mid-Seventeenth Century England'. In *Women in the Church: Papers Read at the 1989 Summer Meeting and the 1990 Winter Meeting of the Ecclesiastical Historical Society*. Ed. W. J. Sheils and Diana Wood. Oxford: Basil Blackwell, 1990. 345–63.

Lewalski, Barbara Kiefer. *Protestant Poetics and the Seventeenth-Century Religious Lyric*. Princeton, New Jersey: Princeton University Press, 1979.

    'Of God and Good Women: The Poems of Aemilia Lanyer'. In *Silent But for the Word: Tudor Women as Patrons, Translators, and Writers of Religious Works*. Ed. Margaret Hannay. Kent, Ohio: Kent State University Press, 1985. 203–24.

    'Imagining Female Community: Aemilia Lanyer's Poems'. In *Writing Women in Jacobean England*. Cambridge, Massachusetts: Harvard University Press, 1993. 213–41.

    'Seizing Discourses and Reinventing Genres'. In Grossman, ed., *Aemilia Lanyer: Gender, Genre, and the Canon*. 49–59.

Loades, Ann, ed. *Feminist Theology: A Reader*. London: SPCK, 1990.

Love, Harold. *Scribal Publication in Seventeenth-Century England*. Oxford: Clarendon Press, 1993.

Lytel, Guy Fitch, and Stephen Orgel, eds. *Patronage in the Renaissance*. Princeton, New Jersey: Princeton University Press, 1981. 191–206.

Mack, Phyllis. *Visionary Women: Ecstatic Prophecy in Seventeenth-Century England*. Los Angeles: University of California Press, 1992.

Mann, Lindsay A. 'Misogyny and Libertinism: Donne's Marriage Sermons'. *John Donne Journal* 11.1–2 (1992): 111–32.

Marotti, Arthur F. 'John Donne and the Rewards of Patronage'. In Lytel and Orgel, eds., *Patronage in the Renaissance*. 207–34.

    '"Love is not love": Elizabethan Sonnet Sequences and the Social Order'. *ELH* 49.2 (1982): 396–428.

    Manuscript, Print, and the English Renaissance Lyric. Ithaca, New York: Cornell University Press, 1995.

Marsh, Jan. *Christina Rossetti: A Literary Biography*. London: Jonathan Cape, 1994.

Martz, Louis L. *The Poetry of Meditation: A Study in English Religious Literature of the Seventeenth Century*. New Haven, Connecticut: Yale University Press, 1954.

Matter, E. Ann. *The Voice of My Beloved: The Song of Songs in Western Medieval Christianity*. Philadelphia: University of Pennsylvania Press, 1990.

McBride, Kari Boyd. 'Sacred Celebration: The Patronage Poems'. In Grossman, ed., *Aemilia Lanyer: Gender, Genre and the Canon*. 60–82.

McBride, Kari Boyd, and John C. Ulreich. 'Answerable Styles: Biblical Poetics and Biblical Politics in the Poetry of Lanyer and Milton'. *Journal of English and Germanic Philology* 100.3 (2001): 333–54.

McCabe, Richard. *Joseph Hall: A Study in Satire and Meditation*. Oxford: Clarendon Press, 1982.

McCullough, Peter. 'Making Dead Men Speak: Laudianism, Print, and the Works of Lancelot Andrewes, 1626–1642'. *The Historical Journal* 41.2 (1998): 401–24.
  Sermons at Court: Politics and Religion in Elizabethan and Jacobean Preaching. Cambridge: Cambridge University Press, 1998.

McCullough, Peter, and Lori Anne Ferrell, eds. *The English Sermon Revised: Religion, Literature and History 1600–1750*. Manchester: Manchester University Press, 2000.

McGrath, Lynette. 'Metaphoric Subversions: Feasts and Mirrors in Aemilia Lanier's *Salve Deus Rex Judaeorum*'. *LIT* 3.2 (1991): 101–13.
  '"Let Us Have Our Libertie Againe": Aemilia Lanier's 17th-Century Feminist Voice'. *Women's Studies* 20.3–4 (1992): 331–48.

McLaughlin, Eleanor. 'Women, Power and the Pursuit of Holiness in Medieval Christianity'. In Loades, ed., *Feminist Theology: A Reader*. 99–120.

Medwick, Catherine. *Teresa of Avila: The Progress of a Soul*. London: Duckworth, 2000.

Miller, Naomi J. '(M)other Tongues: Maternity and Subjectivity'. In Grossman, ed., *Aemilia Lanyer: Gender, Genre and the Canon*. 143–66.

Morgan, John. *Godly Learning: Puritan Attitudes towards Reason, Learning and Education 1560–1640*. Cambridge: Cambridge University Press, 1986.

Morrill, J. S. *The Revolt of the Provinces: Conservatives and Radicals in the English Civil War 1630–1650*. London: Longman, 1980.

Muddiman, John. *A Commentary on the Epistle to the Ephesians*. London: Continuum, 2001.

Mueller, Janel. 'The Feminist Poetics of "Salve Deus Rex Judaeorum"'. In Grossman, ed., *Aemilia Lanyer: Gender, Genre, and the Canon*. 99–127.

Neely, Carol Thomas. 'Constructing the Subject: Feminist Practice and the New Renaissance Discourses'. *ELR* 18.1 (1988): 5–18.

Newman, Barbara. *From Virile Woman to WomanChrist: Studies in Medieval Religion and Literature*. Philadelphia: University of Pennsylvania Press, 1995.

Ng, Su Fang. 'Aemilia Lanyer and the Politics of Praise'. *ELH* 67.2 (2000): 433–51.

Norbrook, David. 'A devine Originall: Lucy Hutchinson and the "woman's version"'. *Times Literary Supplement* March 19 1999: 13–15.
  Writing the English Republic: Poetry, Rhetoric and Politics, 1627–1660. Cambridge: Cambridge University Press, 1999.
  'Lucy Hutchinson and *Order and Disorder*: The Manuscript Evidence'. *English Manuscript Studies 1100–1700* 9 (2000): 257–91.

Okin, Susan Moller. 'Gender, the Public and the Private'. In *Political Theory Today*. Ed. David Held. Cambridge: Polity Press, 1991. 67–90.

Parsons, Susan Frank, ed. *The Cambridge Companion to Feminist Theology*. Cambridge: Cambridge University Press, 2002.

Peters, Christine. *Patterns of Piety: Women, Gender, and Religion in Late Medieval and Reformation England*. Cambridge: Cambridge University Press, 2003.

Phillippy, Patricia. 'Sisters of Magdalen: Women's Mourning in Aemilia Lanyer's *Salve Deus Rex Judaeorum*'. *ELR* 31.1 (2000): 78–106.

Potter, Lois. *Secret Rites and Secret Writing: Royalist Literature, 1641–1660*. Cambridge: Cambridge University Press, 1989.

Power, M. J. 'East London Housing in the Seventeenth Century'. In *Crisis and Order in English Towns 1500–1700: Essays in Urban History*. Ed. Peter Clark and Paul Slack. London: Routledge, 1972. 237–62.

Purkiss, Diane. 'Gender, Power, and the Body: Some Figurations of Femininity in Milton and Seventeenth-Century Women's Writing'. Unpublished DPhil. thesis. University of Oxford, 1991.

   'Producing the Voice, Consuming the Body: Women Prophets of the Seventeenth Century'. In *Women, Writing, History 1640–1740*. Ed. Isobel Grundy and Susan Wiseman. Athens, Georgia: University of Georgia Press, 1992. 139–58.

Purkiss, Diane. Ed. and Introduction. *Three Tragedies by Renaissance Women*. London: Penguin, 1998. xi–xliii.

Rivers, Isabel. *Reason, Grace, and Sentiment: A Study of the Language of Religion and Ethics in England, 1660–1780*. Vol. 1. Cambridge: Cambridge University Press, 1991.

Rogers, P. G. *The Fifth Monarchy Men*. Oxford: Oxford University Press, 1966.

Ross, Sarah. 'Women and Religious Verse in English Manuscript Culture, *c.* 1600–1668: Lady Anne Southwell, Lady Hester Pulter and Katherine Austen'. Unpublished DPhil. thesis. University of Oxford, 2000.

Rowse, A. L., ed. *The Poems of Shakespeare's Dark Lady: Salve Deus Rex Judeorum by Emilia Lanyer*. London: Jonathan Cape, 1978.

Scheper, George L. 'Reformation Attitudes Toward Allegory and the Song of Songs', *PMLA* 89.3 (1973): 551–62.

Schleiner, Louise. *Tudor and Stuart Women Writers*. Bloomington, Indiana: Indiana University Press, 1994.

Schnackenburg, Rudolf. *Ephesians: A Commentary*. Trans. Helen Heron. Edinburgh: T. & T. Clark, 1991.

Schnell, Lisa. '"So Great a Difference Is There in Degree": Aemilia Lanyer and the Aims of Feminist Criticism'. *MLQ* 57.1 (1996): 23–35.

   'Breaking "the rule of *Cortezia*": Aemilia Lanyer's Dedications to *Salve Deus Rex Judaeorum*'. *Journal of Medieval and Early Modern Studies* 27.1 (1997): 77–101.

Schoenfeldt, Michael C. *Prayer and Power: George Herbert and Renaissance Courtship*. Chicago: University of Chicago Press, 1991.

'The Gender of Religious Devotion: Amelia Lanyer and John Donne'. In *Religion and Culture in Renaissance England*. Ed. Claire McEachern and Debora Shuger. Cambridge: Cambridge University Press, 1997. 209–33.

Schüssler Fiorenza, Elisabeth. 'Introduction: Transforming the Legacy of *The Woman's Bible*'. In *Searching the Scriptures. Volume 1: A Feminist Introduction*. Ed. Elisabeth Schüssler Fiorenza. London: SCM, 1993. 1–24.

In Memory of Her: A Feminist Theological Reconstruction of Christian Origins. 2nd edition. London: SCM, 1994.

Seaver, Paul S. *The Puritan Lectureships: The Politics of Religious Dissent 1560–1662*. Stanford, California: Stanford University Press, 1970.

Semler, Liam E. 'The Protestant Birth Ethic: Aesthetic, Political and Religious Contexts for *Eliza's Babes* (1652)'. *ELR* 30.3 (2000): 432–56.

'Who is the Mother of *Eliza's Babes* (1652)? "Eliza", George Wither, and Elizabeth Emerson'. *Journal of English and Germanic Philology* 99.4 (2000): 513–36.

'The Creed of *Eliza's Babes* (1652): Nakedness, Adam and Divinity'. *Albion* 33 (2001): 185–217.

Sharpe, Kevin. 'Private Conscience and Public Duty in the Writings of James VI and I'. In *Public Duty and Private Conscience in Seventeenth-Century England: Essay Presented to G. E. Aylmer*. Ed. Paul Slack, John Morrill and Daniel Woolf. Oxford: Clarendon Press, 1993. 77–100.

'Private Conscience and Public Duty in the Writings of Charles I'. *The Historical Journal* 40.3 (1997): 643–65.

Shaw, Jane. 'Fasting Women: The Significance of Gender and Bodies in Radical Religion and Politics, 1650–1813'. *Radicalism in British Literary Culture, 1650–1830: From Revolution to Revolution*. Ed. Timothy Morton and Nigel Smith. Cambridge: Cambridge University Press, 2002. 101–15.

Shell, Alison. *Catholicism, Controversy, and the English Literary Imagination, 1558–1660*. Cambridge: Cambridge University Press, 1999.

Shepard, Alexandra Jane. 'Meanings of Manhood in Early Modern England, With Special Reference to Cambridge, c. 1560–1640'. Unpublished PhD thesis. Cambridge University, 1998.

Shuger, Debora Kuller. *Habits of Thought in the English Renaissance: Religion, Politics, and the Dominant Culture*. Berkeley, California: University of California Press, 1990.

The Renaissance Bible: Scholarship, Sacrifice, and Subjectivity. Berkeley, California: University of California Press, 1994.

Smith, Nigel. *Perfection Proclaimed: Language and Literature in English Radical Religion, 1640–1660*. Oxford: Clarendon Press, 1989.

Literature and Revolution in England, 1640–1660. New Haven, Connecticut: Yale University Press, 1994.

Steer, Sir Francis W. *Woodrising Church, Norfolk: Notes on the Southwell and Other Families Connected with the Parish*. Norwich: The Diocese of Norwich, 1959.

Steiner, Prudence L. 'A Garden of Spices in New England: John Cotton's and Edward Taylor's Use of the Song of Songs'. In *Allegory, Myth, and Symbol*.

Ed. Morton W. Bloomfield. Cambridge, Massachusetts: Harvard University
Press, 1981. 227–43.

Stevenson, Jane. 'Women, Writing and Scribal Publication in the Sixteenth Century'. Trinity–Trent Colloquium. Trinity College, Cambridge. 29 November
1997.

'Mildred Cecil, Lady Burghley: Poet, Patron, Politician'. Women, Text and
History Seminar. Oxford University. November 1998.

Stewart, Stanley. *The Enclosed Garden: The Tradition and the Image in Seventeenth-
Century Poetry.* Madison, Wisconsin: University of Wisconsin Press, 1966.

Stone, Lawrence. *The Crisis of the Aristocracy.* Oxford: Clarendon Press, 1965.

The Family, Sex and Marriage in England 1500–1800. London: Weidenfeld and
Nicolson, 1979.

Sussman, Charlotte. 'Women's Private Reading and Political Action, 1649–1838'.
In *Radicalism in British Literary Culture, 1650–1830: From Revolution to Revolution.* Ed. Timothy Morton and Nigel Smith. Cambridge: Cambridge University Press, 2002. 133–50.

Thomas, Keith. 'Women and the Civil War Sects'. *Past and Present* 13 (1958): 42–62.

Travitsky, Betty. *The Paradise of Women: Writings by Englishwomen of the Renaissance.* London: Greenwood Press, 1981.

*Subordination and Authorship in Early Modern England: The Case of Elizabeth
Cavendish Egerton and her Loose Papers.* Tempe, Arizona: Arizona Center for
Medieval and Renaissance Studies, 1999.

Trible, Phyllis. *God and the Rhetoric of Sexuality.* London: SCM Press, 1978.

Turner, James Grantham. *One Flesh: Paradisal Marriage and Sexual Relations in the
Age of Milton.* Oxford: Clarendon Press, 1993.

Tyacke, Nicholas. *Anti-Calvinists: The Rise of English Arminianism c. 1590–1640.*
Oxford: Oxford University Press, 1990.

Aspects of English Protestantism c. 1530–1700. Manchester: Manchester University
Press, 2001.

Upton, Bridget Gilfillan. 'Feminist Theology as Biblical Hermeneutics'. In Parsons,
ed., *The Cambridge Companion to Feminist Theology.* 97–113.

Vickery, Amanda. 'Golden Age to Separate Spheres? A Review of the Categories
and Chronology of English Women's History'. *The Historical Journal* 36.2
(1993): 383–414.

Voaden, Rosalynn, ed. *Prophets Abroad: The Reception of Continental Holy Women
in Late-Medieval England.* Cambridge: D. S. Brewer, 1996.

Wall, Wendy. *The Imprint of Gender: Authorship and Publication in the English
Renaissance.* Ithaca, New York: Cornell University Press, 1993.

Watson, Francis. *Agape, Eros, Gender: Towards a Pauline Sexual Ethic.* Cambridge:
Cambridge University Press, 2000.

Watson, Nicholas. 'The Middle English Mystics'. In *The Cambridge History of
Medieval English Literature.* Ed. David Wallace. Cambridge: Cambridge University Press, 1999. 539–65.

Watt, Diane. *Secretaries of God: Women Prophets in Late Medieval and Early Modern
England.* Woodbridge: D. S. Brewer, 1997.

Watt, Tessa. *Cheap Print and Popular Piety 1550–1640*. Cambridge: Cambridge University Press, 1991.

Wilcox, Helen. 'Exploring the Language of Devotion in the English Revolution'. In *Literature and the English Civil War*. Ed. Thomas Healy and Jonathan Sawday. Cambridge: Cambridge University Press, 1990. 75–88.

'"My soule in silence"? Devotional Representations of Renaissance English-women'. In *Representing Women in Renaissance England*. Ed. Claude J. Summers and Ted-Larry Pebworth. Columbia, Missouri: University of Missouri Press, 1997. 9–23.

Wiseman, Susan. 'Unsilent Instruments and the Devil's Cushions: Authority in Seventeenth-Century Women's Prophetic Discourse'. In *New Feminist Discourses: Critical Essays on Theories and Texts*. Ed. Isobel Armstrong. London: Routledge, 1992. 176–96.

Woods, Susanne. 'Vocation and Authority: Born to Write'. In Grossman, ed., *Aemilia Lanyer: Gender, Genre, and the Canon*. 83–98.

Lanyer: A Renaissance Woman Poet. Oxford: Oxford University Press, 1999.

'Women at the Margins in Spenser and Lanyer'. In *Worldmaking Spenser: Explorations in the Early Modern Age*. Ed. Patrick Cheney and Lauren Silberman. Lexington, Kentucky: University Press of Kentucky, 2000. 101–14.

Wolfe, Heather, ed. *Elizabeth Cary Lady Falkland: Life and Letters*. Cambridge: Cambridge University Press, 2001.

Woolf, Rosemary. *The English Mystery Plays*. London: Routledge, 1972.

Woudhuysen, H. R. *Sir Philip Sidney and the Circulation of Manuscripts, 1558–1640*. Oxford: Clarendon Press, 1996.

Zerwick, Max, S. J., and Mary Grosvenor. *A Grammatical Analysis of the New Testament*. 4th edition. Rome: Editrice Pontifico Istituto Biblico, 1993.

Zim, Rivkah. *English Metrical Psalms: Poetry as Praise and Prayer 1535–1601*. Cambridge: Cambridge University Press, 1987.

Index

Index to scripture passages